The Anthropological Study
of Education

Editors

CRAIG J. CALHOUN
FRANCIS A. J. IANNI

MOUTON PUBLISHERS · THE HAGUE · PARIS
DISTRIBUTED IN THE USA AND CANADA BY ALDINE, CHICAGO

General Editor's Preface

The editors of this volume call it a sampler which describes fairly the variety of work that anthropologists of the 1970's are doing in research on education. They modestly disclaim that it is a review of the discipline but their thoughtful introduction and conclusion classify the papers included make a substantial beginning in the work of synthesizing the complex elements of this field. In describing what anthropologists are setting themselves to learn about education and educational institutions, the book (whether sampler or review) has two special qualities: it is brief and compact, yet it is richly international in character. Perhaps its special quality comes from the opportunity which the editors had for full discussion with a genuinely worldwide group of scholars interested in education and related subjects.

Like most contemporary sciences, anthropology is a product of the European tradition. Some argue that it is a product of colonialism, with one small and self-interested part of the species dominating the study of the whole. If we are to understand the species, our science needs substantial input from scholars who represent a variety of the world's cultures. It was a deliberate purpose of the IXth International Congress of Anthropological and Ethnological Sciences to provide impetus in this direction. The *World Anthropology* volumes, therefore, offer a first glimpse of a human science in which members from all societies have played an active role. Each of the books is designed to be self-contained; each is an attempt to update its particular sector of scientific knowledge and is written by specialists from all parts of the world. Each volume should be read and reviewed individually as a separate volume on its own given subject. The set as a whole will indicate what changes are in store for anthropology as scholars from the developing countries join in studying the species of which we are all a part.

The IXth Congress was planned from the beginning not only to include as many of the scholars from every part of the world as possible, but also with a view toward the eventual publication of the paper in high-quality volumes. At previous Congresses scholars were invited to bring papers which were then read out loud. They were necessarily limited in length; many were only summarized; there was little time for discussion; and the sparse discussion could only be in one language. The IXth Congress was an experiment aimed at changing this. Papers were written with the intention of exchanging them before the Congress, particularly in extensive pre-Congress sessions; they were not intended to be read aloud at the Congress, that time being devoted to discussions — discussions which were simultaneously and professionally translated into five languages. The method for eliciting the papers was structured to make as representative a sample as was allowable when scholarly creativity — hence self-selection — was critically important. Scholars were asked both to propose papers of their own and to suggest topics for sessions of the Congress which they might edit into volumes. All were then informed of the suggestions and encouraged to rethink their own papers and the topics. The process, therefore, was a continuous one of feedback and exchange and it has continued to be so even after the Congress. The some two thousand papers comprising *World Anthropology* certainly then offer a substantial sample of world anthropology. It has been said that anthropology is at a turning point; if this is so, these volumes will be the historical direction-markers.

As might have been foreseen in the first postcolonial generation, the large majority of the Congress papers (82 percent) are the work of scholars identified with the industrialized world which fathered our traditional discipline and the institution of the Congress itself: Eastern Europe (15 percent); Western Europe (16 percent); North America (47 percent); Japan, South Africa, Australia, and New Zealand (4 percent). Only 18 percent of the papers are from developing areas: Africa (4 percent); Asia-Oceania (9 percent); Latin America (5 percent). Aside from the substantial representation from the U.S.S.R. and the nations of Eastern Europe, a significant difference between this corpus of written material and that of other Congresses is the addition of the large proportion of contributions from Africa, Asia, and Latin America. "Only 18 percent" is two to four times as great a proportion as that of other Congresses; moreover, 18 percent of 2,000 papers is 360 papers, 10 times the number of "Third World" papers presented at previous Congresses. In fact, these

360 papers are more than the total of ALL papers published after the last International Congress of Anthropological and Ethnological Sciences which was held in the United States (Philadelphia, 1956).
The significance of the increase is not simply quantitative. The input of scholars from areas which have until recently been no more than subject matter for anthropology represents both feedback and also long-awaited theoretical contributions from the perspectives of very different cultural, social, and historical traditions. Many who attended the IXth Congress were convinced that anthropology would not be the same in the future. The fact that the next Congress (India, 1978) will be our first in the "Third World" may be symbolic of the change. Meanwhile, sober consideration of the present set of books will show how much, and just where and how, our discipline is being revolutionized.

As the editors indicate, their book owes much to a pre-Congress conference at the University of Wisconsin in Oshkosh and to several related conferences in the same place at the same time. Readers may share some of this advantage by noting other books in this series on educational theory, adolescence, development, and the variety of regional cultural phenomena and "solutions" to universal problems.

Chicago, Illinois   SOL TAX
March 24, 1976

Preface

This volume consists of several papers presented to the IXth International Congress of Anthropological and Ethnological Sciences in Chicago, September 1973. The aim of the collection is to provide a sampling of the kinds of current anthropological research being done in educational situations. By its very nature it is incomplete. The majority of the papers included were volunteered to the Congress in advance of the organization of the session on the anthropological study of education. While some others were solicited, no attempt has been made to represent a complete picture of the development of the field. Each of the papers being presented here is new, and, we believe, together they are exemplary of most of the kinds of anthropological research being done in education. In addition the papers come from all over the world, and thus give some indication of the breadth of the subject. This book should be seen as an updating of a research area, not as a review.

The papers chosen are all about research. They either have settings in space and time in which they examine a particular set of problems or else they are about methodology. In this way we have distinguished our topics from those of papers concerned primarily with theoretical issues.[1]

We wish to express our gratitude to the Center for the Study of Man at the Smithsonian Institution and to the National Institute of Education of the U.S. Government for their support of a Pre-Congress Conference on Education and Cultural Transmission. This conference was held in Oshkosh, Wisconsin, August 27–30, 1973 under the joint chairmanship

[1] The reader is referred to another volume in the *World Anthropology* series, *Toward a general cultural theory of education*, edited by Frederick O. Gearing and Lucinda Sangree.

of Craig Calhoun, Fred Gearing, and Francis Ianni. A joint session was also held with an NIE-sponsored conference on adolescence chaired by Estelle Fuchs. The Oshkosh meetings provided a valuable forum for the exchange of ideas and information and the introduction of scholars from various parts of the world, in a relaxed setting in which real acquaintance-ships could be formed.[2] In addition, travel funds were provided for a number of those who might not otherwise have been able to attend the Congress. In particular, for their help in Oshkosh, in Chicago, and in planning for both, we express our thanks to Bill Douglass, Jennifer Burdick Stevens, and Sam Stanley of the Center for the Study of Man. We are also grateful to Diane Hoffman, who typed (and retyped) much of the contents of this book, and Karen Tkach, who saw that it turned from manuscript to print. Our debt to Sol Tax, organizer of the Congress, is enormous and obvious. He, together with his "Tax Mafia," performed a magnificent service.

CRAIG JACKSON CALHOUN
Horace Mann-Lincoln Institute
Columbia University
New York, New York

FRANCIS A. J. IANNI
Horace Mann-Lincoln Institute
Columbia University
New York, New York

[2] Participants in the Pre-Congress Conference were:

Alya Baffoun	Laura Harvey	Colin Lacey	Barbara Pischall
Ronald Bucknam	Robert Havighurst	Jean Lave	Marion Pugh
Craig Calhoun	Tamàs Hofer	Norman McQuown	George Spindler
Thomas Carroll	Francis Ianni	Chie Nakane	Louise Spindler
Woodrow Clark	Milada Kalab	Chudi Nwa-Chil	Gerald Storey
Anwar Dil	John King	Peter Ochs	Hervé Varenne
Frederick Gearing	Joe Konno	Sandy Pemberton	Rita Wiesinger

Laura Harvey served as recorder, for which we are grateful, especially for those points at which she continued to write even though her better judgement may have told her nothing worthwhile was being said.

Table of Contents

Introduction

CRAIG JACKSON CALHOUN and FRANCIS A. J. IANNI

The study of education has been a part of social and cultural anthropology almost from their inceptions. As fieldworkers set out to record the structure and content of social life they could not pass up a look at its continuity. This continuity, they said, was learned, and more than that, in every society there existed more or less formalized processes to partially determine the learning of the young.

The study of education has been with us, then, perhaps inevitably, from the beginning of our discipline. As the discipline grew, and techniques were refined, there emerged, however, a specialty area of the anthropological study of education. From something which most anthropologists wrote a little about, education has come to be something about which a few anthropologists write a lot, and the rest feel free to ignore. For better or worse, this is where we find ourselves today.

A variety of approaches to the specialized study of education with anthropological methods is possible. In this book we present essays which cover most of the range of field inquires now in progress. While their diversity is an accurate reflection of the status of the field, we have attempted to provide some order by developing a rudimentary classification of this rather broad range of studies. It is not intended as definitive, but rather as a guide to supplement titles and to provide a sort of framework for viewing a diverse and sometimes little-related body of work.

The categories are:
1. Noninstitutional Education
2. Institutional Education in Society
3. The Organization of Educational Institutions
4. Language and Education

By "noninstitutional education," we refer to the many forms of consciously organized and patterned social mechanisms for the transmission of knowledge and culture which take place outside of "schools" or similarly designated educational institutions. Admittedly this category covers a very broad range of activity — from parents' instruction of children to initiation ceremonies to hunting or herding instruction. In this volume the two papers which represent the area discuss a general framework for the "Oral transmission of knowledge" (Pentikäinen) and a specific example of regularized but noninstitutionalized learning situations for children — Siberian "Fosterage" (Gardanov). These essays give an idea of the range and importance of this area of inquiry, for in many societies, most education, even formal education, is carried out in such noninstitutional settings. There are limits to what can be transmitted and to the utility and efficiency of these methods. But there is also something lost as education becomes more and more exclusively the domain of institutions such as the school. It is in this kind of inquiry that educators will find valuable lessons for their own work, just as anthropologists will find data of interest.

Institutional education is becoming more and more dominant today. Not only is it becoming prominent in the small-scale societies which had previously escaped it but, despite attempts to "open up" the schools, it is increasing its hold on the industrial societies of the world. This is not necessarily either a simply good or simply bad trend. It is, however, one with a number of social concomitants which are not well researched or understood. How, for example, do various forms of institutionalized education relate to national development? Are they sometimes parallel and only partially directional as Wood sees them in Nepal? Is it inevitable that national educational programs cause chaos and in some cases disintegration in the social fabric of local groups? Milada Kalab has traced elements of the fate and functions of monastic education and its supplanters in village Cambodia. Changing traditions seem always to be accompanied by changing patterns and styles of education. The correlation is clear, but the order is not. Many Westerners have become accustomed to viewing education as being the primary agent for social change. There is, however, substantial evidence that educational institutions tend in most situations to be conservative factors in society. Perhaps we too often confuse political stance with social function despite our insistence that education must be apolitical. In any event, governments throughout the world have a great investment in and concern with education. At various levels this seems to result in successful indoctrination while at others it produces active rebellion. In America, social upheavals have been widespread in the last several years, and yet the United States' educational system remains relatively intact. How do members of some of the "alternate life-style" groups which have developed relate to the issues of educating the young? And how do their various choices relate to their internal organization? John King has attempted to answer these questions for groups representative of a classificatory scheme he has developed. America has other sociocultural divisions than those which have resulted from recent rebellions. For hundreds of years black residents of the United States have been receiving a different education from whites. Even though they have lately been formally incorporated into the same educational institutions, there remain a number of differentials. These are both in the relations of the communities and individuals to the educational institutions and in the structuring of what in fact is taught (as opposed to listed in the curriculum) in various schools and classes. Explanations and rationalizations have been offered in a number of different ways. Herbert Ellis undertakes in his paper to analyze one set of these — those which discuss the "failure" of blacks to perform either academically or socially according to the expectations or goals others have suggested.

In quite a different cultural situation, Chudi Nwa-Chil has examined some of the resistances to early Western education in parts of Nigeria. Here an ongoing and neither subordinate nor minority culture was subjected to a sudden influx of aliens who established an educational system which was external to the indigenous system with demands and rewards of its own. That the effects of such an imposition would be dramatic is obvious. Nwa-Chil's paper is an examination of the way members of one society attempted to cope with this interdiction.

Finally, in this section, come papers dealing with the relation of anthropology and education to social planning. First, Robert Havighurst presents a discussion of the contributions of the teaching of anthropology to the development and nature of cultural pluralism in three nations — Australia, New Zealand, and the United States. He is interested both in uncovering the practical significance of anthropological teaching and in learning what factors exist which can help to further a cooperative and successfully functioning cultural pluralism. Edna Mitchell has written concerning education and national planning in Nepal. Here again a form of cultural variety (arguably pluralism) obtains. Nepal is a past of the Himilayan interface. Rather than having any cultural unity, indigenous or exogenous, it is characterized by a variety of social and religious values which exert a powerful effect on both the operation of educational systems and the choice of educational goals. Again the interrelationship between education and the rest of society has broad and far-reaching effects. Anthropologists should be expected and encouraged to turn some of their energies toward the solution of practical problems imposed by this inter-relationship.

There is another side to the study of institutional education, however. This is to focus on the nature and operation of the educational institutions themselves. This is probably the largest of the subsections of the current anthropological study of education. In this study of educational institutions we see an example of a sort of anthropological "microsociology." Traditionally, anthropologists have studied small-scale societies as much as possible in their totality. This is different from either the macro- or microsociological study of large-scale societies. Most social anthropological theory has been developed with an implicit assumption of small-scale and relatively low complexity and an explicit attempt to deal with a complete, integrated social situation. The small-scale assumption has freed anthropologists, for better or worse, from the necessity to deal with statistical indicators of relatively broad societal parameters and complex status sets. Rather, methods have been developed for the observation of actual person-to-person encounters as they are a part of an actual social process, and theories have been developed to account for their generalities as structure. Theories have been both inclusive and tied to actual (as opposed to representational) behavior. As anthropologists now (partially of necessity) turn their attention more and more to inquiries into the nature of particular institutions in larger-scale societies, they are faced with the problem of working out a new relationship between empirical methodology and theory. It is true that anthropological methods of field-work can well and profitably be used in the observation of components of modern societies. It must be remembered, however, that some social subsystems — whether classrooms or street gangs — are not themselves necessarily societies. Although the definition of that term is unclear, it has usually been seen to include, for one thing, generations and reproductive capacities, and neither are usually present in the examples cited. Anthropologists are beginning to face some of these theoretical issues and will of necessity continue more and more to do so.

In the meantime, analysts have focused on occasional aspects of behavior, and sometimes developed entire conceptual frameworks, but not theories, to deal with them. A number of advances are being made in our empirical knowledge of educational institutions, however. In this volume Peggy Sanday has reviewed many of the considerations emerging in the methodology of educational anthropology. Her emphasis is, in particular, on the effort to produce a "harder" sort of data which may be more readily integrated with the works of other social scientists. Several examples of actual research are included which demonstrate the range of both problems and styles of inquiry anthropologist/educationists have operated with. Some studies, for example, have attempted to analyze entire schools as social systems. Others have retained the social system approach but take the classroom as their boundary. Still others have looked at a single facet of the institution — say, teaching practices — or have generalized to an entire cultural situation.

Colin Lacey's paper on his research on a British grammar school, and later on the effects of teacher-training styles on attitudes and practices, demonstrates perhaps most clearly the interplay of two approaches. The first part is a result of intensive social anthropological fieldwork and concentrates on the social ordering — in class and out — of a form (or class) of school boys. The data section deals specifically with teachers and uses questionnaire and attitude-scaling instruments more common to social psychologists. The editors' paper follows something of the same track as the first part of Lacey's paper, but rather than examining an "age grade" it looks at the social organization of entire high schools. It draws its material from a comparative study of three American high schools by a team of field researchers again operating with the assumption that the school can profitably be viewed as a discrete social system. Of course, the school is not a completely discrete system. As Hervé Varenne shows schools in the United States are inexorably related in their fundamental precepts and practices to the rest of American culture. The sorts of classification processes which are important facets of the operation of the school are sometimes similar to, and in any event exist largely for, the systems which compose the rest of the culture. Eleanor Leacock's paper looks at schools in Zambia and contrasts some of their content with practices prevalent in America. Again, it is systems broader than the school itself which she finds most relevant for the understanding of its functioning as an institution.

Woodrow Clark takes for his topic the consideration of violence as a related and perhaps contingent event with public education in the urban areas of the United States. He uses information (seen in the systemic perspective of information theory and generative linguistics) about the organization of school and community to attempt to gain an understanding of a particular set of events he classifies as violence. His attempt is to understand the role of violence in the context of the school and the ongoing social processes of its constituents. He is particularly concerned with parallel societal structures which affect the situation, most notably wealth. Andrew Couch's paper is also concerned with the effect of a parallel system on the operation of an educational organization. In this case, he is considering a college-level program in police science as it is affected by the dual role of instructors and students as professionals in law enforcement as well as members of this educational situation. Rather than being concerned with the operation of the institution as such, Couch, like Leacock, is concerned with the effect of certain institutional factors of the educational and social situations on the content of the teaching and learning processes. Robert Welke, in describing "the radicalization of a conservative community," is again looking at the structure of the school itself. Only implicity does he draw inferences for the effect of the events he describes on the teaching/learning process, but it is clear that this "radicalization" involves a certain educational significance of its own. Further, one can see the extent to which such an occurrence was much more likely in its particular educational setting than elsewhere.

Bea Medicine's paper is concerned with the views of members of one ethnic and political group toward educational institutions imposed on them by another. In Medicine's case, native American educators offer their analyses of the community colleges which serve much of the Amerindian population. Her essay raises the issue of the relation of the actual institutional structure of schools to the needs and culture of the population they are intended to serve. Implicit in the situation, but beyond scope of the paper's analysis, is the anthropologist's recurring confrontation with the problems of a people vastly affected by, but lacking a substantial decisional role in, the political power structure of nation-states.

Thomas Fitzgerald's paper raises (like Havighurst's in the second category) the question of what role can and does the anthropologist play in the development and change of educational institutions. Fitzgerald gives us his observations on his own role in the evaluation of an experimental college set up in the context of a large university. Evaluation, of course, is only one of the many ways in which anthropological studies may directly affect the operation of educational institutions. Each of the other papers presented suggests either explicitly or implicitly its own possible modes of application.

Language is clearly a dominant feature of almost all the definitions — vague and specific — which have been offered for culture. Certainly in education it has been a pervasive influence — so much so that it becomes problematical as a distinct category in this book. Other sections contain papers (Pentikäinen's in particular) which could certainly have been included here. The rough distinguishing factor has been a primary concern with language education. Even this is ambiguous. Henry Torres-Trueba's paper concerns the development of bilingual/bicultural programs for Chicanos. Certainly much that students in these programs are intended to learn is more than simply two languages. Still, the paper is interesting in that its emphasis is clearly on the programs and the training of teachers for the programs which will enable linguistic pluralism to be useful rather than obstructive in the education of some children.

More clearly demonstrating the topic is Eddy Roulet's paper on the more general relations between the ethnography of communication and the teaching of languages, which deals with another of the relations between research and program development. Roulet is concerned with the failure of descriptive and structural linguistics to provide a theory adequate to the applied task of imparting a "competence at communication" to students. They produce knowledge of the rules of grammar, but not of the rules of the application of grammar to communication. Language has often been attached to the realm of "cultural anthropology." Roulet's paper may lead us to see a version of the same error in this classification as in the teaching of mere grammatical rules to students. Language is not simply an artifact of culture, except to the extent that it is NOT used in the interpersonal relations of actual people. If a competence at language is seen as a competence at communication, we have moved into the realm of the social.

These, then, are the papers which compose this book and the classifications in which we will present them. They are lesser and greater, in length, in originality, and in quality. They are all contributions, however, to a growing area of anthropology. This area — the anthropological study of education — needs much more growth and more refinement. It is not hard to see that education is of vast import in society and in the life of individuals, and it makes a great deal of sense for anthropologists to turn their attention to that which is of pervasive influence and dramatic impact.

Educational institutions, it seems, are becoming both ubiquitous and immensely varied in nature. They are not only important, but accessible for the continued study of anthropologists. In addition, they offer the opportunity for some readily defined boundaries — school, classroom — which allow the observer to get a ready focus on his study of complex societies. This sort of "microsociology" is quite likely destined to become more and more common among anthropologists. It has been the emphasis of many studies of modernization and urbanization such as those in the "copper belt" of East and Central Africa. In complex societies it is all but imperative that some sort of group or institution be defined as the parameter of an anthropological study. Educational studies lead the way in much of this work of changing a discipline's orientation.

In a way, anthropology occupies the same position in observation that education does in action. We are all familiar, I know, with the expression of "not being able to see the forest from the trees." So it is with those who would make of anthropology a branch of psychology. On the other hand, some never see trees from a preoccupation with forests. So it is too often with macrosociologists. The particular task of the anthropologist is to look at the relations between trees which organize them into a forest. One cannot do this without seeing individual trees in their differences and similarities. Likewise, one must have knowledge of the whole to realize that it is a forest and not merely an aggregate of trees. Education acts to make the individual a part of society, and to make the forms and knowledge of his society a part of the individual. The anthropologist and educator, then, are to be found posed, looking and working, between the particularity and the regularity of society.

SECTION ONE

Oral Transmission of Knowledge

Editors' Note: Nonliterate cultures do not have well-developed senses of
history although they do have cumulative and transmitted stores of knowledge. In this paper, Juha Pentikäinen analyzes the specific processes of transmission and their situations. While his comments are specifically directed at
"oral societies," it should be noted that they have relevance for consideration
of certain facets of knowledge in literate societies. In the first place, there is
some knowledge which is not written down. In the second place, as Pentikäinen's paper should make apparent, there are certain stylistic differences,
contextual influences, and structural forms which affect the ultimate meaning of various items of knowledge.

A HOLISTIC VIEW OF THE ORAL TRANSMISSION PROCESS

Folkloristics is most emphatically a discipline in which progress to a
large extent follows trends within neighboring disciplines. Stimuli have
been taken from such fields as history, comparative literature, psychology, sociology, cultural anthropology, comparative religion, and linguistics. It would seem, however, that many of the stimulating impulses
available at present will be ignored and not applied to folkloristic problems if folklorists do not recognize that tradition texts should be not
only the object of their study but also the events that accompany the
transmission of the tradition. Today this means that both oral communication and the channels by which mass lore is conveyed need to
be studied and explained together with the interaction that takes place
between written and oral means of communication. In fact, this is but
one basic model of human intercourse. The transmission of tradition

from one generation to another is the process on which the teaching of the knowledge of culture, "social transfer," is based (Hultkrantz 1960: 69–76).

The informing process within a society is usually divided into (1) the action of transmitting tradition information, and (2) action contributing to the formation of information, which can be divided into teaching and upbringing. In a modern civilization, the former is carried out primarily by the school institution, from preschool institutions to universities, the latter predominantly by the primary groups surrounding an individual, such as the family. Upbringing means to make individuals acquainted with or oriented to rules of behavior or norms that are demanded for the security of an individual. The formation of information includes, besides the actual creative sciences, letters, and arts, the free action of information, which is taken care of in modern society by literature, the press, radio, television, etc.

In an oral society, the channels of information are less complicated than in a modern society, and the formation of new information is far less rapid in tempo. Illiterate societies are more homogeneous in their social structure and hierarchy, and then, too, the institutions for the transmission and formation of information are in many cases the same. In cultural anthropology, information transmitted from one generation to another has been described generally by the concept CULTURE. The formation of new information is tied up with the cultures where inventions are made. We can say that an individual who comes by birth to a community does not develop and create a culture of his own, but the culture develops him. The hegemony of man in the world is not secured primarily by his ability to invent new things all the time, but by his capability to adopt, transfer, and apply tradition. In studying the transmission of tradition we can distinguish between ENCULTURATION (the internationalization of culture) and SOCIALIZATION (the integration into society and its norms). In an illiterate society these processes are oral, while in a literate society they are both written and oral.

The concept "oral tradition" is the counterpart to "literary tradition." Albert B. Lord points out that oral tradition — he refers especially to verse tradition — is learned orally and transmitted orally (1964: 5–7). The minimal definition of tradition includes "culture (elements) handed down from one generation to another" (Hultkrantz 1960). The Latin verb *tradere* contains at the root the connotation of continuity. Another criterion of tradition is its social character. Tradition and "individual knowledge" are concepts which are not to be identified with each other. "Individual knowledge" is, in general, information which is retained by man unwritten in his memory; information is tied up with the human mechanism of memory, and for that reason it is prone to different transformations. Those changes may result from the failure of memory and from contamination by the rest of the material collected in the memory. With tradition, the case is similar, but all memory information is not tradition, nor does all "individual knowledge" become tradition. (In the process of adapting into tradition the choices made by the society, the so-called "social control" is crucial.) Besides collective tradition, we can find also group tradition, craft tradition, etc. in a community. The preservation by individuals from one generation to another, of information not generally known by the community, characterizes INDIVIDUAL TRADITION. IDIOSYNCRASIES, pieces of behavior typical of just one individual, are generally excluded from individual traditions. These will only seldom become tradition. If the information carried by an individual has no continuity, if it is not handed down, if the whole society, or one of its groups, does not accept it, we are not dealing with a tradition (Pentikäinen 1968: 109–112).

Historically, the problems of oral tradition have belonged to folklorists. However, not many folklorists actually study "oral tradition," but rather "folklore," which is given different meanings by scholars. It is surprising that many international terminologies of folklore do not even mention the concept "oral tradition." The *Dictionary of folklore, mythology and legend* (Leach 1949–1950: 308–403) gives a list of views of twenty-one scholars concerning folklore and does not define the concept normatively. Even the title of the book is curious, for it places the terms "folklore," "mythology," and "legend," side by side, as if the latter two could not be included in the first. The content analysis of the ideas of the twenty-one writers reveals the heterogeneity of their views. In their characterizations of folklore, the most frequently repeated words are "tradition" (which appears 13 times), "oral" (13), "transmission" (6), "survival" (6), and "social" (6). Most definers (13) agree that folklore is found in both primitive and civilized societies. Some eighteen writers include literature in folklore, twelve include religion, five include crafts, and three writers include folk speech in folklore. The view of the majority is that the definitive criterion of folklore is simply "oral transmission" (Utley 1961: 193–206). Alan Dundes (1965: 1–3) points out that this cannot be the only criterion, and he is undoubtedly right. On the other hand, we cannot approve of Dundes's pessimistic attitude towards operational definitions. In his work, *The study of folklore* (1965), Dundes does not define the concept "folklore" at all, but is contented merely to list some forms of folklore.

The differences between such views may be explained in terms of the difference between literature (esthetics), on one hand, and anthropology, on the other. In the former case, folklore is considered a species of literature, while in the latter case it is considered a central element of culture as an entity. When the approach is esthetic, the folklorist uses text-critical analysis, but an anthropologically oriented folklorist pays principal attention to the context of the tradition and aims at explaining the use, meaning, and function of a tradition. The position of folklore within anthropology has been considered by William R. Bascom in his numerous articles. In his paper "Folklore and anthropology," he writes: "Folklore, to the anthropologist, is a part of culture but not the whole of culture. It includes myths, legends, tales, proverbs, riddles, the texts of ballads and other songs, and other forms of lesser importance, but not folk art, folk dance, folk music, folk costume, folk medicine, folk custom, or folk belief. . . . All folklore is orally transmitted, but not all that is orally transmitted is folklore" (Dundes 1965: 28).

This definition is regarded as too narrow by many folklorists because many categories, e.g. belief tradition and the musicological subjects of ballads and other folksongs, are left outside the concept "folklore." For Bascom, folklore is "verbal art," a label he uses in subsequent papers (Bascom 1955: 245–252). The idea of differentiating the two terms is good. If "folklore" and "oral tradition" were classified as one entity, all information in nonliterate cultures would be included under the term "folklore." Differentiation between the terms is advantageous, among other ways, in that we need not necessarily attach the criterion "oral" to folklore. In practice, a folklorist confronts literary tradition (booklore) as well as either wholly or partly nonverbal material. The meaning of the concept "oral tradition" depends crucially on what is understood by the words "oral" and "tradition," whereas the meaning of "folklore" consists of the meanings of the words "folk" and "lore." The task of a student of folklore is both wider and narrower than that of one who deals with oral tradition. The latter studies all orally transmitted tradition information, the former only a part of it, but the folklore student may, in addition to verbal tradition, also consider nonverbal material and, besides oral tradition, written material as well. The central problem of the study of oral tradition is the process by which tradition is transmitted in speech from speaker to hearer.

In their quest for text materials, folklorists have all too often been content to approach their research as if it were a question of merely locating and examining written documents. The care taken in trying to locate every single item of information on a subject from archives and literary sources for comparative research has been commendable. On the other hand, the questions of how the texts came to be in the archives or in the books, how they came to be noted down, and in what context they existed as living tradition have often been ignored. What Malinowski said as early as 1926 (1926: 24) has been forgotten: "The text, of course, is extremely important, but without the context it remains lifeless." The significance of written variants has also been overestimated when attempts have been made by diffusionists to arrive at the original function of a folktale by, for example, interpreting texts. It is true that a really skillful text critic can make certain conclusions on the basis of the text alone, but a reliable taxonomy of tradition necessitates careful analysis of both source and context at the fieldwork stage. Dundes writes: "One cannot always guess the meaning from context. For this reason, folklorists must actively seek to elicit the meaning of folklore from the folk" (Dundes 1966).

A holistic view of the transmission process means an attempt to arrive at a synthesis by analyzing systematically the different variables of the oral communication. In this way the scholar must direct his attention to all the factors that can influence the transmission of tradition, those factors which concern the culture, the community, the individual, or the deep structure of the tradition itself, and he must further examine the interaction between all these factors.

TRANSMISSION OF TRADITION AS A SOCIAL, COMMUNICATIVE EVENT

Communication theory provides a specialized approach to problems encountered in the study of the transmission (communication) of a message (information) from one source to another. This study is essentially based on the systematics of probability, working with so-called "information-theoretic models." The basic formula of the system of communication has five elements: (1) the information source, (2) the transmitter, (3) the channel of transmission, (4) the receiver, and (5) the destination (cf. Shannon and Weaver 1959: 4–6, 98–99; Cherry 1959: 3–29). The source of information produces messages to be communicated and chooses the desired message from possible alternatives. The transmitter turns the message into a signal and sends it through different channels of communication to the receiver. The function of the receiver is to transform the transmitted and received information into a message again, and to deliver it to the destination. From this point of view, oral transmission can be characterized as a process where the source of information is the brain of the speaker, the transmitter the speech organs, the channel the air, the receiver the ears of the hearer, and the destination the brain of the hearer. Like any information, oral tradition is liable to distortion from different transformations caused by disturbances which are labeled "noise" in communication theory. The concept includes all the factors influencing the transmission and causing the received message to be anything other than identical with the sent message.

The transmission process of oral tradition can be illustrated diagrammatically (cf. Jakobson 1960: 353):

Context

Message

Storyteller .... Listener(s)

Contact

Code

Oral transmission presupposes the existence of INTERACTION between at least two persons. Both a storyteller and a listener or group of listeners are required. In the case (A) in which a story is told to only one listener, the communication pattern is that of a CHAIN, while in the case (B) of a group of listeners, we are dealing with the pattern which is called a CIRCLE. In the latter case we have an active social institution: it has no organization, it is relatively free in its form, and there is no chosen leader (cf. Bavelas 1953: 493–499).

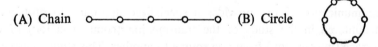

(A) Chain   o——o——o——o——o   (B) Circle

The minimum criterion for a "community" to exist is two individuals. Storytelling is consequently a SOCIAL EVENT (Georges 1969: 317–318) in which the participants do not function simply as individuals but rather control each other and adopt certain role behavior, according to a regular pattern, determined by their social status and relationships. The storytelling situation is also a COMMUNICATIVE PROCESS: the verbal message is transferred directly from the transmitter to the receiver by means of personal contact.

Interaction at the verbal level is not possible if the storyteller and the listener do not understand each other, i.e. if they do not share a common linguistic and paralinguistic code (Hymes 1964: 2–13). A fund of common knowledge and common expectations — a common culture — is also needed. CONTEXT gives the message meaning in a given situation. One of the mistakes made by folklorists in the past has been to regard storytelling as a stereotyped process which could not be changed in its details and which always followed a fixed pattern. Studies in depth have, however, shown that each storytelling situation is unique by nature: it is an event which occurs only once in the same temporal, spatial, and social circumstances (cf. Georges 1969: 316–319).

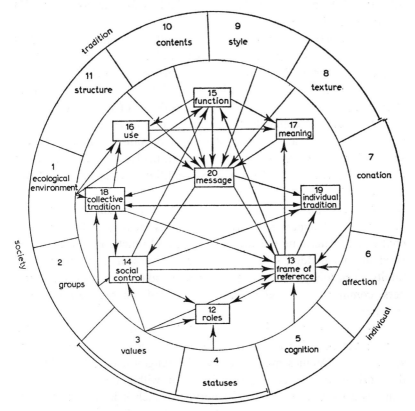

Figure 1.   The dimensions of oral tradition

Figure 1 illustrates my view of the dimensions that should be considered when studying holistically the transmission of oral tradition. The segmental dimensions have been divided into three levels. Level A includes (1) ecological environment and (2) groups. Level B is individually psychological. (The divisions of conscious experience formulated by perception psychologists are the foundation for the level of individual psychology): (3) values, (4) statuses, (5) cognition, (6) affection, (7) conation. Level C includes the depth structure of tradition: (8) texture, (9) style, (10) contents, (11) structure. The variables inside the circle have again been grouped into three levels. The lowest level, D, concerns the individual and social psychological factors which influence the formation of a tradition: (12) social roles, (13) frame of reference, (14) social control. The highest level, E, concerns the context of a tradition message and is divided into (15) function, (16) use, (17) meaning. The central level inside the circle, F, illustrates the phases of social transmission: (18) collective tradition, (19) individual tradition, and (20) transmission of the tradition message.

1. THE ECOLOGICAL ENVIRONMENT includes the cultural-ecological approach which is required for the observation of oral tradition. Tradition has a temporal and local dependence on the cultural environment of its transmission. An ecological study of tradition tends, among other things, to take account of the dependence of a tradition on the local residents, to eliminate the variables due to contacts with other cultures (acculturation), and to shed light on other related questions, such as if membership in a group with a particular source of livelihood bears any consequent influence upon tradition, its context, functions, and contents.

2. GROUPS form the social environment of man and maintain the culture that is taught to an individual. Groups are responsible for social control and determine the values, norms, and sanctions which are desired in an individual's behavior. Characteristics of a group are continuity, reciprocity, an organized nature, solidarity between the members, common norms, aims, and values, and the presence of many members.

3. VALUES are the goals towards which man aims in his social behavior; the behavior of an individual is a choice between different social values. Values may be economic, religious, etc., but whatever their origin, they effect uniform behavior within the community. A value is a goal, whereas a social norm to which it is related is a rule regulating behavior and supported by sanctions. Tradition depends on values in many respects: values influence the role behavior of an individual, his frame of reference, social control by the community, the personal norms he adopts, the social norms maintained by the society, and the context and functions of a tradition.

4. STATUSES are social positions of a system of people with common aims which constitutes a society. A status is a collection of certain rights, duties, privileges, and norms which theoretically, at least, are

possessed and followed by an individual of a certain social standing. Statuses concern both the society and the individual: a society is a system of individuals who occupy statuses, and the individuals in their behavior show a dependence upon their statuses. The dynamic aspect of status is role.

5. COGNITION refers to conscious realization in perception.

6. AFFECTION includes the emotions and the emotional side of the individual.

7. CONATION denotes desire and mental effort. These three divisions of conscious experience can be illustrated as follows: in the case of religious tradition, cognition includes the process of various attitudes and ideas becoming conscious (e.g., the view of the world and the system of values which influences the frame of reference, the dogmas, and the ideas an individual has about the cosmos and supranormal beings); affection includes religious emotion and experience; and conation concerns the behavior of an individual directed toward achieving some end, which in this case might be conducting a rite, by means of which an individual or a community tries to find contact with the supranormal being (Strunk 1962: 39–105).

8. TEXTURE includes the linguistic aspect of oral tradition, the system of phonemes and morphemes that is manifested in every tradition message. This level also comprises the phonetic features typical of each language, e.g. the durational characteristics, the stress, the variations in the fundamental frequency of vocal folds, intonation, and other phonetic coloring of the text. The more marked the textural features of each genre, the more difficult it is to translate it into another language.

9. STYLE includes the use of various formulas, alliteration, rhyme, etc.

10. CONTENT differs from texture in that it usually can be translated, whereas texture is not generally easy to transfer from one language to another. The text is any version of a folktale, proverb, riddle, or rune that still can be analyzed on both the level of "translatable" contents and the "untranslatable" texture. The content comprises, among other things, the plot elements of a story, which may be transferred in tradition messages from one culture to another without obstacles to diffusion caused by language boundaries.

11. STRUCTURAL ANALYSIS is a method useful for the study of both language and content, since it involves the process of distinguishing structural elements out of, for example, narrative entities.

12. SOCIAL ROLES are abstractions which cannot be observed in practice. It is possible, however, to observe a role behavior or role

presentation that belongs to a certain role. There is an interdependence between the status and the role: the occupant of a status is expected to behave in a certain way, or, in other words, to fulfill the role expectations directed to him by society. A great number of "own-roles" and, alternatively, "counter-roles" are attached to every status. The actualization of counter-roles is called the "occupation of a role." Individuals do not often function as independent personalities but rather as occupants of certain statuses and roles. When we speak about any study of oral tradition it is important to bear in mind the roles and role behaviors of the bearers of tradition.

13. FRAME OF REFERENCE is a term from perception psychology denoting the sum of images in the mind of an individual at the moment of perception. The frame of reference considers both the subjective images already in the individual's mind (the primary stimulus for the actualization of the frame of reference) and those coming from outside, the objective, releasing ones. The central values of man may be arranged into frames of reference that remain relatively active all the time.

This kind of active, value-influencing framework can be labeled a dominant frame of reference, and may be religious, economic, etc., in nature. The frame of reference affects the shaping of tradition both at the moment an event takes place and at the interpretation phase following the experience when the experience is either attached to the individual or collective tradition as a part of that body or becomes a mere idiosyncrasy, lacking tradition background (Honko 1962: 96–103; Pentikäinen (1968: 113–118).

14. SOCIAL CONTROL refers to the passing on of norms within a society. Its principal form is teaching, which, even in modern societies, is mainly a task belonging to the family. Social control is control exercised by groups and by certain authoritative individuals within the group and is generally based on collective tradition known and accepted by the society as tradition messages transferred from one generation to another. Social control is regulated by values, and it, in turn, affects the formation of role behavior, frames of reference, individual traditions, and the collective tradition. Material that deviates from the conventional, traditional mass has remarkably slighter chances of being transferred into the collective tradition than material that can show parallels with the tradition information; in other words, a culture exercises active dismissal of certain new information (Cohen 1964: 100–120; Pentikäinen 1968: 107–118).

15. FUNCTION is a concept used in extensive meaning; however, it is also analytically useful to delimit it on two levels of context — use and

meaning — outside the range of scientific terminology. The primary meaning of "function" relates to "task." For example, a specific tradition unit may have a pedagogical, ritual, warning, or entertaining function. If two distinct items of tradition are parts of the same whole of behavior, they are in FUNCTIONAL RELATION to each other; if they may be substituted for each other, they are FUNCTIONAL ALTERNATIVES. If, for example, we consider a religious experience, we can speak about the functional qualifications for its actualization, which might be a certain religious tradition, and different sociopsychological factors, which are to be verified in the memorate material reporting on supernatural experiences. We can also speak about functional consequences, which are caused by the actualization of a tradition (Pentikäinen 1968: 119–121). A very interesting distinction is offered by the pair of concepts MANIFEST and LATENT function, illustrated by the case in which the bearers of tradition themselves may be conscious of the function and the functional consequences and qualifications of the tradition presented by them (Merton 1949: 28–29, 50–53). Considering the tradition repertoire of a single individual, the ADAPTATION TO THE FUNCTION is a useful device: how can the changes in function be explained?

16. USE refers to the presentation and actualization of a tradition. The process involved here is to call the material gathered in archives back to those connections where it can be used in the natural course of the life of people, i.e. to get at the METAFOLKORE, the ideas, and attitudes of the bearer of tradition about the material known by him (Dundes 1966: 506). In the study of individual repertoire it is interesting to explore the attitudes and valuations the bearer of tradition puts on his material.

17. MEANING: refer to point 15 above.

18. COLLECTIVE TRADITION is the tradition material which is generally known and accepted within a society and which forms the basis for social control. The composition of collective tradition can be studied by means of quantitative analysis, i.e. by finding out the frequency and distribution of the tradition unit under study. Features in a clearly popular position can be termed TRADITION DOMINANT (Honko 1962: 129–130).

19. INDIVIDUAL TRADITION is the counterpart of collective tradition. Collective tradition is not the sum of individual traditions — it is quantitatively less because not all individual traditions survive the social control and become common, and at the same time qualitatively more since it is a representative and competent measure of the control. In a study of the tradition bearer, the composition of the individual tradition,

the sources, and the portions of the dominant and latent tradition materials in the whole tradition, the nature of idiosyncrasies must be investigated, since the central problem is the influence of the individual on the formation of his own tradition.

20. THE TRADITION MESSAGE is a message transmitted from one generation to another, which contains traditional information about the culture. It is dependent upon the factors presented in this list. According to the communication theory, it is important in the study of oral tradition messages to explore channels of transmission through which tradition is taught, transmitted, learned, and adopted. Central to the process of transmission is reciprocity between individuals; oral tradition is transmitted as speech from speaker to hearer. The channels of transmission are the bearers of tradition.

THE UNWRITTEN RULES OF ORAL NARRATION

One of the characteristics of tradition is its great stability with respect to form. Content may vary, but form is relatively unchanged and stereotyped. However, despite the stability of form and the opportunities for its study, the formal composition of a folklore item has proved much less challenging to folklorists than has the task of searching for that item's origin (Dundes 1965: 127). The view that has long limited folkloristic research, namely that tradition texts are indivisible units, must therefore be rejected. It would be more useful to analyze the same text from several different angles and at different levels, as, for example, with a focus on content, form, style, structure, texture, function, use, and meaning, as has been done in functional, structural, and formal studies. The question of the interdependence of the different factors must not, however, be left aside. Folkloristic structuralism would find itself faced with a crisis if it were not able to relate its observations to other aspects of folklore research.

The question of the "laws" of narrative tradition has been given special attention by Axel Olrik, who, as early as 1908, put forward his theory of "epic laws" of stories (Olrik 1908). "These laws apply to all European folklore and to some extent beyond that. Against the background of the overwhelming uniformity of these laws, national characteristics seem to be only dialect peculiarities. Even the traditional categories of folk narrative are all governed by these principles of saga construction. We call these principles "laws" because they limit the freedom of composition of oral literature in a much different and more rigid way than in our literature" (Dundes 1965: 131). In Olrik's theory, the concept of *Sagenwelt* and the world of the saga play a central role. In his view "saga" is a comprehensive concept governing all narrative genres such as myth, folktale, memorate, legend, or epic song. By definition then, "epic laws" apply to all other narrative genres and, in principle, to all other branches of folklore as well as to folk tales. As Dundes notes in his introduction to Olrik's article (Dundes 1965: 129–130), "epic laws" are very similar to the superorganic concept, which has been written about widely in cultural anthropology. According to this concept there is not only an "organic" level which is controlled by man but also a superorganic level "above man." Because Olrik's laws are superorganic they control individual storytellers and lie beyond their control. He supposes that the narrators must obey the rules blindly. In an extreme form this concept of "epic laws" may lead to an underestimation of the individual and social contribution made when a tradition is disseminated. Examples of this can be found in the concepts and hypotheses put forward by followers of the geographical-historical method, for example, Kaarle Krohn's concept of "automigration" (Krohn 1922: 21) or Walter Anderson's "law of self-correction" (Anderson 1923: 397–403). Such concepts, however, mean that the practical problem concerning "epic laws" as part of the actual transmission process is disregarded. At what levels can these "laws" be studied? Are the "epic laws" known to the bearer of the tradition? Do they function overtly or covertly? Is transformation of tradition a cognitive or an intuitive process?

A STUDY IN DEPTH: THE "EPIC LAWS" IN MARINA TAKALO'S STORYTELLING

We can answer these questions by analyzing the narrative repertoire of one tradition bearer, Marina Takalo (born in Russian Karelia 1890, died in Finland 1970). Takalo was illiterate, so for her oral communication was the sole process by which information was formed and transmitted. Her repertoire — the amount of the taped material is about one hundred hours — included all the genres of Karelian and Finnish tradition. Mrs. Takalo seemed to be aware of the different meanings and uses of different narrative genres. She categorized the stories using her own "natural" terminology (Honko 1962: 48–64) and seemed to be well aware of the differences when she was relating a folktale (she referred to these narratives as a "tale," "story that has no truth in it," "amusing account"); when she was telling a saint's legend ("story of holy men"); when her story was a secular legend ("story," "hearsay," "event"); and when it was a memorate event ("experienced event," "close event"). She also had a feeling for the meaning, the function, and the use of different stories, and in the course of telling them she selected the code appropriate for the genre from the possible alternatives. In each case this meant a choice between different norms governing content, form, style, texture, and structure. In distinct contrast to what Olrik supposes, most "epic laws" did not seem, at least not on the basis of Mrs. Takalo's material, to apply to all narrative genres. On the other hand, many folktales do seem to follow them.

All the folktales told by Mrs. Takalo contain both a formal beginning and a formal end (the "Law of Opening" and the "Law of Closing"). An existential sentence was used to introduce briefly the main characters of the story and, by means of the "Once upon a time" formula, both the narrator and the audience were transported away from everyday reality to the world of fiction. The action of the story took place between the formal opening and closing sequences. Repetition (the "Law of Repetition") occurs at many levels: for example, events, dialogues, phrases, or single words are often repeated three times (the "Law of Three"). Repetition is also, of course, a kind of rhythmic emphasis at different levels. There were usually only two persons occupying the stage at any one time (the master and each of the brothers in turn; the "Law of Two to a Scene"). Opposed character types (rich and poor) came into confrontation (the "Law of Contrast"). The weakest or youngest proved in the end to be the strongest or cleverest, and triumphed over the others (the "Importance of Final Position"). There can be no doubt that Takalo, guided as she was by tradition, was aware of these stylistic patterns. She knew what the style of each folktale should be and used this knowledge quite consciously in creating autobiographical poems from narrative material or in reproducing complete stories from remembered fragments (cf. Pentikäinen 1971: 90–96).

The "epic laws" operating at the stylistic level correspond to the rhythm of the story and to the language. The most distinctive characteristic of the language used in folk stories is its simplicity and archaic quality; for example, the language used by Mrs. Takalo in her folktales contained considerably more Karelian words and expressions than the ordinary language she used, which had been greatly influenced by Finnish. Language is related to content; the vocabulary is bound to the motif and is consequently foreign to ordinary speech. The form of language is also determined by the epic "Law of Action"; the story is made more interesting by actions rather than by the attributes of its characters, and the story progresses from event to event in accordance with the plot ("Unity of Plot," "Epic Unity"), with the emphasis given to events involving the main character. In its structure, therefore, the language of the story is much more fixed than ordinary language, and permits jumps from one association to another. The storyteller must capture the audience's interest and sustain it, taking his listeners with him and fulfilling their role expectations at the same time. The presentation of a tradition is socially controlled behavior which, in storytelling, means that the story becomes stereotyped, fixed, and has rhythmic tension. The central role played by action means that verbs predominate in the narrative much more than in ordinary language. Mrs. Takalo followed the Karelian style of narration in her abundant use of the historic present.

Linda Dégh writes: "Many have pointed out that the text is nothing but the skeleton of the performed folktale, and that it is necessary to fill out this skeleton by recording the inflection, cadence, and tempo — the rhythm — of the narrator. Gestures, facial expressions, and dramatic interplay must be retained" (Dégh 1969: 53). An examination of the rhythm of Mrs. Takalo's folk tales (Pentikäinen 1973) has shown that rhythm is no random factor in narration but something that is in many ways related to other levels of the transmission of tradition, e.g. the contents, style, form, structure, language, meaning, function, and use. Rhythm is without doubt partly social, formalized style. The individual's idiosyncratic differences, however, are reflected in the rhythm of his narrative. This was shown in Mrs. Takalo's stories by the fact that, as the family mentor, she emphasized the didactic sections of the story.

Marina Takalo belongs to a group of emigrant bearers of tradition. Her stories, like most of her other tradition, stem from the part of Karelia bordering on the White Sea where she spent the first thirty-two years of her life (1890–1922). Her folktales remained latent for about two decades until she was stimulated into recalling them in 1944 by spending two years in her home area. After 1944 she related the stories to great-grandchildren in the family, to other Karelians, and to collectors of tradition. It was principally the direct interview approach of collectors which inspired her to an intensive period of folktale reproduction in the 1960's. This led to a considerable increase in the numbers of folktales on record. In 1960 Mrs. Takalo was encouraged to relate quite freely the folktales she remembered and personally preferred. The collection of folktales gathered in this way was relatively small compared with the final results achieved (only 17.6 percent of the whole material). Systematic interviews carried out in the course of 1962 led to a doubling of her repertoire; furthermore, Mrs. Takalo was also able to recall at this stage a number of sporadic extracts from other folktales without, however, being able to put them together into a single, logical whole. By 1966 several folktales, of which she had only been able to remember fragments earlier, had been polished enough to be included in her REPERTOIRE. (Repertoire refers to the fund of traditions which the informant can actively recall and which he or she can relate without halting, spontaneously, and in a stereotyped manner when the topic of the story is mentioned. It is possible to speak of a REPERTOIRE THRESHOLD which a tradition overcomes once it has been related and ceases, through this activation, to be latent.) In the case of Mrs. Takalo's folktales the development was as follows:

1960: Total number of tales 6 / active repertoire 6.
1962: Total number of tales 25 / active repertoire 12.
1966: Total number of tales 34 / active repertoire 18.

In general Mrs. Takalo was able to relate a folktale simply by relying on her own memory; only on a couple of occasions did she receive help from other Karelians. In spite of the absence of any social control, the stories she was able to recreate in their entirety are very reminiscent of the collections of folk tales gathered in the White Sea area of Karelia.

Sometimes the bearer of a tradition changes the folktale to conform to his or her own individual personality and *Weltanschauung*. When a tradition is reproduced it is a question not only of the preservation of a tradition learned by the informant, but also of TRANSFORMATION. It would seem to be possible, in principle, to study the way in which a tradition is formed in the same way that transformational-generative grammar studies utterances (performance) in order to determine how language is created. The key to creating language is COMPETENCE. A skillful bearer of tradition is able not only to reproduce what he has learned but also to change (transform) the material with which he is already acquainted and to give it different forms. This he does partly by following certain rules he has learned and partly by following his own personality and his own view of the world. An interesting question is to what degree these rules vary for different genres and what degree of individual variation is permitted in different genres. In the case of folktales Mrs. Takalo's example suggests the posing of the following hypothesis: a bearer of tradition who is fully acquainted with the style, structure, rhythm, content, and language norms of storytelling may himself compose folktales or reproduce suitable narratives from memorized material.

REFERENCES

ANDERSON, W.
    1923   *Kaiser und Abt.* Folklore Fellows Communication 42. Helsinki.

BASCOM, WILLIAM R.
    1955   Verbal art. *Journal of American Folklore* 68:245–252.

BAVELAS, A.
    1953   "Communication patterns in task-oriented groups," in *Group dynamics.* Edited by Dorwin Cartwright and Alvin Zander, 493–494. Evanston, Ill.: Northwestern University Press.

CHERRY, COLIN
    1959   *On human communication: a review, a survey, and a criticism.* New York: The Technology Press of Massachusetts Institute of Technology and John Wiley.

COHEN, ARTHUR R.
    1964   *Attitude change and social influence.* New York: Basic Books.

DÉGH, LINDA
    1969   *Folktales and society.* Bloomington, Ind.: Indiana University Press.

DUNDES, ALAN
    1966   Metafolklore and oral literary criticism. *The Monist* 4:505–516.

DUNDES, ALAN, *editor*
    1965   *The study of folklore.* Englewood Cliffs, N.J.: Prentice-Hall.

GEORGES, ROBERT
    1969   Toward an understanding of storytelling events. *Journal of American Folklore* 82:317–318.

HONKO, LAURI
    1962   *Geisterglaube in Ingermandland.* Folklore Fellows Communications 185. Helsinki.

HULTKRANTZ, Å.
    1960   "General ethnological concepts" in *International dictionary of regional European ethnology and folklore,* volume one. Copenhagen: Rosentilde and Baggar.

HYMES, DELL
    1964   Toward ethnographies of communication. *American Anthropologist* 66:2–13.

JAKOBSON, ROMAN
    1960   "Closing statement: linguistics and poetics," in *Style in language.* Edited by Thomas A. Sebeok, 353. Cambridge: M.I.T. Press.

KROHN, KAARLE
    1922   *Skandinavisk mytologi.* Helsinki: Holger Schildts.

LEACH, MARIA, *editor*
    1949–1950   *Dictionary of folklore, mythology, and legend,* two volumes. New York: Funk and Wagnalls.

LORD, ALBERT B.
  1964   *The singer of tales*. Harvard Studies in Comparative Literature 24. Cambridge, Mass.: Harvard University Press.
MALINOWSKI, BRONISLAW
  1926   *Myth in primitive psychology*. New York. (Reprinted 1948 in *Myth, Science and religion, and other essays*. New York: Doubleday.)
MERTON, R. K.
  1949   *Social theory and social structure*. Glencoe, Ill.: Free Press.
OLRIK, A.
  1908   *Nogle grundsaetninger for sagnforskning*. Ringkøbing: Schondergskoe.
PENTIKÄINEN, JUHA
  1968   *The Nordic dead-child tradition*. Folklore Fellows Communications 202. Helsinki.
  1971   *Marina Takalon uskonto*. Forssa.
  1973   "Individual, tradition repertoire and world view." Unpublished manuscript.
SHANNON, C. E., W. WEAVER
  1959   *The mathematical theory of communication*. Urbana, Ill.: University of Illinois Press.
STRUNK, O.
  1962   *Religion: a psychological interpretation*. Nashville, Tenn.: Abingdon Press.
UTLEY, FRANCIS L.
  1961   Folk literature: an operational definition. *Journal of American Folklore* 74:193–206.

Fosterage

V. K. GARDANOV

Editors' Note: Fosterage is the practice of the compulsory rearing of children outside their parents' family. Still practiced by some peoples, the custom at one time was much more widespread. Vladimir Gardanov of the Institute of Ethnography in Moscow explores in this paper the possible origins and forms of fosterage. He looks at the theory of a "primitive community of children" in particular. His paper brings up a whole dimension of regularized educational practice. The key to fosterage is not the content of the education, but its structural characteristic of being carried on outside the family. This has a considerable potentional meaning for individual and group psychologies as well as for sociology. As an educational practice, it shares a major characteristic with institutional forms which also place responsibility for education outside the family (but usually leave the rest of the child's rearing to the parents). It also, however, shares much of its form with other varieties of noninstitutional education. It is not simply in between the two classifications, but an interestingly distinct variety of the latter.

In Soviet ethnographic literature the term *atalychestvo* is used for compulsory raising of children outside of their parents' family; in English this is denoted by the word "fosterage."

The term *atalychestvo* was originally borrowed from Caucasian studies. It was used by scholars to designate the ancient custom whereby a child was given away to another family to be brought up; the head of that family became the child's *atalyk* [foster father]. This custom was widely practiced until the turn of the nineteenth century by some peoples of the Caucasus (Georgians, Abkhazians, Circassians, Abazins, Karachayevs, Balkars, Ossets, and others).

The word *atalyk*, from which the term *atalychestvo* is derived, is of Turkic origin; it consists of the root *ata* [father] and the affix *lyk*, which in Turkic languages forms a whole range of derivatives for kinship terms which all bear the connotation "a person replacing a certain relative, playing his role" (Budagov 1869:8–9; Radlov 1893:455–456; Pokrovskaja 1961:21–22).

Thus the term *atalyk*, widely used by non-Turkic-speaking Caucasian peoples, may be interpreted as "a person (one who brings up children) taking the father's place, playing his part." This translation of the word characterizes the Caucasian *atalyk* who acted like his charges' father not only while they stayed with his family but for the rest of his life.

Atalychestvo in the Caucasus was observed at its strongest among the Circassians (Adigeis). Most of the available written material pertaining to *atalychestvo* in the Caucasus is also related to the Circassians; this is why the subject is discussed here primarily on the basis of Circassian ethnographic material.

Dealing with Caucasian *atalychestvo*, one should never lose sight of its complex composition showing different coexisting historical strata: vestiges of very archaic elements are found side by side with components which crystallized much later under feudal conditions, in a society divided into classes. Only such an approach will give a true insight into the genesis of *atalychestvo* and its social substance and role at the time when it was described in our sources.

The first thing to be noted is that the custom under discussion was compulsory under Caucasian feudal lords, and it was chiefly practiced among them at the time when it first began to be studied by ethnographers. Thus, among the Circassians the parents had absolutely no say in the matter of fosterage; according to custom, it was out of the question for the children of nobles to be brought up by their own parents. Khan-Girej, a well-known Circassian ethnographer who knew his people intimately and himself had been brought up by an *atalyk*, wrote in 1842:

It is without precedent in Circassia that an important man's children be raised in their parents' home, under their parents' supervision; on the contrary, immediately after an infant is born it is given away to be brought up.... (Khan-Girej 1842).

Atalychestvo was almost equally compulsory for the feudal lords of all the other Caucasian peoples among whom this custom was practiced as recently as the past century. It is precisely the compulsory nature of the custom of having one's children brought up in another family that unquestionably constitutes the essential — and archaic — feature of *atalychestvo* in the Caucasus. It is therefore reasonable to assume that in the earlier period fosterage in the Caucasus, and specifically in Circassia, was not confined to the feudal class alone, but was compulsory for all strata of society. This assumption is borne out by the fact that as late as the first half of the nineteenth century *atalychestvo* was practiced by Circassian peasants as well (particularly among the least feudalized tribes); and there is a lingering memory among the people of the time when the custom was universal and each Circassian family was required not only to give its children to some other family, but also to bring up other people's children. Traces of *atalychestvo* as a universal custom are also visible in Abkhazia, where peasants are known to have given their children to *atalyks* as late as the turn of the century. The Abkhazian material is particularly interesting, for among the Abkhazians, just as among the Circassians, this practice played a very important role in social and family life and retained its most archaic features (Al'bov 1893; Smirnova 1951; Inal-Ipa 1960).

Atalychestvo became a purely aristocratic custom in the Caucasus under the impact of developing feudal relations. Among the Circassians, just as among the other Caucasian mountaineers, feudalization occurred comparatively late and at a slow pace (Gardanov 1967), which is why some archaic elements were preserved in social and family life. However, the Circassian variety of *atalychestvo*, too, became fully feudalized. Georgio Interiano of Genoa (second half of the fifteenth century), who was the first to describe this custom as practiced by the Circassians, depicted it as an essential feature of their feudal way of life (Interiano 1502).

Once it had acquired feudal characteristics, the custom of *atalychestvo* was practiced by the Circassians strictly in keeping with the rules of the feudal hierarchy, whereby the children of princes were to be brought up by nobles of the first rank; the children of these nobles, by nobles of the second rank, and so forth; only the children of the lowest-ranking gentry could be raised in the families of ordinary peasants. The Georgians and Abkhazians in the nineteenth century practiced a somewhat different, later form of *atalychestvo*, which developed under feudal conditions; the children of the nobility were, as a rule, raised in peasant families. So in Georgia and Abkhazia, peasants raising their master's children became a sort of feudal duty which survived the abolition of serfdom in the 1860's and 1870's. Nevertheless, the Georgian-Abkhazian version of Caucasian *atalychestvo* was in full keeping with the chief principle of this custom, which had crystallized in the feudal period and under which the children were to be raised in families standing on a lower rung of the social hierarchy.

Although having one's children brought up in another family was compulsory, and this is the most characteristic and the oldest feature of

Caucasian *atalychestvo* which survived until the nineteenth century only among the feudal class, it should be noted that it did not apply equally to boys and girls. In principle, custom required that children of both sexes be given away, but under patriarchal-feudal conditions this custom fell off, with the result that even in feudal families it applied primarily to boys. As far as the Circassians of the nineteenth century are concerned, only princes and nobles of the first rank still regarded fosterage as essential for both boys and girls, with the feudal families of the other categories usually bringing up their girls in their own homes. The same was true of the other Caucasian mountaineers who continued to practice *atalychestvo*. Among these peoples, girls were given to *atalyks* in the nineteenth century only very rarely and only by the highest-born feudal lords. In Abkhazia, however, fosterage for girls had been widely practiced until the 1917 October Revolution by both princes and gentry, and even by some peasants. Such exceptions not withstanding, the Caucasian ethnographic material warrants the conclusion that in general the custom of compulsory fosterage for girls withered away earlier than that for boys.

One of the most important and archaic features of Caucasian *atalychestvo* was that the parents were required to avoid their children when they were staying with *atalyks*; the ban affected both parents to a degree. Not only were the parents to avoid seeing their children, but they could not take care of them in any way whatsoever; they were not even allowed to inquire about their health and in general express their interest or concern. On the contrary, they were bound to stress in every way their estrangement from their children. For instance, if the father or mother had a chance encounter with their child staying with an *atalyk*, they were to pretend that they did not recognize the child. During the whole stay of a Circassian child with an *atalyk*, the mother was allowed to see him only once, when the child was brought to his parents' home for the purpose; and the father had no right to see the child even in this instance.

With time all such rules gradually lost their stringency, and even among the Circassians in the first half of the nineteenth century they were fully adhered to only by the highest feudal class — the princes and nobles of the first rank. There is no doubt, however, that in the past the ancient rules of avoidance were binding on all parents who had given their children to *atalyks*.

Since children were given away immediately after being born and returned to their parents' home only upon coming of age, there was naturally a great deal of estrangement between the parents and the children as well as between brothers and sisters who had all been brought up by different *atalyks*; the *atalyk*'s family remained dearer and closer to the child than his own family even after his return to his parents' house.

The foster child's ties with the *atalyk*'s family were all the stronger since the *atalyk*, as custom prescribed, remained the main counselor and mentor for his charges for the rest of his life. Formally a foster father, the *atalyk* was often actually closer to his charge than the natural father. Accordingly, the *atalyk*'s wife was the child's foster mother, and the *atalyk*'s children were his brothers and sisters.

The ties of kinship between the *atalyk* and his family, on the one hand, and the foster child, on the other, were regarded as equal to consanguineous ties — and were in fact even stronger. This was strikingly manifested when there was a conflict between the ward's father and the *atalyk*: almost invariably the ward would side with his *atalyk*. Of course, such cases were extremely rare: as a rule, *atalychestvo* promoted very close and warm relations between the family giving their child to the *atalyk* and the latter's family. The child's father, enjoying a higher social standing than the *atalyk*, became the patron and protector of the *atalyk* and his entire family. On their part, the *atalyk* and his family became loyal vassals and servants of their ward's father and of his whole family. These relations — purely feudal in character — were cloaked, however, in a mantle of kinship, for two families bound by *atalychestvo* were looked upon as related to one another. The kinship quality of *atalychestvo* ties was emphasized by an obligatory involvement of the two families in each other's blood feuds, as well as by the prohibition of intermarriage between the two families.

The Caucasian *atalyk*, having completed his task (usually as his foster child came of age), was remunerated by the child's father in horses, cattle, slaves, serfs, weapons, and other valuables; sometimes the *atalyk* would also be granted a plot of land. The remuneration was a gift. Its size was not stipulated by custom and depended wholly on the social status and generosity of the father. However great the material value of this remuneration, it was not the *atalyk*'s chief compensation. Actually, when returning his foster child to the latter's parents' home, the *atalyk* would bring gifts, sometimes quite valuable, though certainly inferior to what he got himself. The chief compensation of the *atalyk* was the protection by his foster child's father and subsequently by the foster child. This is why an offspring of a noble family was sometimes claimed by several would-be *atalyks*, who subsequently took turns in bringing him up: the father, too, sought to make use of the custom in order to strengthen the ties of his family with as many vassals as possible, thereby adding to his own stature and importance.

Thus, in the feudal Caucasus *atalychestvo* was above all a means of cementing sovereign-vassal relations by artificial kinship ties. This was particularly important at the initial stages of feudal development, which accounts for the fact that the custom survived longer in its full-fledged form among those peoples of the Caucasus, such as the Circassians, that still remained in an early phase of feudal development.

For a long time *atalychestvo* in the Caucasus was merely described instead of studied, with practically no use made of the comparative ethnohistorical material for other regions. Accordingly, *atalychestvo* was regarded as a curious and rare phenomenon having no analogs outside of the Caucasus. In the light of the now available enthographic material, however, one can safely assert that the custom of having children brought up outside their parents' homes was, and still is, practiced in some form by many ancient and modern peoples in various parts of the world (Giraud-Teulon 1884; Post 1890; Kohler 1884; Steinmetz 1928; Briffault 1927; Kosven 1935). In particular, different forms of fosterage, sometimes quite close to Caucasian *atalychestvo*, occur among a number of Celtic, Germanic (MacLennan 1876; Weinhold 1856; also compare Joyce 1903; Rydzevskaja 1937), Slavonic (Wojcie-chowski 1895; Smirnov 1900–1904; Bobchev 1893; Popov 1904; Gardanov 1959, 1960, 1961), Turkic and Mongolian peoples (Schmidt 1829; *Altan-tobchi* 1858; Goldsunskij 1880; Vladimirtsov 1934; *Materialy po istorii turkmen* ... 1939, 1938; Nazarov 1890). This fact alone convincingly proves that fosterage, even in such a late, feudalized form as Caucasian *atalychestvo*, is by no means a local phenomenon specific to only one ethnic group of peoples, but is rather a widespread institution of a universal nature.

Since the Caucasian, Celtic, and other similar forms of *atalychestvo* represent an archaic custom modified by feudalism but bearing clear vestigial traces of a preclass tribal structure, the question arises regarding the sources of this custom.

Ethnological literature contains a great many hypotheses as to the origin of fosterage (Steinmetz 1928). One of the most popular of these ascribes pedagogical motivation to fosterage; it is assumed that the parents send their children away from home lest they get spoiled and to assure that they are raised in strict discipline in a strange family. Such considerations may have helped perpetuate the custom of having children brought up outside their parents' families in the late feudal and bourgeois epochs, when the children of the ruling classes were usually brought up in special boarding schools, but this explanation fails to give an insight into the ancient roots of *atalychestvo*.

In order to understand the origin of such a complicated phenomenon as *atalychestvo*, which underwent a profound transformation in the course of history, one should distinguish between the primary causes that gave rise to this custom and the causes that provided for the viability of fosterage, though in vestigial forms, under changed conditions. If one approaches the problem of the genesis of *atalychestvo* from this standpoint, one should proceed on those hypotheses which trace this custom to the matrilineal clan.

One of the first scholars to point to the connection of Caucasian *atalychestvo* with matriarchy was Kovalevskij, who observed in his well-known work *Law and custom in the Caucasus*, that *atalychestvo* was among the customs "whose origin cannot be explained by the rules of clan agnation and which presuppose the existence of matriarchy with its associated institutions" (Kovalevskij 1890:10). Noting a number of archaic features in Caucasian *atalychestvo*, Kovalevskij ascribed them to "the system under which patrilineal descendance was as yet unknown," and emphasized the importance of group marriage. Kovalevskij noted that *atalychestvo* had sprung from the clan system and compared this Caucasian custom with similar customs practiced by primitive peoples. Thus, he wrote, among the Maoris "children were never left with their mothers; as they were born they were given to foster fathers and foster mothers charged with the task of rearing and bringing up the children" (Kovalevskij 1890:14).

On the whole, Kovalevskij took the right approach to disclosing the genesis of *atalychestvo*. But he failed to lay bare the causes and circumstances that had brought forth this custom in a primitive society, for he erroneously assumed that the children were given to *atalyks* to be brought up for the simple reason that "the parentage of any of the possible fathers was questionable" (Kovalevskij 1890:17).

Kovalevskij's hypothesis was criticized by Steinmetz who justly remarked that group marriage may have been one of the causes of *atalychestvo*, but not by itself and only during the transition from group marriage to individual marriage. Moreover, criticizing Kovalevskij's hypothesis, Steinmetz, in an article first published in 1893, calls into question the very existence of group marriage, though he does not reject this possibility categorically (Steinmetz 1928:98).

Instead of Kovalevskij's hypothesis, Steinmetz put forward his own theory also centered around the main idea of the Russian scholar — the original connection of fosterage with matriarchy. According to Steinmetz, *atalychestvo* emerged during the transition from matriarchy to patriarchy as a specific transformation of matriarchal rules under the impact of an incipient father's law. Steinmetz writes:

Fosterage in a sense was a means whereby a group of people that hither-to had claimed a child tried to preserve their rights and accordingly protect them from the new growing force; on the other hand, it represented a reduction of this right, a desire to mollify the former right-holders by allowing the child to stay with them for a short while.... (Steinmetz 1928:90–91).

The hypotheses advanced by Kovalevskij and Steinmetz found no response in Caucasian studies in the late nineteenth and early twentieth centuries. In fact the next significant step forward in the study of the genesis of *atalychestvo* was made only forty years later by the Soviet scholar Kosven, who proposed a theory better constructed and better reasoned than that of his predecessors. Developing the views of Kovalevskij and Steinmetz, Kosven regarded *atalychestvo* as

... a very peculiar and specifically transformed old order of the children's transfer to their mother's clan, which had assumed vestigial and largely unrecognizable forms stemming entirely from feudal relations (Kosven 1935:55).

Using concrete material for some backward tribes and peoples of Oceania and Africa, Kosven has convincingly shown the genesis and gradual transformation of the custom of the children's transfer to their mother's clan — to the maternal uncle's family, which points to the original connection of *atalychestvo* with the avunculate (Kosven 1948).

Thus, Kovalevskij, Steinmetz, and Kosven among them have thrown much light on the compiex problem of the genesis of *atalychestvo*. However, the hypotheses advanced by these scholars all fail to pin-point the main factor behind the custom of having children brought up outside of their parents' home. The custom of *atalychestvo* cannot be understood properly unless one remembers a characteristic trait of classic primitive society: the children belonged not to their parents' family, but to the entire body of relatives where the children were born and brought up. This trait, which we suggest terming "the ar-chaic communal claim on the children," was inherent to the early phases of primitive society and stemmed from the very nature of the then current relations based on collective forms of ownership, production, and consumption. This feature was in full accord with all other rules and institutions of primitive society, including group marriage and group forms of kinship.

As the primitive communal system started to disintegrate under the impact of emergent private property and the individual family (which as a rule coincided with the transition from matriarchy to patriarchy), clans began gradually to lose their former unquestionable right to the children, who were increasingly claimed by the family headed by the father. This process, which was taking shape within the matrilineal clan, proceeded in the struggle of the old with the new, and gave rise, by way of compromise, to the custom of *atalychestvo*. The primitive clan family fighting for its rights to the children forced the paternal family, not yet strong enough at that time, to give away its children to another family, at first for good, and then for a more or less lengthy period. Thereby the paternal family symbolically gave up its exclusive right to the children born to it, and since the initial clan was matrilineal, the restoration of its rights to the children took the form of their transfer from the paternal family to that of the maternal uncle, the latter representing the matriarchal system receding into the past. The first form of the upbringing of children outside their parents' family thus emerged historically when the matrilineal clan was still in existence but patrilocal marriage had emerged. So at that stage *atalychestvo* was closely associated with the avunculate. The subsequent course of evolution, however, led to the ultimate disintegration of the matrilineal clan which was superseded by the paternal clan. Under such conditions the connection of *atalychestvo* with the avunculate was naturally severed. At this juncture the custom of bringing up children outside of their parents' home, a vestige of the archaic communal claim on the children, assumed another form, more in keeping with patriarchal rules: the children were given away to be brought up by any family provided it had nothing to do with the maternal relatives, for such a family under matriarchal tradition may have claimed the child.

And finally, during the transition from the patriarchal clan system to the class, primarily feudal, structure, the custom of compulsory upbringing of children outside of the parents' family, preserved above all by the ruling class, assumed the form of having the children brought up by a subordinate or dependent family.

Thus the various phases of disintegration of the archaic communal claim to the children are seen to have given rise to different forms of fosterage.

The question arises, however, as to why it took so long for the archaic communal claim to the children in the form of *atalychestvo* to wither away, and why the custom of *atalychestvo* proved so exceptionally tenacious, having been widely practiced during the decay of the clan system and subsequently in the early feudal period. In our view, as the clan system was falling to pieces there arose the need to make up for the lessening consanguineous ties. In response to that need *atalychestvo* came to the fore as an important means of forming artificial kinship ties, as a basis for protective associations and guilds. Later, with the establishment of feudalism, the custom was utilized by the ruling class to cement the ties between sovereigns and vassals, and this accounts for its being preserved predominantly in the feudal milieu.

REFERENCES

AL'BOV, N.
  1893   Ètnograficheskie nabljudenija v Abkhazii [Ethnographic observations in Abkhazia]. *Zhivaja starina*, vyp.3.
Altan-tobchi
  1858   *Altan-tobchi. Mongol'skaja letopis'* [Altan-tobchi. A Mongolian chronicle] (translated by lama Galsan Gomboev). *Trudy Vostochnogo otdelenija Russkogo arkheologicheskogo obshchestva*, part six. St. Petersburg.
BELL, J. S.
  1840   *Journal of a residence in Circassia during the years 1837, 1838 and 1839*, volumes one and two. London.
BOBCHEV, S.
  1893   *Sbornix na bulgarskit' juridicheski obychai* [Collection of Bulgarian legal customs], part one. Plovdiv.
BRIFFAULT, R.
  1927   *The mothers*, volumes one and three. London: Allen and Unwin.
BUDAGOV, L.
  1869   *Sravnitel'nyi slovar' turetsko-tatarskikh naredchii* [Comparative dictionary of Turko-Tatar dialects]. 1. St. Petersburg.
DUBOIS DE MONTPÉREUX, F.
  1839   *Voyage.... chez les tcherkesses et les abckhases, en Colchide, en Géorgie, en Arménie et en Crimée*, volume one. Paris
GARDANOV, V. K.
  1959   "Kormil'stvo" v drevneĭ Rusi [*Kormilstvo* in ancient Russia]. *Sovetskaja ètnografija* 6.
  1960   O "kormil'tse" i "kormilichitse" kratkoi redaktsii Russkoi Pravdy [On the *kormilets* and *kormilichitsa* of the short edition of the Russkaia Pravda]. *Kratkie soobshchenija Instituta ètnografii Akademii nauk SSSR*, vyp. 35. Moscow.
  1961   "Djad'ki" drevnei Rusi [*Djadki* of ancient Russia]. *Istoricheskie zapiski* vyp. 71. Moscow.
  1967   Obshchestvennyi stroi adygskikh narodov (XVIII - pervaja polovina XIX v.) [Social structure of the Adygei peoples (eighteenth through the first half of the nineteenth century)]. Moscow.
GIRAUD-TEULON, A.
  1884   *Les origines du mariage et de la famille*. Geneva and Paris:A. Cherbuliez.
GOLSUNSKIJ, K. F.
  1880   Mongolooiratskie zakony 1640 g. [Mongol-Oirat laws of 1640]. St. Petersburg.
INAL-IPA, SH.
  1960   *Abkhazy* [The Abkhazians]. Sukhumi.

INTERIANO, GEORGIO
   1502   *La vita et sito de Zychi, chiamati ciarcassi.* Venice.
JOYCE, P. W.
   1903   *A social history of ancient Ireland,* volume two. London: Longmans, Green.
KHAN-GIREJ
   1842   Vera, nravy, ogychai, obraz zhizni cherkesov [Faith, morals, customs and life style of the Circassians]. *Russkii vestnik* 1.
KLAPROTH, J.
   1812   *Reise in den Kaukasus und nach Georgien untergenommen in den Jahren 1807 und 1808,* volume one. Halle and Berlin.
KOHLER, J.
   1884   Studien über die künstliche Verwandtschaft. *Zeitschrift für vergleichende Rechtswissenschaft* 5.
KOSVEN, M. O.
   1935   Atalychestvo [Fosterage]. *Sovetskaja étnografija* 2.
   1948   Avunkulat [Avunculate]. *Sovetskaja étnografija* 1.
KOVALEVSKIJ, MAKSIM
   1890   Zakon i obychai na Kavkaze [Law and custom in the Caucasus] 1. Moscow.
MAC LENNAN, J. F.
   1876   *Studies in ancient history.* London: Macmillan.
Materialy po istorii turkmen ...
   1938-1939   *Materialy po istorii turkmen i Turkmenii* [Materials on the history of the Turkmenians and Turkmenia] 1 (1939), 2 (1938). Moscow, Leningrad.
NAZAROV, P.
   1890   K etnografii bashkir [On the ethnography of the Bashkirs]. *Étnograficheskoe obozrenie.*
NOGMOV, SHORA BEKMURZIN
   1861   *Istorija adykheiskogo naroda* [History of the Adygei people]. Tiflis.
POKROVSKAJA, L. A.
   1961   Terminy rodstra v tiurkskikh jazykakh [Kinship terms in Turkic languages]. *Istoricheskoe razvitie leksiki tiurkskikh jazykov* 1. Moscow.
POPOV, N.
   1904   Iuridicheskie obychai v' Varnesko [Legal customs in Varnesko]. *Sbornix za narodni umotvorenija,* volume twenty.
POST, A. H.
   1890   *Studien zur Entwicklungsgeschichte des Familienrechts.* Oldenburg und Leipzig: A. Schwartz.
RADLOV, V. V.
   1893   *Opyt slovarja tiurkskikh narechii* [Attempt at a dictionary of Turkic dialects] 1. St. Petersburg.
RYDZEVSKAJA, E. A.
   1937   O perezhitkakh matriarkhata u skandinavov po dannym drevnesevernoi literatury [On vestiges of matriarchy among the Scandinavians according to data from old Norse literature]. *Sovetskaja étnografija* 2-3.
SCHMIDT, I. J.
   1829   *Geschichte der Ost-Mongolen und ihres Fürstenhauses.* St. Petersburg.

SMIRNOV, N. I.
   1900–1904   *Ocherk kul'turnoi istorii juzhnykh slavjan* [Essay on the cultural history of the southern Slavs]. vyp. 1–3. Kazan.

SMIRNOVA, JA. S.
   1951   Atalychestvo i usynovlenie u abkhazov [Fosterage and the transfer of foster sons among the Abkhazians]. *Sovetskaja étnografija* 2.

STAL', K. F.
   1900   Ètnograficheskii ocherk cherkesskogo naroda [Ethnographic essay on the Circassian people]. *Kavkazskii sbornik* 21. Tiflis.

STEINMETZ, S. R.
   1928   "De 'forsterage' of opvoeding in vreemde families," in *Gesammelte kleinere Schriften zur Enthnologie und Soziologie*, volume one. Edited by S. R. Steinmetz. Gröningen: P. Noordhoff.

VLADIMIRTSOV, B. A.
   1934   *Obshchestvennyi stroi mongolov* [Social structure of the Mongols]. Leningrad.

WEINHOLD, K.
   1856   *Altnordisches Leben*. Berlin: Weidmannsche Buchhandlung.

WOJCIECHOWSKI, T.
   1895   O piaście in niaści. *Rozprawy Akademii Umiejętnosci, wydz.hist.-filoz.* 32.

SECTION TWO

Resistance to Early Western Education in Eastern Nigeria

CHUDI C. NWA-CHIL

Editors' Note: When European missionaries began in the mid-nineteenth century to evangelize and "civilize" what is today Nigeria, they were met with a mixture of apathy and mistrust. Very few people are likely to be surprised by the resistance of the indigenous populations to these educational efforts, yet a variety of explanations have been posed for the problems which resulted. In the following paper Chudi Nwa-Chil argues that too much attention has been given to the characteristics of the alien educational system itself, and not enough attention to the organization of the indigenous society, particularly to the relations between Europeans and Africans in the preceding years. These relations, it must be remembered, had been largely dominated by the slave trade. Here Nwa-Chil, himself from Eastern Nigeria, although now a lecturer at the University of Dar es Salaam in Tanzania, describes some facets of the institutional background and other factors which affected early educational contacts.

"The public apathy and suspicion that greeted the first efforts to introduce modern education in Africa have given way to an almost mystical faith in education as the indispensable key to personal and national progress" (Kitchen 1962:3). Our aim is to account for the real factors which were responsible for the early reactions (public apathy) of the people of Eastern Nigeria[1] toward Western education in those incipient days of its introduction in the region. It has very often been argued that the main obstacle to the acceptance of Western education in the region had been the innovative characteristics of this form of education. My contention

This is from a series of articles on "Education in Nigeria." A forthcoming one — to be published soon — will attempt to explain why and how the initial resistance to Western education in the region "has given way to an almost mystical faith in education," particularly among the Ibos. This is therefore a study in social change.

[1] To read "former Eastern Region of Nigeria," because after the recent Nigeria-Biafra crisis the Region was divided into three states.

is that while the innovative characteristics of Western education contributed to its nonacceptance, the main factors are to be found partly in
the cultural and institutional set-up of the indigenous society and partly
in the social relations between the Europeans and the Africans prior to
the coming of the first missionaries, the pioneers of Western education.[2]

THE EARLY CONTACTS OF THE PEOPLE OF EASTERN NIGERIA WITH THE MISSIONARIES

The first contacts between Nigerians and European missionaries began
with the first missionary expedition of 1841 — some three hundred years
after the start of slave trade between the whites and the blacks. This
mission, usually referred to as the First Niger Mission, and sponsored
by the Society for the Extinction of the Slave Trade and for the Civilization of Africa, was sent out to promote trade in the hinterland, to try to
establish model farms (through treaties with the local rulers) and, not
least, to spread the gospel and evangelize the Africans. Slave trade had
been going on for more than three centuries and was later abolished by
law, but slavery had continued one way or the other; law and force were
simply not effective.[3] It was believed, therefore, that "the only way to
save Africa from the evils of the slave-trade would be not by law or force,
but by calling out its natural resources" (Crowder 1962: 124).

This mission was a fiasco, as many Europeans in the expedition died
because of climatic and health conditions. But it was significant for at
least one reason: it was from this inception that the missionary activity
in Nigeria really began.

The first European missionaries to enter Eastern Nigeria were from
the Church of Scotland Mission, which arrived in Calabar in 1846. These
were followed by the Church Missionary Society, which began its first
activities in Onitsha, on the Niger, in 1857, and then by the Catholics,
with their first mission also at Onitsha, in 1885. The Qua Iboe (Protestant)
Mission was the last to arrive, and it settled along the Qua Iboe River
area in Uyo.

Although these missionaries had other tasks, such as helping to abolish

[2]   I have chosen Eastern Nigeria because of the Ibos, who are today often cited as
most progressive educationally and the most rapidly and thoroughly Westernized
group in black Africa. Of course, what I have to say also applies, sometimes in large
measure, to other societies in Africa. But I believe that it is especially interesting to
follow the historical development of these people in respect to European-style development, in view of what has been happening in Nigeria.
[3]   Britain had also tried to use force to stop the trade.

slave trade and promoting legitimate trade between the natives and the Europeans, their main objective was to preach the gospel and spread their new religion. They therefore preoccupied themselves with establishing schools and churches through which they could carry out this work of evangelization.

RESISTANCE TO WESTERN EDUCATION

The activities of these early missionaries, however, did not seem to be welcomed by the people of Eastern Nigeria, who not only did not want to go to these schools and were either indifferent or opposed to their establishment and the consequent introduction of the Western[4] system of education, but sometimes even resented the presence of the missionaries in these areas. Thus, these missionaries could not penetrate inland, but remained only along the coasts and in areas of the Niger Delta. And for a long time in the history of the interaction of Western education with the Eastern Nigerian culture, Western education did not make much headway, for it was their traditional social structure that gave the natives a basic reason to reject Western education.

The Religious System

Before the coming of the Europeans in Eastern Nigeria, the native peoples of the region had a way of viewing their world. At the center of the people's view of the world and the place of man in it was the belief in spirits, that the universe was peopled by spirits, some great, some small, some virtuous, and some deadly malignant. All were capable of swift and vindictive actions as well as of rewarding good conduct. These gods either inhabited or were guardians of the land, air, and sea, and everything in them.

Among the Ibo, the supreme deity was Chukwu (or Chineken), who was responsible for creation, fertility, and the rain, and "the source from which men derive their 'chi' or soul". (Forde and Jones 1967:25). Chukwu was also the father of the lesser great spirits: the sun, the sky, lightning, the earth deites, the spirits of water and farms, the spirits of yams and other crops, and the ancestral spirits.

The sun represented good fortune, wealth, and new enterprises. The earth deity, Ani (or Ali), was the most prominent of the great spirits and

---

[4]   Including the Americans' system.

was regarded as the queen of the underworld and the owner of men, whether dead or alive. A shrine for Ani rituals was found in each village, and a senior shrine in the original village of the village group or other wider community.

In Ibo cosmology, every human being had a genius or spiritual double known as his *chi* which was associated with him from the moment of conception, with which his abilities, faults, and good or bad fortune were associated, and into whose care was entrusted the fulfillment of the destiny which Chukwu had prescribed (see Forde and Jones 1967:26).

In very close association with the deities was the belief in ancestral spirits and reincarnation. This belief manifested itself in various ritual practices connected with the ancestral shrines. The dead were reincarnated, and the individual through his death made a transition from the material, tangible, or bodily life to the intangible world of the ancestors. In this process of transition there was usually the carry-over of one's social status and other personal characteristics to the other world. This closeness of the ancestor's spirits helps to explain the Ibo's strong kinship attachments. The cult of ancestors was closely associated with the earth goddess Ani.

But the Ibo world was not just of spirits. It was a dual world in which the spirit world and the world of man were one. The world of man was peopled by all created beings and things, both animate and inanimate. The spirit world was the abode of the creator, the deities, the disembodied and malignant spirits, and the ancestral spirits. It was the future abode of the living after death (Uchendu 1965:11). In the Ibo conception of the dead, the dead were alive and still members of the lineage joined to the real world in a mystic way. There was constant interaction between the world of man and the spirit world. This interaction manifested itself in the behavior and thought processes of the natives, for instance, in their reactions to *imps* and the belief in reincarnation.

Among the Ibibios and some east Cross River peoples, Abassi (Obassi) was the supreme deity. Like Chukwu of the Ibos, Abassi was the sky god and the creator of men. The Ibibios also had numerous other spirits — those associated with animals, sacred places, and objects, and all represented by varying symbols. "Worship of ancestors (Ekpo) is far more prominent. Sacrifices are offered at the ancestral shrine, which is kept in the house of the eldest member of the lineage and consists of wooden stakes two to four feet high driven into the ground. The Oron have carved figures representing ancestors" (Forde and Jones 1967:78). The Ekpo society was a cult group whose members impersonated the dead in public ceremonies.

Among the other tribes of the region, the phenomena of the supreme deity and a swarm of spirits of different denominations and varying functions were as true as among the Ibos and Ibibios. The same was also true of their other religious beliefs and practices.

To summarize, the world as conceived by the people of Eastern Nigeria was a world full of spirits and supernatural powers, a world of the visible and the invisible, a world of the living, the dead, and the yet unborn, a world in which the dead formed an integral part of the social life of the living. To understand these cosmological views of the people is to understand the people themselves: the moorage of their culture; what affected their behavior and thought systems; the framework into which one must fit the beliefs in witchcrafts, charms, and magic so prevalent in this society; the reasons for the respect paid to elders and traditional rulers who form the visible links between the living and the dead. To understand all these is indeed to make sense of the entire living of the indigenous people of Eastern Nigeria.

Then came the European missionaries who introduced their (Western) education. Central to this, at least in its early phases, were these Europeans' religious beliefs: the idea of Christianity, the Divine Trinity, the death and resurrection of Christ, atonement and salvation, the angels, the devils, and heaven and hell. "Almost from the start they condemned the indigenous religions in all their aspects" (Crowder 1962:132). They demanded that the African change to their, the white man's, religion. This demand was unacceptable to the people.

But, it may be asked, what, really, had Western education[5] in its early phase to offer the natives of Eastern Nigeria that would have motivated them to abandon their own system of thought for the European's? Was it the Christian doctrine of atonement and salvation? The practice of atonement was not, of course, unknown in the traditional culture. Among the Ibos, for instance, if a member of the family committed murder or manslaughter, revenge could be taken by the relatives of the murdered man on any member of the murderer's family and the property of the murderer's nearest relatives pillaged in consequence. But if the culprit committed suicide immediately, the whole family were saved from attack and their property from spoliation (Meek 1937:224; 1966:126).

Were the deliverance of the natives from evil spirits, the doctrine of heaven and hell, and the hierarchy of angels new concepts? As will be

---

[5] I consider Western education and the doctrines of the Christian missions (or Western religion) synonymous, the former being only an instrument with which the European missionaries had hoped to effect their proselytization. For example, reading was taught essentially to enable the people to read the Bible.

demonstrated, these were not unfamiliar in the religious doctrines of the Ibo or of any other tribes in the region.

About human sacrifices which the Christians were said to have frowned at, it may be asked whether the idea of sacrifice (human sacrifice) was not known to these Christians. The Christian doctrine taught that "God so loved the world that he gave his only begotten Son to be sacrified for the sins of men." It also taught, amidst messages of love for God and for one another and the abolution of human sacrifice among the natives, that one Abraham, in demonstration of his love for God, was about to sacrifice his only son, Isaac, on the altar but for the kind intervention of a voice in the bush and a ram nearby. So the Christians were indirectly teaching that if you loved God, you would be prepared to sacrifice even your own son to Him. There were then, Christian parallels to the native practice of sacrifice. The killing of twins or the sacrificing of humans was to propitiate the particular god or gods who had been offended, and here it should be reiterated that the birth of twins in those early days was regarded as "an abomination which the gods of the tribe or clan frowned upon" (Nduka 1965:91), just as much as the God of the Catholics would frown upon any Catholic who ate meat on Good Friday or who failed to do his Easter duty — sins usually remedied through prayer and sacrifice to God.

It has often been said that the people of Eastern Nigeria were animists. By this it is meant that they worshipped wood and stone and material artifacts. This description is not quite accurate. They never really worshipped materials objects. These objects were merely symbols of the supreme being, Chukwu or Abassi. Admittedly, there were no shrines or cult symbols for this supreme deity, except the Long Juju Oracle of the Ibos at Arochukwu, and no priesthood or place of worship for him. And it is also true that neither Chukwu nor Abassi, nor indeed any other supreme deity of these people, received any direct sacrifices. But the people knew that they were worshipping the supreme deity, and that this rather than the material and visible objects was the ultimate recipient of the offerings and sacrifices. The lesser gods to whom these sacrifices were explicitly made served only as intermediaries. The following dialogue between a European missionary and one village chief, who apparently understood the basic tenents of the Christian doctrine in those early days, will clearly illustrate this.

Village chief: "You said you had one supreme God who lived on high. We also believe in Him and call Him Chukwu. He is the Creator of everything, including the other gods."
Missionary: "But there are no other gods. Chukwu is the one and only God.

These other gods you mentioned are not gods at all. They are simply pieces of wood and stones, false gods. And you worship them as if they are the true God."
Village chief: "No, we do not. It is true that they are pieces of wood and stones. But we use them only as intermediaries. It is like your angels and saints. As you said, you do not really worship these, but you beg your Chukwu through them. These wood and stone are made by Chukwu for us to approach Him through them."
Missionary: "And the sacrifices?"
Village chief: "Yes, indeed, the sacrifices. We made them first to the little gods. And it is right to do so. They are the messengers of Chukwu. But Chukwu is the Master. These little gods are only his servants who know His will...."
The dialogue continued.[6]

Even if we accept that the natives were, in fact, animists, just how much more animistic were they in comparison to the religion which the Christians had brought to replace theirs?

In the Catholic teaching, for example, one found the angels (or spirits) of God. These angels were the guardians and messengers of God. Everyone on earth had one of them to guide and direct him against evil deeds. If he behaved well, the angel was happy and proud; if he behaved badly, he was ashamed and angry.

Then there were the saints, surrounding God in all His pomp and glory, in a descending order of hierarchy — the most holy of them being nearest to Him, but with Mary, the mother of Jesus, sitting closest. These saints in heaven above were those dead men and women who while on earth behaved exemplarily. Ask them, through prayers, whatever you want, and they will help you to ask God for it. Again, according to the Christian doctrine, beneath the world was hell, a kind of depository for the souls of those who died in mortal sins without repentance and forgiveness. Here these souls were perpetually punished (by burning) in an unquenchable fire. The chief of this territory was Satan or the Devil (or Lucifer) — a former chief servant of God and leader of the angels, who lost his heavenly position through disobedience to God and was cast into Hell.

One wonders, in fact, what significant differences there were between these Christian teachings and the religion of the natives — for instance, between the angels of the Catholics and the *chi* of the Ibos, between the saints in heaven and the ancestral spirits, and between the cross and holy pictures in the Catholic churches and the wood and stone carvings in the homes of the natives. Were not, for example, the saints and Satan just other names for the benevolent and malevolent spirits of the Africans, such as Olisa and Ajo Mmo [Evil Spirit] or the sun and Amadiora.

---

[6] A narration from my great-grandfather, who also was an "animist."

And when an Ibo said, "*Chim do!*" or an Ibibio man, "*Abassi do!*" [God, please!], was he not "raising his mind and heart to God," as the Christians would say?

It goes without saying that if the natives were in any way animists, the European Christian missionaries were no less so. And yet, the latter invited the former to abandon his animism for a belief in the "true" God, in the saints and angels, in the Holy Ghost, in the mysteries concerning the Divine Trinity and the conception of Virgin Mary, and in a better life after death. Whatever the missionaries might have meant, there is no doubt that these culture synonyms with a homonymous outlook[7] brought confusion among the people and contributed to the rejection of Western education in the region.

The Total Culture

It was not just the introduction of another religion that led to the people's initial skepticism toward Western education. The crux of the matter was that, in trying to change the religion of the natives, the missionaries also advocated a complete change in ALL of the indigenous culture. There was nothing good in it, they said; everything was virtually bad. "Native names and costumes, native songs and dances, folklore, art, systems of marriage, were all to be consigned to the scrap-heap" (Nduka 1965:12). It was altogether a revolutionary demand.

According to Crowder, this is, of course, understandable. "The missionaries made a correct appreciation of the fact that West African religions were much more closely integrated with West African cultures than Victorian Christianity with the rest of Victorian culture. To destroy the one effectively it was essential to destroy the other" (1962:52).

These demands naturally undermined the structure of the existing community. To accept them would mean the acceptance of a complete alienation from the entire culture. It would mean the acceptance of the individualism implicit in the Christian faith in contradistinction to the corporate concept of African life. It would make things fall apart. "A cultural group feeling itself threatened by another tends to close itself against the invasion of the other" (Ponsioen 1965:51).

Apart from these direct demands, there were also the indirect ones, arising, for example, from the school textbooks meant for use by the

---

[7] By this I mean that the two religions were quite similar; they only SEEMED to differ. It was this seemingness, essentially, and the missionary's approach to the situation, which caused the whole confusion and the people's reactions.

missionaries in their new schools. For all intents and purposes, these books, and other accompanying materials, were designed not for the people of the region but for the schools in Britain and other countries of Europe and America. Even when meant for the region, they were prepared with little concern about the environment in which the native child lived. They had no bearing whatever on the life of the individual as lived in his traditional enclave.

The earliest European schools in the region were essentially modeled along the lines of the charity schools in England, with curricula over-weighted with religious knowledge — recitation of the catechism, reading passages from the Bible, and singing hymns. When the songs were not religious, they had to be in praise of Britain and her scenery or of events in British history — Rule Britannia, Bonnie Charlie, etc. (Anowi 1965:43). Even in such a fundamental subject as language, not much was made of the vernaculars; "it was proficiency in English that was the goal" (Nduka 1965:37). Indeed, in most schools, not only was English taught as a subject in its own right, but it was made compulsory as the medium of instruction.[8] In such other subjects as the three "R's," the contents were imported unadulterated from Britain or from America, and no attempts were made to use local material in their preparation and teaching. In history and geography, children, mostly the sons of returned ex-slaves, who were understandably the earliest clientele of these missionary schools,[9] were compelled to learn the history of Europe — out of European history books — instead of African history. They were taught more about the Alps, the Thames, the winter and summer seasons, the "land of the midnight sun," etc., than they ever were taught about their own rivers, mountains, the dry and wet seasons, the Sahara, and the equatorial climate.

No doubt these early missionaries tried to give the best of what they really knew anything of — education as it was given in their own countries. The significance of this, nevertheless, is that the education intended for the people simply was not realistic, at least from the people's point of view. It was completely foreign and far removed from their life, or as Nduka (1965:39) put it, "the school and the environment tended to pull in opposite directions." As such, these schools did not arouse the interest and enthusiasm of the native peoples.

---

[8] For example, in all Catholic schools in Nigeria beginning from 1882.
[9] The other early clients of the missionary schools were the children of African traders who were involved in the exchange economy of the coastal region. Anyway, some of the early patrons of the missionary schools were said to have been "literally press-ganged into schools" (Wilson 1966:24).

Conflict with Traditional Education

Also significant in the resistance to Western education was the conflict arising from the traditional forms of education. Before the advent of the Christian missions or, indeed, of Europeans in general, the indigenous people of Eastern Nigeria had their own system of educating their young ones. As in all traditional societies, school and life were one, and education consisted solely in the transmission of the culture by the older members of the society to the younger ones. There were no schools in the formal sense of the word, or any system of organized teaching either for boys or for girls, except in scattered instances of apprenticeship for blacksmiths, medicine men, and fishermen for the boys.

Broadly, education in the traditional social system was "a matter of assimilation rather than formal teaching" (Green 1947:78), and the child learned through contacts, observations, and ACTIVE PARTICIPATION IN DAILY LIFE. This involved him concretely in a meaningful relationship with the entire community. Through his daily activities, he gradually acquired the material and spiritual fundamentals of social life: the values, customs, and traditions of his society, attitudes, beliefs, and world view, and the meaning of life in general.

Mothers played important parts in those aspects of education that concerned girls. They taught them everything relating to the role of the woman — how to fetch wood from the bush, how to draw water from the stream, how to tend certain crops, how to look after their younger brothers or sisters, and how to prepare family meals. Certain crafts, such as weaving and pottery, were strictly in the sphere of women. The distribution of and trade in production were also entirely in the hands of women, and girls usually learned the trade from the older women. All these skills were usually learned without the aid of literacy.

The father assumed most of the responsibility for the education of the boy. He taught him how to be a man.

Thus, a small boy might accompany his father to the farm carrying a wicker container with some fowls in it. He was taught to disintegrate a neighbouring ant hill, and on this the fowls fed. In due course he would take a small hoe in his hand and learn from his father how to clear and till the land and to cultivate the crops. This process of instruction did not end with acquiring the habit and skills of merely the labour involved. Weather signs would be taught, often in the form of runes, rhymes, and sayings. Crop pests, destructive and dangerous animals and reptiles, cross-fertilizing creatures and those advantageous to the soil were identified and their peculiarities taught (Wilson 1966:15).

The task of educating the young was not, of course, exclusively that of the parents. The child was also seen as a member of the community from the educational point of view. Consequently, his education was everybody's affair, and practically everybody took part in it in various ways. For instance, any adult could intervene in the education of any child and in the variously constituted groups for community education. Nonetheless, the parents alone shared the blame for the moral failures of their children.

Available evidence shows conclusively that in the traditional social system of Eastern Nigeria, the child was educated and educated himself in the bosom of society itself through his various contacts with adult life, and in the school of the family. It is wrong therefore to believe that Africa had no schools prior to contact with Western culture. This was exactly what the Europeans, particularly the missionaries, claimed.

When these missionaries arrived in the region, it hardly occurred to them that the natives had cultures of their own; little or no examination or analysis of what already existed in the region itself was ever made. There was, indeed, a naïve belief that the people had no education at all. The fact that education is itself part of the social organization of any society, that all societies, traditional or modern, have educational systems whether or not they are recognized as schools, never really caught the imagination of the European missionaries. No sooner did they arrive in the region than they "stooped to conquer." And so unfortunate misunderstandings arose.

These misunderstandings were reinforced by two other factors: the occupational socialization of the child and the parents' philosophy about education. In those early days children were engaged in various forms of productive activities almost as soon as they could walk. The girls, for instance, participated in various forms of household activities. They carried water from the stream, collected firewood from the bush, scrubbed floors, helped to prepare the family meals, and took care of the babies while their mothers went to the farm or the market. The boys, too, though freer than their sisters, also participated right from childhood. In the season they accompanied their parents to the farms. At home they were called upon to help either in the building operations or in getting food, usually grass from the bush, for the domestic animals, or they simply watched over these animals feeding in the bushes. These daily duties helped to prevent the children from attending the missionary schools and contributed to the resistance to missionary education.

There is one significant aspect that must be mentioned here. Those writers who apply the modern capitalist economic yardstick to traditional African societies have often said much to the effect that, because African children were engaged quite early in life, the African child was no more than "an economic utility" during his early days. This is not quite true, even if the word "labor" is sometimes used in describing the early activities of the traditional African children; one important sociological fact has often been missed by these writers. In the traditional social system of African societies, school and life were one. Children learned mostly through imitation and PARTICIPATION. In taking their sons or daughters to farm or to the market, or in giving them a few odd jobs at home, parents were doing no more than educating their children, as they believed education should be given. No doubt, children did contribute to their families' economy through these activites, but this was not the central objective of parents in these early childhood labor-activities. Education (or, if you like, socialization) was the main concern of these parents at this stage of their children's growth. In such a simple economy with minimal division of labor and specialization, the child had to follow the father (or the mother) in life in general, and in occupational socialization in particular. The economic relationship between child and parent was no more than that of teacher and his pupil, the parent playing the part of the teacher and the child that of the pupil. It was never an employer/ employee relationship, in which the child was an instrument who could be manipulated to perform various tasks merely to satisfy the (economic) needs of the employer. It was the duty of the father or the mother to guide the child when he made his first contacts with his environment, not only in social intercourse with other people but also in work, and to help him benefit from their own experience through his effective participation, according to his capabilities, in the workings of the community.

It becomes obvious, too, from another point of view, why the occupational socialization of the native child contributed to resistance to early Western education. Parents thought it their primary duty to give their children the necessary education. Going to a missionary school was not part of that duty, nor was it, at least as the parents saw it then, a necessary part of the child's education. Rather, as we have already noted, going to a missionary school appeared to have conflicted radically with the child's growing up (or education), not only in that it robbed the child and his parents of the time the child needed to learn at home, but also in that the content of missionary education conflicted with the ideologies of traditional ways of life.

STRUCTURAL STRAIN

To understand more fully the reactions of the people to early Western education in the region, one must look also at the nature of the early contacts between the natives and the Europeans in general and at the pattern of relations which existed between these two peoples before and at the time of the introduction of Western education.

The first large-scale contact of the people of Nigeria with Europeans began in about 1495, with the colonization of the two islands of St. Thomas and Fernando Po by some deported Portuguese Jews, exiles, and converts. These islands were said to consist of a rich volcanic soil and, with the heavy rainfall of the tropics, were found extremely suitable for the growing of some tropical crops and sugar. Sugar, in particular, was a ready market commodity in Europe. But neither São Tomé (St. Thomas) nor Fernando Po had any indigenous population, and as a result these two islands lacked the necessary labor force to work the plantations. Benin, in Western Nigeria, could supply the needed manpower and, by 1510, trade with Benin was almost exclusively in human beings, later slaves.

At Mina, on the Gold Coast, the Portuguese had established a fort and were already trading in gold from this region. Men were also needed to work the gold mines, and the gold merchants were said to be prepared to pay for them at twice their original cost. This meant huge profits for the human traders and soon Benin also was exporting slaves to Mina.

Trade in other goods dwindled after the start in slave trade, and, in fact, before the turn of the century men and gold were the main market commodities in West Africa. The slave population on the two islands of Fernando Po and São Tomé also was becoming so large that it was imperative for the slave dealers to look for markets elsewhere. By this time, fortunately for the traders (and unfortunately for Africa and the world), the Portuguese had begun to settle along the coastal plains of tropical Brazil, which was soon to become another huge plantation center. This was a prospective market for slaves and led most of the original sugar planters on the islands of São Tomé and Fernando Po to transfer their activities — now as slavers — across the Atlantic to South America, where they found a ready market for their goods, a Negro labor force of West African origin.

The silver mines of Mexico and Peru were also discovered by the Spaniards about the middle of the sixteenth century. Here, too, like the islands of São Tomé and Fernando Po and the gold mines of Mina in their early phases, there was a shortage of the necessary labor to work the mines. The population of America was said to be small. The natives of

Mexico and Peru were said to be unable to work in the mines; and the indigenous inhabitants of the West Indian islands had been depleted to almost complete extermination by earlier conquests. Of the Europeans themselves, not many were willing to leave home and work in these mines. The solution to the problem of labor force lay in its importation from the outside. The Spaniards naturally turned to West Africa where there was an abundance of people said to be well-fitted for hard work of this nature, easily adapted to the climate, and adaptable from the mines to the plantations. By the latter part of the sixteenth century the Atlantic slave trade was in full swing. Slaves from Benin joined those from the Congo and Mina — at the island of São Tomé, the center of the seventeenth-century slave trade — in large caravans, for sale in the Americas.

It was said that about 22,000 slaves were shipped annually from ports in Nigeria: 4,000 from Benin and the Colony of Lagos, and 18,000 from Bonny, the New Calabar (the present Kalabari), the Old Calabar, and the Cameroons (see Crowder 1962:63). Such was the first phase of the early contacts of Nigerians with the Europeans, and for many years this human traffic continued.

What were the implications of these early contacts and how did this pattern of relationship affect the acceptance of Western education in Eastern Nigeria?

First, the impact of slave trade on the society made the natives suspicious of any white man, be he a trader or a missionary. Following the history of this slave trade, one hears of the nasty slave raids, inter- and intratribal wars, and the resultant death tolls. One hears also of those killed during the actual slave raids, of those wounded and incapacitated by the wars, of those who died of hardship on their march to the slave coasts, and finally of the millions of souls subsequently shipped to the Americas across the Atlantic to work in the mines and plantations there. More than 40,000,000 people, the majority of whom were able-bodied, were said to have been lost alone to West Africa in this period (see Crowder 1962:63).

As a result of this huge traffic in slaves and the human destruction that went with it, the African developed an attitude of suspicion and apathy toward the European — if not suspicion, then a feeling of insecurity, of uncertainty, and of fear. And since he made no distinction between European trader and European missionary, these facts affected his response to the missionary calls. True, there was slavery in Africa even before the arrival of the first Europeans on that continent. But this was mainly for the performance of servile and domestic duties and relatively on a very small scale. Besides, slavery in those days was never so humiliating or so frightful as it turned out to be during the Atlantic slave trade. In the traditional African social system, slaves were usually acquired as domestic laborers and personal servants to their masters. They often became integrated into the families and were subsequently acculturated and became integrated into the entire community with full rights and duties of free citizenship. In some societies it was even possible for slaves to rise to positions of prominence. One remembers the biography of one Pepple, a slave of Ibo descent, who later became the King of Bonny in the Rivers Province.

The second implication of the early contacts may be summarized as follows: the difficulties of the early missionaries were largely the result of their close association with trading interests. The missions were dependent on the interior traders for transport and supplies, and inevitably in the minds of the local people they became identified with the traders they so hated (see Crowder 1962:147).

With the legal abolition of the slave trade (first by Britain and later by America and other European countries), Britain sought to increase her other trade with Nigeria, buying the raw materials from the country, such as palm produce, timber, and beeswax, and selling her finished products from British industries. But, more importantly, she also sought to deal directly with the inland people and the markets of the interior rather than restrict herself to the coastal regions. She sponsored a number of explorations of the Niger in search of inland highways for this purpose. Before then:

The marketing of goods, including slaves, was handled entirely by the African middle-men of the coastal kingdoms who secured their monopoly on the basis of their exclusive knowledge of conditions in the interior and of the fact that the climate was too unhealthy for Europeans to penetrate beyond the coastal fringe (Crowder 1962:118).

It was then said to be unpopular for Europeans to want to trade directly with the interior. The supply of Ibo slaves to the delta ports, for instance, was under the control of the Aros of Arochukwu who were said to be representatives of the Long Juju Oracle or the supreme deity of the Ibos, Chukwu. Incidentally, this oracle was recognized as the final court of appeal by virtually all the inhabitants of the hinterland and the delta regions so that the Aros acted as mediators between the oracle and the different tribes of the hinterland. Because the Aros commanded great respect among the Ibo and delta states, they were "the only people who could safely travel from village to village unharmed" (Crowder 1962:72). They were therefore the most convenient intermediary between the hinterland and the delta regions.

In genuine fear that they would lose the huge profits that hitherto accrued to them as a result of their intermediary position in trade, these native Aros middlemen did not welcome the idea of the Europeans trading directly with the interior markets. This led to friction and resulted in a number of hostilities against the new traders, as these Europeans were now called. For instance, in the early 1860's, throughout the lands of the Niger Valley, factories set up by the Europeans were attacked and destroyed (see Crowder 1962:146).

The point then is this: it was the very group of European traders, bitterly hated as it were (because of their intrusion into the hinterland), who provided transport, supplies, communication, and sometimes protection for the European missionaries. "As the missionary bodies were not rich enough to own their own ships, these trading firms helped them by transporting them from place to place as the former's ships plied up and down the main rivers and creeks" (Nduka 1965:23). No wonder then that these missionaries became identified with the traders the natives so bitterly hated. No wonder also that the "attacks on the trading posts at Onitsha in 1859 and 1860 brought to a standstill the work of the CMS (Niger) Mission at Onitsha"[10] (Crowder 1962:147).

In conclusion, it can be said then that the difficulties of the early missionary attempts to establish schools in Eastern Nigeria were partly due to the clash of cultures and the resultant culture conflicts between the Europeans and the natives; partly due to the fact that many natives, after more than three hundred years of subjugation into slavery, were not in those early contact days disposed to associate with any Europeans, be they European traders or European missionaries — as they could not distinguish one from the other; and partly due to the fear and insecurity of the native middlemen as their position in trade was threatened and on the point of collapse. As Nduka (1965:10) told us, the missionary "did not want the wealth from the Nigerian soil, nor the fruits of her forests, nor any portion of her soil, but her soul," but this was not enough to induce the native to go to school.

REFERENCES

ANOWI, J. O.
   1965   "The role and function of voluntary agencies in Nigerian education," in *Education in Nigeria*. Edited by O. Ikejiani, 40–53. New York: Frederick A. Praeger.

[10]   This Niger Mission, it should be remembered, began its first activities only two year previous, in 1857.

CROWDER, M.
   1962   *The story of Nigeria.* London: Faber and Faber.
FORDE, D., G. I. JONES
   1967   *The Ibo and Ibibio-speaking peoples of South-Eastern Nigeria* (reprinted edition). London: International African Institute.
GREEN, M. M.
   1947   *Igbo village affairs.* London: Frank Cass.
KITCHEN, H.
   1962   *The educated African.* New York: Frederick A. Praeger.
MEEK, C. K.
   1937   *Law and authority in a Nigerian tribe.* London: Oxford University Press.
   1966   "Ibo law," in *Readings in anthropology* (second edition). Edited by J. D. Jennings and E. A. Hoebel, 221–231. New York: McGraw-Hill.
NDUKA, O.
   1965   *Western education and the Nigerian cultural background.* Ibadan: Oxford University Press.
PONSIOEN, J. A.
   1965   *The analysis of social change reconsidered.* The Hague: Mouton.
UCHENDU, V. C.
   1965   *The Igbo of South-east Nigeria.* New York: Holt, Rinehart and Winston.
WILSON, J.
   1966   *Education and changing West African culture.* London: Oxford University Press.

Monastic Education, Social Mobility, and Village Structure in Cambodia

M. KALAB

Editors' Note: Changing the styles and control of education, the population it reaches, and the methods which support it, all have a considerable effect on the social fabric of a group. In the following paper, Milada Kalab, a lecturer in social anthropology at the University of Durham, England, reports on her research in Cambodia. Established tradition in Cambodia dictated a pattern of monastic education for boys from the local village and a pattern of local village support for the school. As the village became more and more integrated into the social structure of the entire nation, a number of influences began to alter this established pattern. For example, there were conflicts over the meaning and equivalence of various educational credentials. Some children were induced to seek education away from the village, and some of the foundations of the traditional strict monastic education were shaken. Kalab offers not only a record of this process but also insights into the effects and cross-ties of social change.

The hypothesis I present here is that the Cambodian village structure is dependent on the existence of Buddhist monasteries. During the last decades fewer and fewer young men were becoming monks, and this was partly related to the availability of modern secular education. But when the situation became critical in the late fifties, the availability of improved higher monastic education reversed the trend.

My own statistical data come from only one monastery and one small hamlet which form part of a village situated on the left bank of the Mekong River, halfway between Phnom Penh and Kompong Cham town. The Cambodian government had kindly given me permission to copy data

This paper is based on unfinished fieldwork conducted in Cambodia in 1966 and financed by research grants from the Royal Geographical Society and the International Federation of University Women. Many new factors have entered the field during the last few years and my conclusions might not be quite applicable today. To that extent this is a historical study.

from the completed questionnaires of the 1961 census, and I was also allowed to make use of the cadastral records of the village. When, however, in 1967, I wished to augment my incomplete information, I was refused a Cambodian visa. Therefore, if I make tentative generalizations about the whole country on the basis of scanty information about one hamlet, it is not because I am unaware of the limitations of such a procedure, but because I was unable to get more data.

Under the circumstances it might be useful to consider to what extent the village is typical and representative of the state as a whole. Cambodia is not one of the overpopulated countries of Asia. There are about seven million Cambodians living on 70,000 square miles, giving a density of about 100 persons per square mile; but about 90 percent of the inhabitants live in about one-third of the area, in the plains, along the river and lakes. Though at least 80 percent of the people are agriculturists, only about 25 percent of all cultivable land, which is about 10 percent of all land, is actually under cultivation. In Cambodia nobody needs to die of hunger; to be poor means simply to be short of cash.

The village of Prek Por Suosdey (see Maps 1 and 2) lies in the district of Srey Santhor in the province of Kompong Cham, one of the most

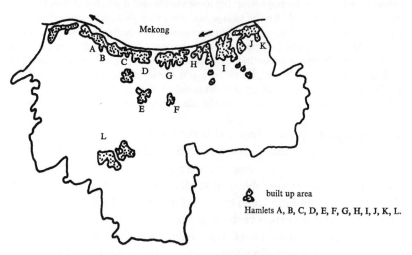

Map 1.   Hamlet distribution in the village of Prek Por Suosdey

fertile areas of Cambodia. There is very little virgin land left in the village but serious pressure on land has not yet started. The village area covers almost 2,000 hectares, and of these about 1,600 are cultivated; the inland crops are mainly paddy and maize and on the river bank there are diverse cash crops. About 1 percent of this land belonged to the crown, 1 percent

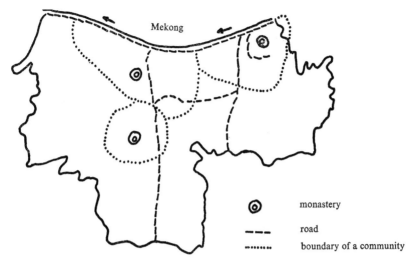

Map 2.   Monastery distribution in the village of Prek Por Suosdey

to monasteries, 1 percent to the village community, and 12 percent to the
state, while 83 percent was privately owned. This privately owned land
was divided about equally between men and women.

The relatively slow and quiet pace of life probably came from the poor
transport facilities. Though a jeep could travel along the river bank and
on a few tracks inland, it was most unusual to see one. No bus service
existed there; transport was mostly by boat, or by bicycle or motorcycle.
One could go by the steamer to Phnom Penh in four or five hours and in
about the same time to the provincial capital, Kompong Cham. There were
at least half a dozen runs a day and the fare was very cheap. But the pas-
sengers on steamers never got off before their final destination, so there
was no mixing of strangers in the village tea shops, as there would have
been if a bus service passed through the village.

Though most villagers seemed to be reasonably well-off, modernization had not made any great impact on the traditional way of life and the
monastery was usually the first to enjoy any innovation. An electricity
generator and loudspeakers were in use during festivals, bottled drinks
were common, but almost the only sophisticated gadgets anybody owned
were a transistor radio or a motorcycle. Everybody still supported the
monastery according to his ability, and even the construction of the medical center was organized largely by the monastery. Only a French-educated
teacher from outside the village expressed doubts about the usefulness
of Buddhist monks. The same informant told me that in villages on
important motorways boys are no longer interested in becoming novices.

This change most likely affects the richer areas rather than the poorer ones where people cannot afford to imitate urban styles of life and remain traditional out of necessity. But in Prek Por monastery support seemed to be a voluntary choice, and that is likely to apply to the majority of Khmer villages.

Prek Por had about 4,500 inhabitants living in 1,500 houses, and the village was subdivided into twelve hamlets. But the boundaries between these communities as understood by the inhabitants themselves are not always identical with those on government maps. This applies even to individual hamlets in areas of dispersed settlement.

A true community is formed by the households supporting the same monastery, and in this sense Prek Por had three monasteries and therefore consisted of three communities. Though in theory any person may support any monastery, in practice — at any rate in this village — the houses giving support to a particular monastery formed a distinct contiguous area. Such a community may overlap the administrative village boundary.

A dyadic relation between an individual household and the monastery is the criterion of belonging to a community, and it is a relation that is easily established or dissolved. It seems to be one of the factors facilitating the spatial mobility of the Khmer peasant. The rate of mobility in the hamlet of Prathnol was almost incredibly high. Between 1961 and 1966, 30 percent of the people moved out and new immigrants arrived who, by 1966, constituted some 40 percent of the total population.

One of the three monasteries in Prek Por was Vatt Prakal, which was supported by seven hamlets, among them the hamlet of Prathnol, which is situated immediately next to the monastery. The villagers are specially organized for the purpose of supporting their monastery. Every hamlet elects its own representative called an *achar*, always a respected man who knows all the Pali formulae and the details of ceremonies, usually somebody who was a monk for a period of time and, moreover, a man who can be trusted with money. The seven *achars* then elect from among themselves a chairman, the big *achar*. They keep in touch with the monastic dignitaries, organize ceremonies and festivals, and address the monks on behalf of the congregation in the temple; they lead recitation and chanting by the lay people. They also collect contributions from the villagers in cash and in grain, and they keep all the accounts.

As in other Theravada countries, only older people attend the weekly services on Buddhist holy days and attempt to keep the precepts. The young and the householders, who contribute most of the offerings and labor, attend services only on special occasions, and though they then repeat the eight precepts after the monks, they make little effort at observing them. Very young boys may become pagoda boys, doing minor services for some particular monk and either living in the monastery or spending only the day there. Older boys may become ordained novices. Only older people attend meditation retreats during the rainy season and of the nineteen people in Prathnol who did so, sixteen were women. Of course men interested in the contemplative life can become monks, and some do so later in life, especially widowers.

I mentioned the committee of *achars* which acts as the liaison between the lay community and its monks. The inhabitants are connected through quite a different system with the administration of the country. An elected headman acts as the representative of the villagers to the administration and he also represents the administration to the village. He is responsible to the district officer, who is responsible to the governor of the province, who is responsible to the central government. The headman is the only member of this hierarchy who has any grasp of the local affairs; all other officials are members of the civil service, bureaucrats moved every few years to other locations. The headman is a local man and he is elected.

The other elected person who represents the people directly at the center is their member of parliament. Under Prince Sihanouk, a third link with the administration was the National Congress, a public meeting attended by all the ministers and other officials. It was held twice a year in the capital and any citizen had the right to attend and bring up a question or a complaint to which the officer responsible for the matter had to answer in public.

The secular administrative hierarchy is paralleled by a monastic hierarchy. As in Thailand, there are two monastic orders in Cambodia, the Thommayut and the Mohanikay, but unlike Thailand, in Cambodia each of these orders has a separate hierarchy of dignitaries, with a *sanghanayaka* at the top of each order. The Thommayut monasteries are virtually limited to towns, with a very few exceptions (Ebihara 1966:176) and their supporters are the royal family and most officials. Out of about 3,000 monasteries, only about 110 were Thommayut. There were none in Prek Por.

On the village level, every monastery is headed by an abbot and his two deputies. Only some abbots are permitted by the central organization of the *sangha* to act as preceptors at ordination ceremonies. In every district there is an *anukon*, a monastic position corresponding to the district officer of the secular hierarchy. In the district of Srey Santhor this official resided in a different village from that of the district officer. On the provincial level there is the provincial monastic head, called a *mekon*, who resides in the provincial capital. There is a council of monastic dignitaries at the center, and there are also councils on the provincial and district levels. The provincial and higher dignitaries were nominated by the king, the lower ones by the head of the order (Chau-Seng 1962).

In most matters concerning the *sangha* both the secular official and the monastic official cooperated; for instance, teachers in the monastic schools had their nominations countersigned by the governor and the *mekon*. In theory this harmonious cooperation was essential for the life of the Khmer nation, which was likened to a chariot with two wheels, one of them being the state and the other religion. But sometimes there appeared to be a slight tension between the two hierarchies.

Though the main aim of a monk's life is the attainment of nirvana and the villagers support him materially to gain religious merit, the monasteries always provided many more immediate services. The monks were the most trusted advisors of the people, who discussed their agricultural work with them, borrowed money from them, and sometimes received medical advice. Today if a monk takes charge of a community project, people do cooperate with him and the project is likely to succeed. Though monks are supposed to keep aloof from politics and have no right to vote in a general election, during the last electoral campaign in 1966, all four candidates in Prek Por's electoral district, instead of holding public meetings and delivering speeches, spent their time visiting the abbots in all the local monasteries. Grass-roots politics were in the hands of the influential monks in the villages and this was one of the reasons why Prince Sihanouk and other politicians, even when followers of the Thommayut order, paid more and more attention to the Mohanikay hierarchy. But while the head of state showered special favors on the late *sangharaja* of the Mohanikay order, tensions occasionally developed on a lower level.

For instance, the district officer at Srey Santhor and his family were supporters of the Thommayut order. When attending a Mohanikay service in the village, they complained to me that the Mohanikay pronunciation of Pali was quite unintelligible to them. Later I witnessed a clash during the funeral of the *anukon* of the district. Cremations of important personalities are always accompanied by a series of ceremonies and entertainments lasting for several days. These are planned well ahead to avoid any clashes. This time one of these special events was the distribution of gifts to poor people by the district officer, but he was delayed by some family matter and missed the fixed time in the morning. He then decided to hold the distribution at the time when the *mekon* was giving his sermon. It would have been quite easy to postpone the occasion for an hour, but as neither dignitary would give way, both ceremonies proceeded at the same time, about one hundred yards from each other, and both used loudspeakers to their fullest advantage. The appointed bureaucrat had obviously much less reason than the elected politician to be polite to a monk. Even so, the *mekon* had a larger audience than the district officer. The introduction of compulsory secular primary education was a more serious blow to the power of the *sangha* than such personal skirmishes.

Education was always one of the traditional functions of the Buddhist monastery. Various monastic institutions founded by the kings of Funan were seats of learning and places for the education of the young. Their inscriptions mention not only how much food and incense each resident was to receive every day, but also the number of blank leaves, ink, and chalk needed for students (Chatterji 1964:115), while among other servants attached to these institutions there were preparers of leaves for writing (Chatterji 1964:123).

As it was the practice until recently for every boy to become a novice or monk for a period of time before marriage, and as every monk must be able to read sermons, almost all Khmer men were literate and all women were illiterate. The term literate meant in this context a man who could read, not necessarily one who could also write. This distinction is so important that the census questionnaires make a distinction between those who can read and write and those who can read only. More significantly, the census taker questioning monks in Vatt Prakal indicated that all the monks could read only, though I know that at least some of them are good at writing.

When King Chulalongkorn in Thailand decided to modernize the Thai educational system, he continued to use the monasteries for the purpose (Wyatt 1969:116), gradually training more and more teachers, both monks and laymen. This system started in 1884, and it was introduced into the Cambodian provinces of Thailand in 1900. When Battambang and Siemreap were returned to Cambodia in 1908, the people there wished to continue the modern pagoda schools, so the French adopted the idea in 1911. Thus for some time the traditional function of the monastery continued in a modernized version. Later, however, more and more secular primary schools were founded, and this happened at a time when the other functions of the monasteries such as giving medical help, banking facilities, and architectural assistance, started to fade away as well.

Education was always one of the means of social mobility. Now not only could education be had without monastic training, but the certificates from the secular schools were more useful in getting employment. So fewer and fewer boys became novices. This was the situation in the middle of this century and it seemed at one stage that the monasteries might die out, which in turn would necessitate drastic changes in the village structure.

Meanwhile the level of literacy was constantly improving. The primary school sector has been enormously expanded during the last dozen years, so that mere literacy has ceased to be a problem for the younger generation. In 1964 an adult education campaign was started with the target of teaching every Khmer person how to read and write within one year, and every foreigner within two years. In Prathnol this effort was very successful, partly due to the fact that the district office was in the neighboring hamlet, but also due to the genuine enthusiasm of several local teachers. Except for some very old ladies, everybody could now read and some people actually did read books — middle-aged ladies read tracts on religion, young girls read love stories and manuals on writing love letters, men preferred historical novels, and everybody read the election manifestoes of parliamentary candidates. In 1966 nobody was interested in reading newspapers. Though at this time there were only three adults below the age of forty at Prathnol who were illiterate (Kalab 1968:533), only three persons had some secondary education: one man and one woman in their twenties and one man in his thirties, who had monastic secondary education.

It was at the stage when the monopoly of primary education was passing away from the monasteries to secular schools that the *sangha* started paying more attention to higher education. They had always had some Pali schools in the capital. From 1933 on they had introduced a system of elementary Pali schools into village monasteries. In 1962 there were 570 primary Buddhist schools in the country. Apart from Pali and elements of the Buddhist doctrine, the students also learned mathematics, science, history, geography, civics, and administration. If after three years they passed the state examination, they received the title of *Maha* and could take part in the entrance examination to a Buddhist lycée.

In 1962, there was only one Buddhist lycée in Phnom Penh which admitted 150 new students every year (Vajirappano 1962). Later a Buddhist lycée was opened also at Battambang. There students study, apart from Pali, physics, chemistry, mathematics, religion, history, geography, hygiene, Sanskrit, French, English and Khmer. Later, as more monks were able to go for higher education to India rather than to France, there was a tendency to choose English rather than French as their European language. After four years at the lycée there is another state examination and successful candidates are allowed to sit for the entrance examination to the Buddhist university. Each year forty new students are admitted. The study at the university lasts ten years and is divided into three parts. During the first three years the student has to master fourteen different subjects. After the first degree he specializes, choosing one of six courses. After four years he can obtain a master's degree. After three more years and a thesis he may receive a doctorate.

The Buddhist secondary schools and the university were started with the intention of creating an up-to-date Buddhist intellectual elite, because the monks were losing their intellectual leadership to the French-educated scholars. But the effect of this new network of schools was much wider.

The decisive move was the recognition of the certificates issued by monastic institutions as equivalent to those issued by secular institutions. This happened, according to Choan and Sarin (1970:139), in 1963. According to the Cambodian secular system, a child starts school at the age of seven in class 12, and the first grade of the Pali elementary school corresponds to class 9, the third grade to class 7. The Buddhist lycée corresponds to classes 6, 5, 4, and 3 of the French lycée.

There was one schoolteacher resident at Prathnol who had a diploma from what was known in his time as the Higher Pali school. According to him it should have been recognized as equal to a certificate from class 3 of a French lycée, and he should have been paid as a full teacher; actually it was recognized as only a certificate from class 6 and he was employed as an assistant teacher. He believed that this situation would be mended soon by yet another new law. But whether these certificates are recognized completely or incompletely, the main thing is that they are recognized.

Despite the success of primary education and the literacy drive, poor children still found it difficult to get secondary education. The school might be far away and the student would have to reside near it and pay for his board and lodging. It might be a little cheaper if he lived in a monastery, but even then he had to pay for his books and uniforms. According to Choan and Sarin (1970:140), most of these schools were new and expected the students to contribute between 1000 and 4000 riel to the cost of construction. I was also told that some teachers demanded bribes. Girls are helpless here, but poor boys who desire an education can become ordained novices and join one of those monasteries which have Pali schools.

Rich people in Phnom Penh complained about this development, which deprived their Paris-educated children of a complete monopoly of certain jobs. This development also may not be true in all areas of Cambodia. In cities and on the main roads monkhood presumably continued to decline in popularity among the young. But the situation at Vatt Prakal seemed to confirm the renewed interest in the novitiate. According to the census of 1961 there were eighteen monks and eighteen novices in this monastery. In 1966 there were fourteen monks and thirty-eight novices there.

Though I have no information about the number of monks in Vatt Prakal before 1961, one can deduce indirectly that in the past their number must have been higher in relation to village population. I have the statistics for men from the hamlet of Prathnol who were or were not monks (Table 1).

Table 1.   Men of the hamlet of Prathnol

Age group	Number of males	Number who are or were monks or novices	Number who never were monks or novices
11–15	17	3	14
16–20	11	5	6
21–25	9	1	8
26–30	10	6	4
31–35	11	7	4
36–40	10	8	2
41–45	5	4	1
46–50	4	3	1
51–55	5	4	1
56–85	9	9	0

We may disregard the 11 to 15 age group, because few boys join before they are 14 or 15 years old. In the 16 to 20 age group almost half the boys are novices. This contrasts with the 21 to 25 age group where only 10 percent became ordained.

From this Table it appears that before 1930 or so everybody became ordained. Later the numbers shlowly declined. For the 36 to 55 group it is still 80 percent, for the 26 to 35 group 60 percent; then suddenly the lowest point is reached at 10 percent, which happened probably around 1960. It seems that the recognition of the monastic certificates around 1963 had considerable effect, bringing the figure of boys becoming monks to 50 percent.

Most of the new novices stay as long as they can continue their studies. After two or three unsuccessful attempts at an entry examination either to the lycée or to the university, they are likely to disrobe and to seek government employment with the help of the last certificate they were able to obtain. According to Choan and Sarin, most of them stated they wished to return to agriculture when they disrobed. This is a rather surprising wish, even though most of them might have to do so in the end. I remained in correspondence with a few monks, of whom two have disrobed. One of them had attended only an elementary Pali school and also studied some English. After disrobing he worked as a mason at the Angkor conservation project and later as a cycler, taking tourists around to the monuments. His aim was to become a tourist guide. The other monk had completed the Buddhist lycée, but was not admitted to the university. After two years as a Pali teacher he disrobed and became a clerk in a government office.

Obviously, the monastic system of education does offer a channel of upward mobility to the poor boy, but it is not a soft option. There are good reasons why some sons of well-to-do parents do not choose this path, except when they genuinely wish to become monks for life.

The novices are kept under strict discipline by their teacher and by the abbot. At Vatt Prakal, in addition to their studies, daily alms rounds, and chores within the monastery, they also worked daily on the construction of the medical center, carrying stones, mixing cement, and the like.

Attendance at a monastic school is no guarantee of a final certificate. Places in the higher institutions are very few and the competition is intense. There were about 10,000 students in the elementary Pali schools in 1961 (about 3,500 in each grade), and about 3,500 would appear for the final examination each year. Of these, only about 2,000 were successful, or approximately 57 percent. Of these 2,000, only a fraction could be admitted to a Buddhist lycée — 150 students in 1961, maybe 500 today. Of these again, about 60 percent would pass the final examination, though the statistics are not very clear on this point. But whatever the number of successful candidates, only 40 can be admitted to the university each year. Only the very best get that far.

Having worked so hard for so many years, what have they learned? Much of their study is still done by rote rather than by understanding, and though some secular subjects are taught, this is probably on a very elementary level. Most of their time is spent, understandably enough, on the Pali language and Buddhist doctrine. Tambiah (1968:101) mentions that the monks in northeast Thailand often do not understand what they recite. This does not happen in Cambodia because, since 1926, Pali recitations by both monks and laymen are followed by a Khmer translation of all texts except the precepts. This, of course, does not mean that the person knows which word means what. Some monks have a very vague idea about the grammar even after several years of Pali studies. But no doubt the Pali schools have made some improvement here.

In the secular sector the government wisely encouraged technical education — science, medicine, and agriculture — so that Cambodia probably does not have the surplus of lawyers and economists that India used to have. A Buddhist education, however, is of necessity geared towards the humanities, so that the most useful employment, like agriculture and engineering, is closed to the poor student with monastic training who is obliged to indulge in such luxuries as philosophy, linguistics, or archaeology. Of course this paradox applies only to the few at the top; the majority probably end up as teachers. As monks study all subjects through the medium of Khmer and not French, they may be specially well-qualified to help with the Khmerization of instruction (Vann Molyvann 1967).

This whole development was disrupted in Cambodia in April 1970. In 1952, the Khmer branch of the Viet Cong claimed to be following the tradition of revolutionary Buddhist monks, and it was proud of having several Buddhist monks of repute on its committee. They also wrote that "the schools opened in liberated areas taught people how to read and write Pali" (Khmer Peace Committee 1952:21). Now it seems, at least according to the official *Cambodian News*, that the communists are concentrating on liquidating the *sangha*. They destroyed 208 pagodas and after a year of war only one-half of the original 70,000 monks were still in robes and alive (*Cambodian News* 1971). Those monks who did not disrobe under pressure or were not killed are said to be concentrated in the towns where army protection is available. As all higher schools were always in towns, many more monks may be using this unfortunate situation to study, or at least the numbers of students would not diminish. But the elementary Pali schools are bound to be affected.

According to information received in July 1972,[1] the interest in monkhood is indeed increasing, at least in areas under government control.

While the Khmer Rouge do not persecute monks in the same way as the North Vietnamese, they do not allow members of the *sangha* hierarchy to attend their annual congress in Phnom Penh, they nominate their own monastic dignitaries with a *sanghadhipati* at the top of the hierarchy, and they hold their own monastic congresses every six months in the forest. They also stop young men from becoming monks.

In the Khmer Republic parents now encourage their sons to enter the *sangha*, partly in the hope that in this way they will not get involved in fighting. On the other hand, the qualifications gained through monastic education are recognized by the Khmer government, and in the army a bachelor's degree leads to the rank of sublieutenant; a master's degree to that of lieutenant. Though until now military service has not been

[1] Personal communication from the Venerable Tor-Ann Aggarato, lecturer at the Buddhist University in Phnom Penh (to whom I am also obliged for several corrections in this text).

compulsory, there is no shortage of volunteers, and especially in the military police there are fewer places than applicants.

The increased interest in ordination is best seen in peaceful Battambang province where the number of monks doubled. In July 1972, it was proposed to increase the salary of Pali school teachers from 1,500 riel to more than 3,000 riel per month. The Buddhist lycée in Battambang prepares students only for their diploma; at the lycée in Phnom Penh they study only for the bachelor's degree, while the university has now only master's students. Apart from the two Buddhist lycées, three Dhammaduta colleges were started, two in Phnom Penh and one in Battambang. In these colleges teaching is done by unpaid volunteers, mainly university students.

The number of students admitted to the Buddhist University each year has also been increased. In 1971, sixty new students were admitted, and, in 1972, there were 200 first year students, divided into four classes. As of 1972, the entrance examination to the Buddhist University has been abolished. All students now receive scholarships which are fixed at 300 riel per month for a bachelor's degree and 600 riel for a master's degree. (A lay master's student in the Arts University in Phnom Penh receives 900 riel per month.)

These developments seem to confirm my hypothesis at least for the government-held areas. Whatever may be happening now in other parts of Cambodia, in 1966 it seemed that the improved system of higher monastic education saved at least some monasteries from extinction and so preserved the traditional focus of village life and the traditional village structure. Social change initiated by modernization in the secular education field was cancelled out by modernization in the monastic system.

REFERENCES

Cambodian News
    1971   *Cambodian News*. August 19th. Embassy of the Khmer Republic in London.
CHATTERJI, BIJAN RAJ
    1964   *Indian cultural influence in Cambodia* (reprint of 1928 edition). Calcutta: University of Calcutta.
CHAU-SENG
    1962   *L'organisation buddhique au Cambodge*. Phnom Penh: Université Buddhique Preah Sihanouk Raj.
CHOAN; SARIN
    1970   Le vénérable chef de la pagode de Tep Pranam. *Bulletin de l'École Française d'Extrême-Orient* 57: 127–154.

EBIHARA, MAY
  1966   "Interrelations between Buddhism and social systems in Cambodian peasant cultures," in *Anthropological studies in Theravada Buddhism*. Edited by Manning Nash, et al., 175–196. New Haven: Yale University Southeast Asian Studies.

ÉTUDIANTS DE LA FACULTÉ ROYALE D'ARCHÉOLOGIE DE PHNOM PENH
  1969   Le monastère buddhique de Tep Pranam à Oudong. *Bulletin de l'École Française d'Extrême-Orient* 56: 29–56.

KALAB, MILADA
  1968   Study of a Cambodian village. *The Geographical Journal* 134:521–537.

KHMER PEACE COMMITTEE
  1952   *Khmer armed resistance*. Cambodia: Khmer Peace Committee.

L'ÉDUCATION
  1964   Cambodge d'aujourd'hui. *L'Éducation* 3:23–25.

TAMBIAH, S. J.
  1968   "Literacy in a Buddhist village in northeast Thailand," in *Literacy in traditional societies*. Edited by Jack Goody, 85–131. Cambridge: Cambridge University Press.

VAJIRAPPANO, HUOT TATH
  1962   *L'enseignement du buddhisme des origines á nos jours*. Phnom Penh: Université Buddhique Preah Sihanouk Raj.

VANN MOLYVANN
  1967   La khmérisation de l'enseignement. *Le Sangkum* 26:54–59.

WYATT, DAVID K.
  1969   *The politics of reform in Thailand*. New Haven and London: Yale University Press.

Patterns of Enculturation in Communal Society

J. MICHAEL KING

Editors' Note: Communalism is a form of social relations which has been discussed and attempted for much of human history. Recently it has received particular attention and involvement in the United States, particularly on the West Coast. John King has for some years been involved with this "movement" and has collected data on hundreds of transient and more enduring California communal groups. In this paper, he gives background material on three groups which have maintained a certain amount of continuity over time. He constructs a typology of communal organization and then analyzes some of the processes of enculturation and education which take place in his three examples. He also compares these groups with Hostetler's well-known research on the Hutterites, one of the few communal groups maintaining an existence in America over a number of generations. King's paper provides interesting new data on this social phenomenon and a productive scheme for its analysis. In addition, he provides one of the few professional observational accounts of the processes of education in these alternative social groupings which have achieved so much popular attention in recent years.

Attempts to live communally have been made throughout history, and while most have failed to perpetuate themselves for long, such groups as the Hutterian Brethren and the Bruderhof have demonstrated that they can be successful. Given the current intense interest and experimentation in such forms and ways of life, I have elected to examine some aspects of the phenomena. It is hoped that through this brief analysis of communitarian processes of enculturation, or education, that some light might be thrown on the mechanisms by which some communes fail and others succeed. It might even prove possible to hazard a prediction on the relative chances for the continuation of such groups as we now have in North America.

In planning the research phase of this study, I chose to explore what I thought represented a reasonable cross-section of the communitarian scene in the United States today. Although I restricted myself to the investigation of communes in California, I examined all such groups for which there was any data in three of the eight major ecological zones into which the state is usually divided. These were chosen to represent urban, intermediate, and rural environments. From each of these regions one group was randomly selected for detailed analysis — it is these which form the basis of this presentation and which are described in the following three sections.

Before commencing with the main subject matter of this article, I feel that it would be desirable for me to present some general background information. On the basis of the study of these communes, I came to differentiate between three major forms of communal organization, with each being found in greatest abundance in a particular region (though far from exclusive to any). These I categorized as: acephalous commune, charismatic or centralized commune, and corporate or institutionalized commune, and define each as follows:

1. Acephalous commune: composed of at least two families (of procreation), usually of the same generation, who are related to each other on the basis of simulated consanguinity (fictive kinship). A polygamous union represents a single such family of procreation, and all must claim a common homestead or domicile.

2. Charismatic commune: composed of one individual in a superior social position with all others sharing a subordinate one. Frequently the superior individual is also older than the others, and his entire family may be dominant over the others. The rest of the group can be defined as for an acephalous commune.

3. Corporate commune: a corporate aggregation of smaller family units occupying a single dwelling, a number of adjacent dwellings, or a common territory; and normally composed of at least two families of procreation who are related to each other on the basis of fictive kinship. Frequently such families occupy at least two adjacent generations and usually possess a centralized decision-making body which is considered to be formally independent of the family units.

As I am contending here primarily with a social structural perspective, the definitions I have given have been designed to closely replicate concepts employed by Murdock (1967) in his description of more traditional forms of community and familial organization. It is intended that this device will extend greater comparability to the data at hand through at least the implication of a somewhat cross-cultural approach.

The term "commune" is retained, as against the more general "community," to draw attention to one of the specific and particularly significant characteristics of the family units being examined: that these families tend to be united with one another on the basis of simulated, rather than consanguineally determined bonds of kinship.

Within the many other communitarian studies, comparable forms of categorization have been cited by Turner (1969) and Zablocki (1971), among others. Turner's analysis revolved around his concept of "communitas," which had the three dominant types classified as existential or spontaneous, normative, and ideological "communitas." His definition of "communitas" is "a relationship between concrete, historical, idiosyncratic individuals" (1969:131), and "an unstructured or rudimentarily structured and relatively undifferentiated comitatus, community, or even communion of equal individuals who submit together to the general authority of the ritual elders" (1969:96). This comes close, but gives the phenomena a greater philosophical emphasis than necessary — although it certainly fulfilled his intentions. I have some reservations concerning the applicability of his typology, as it stands, to the current communitarian scene. Most assuredly, his analogy between "communitas" and the early "hippie happenings" must beg the issue. Turner failed to grasp that such "happenings" occurred only external to the established residential groupings of the time, which were in themselves usually not communal. Most of those who attended such congregations would return soon afterwards to their parent's or their own homes in the city or suburbs and to their regular white collar or student status — it was not through chance that almost all such "happenings" took place on weekends. A modified use of the concept, e.g. as fraternity, might nonetheless still prove quite beneficial.

Zablocki's description of the Bruderhof, a third-generation communal group now centered in upstate New York, explores the historical development of this corporate commune utilizing concepts much akin to those offered here. In retrospect, the author saw the Bruderhof as having grown along the lines established by the following organizational phases: communion, charismatic community, transitional community, and church.

These phases can be contrasted with my scheme as follows: communion — a definite, acephalous communal stage which involved the original group of persons who were to eventually found the Bruderhof. No one individual present was considered ultimately to be more in authority than any other. Charismatic community — what I also call a charismatic or cephalic (centralized) commune, based on the sociopolitical, and sometimes theocratic, dominance of a specific individual over all others, who are his followers yet unified amongst themselves as would be an acephalous group. Transitional community — by definition only sociologically "visible" in retrospect. Zablocki saw it as a period of emerging collective leadership which eventually resulted in the Bruderhof becoming a formal church, which is the last, or current, stage. These phases yielded a quite accurate depiction of what was in this case a religious, corporate commune.

Finally, the study of the Hutterites (e.g. Hostetler and Huntington 1967, 1968) can be contrasted with such analyses of communitarian groups in that, although they live communally, they are no longer members of a commune. By definition, such communards are together by reason of choice, not kinship — as is the case with the Hutterites who have become an ethnic group. Such a group is identified by reason of the biological or consanguineal — whether actual or assumed — kinship of the greater percentage of its membership. Although a commune's membership is often biologically unrelated, its constituent members may consider themselves to be related on other grounds, such as psychic or spiritual affinity.

In reading the rest of this paper, the preceding discourse should be kept in mind. Each of the next three sections shall be devoted to a description of a particular, representative form of the three types of communal organization I have referred to. In the last section, these will be contrasted with a brief depiction of Hutterian life, in an attempt to illuminate more sufficiently the sociological and enculturative questions in mind.

In referring to enculturation, it must be made explicit that I am thinking in terms of both the generic process of education, formal and informal, and the particularistic nature of cultural transmission. That is, I am continuing the distinction made by Mead (1963) several years ago, when she contrasted socialization, or the analysis of universal processes of learning, with enculturation, or learning as it occurs in a specific cultural setting. I shall return to this distinction at a later point in this paper.

THE KOBOLD COMMUNITY: AN ACEPHALOUS COMMUNE

Kobold is a small, urban commune in a predominantly residential district of San Francisco. Founded in early 1967, it is typically composed of about twelve adults with six children, although its specific composition has fluctuated several times over the years. Generally, the group is broken down into six nuclear families, with one child in each; however, there have been exceptions. A solitary adult male is commonly found on an extended visit there; sometimes he also invites a lover, would-be or actual. At another time for about seven months, the entire adult population, consisted of women — the men having relocated elsewhere. In time three women were rejoined by their husbands, two women found replacements, and the last left on her own.

This commune occupies a seven-room flat on the top floor of a two-story, aged tenement house. Four of the rooms are permanently employed as bedrooms, one is the kitchen, and the other two alternate according to need and whim as bedroom, guest room, studio, or child's playroom.

The communal economy is entirely dependent on the sum total of every individual's relative success in obtaining funds through extra-community enterprise. Three women receive welfare contributions for the care and support of their children; one has a reasonable, part-time position with a downtown department store; the other two are sometimes employed, sometimes not. The men seem to vacillate not only in their residence, but in their ability and willingness to seek employment. The most stable individual male over a period of time is one who has maintained a comparatively lucrative arrangement as a construction worker for the city. Others are commonly unemployed: sometimes supplementing their meager incomes with food stamps, sometimes surviving off one-shot jobs with various weekly newspapers (as delivery men) or other sporadic and low-paying sources of employment for unskilled labor.

The economic arrangements at Kobold readily reflect the group's emphasis on individualism and equivalence. The rent is divided on the basis of the number of bedrooms in use — usually, with four being occupied, the rent is charged to what is referred to as the "primary resident" of each bedroom. Initially, the five or six men each payed equal shares, whether they had children or not. Later, with the temporary departure of all of the adult males, the "primary resident" category came to refer to the adult women present, and has remained the case since the return of the men.

Since 1969 the group has participated in a local "food conspiracy" which enables them to purchase food with the buying power of several hundred consumers. The food may be paid for either with cash or food vouchers. In this sense, food is reckoned as being comparable to utilities in that the expenses for both are divided equally among each adult resident (irrespective of other status). A certain, fixed amount is put aside every week by and for every member; what remains is used for additional expenses incurred for items not obtainable through the conspiracy, or for unforeseen necessities. In addition, each individual is, of course, free to pursue his own particular needs or desires and, thus, to purchase and put aside anything he might especially want, so long as the cost of this does not impair his ability to meet his share of the rent and utility (including general food) costs. Special food for children has usually been considered as being in this latter category.

The most readily apparent motive for the residents of Kobold to live where and how they do (i.e. communally) is economic convenience. None of the individuals present is especially secure with regard to income; and this form of life-style allows each the possibility of having access to a greater, and hence more stable in overall terms, resource base than any one individual or conjugal pair could manage.

Furthermore, there is the somewhat obvious factor that each shares a common ideological and cultural background. None follow a particular religious creed, yet there is unity in their individualism: each accepts a belief in a "cosmic reality or consciousness," which is attainable through the use of hallucinogenic drugs and/or the practice of certain styles of living, especially those conducive to meditation. There is in this an understanding that communal living is of great importance for the proper development, perhaps the ultimate self-realization, of the individual.

Maintenance of the household, in terms of domestic services as well as general decision making, is theoretically communal. Originally, the women did essentially all of the household work, even when employed outside of the group (and when their husbands were not). Now, with the concept of "primary resident" in force, they have been able to push more of the responsibility and labor onto the men, retaining only those tasks specifically related to child rearing (as exclusively woman's work). General household work is done on a rotating basis, with each person being held responsible by the group for a particular day and night of food preparation, dishwashing, overall cleanup, etc. In practice, each individual is pressured to show responsibility for himself through cleaning after his activities. This includes even the younger children, who are expected rather early to take care of themselves. Thus, the "daily boss" usually has only to supervise for the day and tend to major, communal "messes" and he is quick to point out when an individual is derelict in his duties to the group.

Most social control and decision making can be made on an impromptu, immediate basis. When further arrangements or clarifications must be made, they are decided upon, as a rule, by the group while at their one, daily communal event: supper. Periodically a more specific decision-making meeting — a "blood session" — must be held; these usually occur almost weekly, typically on Sundays. Communal projects are also discussed at these get-togethers, and the actual form of arriving at decisions has been labeled participatory democracy.

Because the social organization of Kobold is based on what may be referred to as individual, adult equivalence, the ordering of authority and formal decision making tends to be somewhat "democratic." By this it is meant that at any given time the carrier of responsibility in terms of economics (who pays the rent or sees to it that it is paid) and authority (whose opinions are most highly regarded and most frequently respected) is always dependent on the group and must act within the bounds established by their perceived needs. Hence, such an individual is, at most, the spokesman for the group; and even this is likely to be so only relative to a specific, limited circumstance. Such "authority" changes hands almost as rapidly as decisions are faced, partly as a result of the group's inability to endure what are seen as transgressions against each member's inherent rights to self-reliance.

Despite the "primary resident" concept, within the nuclear family units decisions tend to be made with a sense of finality most frequently by the men. The adult males here have retained an authoritarian status in regard to the common, day-to-day affairs of the family. But the woman generally has the last say concerning the raising of her child, which is justified through time by the relative instability of marriages at Kobold. In the end, the women and children are the basis of the group; the adult male population is more transient.

For the child this means that he is ultimately rewarded for recognizing the authority of adult males, but not for taking any particular one too seriously. The children do tend to envy a man's relative freedom concerning his extracommunity activities and his obvious position of intimacy with their mother, and this reinforces their willingness to identify with the male role. But their first several years are almost entirely in a woman's world, and it is not until they enter school that the picture changes.

The Kobold child's first encounter with a parental surrogate is usually with an older (generally fictive) sibling acting as babysitter, while his mother is elsewhere in the house. Next, there is an occasional exchange of assistance between the women of the commune, in terms of watching and caring for each other's children while one has to be away; so the child soon has to adjust to a mild form of "communal motherhood."

This situation does not change significantly until the child is put in a day-care center, typically sometime in his third year. By that time his mother has begun to experiment, out of need or for a respite from the house, with part-time employment or attendance in school. And so the child is brought to one of several available centers: the Kobold mothers seem to prefer a particular, neighborhood one, where they periodically volunteer their services in exchange for their use of the place. One mother has also begun to use the center at the university she is now attending. In either case, overall convenience seems to be the deciding factor as to which one to use.

At this day-care center the child not only is left in the hands and care of strange women for the first time, but meets the first strange men as well (short of occasional visitors to the commune). These men are usually volunteers at the center and assume positions of assistantship to the women who actually run the program. None of the men present at this center are actually fathers themselves.

Although the children, boys especially, are generally fascinated with the men at the center, there simply are not enough to go around. Almost all instruction and most supervision derive from the women present, many of whom are well-known to the children (at some time every child's mother will be one of these). So the net result of the formal structure of the school is not substantially different from that of the home — with the important exception of the child's new peer relations. Here, for the first time, the child has the opportunity to meet and gather with others of his age who are not fellow members of Kobold.

The equivalent of the first three years of elementary school have to date been completed in attendance at the local "free school." This school is structurally much akin to the day-care center, with the important modification that here men are at least as significant as women: numbers and positions are essentially identical.

All grade levels are taught in one building, divided according to interest group rather than age or level of competence. This, as the child soon discovers, is admirably suited for peer-group patronage; and when a particular clustering of children feel they have a common interest, they can usually find an adult who will comply. Rather than having to learn to conform to the teacher's program, the students can frequently make matters go the other way.

In the past, from fourth grade on the children have entered public schools, with various reactions. Some have made the adjustment relatively smoothly; others have tended to withdraw in shock, finding satisfaction from their fellow communards rather than their schoolmates. Such children have been able to reenter an alternative school system by their sixth grade — all others have done so again with high school.

Thus far, none of the children have completed high school, and it is questionable if any will — at any rate, not in an "orthodox" manner. It seems that by this time in their lives they are already considered adults in the communard world and have little to compel them to go through those last years of school. By sixteen they will probably already be accustomed to sexual relationships and the use of hallucinogenic drugs; they will be all too aware of what to look forward to in terms of employment: very little, with or without a degree. If they return to school at all, it will be at the community college level, either for specific technical training or for general avocational interests.

For those of Kobold, the early phase of childhood, immediately after birth and through the preschool years, has stood out in marked contrast with later childhood. At that time the child is suddenly, almost violently, confronted with the need for seemingly spontaneous attainment of adulthood. Whereas before, as a "house child" or "knee baby," he was avidly fondled and cared for by most adults who wandered into his life, now he is at best ignored, or more often the object of frequent complaints and orders. In response he generally falls back for the first time on children his own age — initially those in his own home, then, those of his school. Forming steady peer groups is his hope for getting through the years ahead. Insecurity in this prompts him to continue his interest in his superiors, now transferred to an increasing degree to the adults at his school. If this is reciprocated, he may become an exceptional child in terms of the intellectual direction he follows — or in whatever other area he is capable of acquiring emotional support. At this time, while yet in the day-care facility, the child begins to spend most of his time in the company of others of his own sex, both adults and peers; and this tendency is likely to increase as time goes by. If the child is able to combine the value system of his adult fellow-communards with an interest and involvement in his peer group, then he is likely to continue the pattern and spend his adult life in fictive-fraternal households rather similar to that in which he spent his childhood. For many of the others, those who fail, the future lies in "open-land communities," squatter shacks, "crash pads," drug-induced oblivion, and/or jail.

HARMONY HILL: A CHARISMATIC COMMUNE

In contrast to the more rigidly structured, corporate community of

Matra devo bhava (discussed in the following section), Harmony Hill first strikes the observer with the impression of extreme looseness, even anarchy. While founded as a Hindu community, it relatively soon established itself as being absorptive in religious matters: synthesizing elements of Hinduism and Zen Buddhism with those of fundamentalist Christianity and occultism. In all of this, it actually reflects a more prevalent, representative form of contemporary American communalism than does the somewhat dogmatic organization of *Matra*.

Harmony Hill began in 1966 with the formation of a small group by individuals with related interests in the Wailua University, a Hindu-oriented center originally founded in India, whose main office today is located in Hawaii, with others in San Francisco and Virginia City, Nevada. Theologically, it is similar in focus to certain traditional veins within Hinduism generally, differing noticeably in its greater outward, goal-directed character. Of special significance for us is its application of *shūm* or *shūm-shūm*, a ritual language created by the Master of the University, who is said to have conceived of it during a vision.

The use of *shūm* played an important role during the initial development of Harmony Hill, though its overall use now appears to be gradually diminishing. It still figures prominently in several communal rituals, but it is used commonly only within a restricted, special social grouping (those who have been with the community since its origin).

Harmony Hill was originally an urban commune in Southern California, but relocated to the Santa Cruz Mountain area in early 1969. At that time, the leader of the community purchased six acres of land on a steeply sloping, redwood-covered hillside. His house was the first constructed and since has been adapted as the communal center; the structure of his household was distinctively polygynous. This is in contrast to all others, which remain monogamous. Little analysis is needed to identify this polygynous situation as an aspect of the leader's "special person" image: when his household disintegrated two years ago, he chose to remain alone, rather than in a monogamous relationship with the one woman he could have retained. Recently, he has indicated interest in two additional women, though their relationship is not as yet codomestic. Curiously, neither woman is a member of the community, though both occasionally participate in the period, intensive spiritual sessions which are sponsored for the benefit of group members and outsiders as well (the latter are largely included for the monetary benefit of the former).

As a rule, the community is composed of nineteen adults and seven children. These are broken down into the one polygynous household already cited and eight conjugal dyads. Typically, two or three of these monogamous pairs share a common household, but every adult individual has constructed and possesses a particular meditation platform of his or her own.

As of this writing, the group has undergone two major vacillations in population, in addition to the seemingly continual minor alterations which take place. They have incorporated a further four acres of land into their holdings and are currently in the process of making another extension. Sufficient housing for all has been built, and their platforms are scattered throughout the area for individualized mediation practices. Their greatest communal enterprises consist of having three taps sunk into a nearby creek — to insure an adequate water supply (which it does not do) — and creating a garden from which to feed themselves (which it is not capable of doing). The home of the community leader is also the communal center. The houses radiate out from there, and from them fan out the meditation platforms. The theme of individuality is reflected in these platforms, the independent houses, and the inability to organize the body of people for concerted, communal activities or to maintain their interest in group enterprises, especially if these latter concern general economic or political activities. Other than the purely social level, ritual is the only major level that these people seem to be able to share.

Cutting across all of the themes of individuality is the group concession regarding certain forms of ritualized expression: not only the ritual language (*shūm*), but also occasions such as their tea ceremony; the occasional communal meals; group meditation; and the ritualized use of various psychotropic drugs, specifically, marijuana and hashish (though these are not used by everyone in the community).

While much of the day is obviously related to personal pursuits, there is generally also a noticeable proportion of it devoted to cooperative activities. However, these can usually be considered as individualized acts as well, in that they most frequently take place between localized subgroups of people who have taken particular interest in one another. The bonds of friendship and association unite the community, but often only in a rather obscure fashion — via a circuitous route, with the entire group included only on an abstract level of perception or reasoning or through the eyes of an uninitiated observer.

In summary, Harmony Hill is composed of a group of households which are, in their turn, constituent units in a network of main and branch ties, relating each house to the other on the basis of short-term contractual bonds, with the emphasis on ritual cooperation and economic assistance. Each household is seen as being essentially independent, but linked to the community on a spiritual level. Within the specific homes are the family units, normally two or three conjugal dyads, with one having a polygynous tendency. Three households contain children, seven in all. Four were born at the settlement; two older than the community itself arrived with the original adult population; the last, born elsewhere, arrived there while still an infant. The community is perceived by its members as "owning" all of the children; nevertheless, with the relative instability of the population content in mind (i.e. specific people rather than the demographic structure), one sees the social framework as entailing the presence of nuclear families with children and relative equality between the sexes (some measurably greater authority attributed to the male household heads).

The household at Harmony Hill is characteristically composed of two or three nuclear families, each being considered as unique and distinct from each other as the household is from other households in the settlement. Sharing is generally restricted to coresidency status, though other select tasks are frequently treated in a cooperative manner, particularly among women of the house regarding certain domestic activities including childrearing. The men, on the other hand, cooperate with occasional construction and maintenance duties, but more often strike out on their own each day.

The sexes are considered comparatively equivalent, although the adult males are regarded as possessors of final authority and have a considerably lighter specified workload than their mates. The women take it upon themselves to maintain the order and continued functioning of the home, to care exclusively for the children, and to meet whatever shortcomings their husbands may have in terms of household subsistence. In a few cases, this means that the women, in addition to their other tasks, work harder and longer than their mates just to meet these shortcomings. Such arrangements are marked by instability.

Subsistence is achieved through a broad-spectrum approach: from gardening and gathering (wild foods and other surplus commodities), outside employment (full or part-time), or receiving government assistance (especially welfare payments). In addition the community sponsors several periodic activities which are oriented towards securing funds from outside — these are predominantly concerned with lessons in meditation and the like.

Given the women's usually demanding schedule of duties, children are assimulated into the work force at an early age. While still "knee babies," they are introduced to the world of domestic labor and are carried everywhere by their mothers. By age three, or when mobile but still a preschooler, these children routinely attend to personal and household tasks, with girls frequently responsible for other, younger infants. Since these children are commonly from different families and, again, considering the excessive work load of so many women, there have been motivations for the formation of child-rare collectives.

The most elementary form of such a collective pursuit at Harmony is that of the alternating assumption of responsibility taken on by women of a common household for their own children. The main collective, however, is that which is localized at the community center. Here is the only building which is really adequately heated during the long, cold and wet winter, the only building with plumbing at all, and that with the greatest daily turnover of visitors — thus, one is usually assured of being able to locate someone willing to assume charge of the younger children for a while.

Here, also, the child has the greatest exposure to cooperative and communal activities. He finds himself, while at the heart of the community, also at the center of his parents' ritual world. He is able to witness, and with increased age to participate in, all of the major group practices and, through the lectures and conversations which continually go on there, is made aware of the adults' values and world news. Through observing social interaction, he also soon learns the local patterns of friendship which to some degree contradict what he hears in terms of communal values — thus learning the lesson of relativism.

While child-care collectives are strictly a community pattern, formal schools are a different matter. In this matter community members have had to work together with other communes in the area on the construction and continuance of a "free school." This is located in a small town, about six miles from Harmony, and cares for the elementary grades. Here, community children first encounter strangers on a fairly large scale, though most are associated with other communes.

Entrance into school inevitably produces new contacts for the child, who soon begins to develop his own extracommunity social network (in contrast with his parents). Within a few years this will have progressed to the point where the child, usually from age ten on, will be allowed a considerable degree of freedom in arranging his life-style: where he will sleep; how he will get to and from school, or if he will go at all; whether or not he will "turn on," or eat meat (community adults are vegetarian); and with whom he will generally associate.

Anywhere from between the ages of twelve and sixteen, the child will be considered to be on his own. Henceforth, he will succeed according to his own merits, or so it is said, though he always has the option of

remaining with his parents. In point of fact, no child has yet done so —
by that age his peers apparently mean more to him than his parents,
and they have usually set off to form their own group (either within
the community, or at another).

The organization of the "free school" that children are sent to is
rather basic: there are four licensed instructors involved and a rotating,
volunteer staff of eight additional adults. All are considered to be teachers,
in the sense of being guides or educational facilitators. For legal purposes,
those with their teaching credentials are conceptually distinguished from
the others, though all are also parents of children in attendance and are
seen from that perspective as well.

The content of the instruction emphasizes such skills as reading,
writing, elementary mathematics, and the like. In addition, the child
is exposed to the intricacies of social and personal relations, his own
inner and social needs, and ways for attempting to satisfy them. Involvement is favored over lecture, spontaneity over regulation, independence
and creativity over dependence and memorization. The results suggest
an individual not unlike his parents: one who feels free to pursue his
own path and recognizes a need both for spiritual and self-realization
and for meaningful cooperative social interaction. These values will
likely be reinforced at the experimental high school he will attend,
irrespective of whether or not he satisfactorily completes his stay there;
by then he will have created his own world around his personal networks
of relations.

MATRA DEVO BHAVA:
A RELIGIOUS CORPORATE COMMUNE

Matra devo bhava [Mother should be treated as God] had its inception
as a formal, corporate community in 1966, with the purchase of twenty-
four acres of land in the central foothills of the Sierra Nevada, twenty
miles from the nearest city. The initial purchase was made by one
individual, since acclaimed the spiritual leader of the community. This
was followed the next year by the additional purchase of forty-eight
acres through the further efforts of the same individual, now joined by
several of his followers from his former temple in San Francisco. In
July 1968, over four hundred acres of land were obtained six miles away
from the first area; these were developed into what was to become a
cooperative farm, while the first holding was converted into a meditation
center/retreat (hereafter, specific reference is made to either the Farm,

or the Retreat, respectively; and generically, to the Community).

A prerequisite to joining the Community is that one has already become affiliated with the Self-Realization Fellowship and successfully completed either their or *Matra*'s own six-month correspondence course on meditation. Founded by Paramahansa Yogamanda, who called it, "the faith of all religions," it represents, in effect, an attempted synthesis of Hinduism and Christianity, with an emphasis on forms of "self-realization" through meditation and group ritual. The SRF has been in the United States since 1920, primarily centered in Southern California, but with branches throughout the nation and in more than twenty other countries (including India, where it is known as the Yogada Satsanga Society).

At the Farm new or prospective members must also contribute $1,000 to the Community, or $1,500 for married couples, before their official acceptance. Invariably, new members also bring in further capital of benefit to the Community, such as tools, machines of various kinds, building materials, and so on. Cancellation of membership entitles the person to whatever refund can be made from the sale of his membership, with a transfer charge being deducted. The Community will also sell whatever he leaves behind, such as a house, and reimburse him for the amount, except for a similar transfer fee as well as a "small" service charge; or it may choose to condemn the house and do with it as it pleases, without such compensation.

The people of *Matra* have developed a dual economic system, based on the standards represented by the United States dollar and the chit. The former is employed specifically for extracommunity affairs, i.e. for use outside the Community: payment of taxes, purchases made from professional distributors, and for the renumeration of services rendered by a nonmember. The chit is for purchases made within the Community and for payment of services rendered by a member either within a particular colony or between the two. It is a negotiable voucher, par to the dollar for purchases within the Community, but exchangeable for half the amount should a member prefer legal, i.e. United States currency.

The Retreat and the Farm have independent and quite distinct means for obtaining funds from outside of the Community. The Retreat depends primarily on its services as a meditation center and place of yoga instruction for the major part of its income. The Farm is involved in agriculture, manufacturing, and publishing. In the first category, it is concerned mostly with semiintensive horticulture for subsistence purposes (i.e. personal consumption), with some of its produce being sold to the Retreat and on the local market. A considerable portion of its lower grassland is also leased to neighbors for cattle grazing, though this is essentially a public relations endeavor — the rent charged is quite nominal (the people of *Matra* are vegetarian and, thus, have no use for the land themselves). The manufacturing business includes a variety of crafts including candlemaking, weaving, sculpture, and ceramics. There is an especially active incense and luggage ("steamer best") industry. They have their own record and publication company which prints and distributes a number of writings and recordings of various members of the Community and puts out their correspondence course in meditation and yoga.

What I have been referring to here as *Matra devo bhava* is composed of several dozen homesteads clustered in and around the two primary communities, or colonies, of the Farm and the Retreat, which are separated from one another by a distance of six miles. In addition, there exist a number of individually owned homesteads geographically, or at least technically, isolated but sharing in their religious and economic activities.

In all, there is an effective population of about one hundred and seventy-eight individuals, but only the forty in residence at the Farm directly concern us here. In contrast to the Retreat, the Farm has households with both child and adult population content (continued residence of particular persons) of a comparatively permanent character. Furthermore, as an arbitrary dividing line in terms of a test of durability and adaptation to the local way of living, we are only treating those forty who have been in residence at the Farm for five years or more (and whom I have been able to follow through those years).

I find it valuable to distinguish between certain categories of participants regarding residence, basing this on distinctions made by the members. Primarily, this involves dividing the total population into permanent and participating members, with the recognition of several functionally derived grades in each. The first category includes those who have resided in the Community for one year or more; have completed all necessary payments of dues; and in the case of a minor, has Community recognition that he is capable of assuming adult responsibilities. The age of obtaining majority is approximately fourteen, but one must, theoretically at least, be voted into adulthood. On the basis of actual observation, it appears that this is considered important only for males reaching adulthood; females have not yet found it necessary.

The second category includes all those who happen to be at the Community at any given moment; that is, it is comprised of transients and new arrivals, their number being calculated as an average figure. At the Retreat these are usually transients or visitors, and at the Farm these are usually guests (in season) or initiates (potential replacements or additions). Satisfactory completion or commensurate enrollment in either the SRF or the local Hindi correspondence course is mandatory for all.

An important subcategory of permanent membership is that of the trustee. This term is employed for the elected representatives of the members of the Community. There are five such officers, three for the Farm, and two for the Retreat. Those concerned with the Farm, one male and two females, represent the three major territorial divisions or wards of that colony. Territorial distinctions are not made within the Retreat, hence the two representatives here are chosen randomly from the population. In addition, the spiritual master of the Community, in effect, operates as another trustee (though never referred to in that fashion) in that his opinion is always sought or known. All permanent members are capable of voting in the Community elections. Elections for offices occur annually.

Participating membership allows one to take part in various Community activities without charge and to vote in special elections. All members, permanent and participating, are supposed to be consulted in cases of important political and economic decisions. Thus, participating membership, though highly conditional, is to be distinguished from casual visiting relations.

On the Farm a planning board is emerging along the lines of the official political structure of the Community. Thus far it is only loosely organized with self-elected members. The work of this group primarily concerns the direction and execution of housing and community layout. This involves regulating standards as well as the zoning of the colony into residential, agricultural, industrial, and natural areas — principally to insure the colony's control over its own future. At the present time the board is composed of four men who each possess the training and skills most related to the concerns of the group: one is an architect with additional experience in carpentry, one is a professional mechanic, another a plumber, and the fourth is the informal spiritual leader of the Farm and main assistant to the Community leader.

There are four basic structural, dyadic relationships in the social organization of *Matra devo bhava*. The first three, based on principles of kinship, are consanguinity, affinity, and simulation; and the fourth is association or contract. Of the several possible forms in the first category, consanguinity, the maternal and sibling dyads, are most prevalent. In addition, these are extended somewhat through the simulated, or fictive-kinship, arrangements made with would-be siblings. Affinal connections tend to be serial and temporary, while association affiliations are simultaneously short-term and prevalent.

Of the twenty adults at the Farm, sixteen are women, and only four are men. Two of the men are single; one, in fact, has taken a vow of celibacy. Thus only two nuclear family units remain intact. This leaves sixteen women and their twenty children to be accounted for. Two of these women are single, without children — they live together at the Farm center. Thus, we have a total of fourteen women with the twenty children.

Eight of the women have one child each; most of these women have paired domestically. Two of the women have two children apiece, one has three, and the last has five. Nine of these children have been born at the Community; all others came here with their parents. In most cases their fathers also came originally, but left soon after. Four women live with only their own children at home; the rest share a house with one other woman and her children. Both single men live alone and somewhat removed from the center of the Community.

In traditional American social organization, one of the crucial sets of obligations inseparably linked with the roles of husband and *pater* is the image of provider: the man sees to it that his wife and children are well taken care of. Apparently this is felt by the new arrival at the Farm, because one of the first programs the adult male in a recently arrived family engages himself in is that of constructing a sound, reasonably spacious home for his family. This is usually also the best major work program that he will complete, for no sooner is he through than he bids his family good-bye.

It has been pointed out to me several times that there is an assumption (on the part of the women) that a new man will only stay at the Farm for approximately three months, or the length of time required to finish constructing a durable building. This is despite the fact that he may come as a part of a family, that he was probably married for several years prior to arriving, and that he had to pay fifteen hundred dollars for membership and the right of his family to move there.

The enculturation process at *Matra* revolves mainly around the following three primary elements: (1) personal adaptation to approved roles facilitated through identification with established images; (2) the regular use of individualized and intimate group rituals; and (3) the institutionalized educational system. All of these are characterized by an emphasis on personal guidance, the use of examples (models), and repetitive actions. It is considered important for the child to develop definite values based on his identification with a model adapted from the local, formalized system of role-imagery, and tempered with personal (but supervised) experience.

In addition to the personalized, informal guidance begun at a very early age, the people of *Matra* provide their children with a day-care facility and primary school, to which they are consigned by the age of three. Prior to that, it is also common for mothers to exchange baby-watching services, and there is one collective infant-care center. For the last three years they have also operated their own high school in conjunction with another such community. During his fourth- through eighth-grade years, the *Matra* child is faced with attending a local, public elementary school. This is seen by his elders as a necessary public-relations move and an opportunity for extracommunity experience, and by the child as a chance for advancing. Generally, by the end of the last year at this school, the child is more than happy to be allowed to remain at *Matra*: his encounter with the outside world is guaranteed to shock him into an appreciation of his own life-style and community. It is felt by the people of *Matra* that it is initially up to a child's guardians, usually his mother, to assist him in his personal and social development and to prepare his way for later participation in the formal educational system. Even the school system is such that through the completion of third grade, the child will almost always be in association with, and under the supervision of, women who are known to him and are much like his mother. The rotating instructor arrangement at the day-care center and school also provides that he will be taught at least once a week by his own mother.

Children are, by and large, confronted from infancy with strong and explicit rules concerning the prevention of antisocial behavior, which is usually defined as excessive self-assertion, aggression, disrespect for others, and disobedience. Should a child exhibit such behavior, he is most apt to be reprimanded in a nonpunitive manner — praise and affection being balanced against the threat of withdrawal of love or attention.

Up until the age of eight or nine years, the children at *Matra* are prone at times to being somewhat boisterous and loud, even aggressive. When a child is thus acting out of line, his mother is apt to insist on his staying either near her or close to the home — keeping him away from the opportunity to fight with other children. Aggression directed toward peers is discouraged much more overtly and immediately than that directed against a parent; however, both are considered negatively and are equally likely to prompt corrective measures.

Two final factors are of extreme importance in the life of this community: these concern the concepts of mutual dependence or reciprocity and personal responsibility. In reacting to the reduction of family units to matricentric ones, the women here have come to reinforce their values regarding mutual interaction and dependence, at the expense of individualism. These women have banded together into common households and share a great wealth of material and economic interests.

The close mutual dependence of these women on each other is a dominant aspect of life with ramifications in most other areas of community organization. The children are made cognizant of this at an early age and are introduced to their place in this system through an equally early exposure to chores and the need for personal responsibility. Initially, most tasks concern household matters, eventually extending into agricultural labor. Girls are expected to aid in caring for other, younger children, first just those near to home, then at the community center. Boys move quickly into technical work and spend much of their time during their early school years with the men working together on the mechanical and industrial maintenance of the Farm. By high school age, all have assumed their appropriate places within the social structure: the girls, still at their mother's home, will spend their days in the gardens, factories, and religious centers; the boys, now living alone or at the center, will work on the technical and hard-labor side of life — or will relocate to the Retreat to practice a spiritualist's existence.

PATTERNS OF ENCULTURATION

In order to reduce the preceding descriptive sections to meaningful size and form, we shall now attempt to analyze them in terms of certain broad characteristics of their systems of enculturation. From this perspective we will be concerned more with the range of variations found between these three communes than with constructing seemingly all-inclusive categories. Thus, we should be able to recognize the nine basic patterns delineated as follows:

1. THE NATURE OF THE CHILD Generally, all groups considered their newborn children in much the same light as that recorded by the Fischers for the parents of Orchard Town, where the child was rated in regard to his supposed "potential" (see Whiting, et al 1966). Such a child is not so much the object of parental affection for what he is, but for what he is to become. There are many means for evaluating him in this regard. At each of these three communes, the child is typically rated in terms of his ability to adapt to, or at least accept, the local life-style. At Kobold and Harmony this is seen particularly in the area of the child's attempts at self-realization (including his ability to care for himself at an early age); at *Matra* this is more frequently a matter of the child's obedience and responsibility.

2. THE NATURE OF PARENTHOOD   Significant variations in attitude exist in the three communes examined in detail. At both *Matra* and Harmony, the mothers tend to see their giving birth to a child in terms of personal fulfillment and realization of new or increased status; at Kobold the perspective reflects a sense of motherhood as inconvenience or even personal affliction. Children there are seen as being accidental by-products of life, although ultimately inevitable. Overall, they are considered to be something of a burden.

At Kobold a sense of fatherhood is, at best, weakly developed or has little opportunity for display. Adult men are impermanent, usually transient elements of the group — those who remain are frequently not at home. At Harmony this is not the case at all; although particular occupants of the role may be replaced, the role of fatherhood and its attendant status are prominent and closely associated with the sentiments regarding motherhood as self-fulfillment. At *Matra*, fatherhood is nonexistent, though there exists what may be referred to as an institutionalized mother's-brother role. This is assumed by all adult males present for any length of time and is characterized by an informal, playful, and advisory or guidance relationship between these men and male children. Interaction of this sort between the adult males and female children is essentially similar, though the girls remain somewhat aloof at most times. The men frequently give lectures and demonstrations of special tasks to the children, but never reprimand.

3. DOMINANT VALUES AND PERSONAL ATTRIBUTES   This might alternatively be called, "The nature of the individual," and concerns the interplay between value emphasis and behavioral norms in each of these groups. At both Kobold and Harmony this would have to be considered within the concept of self-reliance: including such manifestations of this as self-realization, achievement, and independence. Both groups actively seek attempts at self-realization or enlightenment, which they further correlate with a struggle for personal dignity through mastery of spiritual integrity (which amounts to independence).

At *Matra* such is not quite the case. That is, whereas all groups claim to appreciate interdependence, it is actually realized to any substantial degree only at *Matra*, where the households are inseparably linked with one another and with the greater Community through complex sets or networks of obligations. Allied with this and with the composition of the household groups (which are matricentric), the emphasis here is on dependence and obedience. Once the individual has been accepted into the Community, bonds of reciprocity coalesce and grow, and they will only be broken at the expense of having to undergo complete Community rejection — of having to depart immediately and permanently. Given this, appreciation of a sense of responsibility is inculcated early into any new member's attitudes, whether he is young or old.

4. HOUSEHOLD COMPOSITION   Already alluded to above, this primarily involves the codomestic units indicative of each commune. Kobold actually represents a single household in a technical sense, though there are distinctions within the groups as to roommate-relations (including conjugal dyads). Sexual dyads are considered to be the foundation of the commune, but of the adult population only fictive sororal and maternal dyads have demonstrated any duration through time. Nevertheless, the operation of the commune implies a masculine presence, though this is characteristically met through the use of surrogates (the women presenting both male and female images).

At Harmony the household is usually divided between two or more conjugal couples, or nuclear family units, with the male heads of each taking definitely leading positions. At *Matra* the household is typically a fictive sororal one, with two women and their children occupying a cooperatively arranged dwelling. The woman present for the longer length of time has the greater voice in household decision-making situations, but this is not indicative of a pervasive sense of superiority or masculinity on her part (or not necessarily so).

5. DIVISION OF AUTHORITY AND LABOR   The typology of communalism cited at the beginning of this paper, and which supplied the format of it, directly concerned this aspect of community organization. It has been illustrated how, as communities, Kobold largely emphasized decision-making equivalence, and Harmony did essentially the same, with the notable exception of having an ultimate or last representative of authority — the community leader. *Matra*, on the other hand, had segmental community organization with separate political bodies governing each colony. The Retreat closely resembled Harmony in its structure; the Farm had a board of representatives, planning board, and additional, formalized channels of authority.

As for labor, all maintained distinctions in practice, though not necessarily in conscious orientation. At Kobold the women did the overwhelmingly greater amount of work, although the particular tasks anyone was likely to undertake were not stringently sex-typed. Within the household men and women were equally likely to perform most chores, in terms of the nature of the work; but outside labor was usually distinct as to sex — with men performing construction jobs and manual or unskilled labor and women following secretarial and academic pursuits. In the house itself only specifically child-rearing activities were considered to be "women's work."

At Harmony the amount of labor was for all purposes equal for the sexes, with tasks generally also being reciprocal, i.e. interchangeable between the sexes and between individuals within any given household (which was the labor or production and consumption unit). At *Matra* activities generally were comparatively rigidly sex-categorized, with the women performing by far the greatest amount and variety of tasks. Their labor was predominantly concerned with household and factory activities, as well as all chores strictly related to children. The men were concerned with specialized production and maintenance jobs, such as mechanized work and construction.

In all the communes, children are inducted fairly early into household tasks, considering the country at large where children are generally not part of the work force at all. Their chores are usually concerned with menial and repetitive matters, such as sweeping — with the notable exception that young girls are commonly given the care and supervision of yet younger children, sometimes for long periods of time. Both at Kobold and Harmony children of both sexes are expected from an early age to make some effort at keeping watch and care over their own effects. At *Matra* such is not felt to be important — mothers are usually quite willing to pick up after their children within the house so long as the children show proper attentiveness to their outside activities (gardening and schoolwork mostly, but also labor at the incense factory at about school age).

6. SOCIAL STRATIFICATION Closely allied in part with the immediately preceding pattern, here we are concerned with the categorization of roles that at communes largely reflect sex- and age-based distinctions. The previous section has treated the first problem in some detail; to recapitulate here briefly, I shall simply point out that such sexual distinctions are not felt to be especially significant at either Kobold or Harmony, though they are certainly more in evidence at the latter than the former. They are quite clear and pronounced at *Matra*, pervading all aspects of life there.

However, the primary form of stratification found in any of the groups is that which reflects age grading. At Kobold it is the most apparent form of communal organization amounting to an overt opposition between the adult and minor segments of the population. Both are perceived as occupants of what are essentially quite different worlds, members of each relying most on their particular age-peers. At Harmony the situation is comparable, though there is a more evident tendency for age-groups to grade into one another — partly correlated perhaps with the relative isolation of the commune, which would especially effect the children.

At *Matra* the adult members are felt to occupy a particular social stratum on the basis of the degree to which they have satisfactorily completed or met the requirements for membership. On the other hand, children are categorized by age at the following levels: infancy ("lap" or "knee-babies"); preschool ("housechildren"); school children; and adolescents ("teens"). All of these classes are considered to be hierarchially arranged and functionally derived and are reinforced through religious symbolism.

7.   BELIEF CONCERNING THE NATURAL WORLD   Here we are especially concerned with the perspective of belief in regard to matters of health and physical well-being, which was demonstrated to be a significant variable by the work of the scholars in the Six Cultures Series (Whiting et al. 1966). Generally, for all groups, the focus seems to be a matter of belief in man's intimate relationship with nature. Hence, illness is correlated with a lack of personal harmony with the natural world. In order to be reinstated to good health, one must become reconciled with nature, and this must be obtained in more or less proscribed means such as through certain practices of hatha yoga and meditation, as well as by the use of herbs and "natural" medicines. There appears to be a somewhat greater emphasis on prevention than in the dominant society, if such approaches as yoga can be taken as indicative. No one in any of these three communes claimed total rejection of standard American medical services, though these were usually claimed to be only for last resorts. Those at Kobold were noticeably more inclined towards such measures than the others.

8.   FORMALIZED EDUCATIONAL SYSTEMS   The pattern of communal adaptation to an external and formal educational system is of key significance. In the United States attendence at a state-licensed school is compulsory through the age of fourteen (eighteen in the state of California). Thus, they have had to find the means to cope with this further requirement. This has been aided through the widespread formation of the so-called "alternative" schools.

All three communes make use of child-care centers and send their children to alternative elementary and high schools at some time in their lives. Variations primarily reflect discrepancies in the regional availability of such schools, especially those which continue through high school. At Kobold the children attend public school through most of their elementary and junior high school years; at Harmony they skip child-care centers but attend school through junior high school in most cases. At *Matra* they attend public school only in the fourth through eighth grades, having their own high school. Only at *Matra* are the alternative schools that the children attend actually owned and run by the

Community. Both Kobold and Harmony utilize independent "free" schools, a practice that makes the school years a discontinuous process for the children, since they must go through at least three separate schools over the years (with substantially different student bodies in each).

9. RECRUITMENT OF NEW ADULT MEMBERS Recruitment includes advertisement, selection, (re-)education, and assimilation. The preceding sections have emphasized the adult-child or child-rearing aspects of enculturation, which has unfortunately lent a degree of lopsidedness to the discussion at hand. The transient element found to a certain degree at all the communes described necessitates some recognition of personnel replacement or the recruitment of new adults from an outside population.

At Kobold and Harmony this has proved to be the greatest area of expansion and even continuance. The Kobold population of women has remained constant, with only minor modifications since its origin. The men there have tended to enter the group as lovers of these women or, rarely, as a friend of one of the men. At Harmony membership is achieved through affiliation with the commune's ritual and spiritual practices; then, after acceptance by the leader the person must find someone who is already there to take them into their home (at least until another residence becomes available). Adaptation to and absorbtion into the commune is reckoned on the basis of the individual's success at finding a niche for himself and maintaining it thereafter.

At *Matra* one joins only after completing a six-month correspondence course on meditation and yoga, through sharing an awareness of the basic tenets of Hinduism (as interpreted by the Community's Master), through acceptance by the planning board and the board of representatives (the Community leader or Master has only one official vote in the latter board, none in the former), through the satisfactory completion of all membership payments ($1,500 for couples), and through meeting acceptable housing arrangements, which must be accomplished on one's own and yet must still be approved by the planning board. After all this the individual is voted into complete, permanent membership at a general election.

To provide a constant of sorts, against which to contrast the foregoing, and hence to arrive at a better comprehension of the data, I aim here to describe briefly one last communal group from the perspective that has just been employed. Of the many scholars who have shown an interest in the field, Hostetler and Huntington (1967, 1968) have made the largest contribution to the anthropological study of North American communalism. Their work has been concerned with the Hutterian Brethren who, according to Hostetler's and Huntington's description, are the largest and most successful of the communal groups in the United States and Canada. They have also the longest history, extending back to A.D. 1528 in south Tyrol and Moravia, having come to this country in 1874. From the original three colonies which settled in the Dakota area, they have grown to a number in excess of 170 colonies, including over 18,000 people. They have many unique characteristics as a social order, but only those which immediately pertain to the previously cited patterns shall concern us here.

1.   THE NATURE OF THE CHILD   This is correlated with the Hutterite conception of the universe which is dualistic — divided into carnal and spiritual spheres. The child is considered to be predominantly carnal at birth, or selfish, and in need of nurturance which is directed to lead him to his spiritual, or selfless, fulfillment. This is attainable simply through maturation, in the Hutterite sense, reckoned, in turn, in terms of the child's gradual renouncement of individual will coupled with the assumption of voluntary conformity to colony ends.

2.   THE NATURE OF PARENTHOOD   The Hutterites tend to regard themselves as Christian believers who maintain the proper life-style and social order, which is oriented towards obedience to and worship of God. As an aspect of this, sexual relations are considered to be good only for married couples. Remarriage after divorce is not allowed (there is only one divorce on record since 1875), and no birth control practices are permitted. Parenthood, then, is perceived in terms of the production of new souls for God, and for their initial and very important nurturance.

3.   DOMINANT VALUES AND PERSONAL ATTRIBUTES   Individualism is not accepted; instead value is placed on dependency and nurturance, responsibility, obedience, and sociability. Individuals are taught early to be dependent and obedient to the formalized system of authorities; they are to be of help to one another and responsible for performance of assigned duties. A child is often rewarded, even when as young as two, by being allowed to hold an infant — this is considered to be a display of responsibility and is thoroughly enjoyed. Sociability is linked with the belief that aloneness is unpleasant and to be avoided. The individual becomes aware early that to be with his fellow Hutterutes is pleasurable in itself.

4.   HOUSEHOLD COMPOSITION   Each colony is based around nuclear family units, with children usually staying with their parents until marriage, which is normally in their early twenties. Often married couples remain in the apartment of the man's parents until other accomodations can be made — perhaps with the next branching activity of the colony.

5.   DIVISION OF AUTHORITY AND LABOR   Within the family units the male is definitely the head — above both his wife and children. The woman is

considered to be "naturally inferior" to the man, with both assuming a superior position with regard to the children. The situation is decidedly patriarchial, though women are felt to be more competent than men in certain, specifically feminine activities. These attitudes of differential abilities for the sexes extend into the characteristic forms of labor so that men are typically concerned with the extracommunity and economic pursuits, while women are restricted to the household and child-rearing functions.

Within the colony at large with reference to authority or politics, we have several categories. All such authority is seen to originate from a single, supernaturally derived source of wisdom. After that the major distinction is felt to be between baptized and nonbaptized individuals (Hutterites practice voluntary, adult baptism). Within the former category they have developed a rather rigid set of distinctions with regard to the following levels of authority: all baptized members form the Church, but women have no actual voice in decision-making gatherings. Some of the adult, baptized males occupy departmental positions. There is a council, composed of five to seven men who are in the top positions (which are themselves hierarchially arranged). The preacher assembly is the ultimate political body for the entire Church and is composed of a gathering of elders (particular colonies retain the right to reject through unanimous vote any decisions made by this assembly which they feel negatively effects communal ends).

6. SOCIAL STRATIFICATION   Essentially this has already been examined with reference to the preceding two patterns. However, there is the matter of the functionally derived age-grading system which breaks down as follows: house child (birth to three); kindergartener (three to five); school child (six to fifteen); the casual years or adolescence (fifteen to baptism); adulthood (baptism and marriage); and aged (the retirement from mandatory labor until death). Each of these sets is believed to be ordained by God, and all are related to particular qualities of status and obligation. They are in addition to the sexual and political or authoritative levels already described, though inseparably tied with them.

7. BELIEF CONCERNING THE NATURAL WORLD   For the Hutterites this is associated with a conception of the world as being of two natures, duality: one carnal and the other spiritual. It is man's duty to develop his spiritual side, having both at birth (when his carnal aspect is more developed). Eventually the spiritual side of the universe is to win out over the other, and it is up to the particular man to be on that side when it happens (through living the proper life, the Hutterite life).

Concerning health, this is perceived somewhat differentially. To some degree illness is thought to be a test by God of one's fortitude and trust in Him. But it is likewise felt to be essentially inevitable — such is the nature of flesh. Corruption and weakness are indicative of carnality and are only to be conquered through attainment of total spirituality, at the death of the body.

8. FORMALIZED EDUCATIONAL SYSTEM   Like the contemporary communes, the Hutterites are faced with an external governing force which demands that their children attend licensed schools. Unlike most of them, however, the Hutterities adapted to this through a unique compromise. In addition to correlating schooling with their system of age-grading, the Hutterites created their own schools for instruction in the communal rituals of life and esoteric knowledge (also of their particular version of south Tyrolese and the High German dialect). They also stepped in and took over the local public school, which they refer to as the English school, and which is kept near to the colony though symbolically separate from it. The English teacher is paid by the colony, and he and his family have their residence supplied for them (off the colony grounds).

The child first attends the colony kindergarten, which in our usual sense is actually a preschool or nursery-kindergarten combination. He will remain there for two or three years before entering the distinctively Hutterian German school, and he will stay there for one year prior to going to the public, or English, school. All during his years there he will continue to attend the German school as well, returning to it for an hour's instruction every day after regular school attendance (and all day Saturday).

9. RECRUITMENT OF NEW ADULT MEMBERS   Today the Hutterites have come to accept only a very few converts, not having practiced any substantial missionary efforts since the seventeenth century. Instead, they have learned to rely on their own natural, or biological, rate of increase and expansion. They are an ethnic community, though they pursue communitarian values.

SUMMARY

In conclusion we must appraise the preceding patterns as they relate to the relative successes of the particular group in regard to their systems of enculturation. While these patterns are to a large extent interdependent, certain distinctions remain. These can be delineated with reference to the differing abilities of the communes to transmit their ways of life to other individuals, both of the same generation and cross-generationally.

Both Kobold and Harmony Hill have proven to be, for all purposes, incapable of circumventing their dependence on the continual assimilation of new, adult members. *Matra devo bhava* and the Hutterian Brethren have come to trust their processes of child-rearing and natural increase over, and even instead of, the admittance of new adults.

Tentative, preliminary analysis would seem to indicate that the first two types of communal organization (acephalous and charismatic) have failed to develop satisfactory means of educating their young for a life of mutual dependence and reciprocity, as contrasted with the emphasis on self-reliance as it is found in the greater society, and hence must depend on forms of adult recruitment for their survival. Only in the corporate, large-scale, and highly complex communes do we find the means for maintaining sophisticated educational approaches to communalism. In the current, recently developed forms such as *Matra devo bhava*, this has been reinforced through a modification of the social organization and structure of the domestic unit so that the mother-child relationship is paramount. In such traditional forms as the Hutterian Brethren, success has been aided through the inculcation of belief in an absolute, supernaturally ordained system of social control.

We have seen how some of the contemporary, or "hippie," communes, as they are sometimes called, stress processes of self-reliance including self-development and realization. As a consequence, they tend to enculturate their children more in terms of the larger society, than as future bearers of their own, unique way of life. Kobold and Harmony Hill have, due partly to their emphases on self-realization and the like, come to depend on recruitment of other adults for their continuance as social bodies. Their very success in teaching this approach to their young ultimately requires them to look elsewhere for new members.

Among the people of *Matra devo bhava* the value of self-realization is also taught, but here it is distinguished from self-reliance (emphasis, instead, is on obedience and dependence), and the process itself is considered to be linked with Community membership or at least participation. Hence, those raised within this system tend to continue to seek personal enlightenment, yet still remain within the Community.

The Hutterites, in significant part due to their belief that the individual must come to accept a supreme, supernatural source of authority and must voluntarily surrender his will to the Church, have succeeded in transmitting their life-style cross-generationally. In contrast, there is virtually no attempt or desire to bring converts into the colonies — having become an ethnic group which predominantly perpetuates itself biologically.

In terms of its educational processes it might then be said that a society is successful when its forms of socialization become secondary to enculturation: that is, when an individual is brought up not in human society *per se*, but into the particular culture of his parents. In order to perpetuate itself, the society must have its members believe that that society, as it stands, is necessary for the survival and success of the individual. Such a person must come to incorporate the social and cultural system into his self-identity.

REFERENCES

HOSTETLER, JOHN A., GERTRUDE ENDERS HUNTINGTON
   1967   *The Hutterites in North America.* New York: Holt, Rinehart and Winston.
   1968   Communal socialization patterns in Hutterite society. *Ethnology* 7 (1):331–355.
MEAD, MARGARET
   1963   Socialization and enculturation. *Current Anthropology* 4:184–188.
MURDOCK, GEORGE PETER
   1967   *Ethnographic atlas.* Pittsburgh: University of Pittsburgh Press.
TURNER, VICTOR
   1969   *The ritual process.* Chicago: Aldine.
WHITING, JOHN, *et al., editors*
   1966   Six Cultures Series, seven volumes. (See especially volume six: *Orchard Town, U.S.A.* Edited by J.L. Fischer and A. Fischer.) New York: J. Wiley and Sons.
ZABLOCKI, BENJAMIN
   1971   *The joyful community.* Baltimore: Penguin.

Theories of Academic and Social Failure of Oppressed Black Students: Source, Motives, and Influences

HERBERT G. ELLIS

Editors' Note: Herbert G. Ellis is a black, an educator, and a social scientist. In this paper he treats one of the most important concerns of members of each of those three categories. Why do certain observers find certain problems and label them failures for black students? A number of scholars and practitioners have offered theories to explain what they felt were the failures minority students encountered. Here Ellis, who has himself taught in Chicago, attempts to give one perspective on the nature of, and reasons for, these theories. He finds most to be rooted in the biases and inequities of the culture of their proponents and to be inadequate tools for the explication of problems which may exist in educational situations.

THE PROBLEM

Inasmuch as my formative years of academic training and teaching experience took place in the tradition of the dual southern school system, it was not until I experienced teaching and counseling juvenile delinquents and youthful offenders[1] in an urban setting that I was compelled by

[1]   In the context referred to here, the term juvenile delinquents connotes boys under the age of seventeen and girls under the age of eighteen (usually the case in most states) who fail, shirk, or neglect their duties and responsibilities in the home, school, or community. Such youngsters are said to be incapable of functioning within and benefiting from the instructional programs provided in the regular elementary and secondary schools such that they are placed either in a social adjustment school run by the local school board or in a custodial state institution.

Youthful offenders, however, are those males and females between the ages of seventeen and twenty-one and eighteen and twenty-one, respectively. These are persons who are classified as neither juveniles nor adults, and who are involved in the correctional process (i.e. lockups, detention homes, probations, jails, paroles, etc.) by having committed a felony and/or misdemeanor. For an interesting discussion of the interchangeable usage of the terms juvenile delinquent and youthful offender, see Luger (1970).

experience, curiosity, and reason to question and study the meaning and essence of contemporary urban education for black and other minority students. During this process of inquiry,[2] several observations became more apparent to me than ever: (1) that certain general propositions used as principles to explain the nature of black minority students have been concocted by social scientists, (2) that such principles are used by many professional educators as the basis for constructing models to implement educational and work programs for oppressed black students, (3) that the practical significance of the assumptions underlying the principles is skewed in favor of those persons who concocted them and those educators who use such principles or conceptual orientations to guide their behavior when having to perform services for or deal with blacks, and (4) that the principles have far-reaching consequences on the academic achievement and social development of black students.

THE PURPOSE

This paper, addressed to the problems stated above, will bring to bear the predominant theories advanced by social scientists in their attempt to provide educators and scholarly audiences with explanations for the academic and social failure of black students. Moreover, this paper will attempt to explain what the writer believes to be the motives for formulating theories and the influence of the theories on designing educational work programs and implementing teaching strategies for oppressed black students.

The reader, however, should keep in mind that the writer's personal points of view were derived from empirical data and that they are stated in this paper merely as a means of stimulating viable discussion that will, I hope, lead to a reevaluation of the social scientist's role and its relationship to that of the educator.

DEFINING SOCIAL SCIENCE THEORIES THAT INFLUENCE PUBLIC EDUCATION FOR BLACK STUDENTS

There are at least five positions advanced by social scientists as to the causes of academic and social failure of oppressed black students.

[2]   The process of inquiry encompassed my involvement in seminars, in-service meetings, private conferences with administrative personnel, general discussion sessions with teachers, counselors, and other professional personnel, and innumerable formal and informal "rap" sessions (interviews) with juvenile delinquents and youthful offenders. It also included innumerable home and agency visitations, involvement in curriculum planning, and a survey of the literature.

The Evolutionary Theory

The theory which has done more than any other to shape the treatment black students receive from their teachers and school administrators and to shape their performance in school and their feelings of self-worth and self-actualization is the evolutionary theory. This traditional theory implies that blacks have not evolved biologically to a point where their mental and physical organisms are capable of adapting to and coping in a sophisticated manner with the rigors of their environment (Putnam 1961).

Predicated on the assumption that blacks have not evolved beyond the primitive stage of natural development, this theory advances the notion that the behavior of blacks is governed primarily by impulse and immediate gratification. However, the similarity between the physiological and the biological characteristics of blacks and that of their white counterparts, plus the demonstrated ability of blacks to withstand extremely hard labor and mental torture have destroyed the credibility of the evolutionary deficit theory.

The Genetic Theory

This theory came into being as a replacement of the evolutionary theory. It postulates that blacks are intellectually inferior to whites and that the differences between the intellectual endowment of the two races can be attributed to hereditary causation (Jensen 1969). From a genetic point of view, this position implies that blacks are less than human, and since they do not belong to the species of man, whatever traits they possess are unique to their genetic configuration. In more precise terms, this means that the learning characteristics (i.e. cognitive and perceptual development, degree of motivation, and mental maturity) of blacks and their mediating processes (i.e. conflict, anxiety, drive, thinking, etc.) therein are basically the same from one black individual to the next.

This also means that there is a predictive similarity in the cognitive, affective, psychomotor, and action pattern responses of blacks to similar situations and conditions. For example, it is said that black students who are "culturally deprived" are antiintellectual, less interested in art and music, excitement oriented (Riessman 1962), and good at performing physical or motoric tasks (Miller and Swanson 1960). Although these scholars would tend to attribute such traits to a self-perpetuating "culture of poverty," proponents of the genetic deficit theory would attribute them to a fixed genetic code. In short, the genetic deficit theory assumes that no form of external motivation, guidance, and positive reinforcement will modify the behavior of blacks.

The Environment Deficit Theory

This position asserts that blacks are unable to take full advantage of the opportunities afforded them by white society primarily because of social disorganization and disease within the black community. It focuses on the menacing and insidious conditions of poverty as they affect the physical and mental well-being of blacks. Proponents of this position contend that inadequate housing conditions such as limited space to accommodate the size of the family, poor heating systems, defective plumbing and wiring, falling plaster, as well as inadequate food supply and nourishment are the basic factors which attribute to the social disorganization and disease within the black community and consequently contribute in a negative way to the academic performance of black students. Unfortunately, supporters of this theory unwittingly suggest that the physically impoverished conditions of minority groups and blacks particularly may very well be the kind of conditions they choose to live under (Foster 1972).

The Inadequate Life-style Theory

The general assumption underlying this position is that blacks are devoid of a culture; therefore, they are in need of acculturation (Glazer and Moynihan 1963). Moreover, supporters of this position credit the socioeconomic plight and accompanying academic failure of blacks to the self-perpetuating primitive nature of black life-style. This life-style is allegedly characterized by permissiveness, hedonism, impulsive antisocial behavior, bad and improper language, and disorganized and nondirected pursuits. Thus such traits are perceived as "pathological versions" of the white American culture.

The Cultural Difference Theory

In contrast to the inadequate life-style or the cultural deprivation theory, the supporters of the cultural difference position have the notion that whatever life-style blacks possess is indeed indicative of a distinctive culture and that the major difficulty blacks have in adapting to the demands of the larger society arises out of the conflict of values and meanings between the two cultures (Baratz and Baratz 1970; Riessman 1962; Havighurst 1971).

MOTIVES: RESTRICTIONS, DEMANDS, AND CUSTOMS

Before discussing the motives underlying these theories, it would be beneficial to examine some of the social restrictions, demands, and customs from which the theories emerged.

Since the inception of American history, slavery, segregation, colonialism, and social discrimination have been the major institutions directing the course of the American social order. These institutions and the conditions of these institutions span a period of more than three hundred years and exemplify in a dehumanizing manner the Euroamerican supremacy and dominance over its black populace. The edicts of these institutions not only place certain demands and restrictions on blacks but they also relegate blacks to a subservient position in the scheme of American life.

To maintain these institutions from a pragmatic point of view, several strategies were devised. During the early years of American history, blacks were denied identity specification and group cohesion. This was willfully accomplished by separating those blacks who had a native language in common, by separating black males and females, except to propagate the species, and by denying blacks the privilege to congregate in places other than church. Other earlier means to achieve the same objective were to isolate the so-called "house niggers" from the "field niggers" (the former being the maids, butlers, valets, midwives, and nannies, and the latter being those field hands who picked cotton, crushed sugar cane, etc.) and to isolate the more aggressive blacks from the docile and nonassertive (the former being the readers, writers, and activists and the latter being those who were strictly illiterate by Euroamerican standards).

Another practical approach to maintain and solidify the institutions of slavery, segregation, colonialism, and social discrimination was to deny blacks any form of interaction with whites. Thus the notion was concocted that any form of human associations of whites with blacks would indubitably retard the intellectual and social growth and spiritual development of whites and that it would presumably contribute negatively to furthering the goals of the white institutions.

From this notion came a number of restrictions, demands, and customs. *De jure* segregation became the practice in Southern states, while the Northern states invoked *de facto* segregation. Inasmuch as the school is charged with the major responsibility of transmitting the culture, black students who lived in predominantly white districts in Southern states and who were allowed to attend school were given vouchers to attend schools in predominantly black districts.³ Whites in Northern states practiced gerrymandering school districts to avoid physical and social contact with blacks. It should be noted, however, that *de jure* and *de facto* segregation still exist in many sectors of public education in spite of the Supreme Court's 1954 *Brown* decision and subsequent legislation.⁴

In the domain of public accommodations, blacks were forced to drink at separate water fountains and eat at separate restaurants. They were compelled to utilize separate toilet facilities and sit in the rear of buses. They were forced to worship in separate churches and even be buried in separate cemeteries.

However, the recent activist movement, the social legislation, and the rapid migration of blacks from rural to urban communities have ushered in a relatively new strategy to further divide and conquer blacks and to maintain the white status quo. This strategy is known as the "conspiracy." It comes in many disguises under the aegis of integration,⁵ and it is evidenced in many sectors of contemporary American society. For instance, in the economic sector, blacks are not afforded the same choices of job selection and limitations of job performance as their white counterparts. In cases where blacks are allowed to demonstrate their ability and expertise through written examinations, they are often told that they fail to pass the performance tests. Blacks are often told that they do not possess the training or skills to perform even the most basic job performance tasks. In other words, they are frequently told that they are either too old or too young for certain jobs and that they do not fit the job description academically, emotionally, and socially.

The irony of this condition and treatment is that a different yardstick

³ The extent to which the voucher plan was ingrained in public education in many Southern school systems can be inferred from the fact that prior to the 1954 Supreme Court decision (*Brown* vs *Board of Education in Topeka*) all black high school students in the county of St. Louis, Missouri, were given vouchers to attend either Douglass High School in Webster Groves, Missouri (i.e. the only accredited black high school in the county), or one of three black high schools in St. Louis proper.
⁴ A recent report prepared by the Center for Metropolitan Planning and Research of Johns Hopkins University and obtained exclusively by the *Chicago Sun-Times* attests to widespread segregation in Northern city schools. According to the *Sun-Times*, this report concludes that desegregation of Northern city schools has been small and is yet declining. Of the ninety-one school systems studied, Chicago was found to rank highest in segregation (*Chicago Sun-Times* 1973:3,50).
⁵ Integration in this context refers to the act of HIRING blacks but restricting their interpersonal involvement in the business-industrial complex, thus minimizing their chances for economic and political advancement. Integration in this sense also means the training of blacks for performance tasks but with antiquated technical equipment, as well as allowing blacks to take job performance tests that are systematically designed to fail them.

is used to measure the ability and expertise of blacks from that used to measure the same variables of performance by whites. This point is clearly evidenced in the fact that there exists a widespread attack on the personal appearance and language of blacks. The personal appearance and the language of blacks must be impeccable. For example, black teachers must never make such mistakes as: "BRING this note to the teacher next door," "My class is in the LIBERRY," or "INregards to ...." Yet these are but a few of the mistakes in pronunciation and usage that many white teachers frequently make. The black individual who wears the natural hair style, the daishiki, pendants, or love beads is immediately classified as a militant, whereas the white youngster who decides to wear his hair long, join a commune, and rusticate for days without combing his hair or bathing is said to be merely defying his parents who have neglected him.

All of these are systematic schemes tacitly devised by white labor and management along with educational institutions to exclude blacks from all but menial roles in the economic system (Clark n.d.) In short, this economic conspiracy is characterized as the "relegation of blacks to the hot, dirty and low-paying jobs" on the labor market (Bennett 1972).

In the sphere of communications, scholarly audiences and the mass media along with other establishment institutions conspire to socially distribute information and knowledge about the life-style of blacks as well as the world about them. This simply means that the kinds of information and knowledge disseminated and distributed to blacks or about blacks are generally those which appeal to racists and oppressors and thereby tend to dehumanize blacks. Cogent examples of this ploy are Glazer's and Moynihan's original thesis (1963) that blacks "have no culture to guard and protect" and Jensen's former thesis (1969) that the IQ of blacks is controlled 80 percent by genetic code and 20 percent by environmental variables.[6]

Now that we have focused, at least in part, on the source of the theories used to explain the social behavior and academic failure of blacks, the question comes to mind as to what are the possible motives underlying the theories.

Obviously, there are at least two motives. First, the theories function

---

[6]   The uncertainty of Jensen's and Moynihan's positions is evidenced by their responses to the challenges they have received from critics. Some indication of Jensen's modified position is discussed in the recent work of Yette (1971). Moynihan's response to his critics came in the form of modifying his original position regarding the status, values, and culture of blacks (Glazer and Moynihan 1963). This socially harmful manner of distributing and disseminating knowledge and information has been discussed by Rowan (1970).

as a practical therapeutic device. This means that the theories serve as the basic tools to perpetuate a closed society,[7] which manipulates, dominates, and controls blacks. In this sense, these theories not only dehumanize blacks by destroying their self-identity, their personal worth, and their aspirations to become self-actualizing, but also subjugate blacks to the extent that they become the political and economic prey of the dominant society. To this extent, blacks must attend school longer and receive fewer rewards. They must work harder and get less. They must earn less, spend more, and receive merchandise of inferior quality.[8] All of these conditions are to the economic and political advantage of the white power structure.

Second, these theories serve a dual psychological therapeutic function in the sense that they are devised to justify morally racism and oppression while at the same time allow racists and oppressors to cope with their own fears, inadequacies, self-hatred, contempt, and primitive instincts (e.g. the urge to dehumanize black males and females).

As racism and oppression, which are acquired beliefs and conditions, respectively, have a pernicious influence on the psyche of their recipients (Poussaint 1968), they also affect the psyche of their perpetrators. Such beliefs that blacks are evolutionarily inferior to whites and genetically deficient, that the black community is disorganized by virtue of conditions of the physical environment, that the socioeconomic conditions of blacks are attributed to their way of life, etc. are all notions that permeate the social order and are notions that must be justified to maintain the social order.

Therefore, as racists and oppressors attempt to perpetuate the status quo, conflict arises between their desire and need to exploit, control, and dominate blacks, their knowledge in knowing that it is human for the oppressed to fight back, and their pretentious belief in the egalitarian ideology. This conflict gives impetus to the exemplification of a set of covert and overt types of behavior on the part of the racists and oppressors.

For purposes of clarification, I shall classify these forms of behavior into two categories. The first category constitutes the "up-tight" syndrome. It is characterized by such pervasive symptoms as anxiety or unwarranted frustration, projection of personal conflict and delusions on the part of

[7]   A closed society here refers to societal organizations which place restrictions and limitations on various members of the total populace because of race, religion, ethnicity, and sex.
[8]   The economic exploitations of oppressed peoples is documented in a survey conducted by the Federal Trade Commission. Some significant insights of this report are cited by Yette (1971).

white racists and oppressors when they are in the presence of, or have to deal with, blacks who possess and exemplify such middle-class traits as assertiveness, aggressiveness, sensitivity, creativity, and intelligence.

In precise terms, the intrapersonal conflict (i.e. guilt, self-hatred, desire to destroy others) of the white adversaries reaches such intensity that they unconsciously believe their economic security, political power, prestige, and social status are in jeopardy. For they cannot afford to have nor will they allow, any black person to outshine or outwit them. They therefore feel compelled to devise ways to deal with their intrapsychic conflict as they are forced to react to blacks within their environment.

The second set of behavior types constitutes the "coping" syndrome which is used to infer the nature of the "up-tight" syndrome. The "coping" syndrome encompasses a variety of symptoms which are as follows:

1.   THE INGRATIATING DEMEANOR   It characterizes the behavior of those individuals who on the one hand attempt to gain by pretense the good graces of blacks while on the other hand feel committed to maintain power, dominance, and control over them. Because of guilt and anxiety, such individuals are compelled when in the presence of blacks to espouse blacks. These are the individuals who often talk about the "many" black friends they have and the nature of their social relationships. These are the individuals who must tell other blacks about how good, intelligent, or how unlike other blacks their black friends are.

2.   THE COMPLIANCE DEMEANOR   It characterizes those individuals who feel because of their delusion (i.e. false impressions and beliefs about blacks) and their feelings of impending danger when having to deal with blacks that they, whites, must comply with the demands of blacks. These individuals never or rarely take into account the significance, practicality, and applicability of the demands made of them by blacks. They respond to the demands strictly on the basis of fear, unwarranted frustration, or feelings of inadequacy. Their behavior generally evidences little if any knowledge about blacks. As a result, they overcompensate by giving blacks an abundance of TOKEN REWARDS[9] which blacks in many instances do not need and certainly do not desire.

---

[9]   Token rewards come in many forms, and as far as oppressed blacks are concerned, such rewards have no practical significance toward improving their lot. For example, to bus blacks into white neighborhoods as a means of promoting desegregation or racial balance, and to decentralize urban school systems are both forms of tokenism. These are so-called because it is a known fact that many whites do not want blacks on their "turf," or "hallowed grounds," because many blacks feel uncomfortable in such a position, and these systems often place a physical burden on blacks. Also, these are so called because many schools in black communities literally refuse to involve the community in the activities of the school.

3. THE PATERNALISTIC DEMEANOR   It is a conscious or unconscious state of mind in which the individual feels he has inherited the responsibility of overseeing blacks. Here the individual strongly believes that he is more capable of making decisions about blacks and structuring their destiny than blacks themselves. Such a person feels with no uncertainty that he is superior to blacks.

4. THE DENIAL DEMEANOR   This symptom characterizes the individual who finds himself intolerable. He is fraught with guilt and self-hatred to the extent that he denies racism and oppression as being at the root of the treatment blacks receive. He consequently conjures genocide theories to justify his beliefs about blacks and the treatment he imposes on blacks.[10]

5. THE ANTISOCIAL AGGRESSION DEMEANOR   This behavior characterizes the ACT of plotting either covertly or overtly to destroy by any means necessary all blacks who pose a threat to those persons who dominate, manipulate, and control blacks.[11]

6. THE IDENTITY CRISIS DEMEANOR   This is a state of behavior in which the individual wittingly or unwittingly seeks to ingratiate blacks by identifying with them. This behavior is more often evidenced among the white middle- and upper- classes, and it takes the form of attempts to walk, talk, and even dress like the poor class of blacks. The individual exemplifying this behavior generally thinks he knows what it is like to be black and poor. In other words, he walks, talks, and dresses as he thinks blacks walk, talk, and dress. The sad point is, however, that he doesn't know what it's like to be black and poor, nor does he know that he doesn't know.

7. THE RATIONALIZATION DEMEANOR   This coping technique characterizes those individuals who are compelled unconsciously to find within the social sciences and elsewhere superficial, unreasonable, and invalid reasons, concepts, and assumptions to justify their fears, inadequacies, contempt, and primitive instincts.

Finally, two points should be remembered: (1) Just as "the ghetto's existence, and its dynamics, make necessary the development of peculiar survival techniques and styles," (Clark n.d.) so do the institutions of

---

[10]   It should be noted that the term genocide as used in this paper has reference to the systematic ways of destroying the minds of a people — the deterioration of one's aspirations, values, customs, potentials, etc. to the extent that it produces a paranoid state of mind.

[11]   As far as the writer is concerned, each of the theories discussed in this paper are conscious or unconscious expressions of white hostility toward blacks. Even as laudable as the cultural conflict theory seems, it exposes its true meaning by virtue of the fact that it addresses symptoms and not sources of academic and social failure.

segregation, colonialism, and social discrimination make for a peculiar survival technique and style on the part of white racists and oppressors. (2) The types of coping behavior mentioned here are by no means exhaustive, nor are they mutually exclusive.

THE INFLUENCE OF THE THEORIES ON EDUCATING OPPRESSED BLACK STUDENTS

If the foregoing discussion is at all indicative of anything significant, it is indeed the notion that the sociocultural theories mentioned here are inimical to the prime concerns of oppressed blacks (i.e. their desire and need to become self-actualizing, to determine their own destiny, to grow intellectually and socially, and to gain political and economic power). Inasmuch as these theories are designed to maintain and perpetuate the institutions of segregation, social discrimination, and colonialism, they are destined to have a pernicious effect on the total educational process as it relates to and "involves" oppressed black students.

How then, are the underlying assumptions of the theories brought to bear on the problem of educating oppressed black students? Significantly, the answer to this question lies in the context of mental health, early education, and the specialization models as they are endemic to the operational phase of the educational process.

The MENTAL HEALTH MODEL supposedly focuses on prevention and eradication of mental illnesses and behavioral disorders in black oppressed students. This model has four stages. The first stage is the identification of the behavioral-types stage, during which time the classroom teacher and a variety of other specialists (i.e. remedial teachers, social workers, psychologists, speech and hearing specialists, teacher nurses, and guidance counselors) endeavor to specify and explain in educational parlance the social science interpretations of the academic and social behavior of oppressed black students.

During this stage, major emphasis is placed on gaining insight into how oppressed black students perform cognitive, perceptual, and oral language skills. Consideration is given here to the attitudes, values, appreciations, interests, and motivations of black students. Also during this stage, a great deal of attention is focused on the failures of oppressed black students, rather than on their strengths and achievements. The basic strategy used at this stage is the child-study approach in which a variety of experts in the educational profession collectively study the physical, mental, social, emotional (Kowitz 1969), as well as the academic status of oppressed black students.

Labeling the behavioral types is the second stage. This is the stage in which the observed behavior is evaluated in accordance to criterion established by the white middle class. Succinctly stated, oppressed black students must adhere to the following guidelines: (1) Since they are expected to be disorganized and deficient in thought processes, poor in linguistic abilities (Deutch 1965; Hunt 1964), inattentive and lacking the motivation to achieve (Zigler and Butterfield 1969), oppressed black students must be willing to accept an education regardless of how inferior in quality it may be. The significance here is that while oppressed black students are required to read, write, and speak standard English, they are not expected to perform these skills with the same degree of expertise or proficiency as their white counterparts. (2) They must accept the Janus-faced policies and social standards placed before them by racists and oppressors. On the one hand, this means that while it is all right for whites to exploit blacks through such means as inflated insurance premiums, control of illegal activities within the black community (e.g. prostitution, narcotics, and the numbers racket), the sale and rental of inferior and substandard housing, and overpriced and inferior quality of food and other kinds of merchandise, it is, on the other hand, antisocial and criminal for blacks to engage in such activities as snatching purses, burglarizing, holdups, etc. (3) They must conform to what the dominant society establishes as the proper standards of hair and dress styles. (4) They must respond to authority figures in a docile, nonassertive, and subservient manner. (5) They must accept themselves and the conditions of their indigenous milieu as the major source of their problem. Strict adherence to these guidelines is imperative, and any deviation from them allegedly evidences a mental deficiency and/or an emotional and/or social disturbance. It is during this stage that the "deviant" forms of behaviors are labeled accordingly (i.e. emotionally disturbed, socially maladjusted, educable mentally retarded, trainable retarded, learning disabled, etc.).

The third stage of the mental health model is the separating and regrouping stage. It is during this stage that each oppressed black youngster is placed in a specific type of educational, work and/or treatment program. If he is of preschool age, the prevailing tendency is to place him in a Head Start program or its equivalent to make up for his asserted deficits. If he is of primary age and he is classified as a youngster who is unable to adjust to the emotional and social climate of the regular classroom or the academic rigors therein, he will be placed in a remedial class beyond the primary grades; or if he is placed in it during his intermediate years of school, and he doesn't seem to be making "satisfactory" progress, he is then sent to either a vocational guidance center or a social adjustment school.[12]

When a black youngster reaches the age of sixteen and he demonstrates continued scholastic failure, chronic absenteeism, and "social and emotional" aberrations, he is then sent to a continuation school[13] or he is put out of school completely. The pattern of behavior and treatment that follows is certainly obvious. "Criminal" tendencies generally set in, if they have not done so already, or such tendencies become crystallized, and the youngster more than likely terminates his education as a juvenile delinquent or youthful offender in a "criminal prep" school (i.e. youth reformatories and adult penal institutions).

Sadly enough, in such instances as mentioned above, the black child and his environmental conditions are said to be responsible for his academic failure and social alienation. Seldom is the school considered an integral part of that environment which contributes to his academic failure and social alienation.

The fourth stage is the actual teaching and counseling stage. This stage is significant because it is the time when teachers, counselors, and supervisors must apply to the learning process the research findings, theories, and concepts derived from a variety of disciplines. This is a crucial stage because the research findings, theories, and concepts each teacher and counselor selects to guide his method of instruction and to establish a climate conducive to learning whatever the teacher or counselor has in mind reflect his value orientations which in themselves are largely derived from theories, assumptions, concepts, and administrative and supervisory

[12]   In the parlance of education, social adjustment schools operate within the purview of special education. Theoretically, they are of two types — residential and nonresidential. The former type of school is designed to service juvenile delinquents and youthful offenders. The educational facility is usually located in juvenile detention homes, residential treatment centers, camps, correctional institutions, jails, and the like. The latter type of school is usually run by the local school district. The youngsters attending such a school have the privilege of going home each day. The nonresidential schools are designed to accommodate those students who have been diagnosed as being incapable of functioning within and benefiting from the instructional programs provided in the "regular" elementary and secondary schools. Such students are generally referred to as chronic truants and/or socially maladjusted and/or emotionally disturbed.

Moreover, the educational philosophy of both the residential and nonresidential social adjustment schools is basically the same. It is the exposure of deviant students to an entirely new educational milieu from which they can acquire self-esteem, realistic goals, social success, and academic achievement through counseling and instruction commensurate to their individual needs and capabilities.

[13]   The continuation schools have been defined as institutions working in cooperation with the "regular" schools to provide an alternative approach to common educational goals, to utilize human resources fully, and to give ALL youth the knowledge, skills, and attitudes necessary to achieve worthy personal and social goals (Reed 1969). Reed states that the philosophy of these schools focuses on understanding the youth as a "divergent being."

values and practices. Moreover, this is a crucial stage because the behavior of oppressed black students is affected by the values held by all persons (teachers, counselors, psychologists, supervisors, etc.) involved in modifying their behavior.

The case which follows serves as a cogent example to dramatize the values of teachers, the source of their values, and the influence of their values on the behavior of their students. To inform the regular teacher of the academic performance and the deportment of a group of black boys enrolled in a "remedial" class in an urban social adjustment school, a white male substitute teacher left this report:

> This is better than a trip to the zoo; they don't let you inside of the cage. This group is beyond belief — not that anyone need say it again! The only one who evidenced any signs of intelligence was Sam. That's easier than listing the rest. I had to send Joe to the office for the remainder of the day at 1:30. I was so saturated with violent behavior that I couldn't stand it any longer. We didn't get any books opened. I just sat here and tried to keep them inside of their cage and from killing each other.

Interestingly, each of these students behaved in precisely the manner in which he had been expected and allowed to behave. For this particular teacher, at this particular time, this was an ego trip which reinforced his preconceived image of black students. For the students, it was a day of "put down" (i.e. to suppress the natural urge to learn, to humble oneself to the pleasure principles) and failure. If these same students had exemplified the typical middle-class model, this same teacher would have been just as astounded. Of course, in this case, the chances are that he would have classified these students either as exceptionally bright or he would have associated their behavior with the influence of a white teacher.

The case of the white substitute teacher can be multiplied a thousand-fold, and the sad truth of the matter is that many teachers of oppressed black students are given the mandate to simply contain and restrain these students. This mandate seemingly emerged with the recent migration of blacks to urban communities and the postwar "baby boom" of the last two decades. Prior to this time, the standards for teaching in most urban public school systems were strict and followed to the letter of the law insofar as selecting those who are best qualified to perform the teaching task. In substance, the standards have been lowered. The cases which follow further attest to the notion that teachers in urban public schools should be primarily concerned with containing and restraining oppressed black students.

While being interviewed for his first teaching position, and while possessing only the minimum requirements, a black applicant was offered a job teaching boys who had been classified as socially maladjusted and emotionally disturbed. When he attempted to discuss with the interviewer what he thought were his academic deficiences, the interviewer replied, "Oh! You aren't expected to teach those kind of boys anything. Just keep them out of the principal's hair."

The next example is the case of a white teacher, who was automatically certified (i.e. certification without having to take written or oral examinations) in a social adjustment school for boys where he had worked three years before as a substitute. During the three-year period, this teacher often expressed in conferences his guilt for the plight of blacks. He felt that to make his life more meaningful, he had to ingratiate blacks. Thus, he would frequently bring shirts, sweaters, trousers, and ink pens to give to the black students regardless of actual need. However, when the teacher became angry with these students, he would often throw their carfare (i.e. tokens, coins, and transfers) out of the second floor window of the school building. Such behavior was usually followed by attempts to explain and make up for his actions.

It should be remembered that while teachers often express dissatisfaction with the behavior of oppressed black students, they seldom attempt to prevent the occurrence of undesirable behavior or rectify it if it does occur. For disruptive or antisocial behavior will prevail in any group situation which lacks purpose, practical and meaningfully significant activities, shared responsibilities, value analysis (both those of the students as well as those of the teacher), and productive responses. Any teaching and counseling setting which falls short of these directives is destined to be a detriment to the social and intellectual growth and development of any student, regardless of his race, ethnicity, abilities, interests, and social status.

The EARLY EDUCATION MODEL is built on the notion that oppressed black students, particularly, are devoid of the skills necessary to cope effectively and efficiently with the demands of highly advanced sociological and technological urban societies. In precise terms, the early education model is viewed as a series of specialized academic and training programs implemented in specified institutions under specified conditions for the purpose of helping oppressed black students develop as early as possible perceptual, cognitive, and social skills.[14]

[14] Gordon and Wilkerson (1966) give a detailed description of a variety of special programs and institutions in operation in urban communities throughout the United States. Though the special programs and institutions listed appear under different titles from one section of the country to another, many of them are designed to compensate urban blacks for their so-called cultural and/or environmental deficits or differences.

Inasmuch as the early education model exposes to scrutiny the myth of the egalitarian creed and the reality of nonequal treatment, social scientists as well as educators were forced to construct this model in a manner that would justify the dichotomy between the philosophy of education and educational practice in low-status urban public schools.

In constructing this model, four points of view were considered: (1) that oppressed black students are without a cultural base and therefore have no culture; (2) that the language (i.e. verbal and nonverbal behavior), child-rearing practices, music, art, literature, and other indigenous patterns of life-style are all indicative of a rich and viable black culture; (3) that the major problems (i.e. poor scholastic achievement and social development) oppressed black students have in school arise out of the conflict between their indigenous cultural demands and those made of them by the dominant society; and (4) that teachers and other persons in the educational profession lack a basic knowledge about black culture and that ignorance of this kind contributes considerably to the academic and social failure of oppressed black students.

To reconcile somewhat these differences of opinions, an education-disadvantaged rationale was adopted (Erickson, Bryan, and Walker 1972). This rationale has two strands. The first strand focuses on the kinds of academic and social readiness skills oppressed black students "need" but do not receive outside of their immediate school milieu. The second strand concerns the kinds of training school administrators, supervisor teachers, counselors, and other related school professionals and para-professionals receive in their preparation for the kinds of services they are to provide for oppressed black students.

In other words, this rationale says two things: (1) that oppressed black students are at a disadvantage when they are called to respond to stimuli emanating from the middle-class value system which they have not been prepared to handle, and (2) that professional personnel in educational settings are likewise at a disadvantage when they are called to provide services to oppressed black students. As Erickson, et al. assert, this rationale shifts the emphasis from cultural and environmental differences or deficits to education-disadvantaged.

Therefore, the early education model proposes the following strategies for the acculturation of oppressed black students: (1) Expose such students to as many middle-class cultural, social, and intellectual stimuli as soon and as often as possible; the point of significance here is that there is a vast difference between exposure and involvement. (2) Provide for these students the proper nourishment and financial assistance; often-times blacks are not involved in the process of determining whether or not they need the assistance offered. (3) Provide homemakers to assist the parents of these students; the assumptions on which homemakers are sent into these homes are generally derived from materialistic values rather than from the fact that the conditions that prevail in many oppressed black homes derive from racism and oppression. (4) If the homes of these students are totally "inadequate," then remove them from their homes; the irony of this situation is that oftentimes many such students are sent to facilities (i.e. detention homes, parental schools, camps, correctional institutions) which breed problems far more serious than the ones the youngsters encountered in their homes. (5) Remove the "atypical" oppressed black student from the regular classroom as soon as possible. (6) Provide within the school as many professional services as possible. (7) Teach standard English to these students either as a second language or as a replacement of the black idiom. (8) Provide in-service meetings, seminars, and courses to acquaint and sensitize teachers and other related personnel to the needs, characteristics, strengths, and weaknesses of these students; in most instances, the strengths of these students are rarely considered, for very little research has been done to determine such — a person's strengths are generally less obvious than weaknesses and more difficult to discern. (9) Provide more vocational guidance and training for these students. (10) Provide more social adjustment schools and remedial classes for these students.

Although this by no means exhaustive list of strategies or recommendations seems laudable and acceptable, careful scrutiny of the recommendations reveals a number of implications that ought to be of paramount concern to educators and social scientists as well.

To focus attention on the education-disadvantaged is a subtle and tacit way of ignoring the types of behavior and conditions which directly contribute to the academic and social failure of oppressed black students. By adopting the education-disadvantaged scheme, educators and social scientists are then able to avoid personal confrontation with such conditions (i.e. the locus of poverty) as substandard housing, menial jobs, inferior qualities of education, inadequate medical services, limited and inadequate recreational facilities, inferior qualities of foods and other merchandise, and limited physical and social mobility.

This scheme also affords educators and social scientists the privilege to deny racism (i.e. race as the primary determinant of capabilities, traits, capacities, interests, and superiority) and oppression (i.e. political and economic dominance, power, control, and manipulation) as the possible sources of academic and social failure of oppressed black students. These circumstances preclude any chance of genuine acculturation and they insure annihilation of black cultural values.

In a behavioristic sense, oppressed black students who are exposed to these circumstances are in a marginal position which they find very difficult to handle. Fluctuating between a denial of inclusion into the mainstream of contemporary American life and the continuous genocide of black culture, such students find themselves without two basic necessities for survival and inclusion. These are identity specification and group cohesion.

Another implication of the early-education model is that it allows educators to employ "gimmicks" against oppressed black students. To illustrate the point, the following example is in order: In response to the notion that "culturally deprived, culturally different, or education-disadvantaged" students in inner city schools are undernourished, which ultimately leads to poor performance in school, a breakfast program was instituted in an urban social adjustment school for boys. All of the students were given not only a free breakfast but also a free lunch. No criteria were established as guidelines to determine who would actually benefit from the free meals nor was the community consulted before the plan was put into effect. While on duty during the periods in which the meals were served, a teacher noted that many of the black students did not eat the free meals. When asked why, several students replied that they had had either a full meal at home or that their parents had given them the money to buy their own lunch or breakfast.

This type of ploy is certainly detrimental to oppressed black students inasmuch as it destroys self-worth and assertiveness. It tends to make the oppressed dependent rather than independent. In essence, it is a manipulative device.

The SPECIALIZATION MODEL addresses two serious issues: (1) Who should be responsible for making decisions which directly affect the acculturation process? (2) Who should be assigned the task of distributing and disseminating knowledge, information, and skills to those who are being acculturated?

The designers of the specialization model contend that because it is blacks who are in "need" of taking on the cultural values of the dominant society, then it is certainly logical for whites to show blacks the way of acceptance into the dominant society. Therefore, this model advances the following tenets: (1) White expertise should be used to diagnose and assess the extent to which black students are different, deficient, or disadvantaged in terms of white middle-class values, attitudes appreciations, emotional and social adjustment, and language-motoric skills (i.e. forms of communication such as reading, writing, and speaking).

(2) They should prognosticate the behavior of these students and also make recommendations for bringing about the necessary changes in their behavior. (3) They should be empowered to manage and supervise the various programs and services which are designed to ameliorate the academic and social disparities of these students. (4) They should implement the teaching and counseling strategies of ameliorative programs.

We may conclude from these tenets that the specialization model is essentially an exclusion model which was designed to support and perpetuate racist and oppressive objectives. Adapting a phrase of Sizemore (1972), this model is a means by which many institutions of formal education "promote and protect an authoritarian decision-making hierarchy based on the values of white European superiority."

James's explanation (1970) of the treatment black teachers, counselors, and administrators have received in Southern public schools since the advent of desegregation may seem paradoxical to the tenets of the specialization model, yet they are cogent examples of this model in operation. He states that while it is quite all right for blacks to administer or supervise Southern schools which are all black, the moment the schools become substantially desegregated, the principals must be white. He further states that though black teachers, counselors, and administrators are as qualified and in many instances more so than their white counterparts, they have only one of two alternatives in the desegregation process: (1) They may either accept token integration by being placed in a position where they are few in number and where they have no title of respect or specified responsibility and authority, or (2) they may be given a title, but at the same time they are exposed to embarrassing circumstances which consequently force retirement. For instance, many black educators in Southern public schools and elsewhere have been given administrative and supervisory jobs which were morally debased in terms of mediocre facilities, inadequate staffing, unimaginative curriculum, and low academic expectations long before they took these positions. Yet they are expected to play the "super nigger" role, which means to clean up the mess that their white adversary created or was unable to handle.

In Northern public school systems, a modified version of the specialization model used in Southern public schools is employed. The general opinion here is that schools which service exclusively black communities can best be run by white educators. However, in instances where black professionals are given positions in the administrative hierarchy, they find the security of their positions dependent upon circumstances and chance factors. Because they are often hired not on the basis of their qualifications, but rather on the basis of how well they ignore and accommodate the culture of poverty (i.e. its nature and source), these educators find their positions quite risky and full of uncertainty. This precarious position leaves these educators vulnerable and subject to manipulation.

What are the educational outcomes of the specialization model? It can be said that debasement of black identity and self-esteem is perhaps the most obvious result of this model. This is accomplished via removal of black leaders from positions of authority and placing them in positions where they can be declared incompetent, or by "window dressing" (i.e. carefully selecting the nonaggressive, nonassertive, and passive blacks to positions in the administrative hierarchy). In essence, what happens is that black leaders lose in the view of other blacks their status, prestige, and oftentimes a secure economic base, and black students lose the valuable image such black leaders provide for social, emotional, and intellectual growth and development.

Having no one with whom to identify, oppressed black students soon become conditioned to feel weak and cultureless. Their motivation becomes retarded and their aspirations become limited. Feelings of white superiority and black inferiority are engendered. Thus, social and academic achievement is rarely achieved. Moerover, the school loses its holding power, and chronic truancy and other serious behavior problems emerge.

CONCLUDING COMMENTS

From the arguments posed in this paper, several significant points are suggested. First, the theories discussed here are a clear indication that social scientists have not been collectively responsive to the challenge of dealing directly with the source of the problems involved in educating oppressed black students. Second, to focus attention exclusively on the symptoms of failure is a pernicious ploy to sustain and intensify the institutions of colonialism, segregation and social discrimination. Third, many public schools in oppressed black communities paradoxically accommodate the institutions of colonialism, segregation, and social discrimination by assuming that black youngsters can only function at the concrete level, by lowering academic and social standards, by labeling and stigmatizing the behavior of these youngsters, and by using punitive measures (e.g. exclusion from school), coercion, and ridicule to settle conflicts that arise between oppressed black students and school. Fourth, the strategies used to educate oppressed black students contribute considerably to producing an educational product that is nonassertive, dependent, and poor in self-esteem and personal worth. Indeed, each of these traits is synonymous with failure.

It is therefore my contention that educational work programs for oppressed black students will not meet with any significant degree of success until such time as the points suggested are dealt with genuinely and intelligently by social scientists, educators, and the mass media as well.

REFERENCES

BARATZ, STEPHEN, JOAN BARATZ
  1970   Early childhood intervention. *Harvard Educational Review* 40:29–50.
BENNETT, LERONE JR.
  1972   The black worker. *Ebony* 73 (December).
Chicago Sun-Times
  1973   News item, February 25, 1973.
CLARK, KENNETH
  n.d.   "No gimmicks whitie." From a speech presented at the National Conference on the Effective Utilization by Industry of the Hard-core Unemployed. Mimeographed.
DEUTCH, MARTIN
  1965   The role of social class in language development and cognition. *American Journal of Orthopsychiatry* 35:78–88.
ERICKSON, EDSEL L., CLIFFORD E. BRYAN, LEWIS WALKER
  1972   The educability of dominant groups. *Phi Delta Kappan* 53(5): 319–321.
FOSTER, ASHLEY
  1972   Home environment and performance in school. *School and Society* 100:236–237.
GLAZER, N., D. P. MOYNIHAN
  1963   *Beyond the melting pot* (first edition). Cambridge, Mass.: MIT Press (second edition 1970).
GORDON, E. W., D. A. WILKERSON
  1966   *Compensatory education for the disadvantaged.* Princeton: College Entrance Examination Board.
HAVIGHURST, R. J.
  1971   "Minority subcultures and the law of effect," in *Educating the disadvantaged, school year 1969/1970*, volume two, part one. Edited by A. C. Ornstein. New York: AMS.
HUNT, J. MC V.
  1964   How children develop intellectually. *Children* 83-91.
JAMES, J. C.
  1970   The black principal: another vanishing American. *The New Republic* (September): 17–20.
JENSEN, ARTHUR
  1969   How much can we boost I.Q.? *Harvard Educational Review* 39:1–123.

126 HERBERT G. ELLIS

KOWITZ, GERALD F.
1969 The trends in elementary counseling. *The Educational Forum* 34:87–93.
MILLER, D. R., G. E. SWANSON
1960 *Inner conflict and defense.* New York: Holt.
LUGER, M.
1970 "The youthful offender," in *Crime, criminology and contemporary society.* Edited by R. D. Knudten, 42–43. Homewood: Dorsey.
POUSSAINT, A. F.
1968 "A Negro psychiatrist on the black psyche," in *Is anybody listening to black America?* Edited by C. E. Lincoln, 24–28. New York: Seabury.
PUTNAM, C.
1961 *Race and reason: a Yankee view.* Washington: Public Affairs.
REED, DONALD R.
1969 The nature and function of continuation education. *Journal of Secondary Education* 44:292–297.
RIESSMAN, F.
1962 *The culturally deprived child.* New York: Harper and Row.
ROWAN, CARL T.
1970 How racists use science to degrade black people. *Ebony* 40 (May).
SIZEMORE, BARBARA A.
1972 Is there a case for separate schools? *Phi Delta Kappan* 53 (5):281–284.
YETTE, S. F.
1971 *The choice: the issue of black survival in America.* New York: Berkley.
ZIGLER, E., E. C. BUTTERFIELD
1969 "Motivational aspects of changes in I.Q. test performance of culturally deprived nursery school children," in *Annual progress in child psychiatry and child development.* Edited by S. Chess and A. Thomas, 353–366. New York: Brunner/Mazel.

Contributions of Anthropology to Cultural Pluralism. Three Case Studies: Australia, New Zealand, and the United States

ROBERT J. HAVIGHURST

Editors' Note: Robert Havighurst has long been involved with work in human development and the social sciences. In this paper he examines some of the results of a specific institutional teaching enterprise — that of the teaching of anthropology in plural or potentially plural societies. This brings the anthropological study of education very close to home, and anthropology teachers may find some reassurance in Havighurst's conclusions. A member of the Committee on Human Development and the Faculty of Education at the University of Chicago, Havighurst explores both the results of three case studies and the potential for anthropological teaching to help in the creation of productive cultural pluralism.

There have been three remarkably parallel cases of the interaction of a Western, "modern" culture with a primitive culture — in what are now Australia, New Zealand, and the United States. Commencing at various dates between about 1600 and 1800, this interaction appears to have followed a similar sequence of phases in all three areas, with the contemporary phase — movement toward cultural pluralism — having started at about the same time, around 1960.

The purpose here is to examine the functions of research and teaching of anthropology in the evolution of the cross-cultural interaction in these three cases.

In these three cases the British-American society wanted land which its members could settle and exploit. This meant uprooting and pushing out a resident society which was not equipped by technology or value orientation to cope with the aggressive and instrumental Anglo society. In each case the invading society came in such numbers that the native society was soon vastly outnumbered. At present the proportions of the native people are: New Zealand, 8 percent; Australia, 0.8 percent; and the United States, 0.4 percent.

The interaction between the Anglo and the native societies has followed a similar course in all three cases, as has been pointed out by anthropologists who have studied the process. Two men took the lead in making this analysis in Australasia: Firth for New Zealand and Elkin for Australia. A number of Americans have used a similar conceptual scheme, though it has not been stated so explicitly.

Briefly, the sequence of phases, or stages, is:

1.   Tentative and cautious initial contacts, generally with an emphasis on trade rather than settlement of the land.

2.   Settlement and colonization by the Anglo society, which takes land from the natives.

3.   Resistance from natives to land takeover, physical conflict, and defeat of the natives.

4.   Native retreat and withdrawal to reserves, reservations, or isolated strongholds. Native population reduced to its lowest number.

5.   Anglo society develops a policy of assimilation of the dwindling native society, which is accepted by a minority of the native people.

6.   Assimilation policy is seen as inadequate by Anglos and natives. Problems of socioeconomic adjustment arise, with rapid population increase of native people, migration to the cities, and protest movements.

7.   Rise of a movement for cultural pluralism — a plurality of cultures with their members seeking to live together in amity and mutual understanding and mutual cooperation, but maintaining separate cultures.

The writer has studied this interaction of Anglo with native cultures in all three countries and sees anthropologists as the central ideologists in the movement from a policy of ASSIMILATION to one of CULTURAL PLURALISM. The seven phases, or stages, appear in all three countries, but with significant differences. The writer has been studying the differences as well as the similarities. He proposes to trace the interaction of anthropologists with the political and intellectual leadership of the country, as well as with the leaders of the native cultures. In this process the educational system has been the major instrument of social change — through university teaching and research; through education of native people; and through the activity of anthropologists as advisers, administrators, and political activists.

ANTHROPOLOGY AND INTERACTION OF CULTURES AT THREE POINTS IN THE SEQUENCE

There are three points in the sequence of interaction where a policy aimed to control the relations between the two cultures is evident, though sometimes more implicit than explicit. The first of these is the period after the defeat of the natives, when they withdraw voluntarily or under pressure to relatively isolated areas. This is the period of minimum population. The natives are especially vulnerable to contagious diseases to which the whites have some resistance: influenza, pneumonia, tuberculosis, and measles. Furthermore, if there is such a thing as a "will to live," it is at a low ebb at this juncture.

While there was no branch of social science by the name of social anthropology at the time of this situation, there was interest in the conflict of cultures, and there was need for decisions on the part of the Anglo society as to what they should do about the native society, which was very much in their way — a kind of pest, at the least. The date for this period, in New Zealand and Australia, was about 1850 to 1890, and the Indians of the eastern United States were also by this time subdued and confined on reservations. There was what would now be called a pseudo-anthropology, growing out of the success of Charles Darwin's theory of human evolution.

The descent of man was published in 1871 and immediately gave birth to a sociological version of evolutionary theory, namely, the doctrine of the survival of the fittest applied to societies and social institutions. Weaker forms of social organization were destined to disappear in competition with stronger and more efficient forms. Herbert Spencer's writings were thought to support this view of history. And it was easy for the European leaders of the colonization and settlement of lands inhabited by simpler societies to believe that the European form of society was destined to survive, deserved to survive, and the sooner the process of dispatching the weaker society, the better.

This attitude can be found expressed in various tracts that were written at the time as apologies for what was taking place, which would now be branded as GENOCIDE. For example, a letter published in a Melbourne newspaper in 1876 went as follows:

We invoke and remorselessly fulfill the inexorable law of natural selection when exterminating the inferior Australian and Maori races.... The world is better for it: and could be incalculably better still, were we loyally to accept the lesson thus taught by nature — by preserving the varieties most perfect in every way; instead of actually promoting the non-survival of the fittest by protecting the propagation of the improvident, the diseased, the defective, and the criminal. Thus we surely lower the average of, and tend to destroy, the human race almost as surely as if we were openly to resort to communism (cited in Rusden 1972:16).

The actual disappearance of the native society did seem imminent, for the numbers of natives were decreasing, and the natives seemed weak in almost every sense. The Australian policy was "to ease the dying pillow" for the Aborigine. This could be done partly by feeding and clothing the people who would come to a depot on a reservation, without expecting them to do anything constructive about their own condition. Furthermore, if there had been much miscegenation, as there had been in the Australian case, and to a considerable extent in some areas of major contact in the United States and New Zealand, it was assumed that the mixed bloods would continue to intermarry with whites. Thus the native "blood" would become absorbed in another two or three generations, and the race would be effectively "whitened."

In the United States, between about 1865 and 1890, there was a similar belief on the part of many people in positions of power that no feature of Indian life was worth preserving and that Indians would never contribute anything vital or distinctive to American life, so long as they remained in the tribal state. An American by the name of Thomas J. Mays, writing in the *Popular Science Monthly* in 1888, said, "Nature was doing more to solve the Indian problem than statesmen had ever accomplished," meaning that the Indian race would soon disappear by a process of miscegenation, aided by disease that would take off the full-bloods.

Forty years before, President Andrew Jackson had struck a similar note in his Farewell Address upon retiring from the presidency in 1837. He took credit for ridding the eastern and central states of the Indians, saying:

The states which had so long been retarded in their improvement by the Indian tribes residing in the midst of them are at length relieved from the evil, and this unhappy race — the original dwellers in our land — are now placed in a situation where we may well hope that they will share in the blessings of civilization (Morison 1965:451).

Assimilation Theory

The second point at which a new policy had to be created was when it became clear that the native race would not disappear of its own accord, but was growing in numbers and was meeting adjustment problems which were also problems for the dominant society. At this point, anthropology was developing rapidly as a social science, and anthropologists were studying the native races in terms of social organization and social change. They, of course, became intensely aware of the problem of interaction of vigorous cultures, and a number of them became involved as advisers, policy makers administrators and educators. Furthermore, they appreciated the native cultures and were disposed to speak for them, if there should be a controversy.

At this point, ASSIMILATION policy emerged with support from anthropology. The policy assumed that the native group would become merged into the dominant society through processes of education, employment, citizenship — all by forms of joint participation in which the natives learned how to take part efficiently in the dominant society. For example, in Australia in 1951, a Conference of Commonwealth and State Ministers on Native Welfare declared as policy that Aborigines "shall attain the same manner of living as other Australians" (Native Welfare Conference 1951),

Elkin, the Australian anthropologist, was a leader in the drive for a policy of assimilation. He came to the University of Sydney as professor of anthropology in 1934 after a period of fieldwork in the north and center of Australia. He then spoke and wrote vigorously to support his thesis that the Aborigines had a culture which should be respected, and that a positive policy of health services, education, and employment should be put into effect, with the aim of preparing Aborigines for life in the general Australian community. His book (1959) on the Australian Aborigines, first published in 1928, was influential in giving people a more positive attitude toward the Aborigines. His position was taken up generally by younger anthropologists, and he was consulted by government officials. At about this time, the name of the Aborigines' Protective Board in New South Wales was changed to Aborigines' Welfare Board, signifying the change of policy. The term "assimilation" was written into the New South Wales law, which declared officially for the first time that the future of part-Aborigines lay in their assimilation into the economic and political life of the general Australian community.

When he revised his book, Elkin wrote a new final chapter with the heading, "Epilogue: the Aborigines on the march." In this chapter he said: "This book has been written because it should be the desire, as it is the duty, of non-Aboriginal Australians to understand the Aborigines" (1959:321). He goes on to say (1959:322):

The future of the Aborigines, whether full-blood or other, lies within the general framework and current of Australian economic, political, social, and religious life. The old order is passing, and a new order is being entered through a process of assimilation; but the rate varies according to the types of Aborigines and their geographical position.

But he qualifies the meaning of "assimilation" a few pages later, when he says,

Although the Aborigines more and more want to be a part of Australian life in their own right they want to reach this goal as Aborigines.... The nearer goal, however, is that while still Aboriginal in many social and spiritual aspects of life, they will become full and responsible citizens not offending against essential features of our social behavior (1959: 337–8).

Assimilation policy developed in New Zealand together with the rise of the Young Maori Party after 1900. Sir Peter Buck and Sir Apirana Ngata believed that the Maori population could be assimilated as a rural citizenry. They should have education, and they should have financial help from the government in establishing themselves as farmers.

Assimilation was seen as the appropriate goal by Firth, in his monumental *Primitive economics of the New Zealand Maori* (1959), first published in 1929. He noted the "reshaping of their social institutions" that took place among the Maori in the period from 1910 to 1930 and saw it go even further toward assimilation by 1959, when he revised the book. Like Elkin, however, he made some qualifications of the assimilation policy as he saw it. The Maori had rebuilt their community meeting halls (*marae*) and were still applying community controls to much of their social behavior, in contrast to the more individualistic economic and social behavior of the Pakehas. He wrote:

If the watch-word be not assimilation but incorporation into the political, social, and economic body of the New Zealand community, then the Maori and the Pakeha with whom they share the country should hope in the long run for a working solution to their relationships (1959: 482).

The native culture is not being mixed mechanically into the dominant society and thus losing its identity, he seems to say. Rather, important elements of Maori culture are being INCORPORATED, without losing their Maori character.

The anthropologists who followed Firth on the New Zealand scene in the 1950's and early 1960's were engaged in stretching the concept of assimilation to make it more inclusive of Maori cultural characteristics. Piddington is a leader of this group. He applied the term "social symbiosis" to describe a situation in which European and Maori culture traits could mutually support each other. This could hardly be called assimilation of Maori culture into European culture. In a recent essay he used the concept of EMERGENT DEVELOPMENT of new culture forms in the Maori society. Emergent development, he said, consisted of "positive and spontaneous emergence of new types of social institutions within cultures undergoing change" (1968:260). Such developments combine elements from both cultures, and this can hardly be seen as assimilation of the native culture into the Western culture.

Assimilation policy in the United States had less support from anthropology than it had in the other two countries. When there was major controversy over ASSIMILATION POLICY, in the period from about 1870 to 1930, we do not find anthropologists taking much part in the controversy. They studied Indian cultures as ethnographers and had plenty of work to do, because there was a wide variety of Indian tribes. There was greater pressure for assimilation in some areas than in others, and the anthropologists seem to have been absent where the controversies were.

Assimilation was the issue in the allotment of Indian lands to individual Indian owners. Those whites who favored allotment for unselfish, i.e. non-land-grabbing, reasons did so because they thought that individual ownership and responsibility for land would make the Indian more thrifty, more individualistic, more foresighted — more like the "ideal" American farm owner. Those who were opposed to allotment believed that the "Indian way" of communal use of land, communal decision making, and extended family responsibility for the welfare of individuals was worth maintaining, at least as long as Indians preferred it that way. They trusted the Indians to know or to find out what was best for them.

The passage of the Dawes Act, in 1887, provided for the allotment of Indian land to individual owners, who were expected to use the land efficiently; land they could not use as individual farmers was to be sold to white farmers, or leased to cattlemen, with some cash payments to tribal members. These actions would tend to push the Indian into the economic position of the American landowner. He and his children could learn to use land efficiently, or they could use education to learn some other occupations.

The fact that this policy did not work out well was anticipated by some people and recognized by others as the decades passed, and eventually, in 1934, the allotment practice was discontinued by Act of Congress. But the Indians had lost most of their land by that time. They were poor, ill-educated, and ill-adapted to participate in American-Anglo society. These facts were pointed out in the Meriam survey, published in 1928, but further attempts at assimilation were recommended. The Meriam report concluded:

The fundamental requirement is that the task of the Indian Service be recognized as primarily educational, in the broadest sense of that word, and that it be made an efficient educational agency, devoting its main energies to the social and economic advancement of the Indians, so that they may be absorbed into the prevailing civilization or be fitted to live in the presence of that civilization at least in accordance with a minimum standard of health and decency (Meriam 1928:21).

Margaret Mead (1960) presented an acute critique of assimilation policy along with some of the complexity of cultural pluralism in an essay on community education programs. She illustrated her thinking about culture change and culture contact with three case studies of native societies, one of them being the "Antler" tribe of Plains Indians who have suffered from assimilation policy gone wrong.

Cultural Pluralism

Assimilation as a policy had been tried and found inadequate. Even though some people of the native race did assimilate into the dominant society successfully, they were few in number. Meanwhile the native population was growing rapidly in numbers, was emigrating to the cities, and was becoming a kind of semipermanent lower working class — poor, under-employed, and dissatisfied. Some of the younger members of the native group became militant, demanding more positive attention and assistance from the dominant group. Anthropologists took an active part in defining and promoting the next policy step, toward cultural pluralism.

This was seen most clearly in the Australian case. Three anthropologists were especially important in this connection. Professor W. E. H. Stanner of the Australian National University was a member of the three-man Commonwealth Council on Aboriginal Affairs, which advised the government on Aboriginal affairs policy. A husband-wife team of anthropologists at the University of Western Australia, Professor Ronald M. Berndt and Dr. Catherine H. Berndt wrote and spoke effectively. Also, Professor C. D. Rowley, a specialist in government, became the organizer and editor of a three-volume series on Aboriginal affairs, sponsored by the Social Science Research Council of Australia (Rowley 1970, 1971a, 1971b; see also 1972). In fact, the departments of anthropology at all of the Australian universities had one or more staff members doing research and writing and speaking on aboriginal affairs that focused on a policy of cultural pluralism.

Excerpts from writings by Stanner and the Berndts will help to clarify the policy which went under various terms and is being called cultural pluralism by this writer. Professor Stanner (1967:56–57), explaining the complexity of the problem of creating a true cultural pluralism, said:

Over the last thirty years we have been trying to attract them (Aborigines) into some sort of union with us. We call it "assimilation" and think of "integration" as an intermediate stage or perhaps a less complete union. But it is easy for us to overlook that a long humiliation can dull the vision, narrow the spirit, and contract the heart towards new things. Some of the Aborigines do not understand our offer; some think it is not genuine; some, that its terms are not very attractive; some prefer to cling to their old identity until they are more sure what identity they will have within our new proposals for them. There are deeper difficulties still. We are asking them to become a new people but this means in human terms that we are asking them to un-be what they now are. But many of them are now seeking to rediscover who and what their people were before the long humiliation. It is a search for identity, a way of restoring self-esteem, of finding a new direction for the will to survive, and of making a better bargain of life on a more responsive market at a more understanding time.

Berndt (1969:xvii) clearly hopes for a viable form of cultural pluralism. Introducing a symposium on current problems among aborigines, he stressed the obstacles to a cultural identity for the aborigines and described conditions under which a fairly satisfactory Aboriginal identity might be achieved within a policy of cultural pluralism.

He pointed out the following facts:

1.   People of Aboriginal descent are participating much more positively in their own affairs, despite limited opportunities for communication with others, general socioeconomic deprivation, and circumscribed opportunities for choice.

2.   Socioeconomic disadvantage. A high proportion of people of Aboriginal descent have remained virtually anchored at a low socioeconomic level — in many cases at a bare subsistence level.

3.   The provision of improved educational facilities is a major need. This is especially important for the part-Aboriginal people who live in or near the town and cities. They have become divorced from traditional Aboriginal life, but they suffer from restricted opportunities for education, training, and employment.

In general terms, for children of Aboriginal descent, basic teaching about the wider Australian society needs to be strengthened and supplemented, to overcome the limited horizons of small-scale and often very narrow mission and government settlement living. And with this should go training in basic skills, and special help to cope with adaptation to changing conditions and to sophisticated economics..... Additionally, where broader issues of understanding and appreciating differing views and values are concerned, education is, or should be, a two-way process — relevant not only to people of Aboriginal descent but to other Australians as well.

4.   At present, "there are two contrasting trends in Aboriginal life." One is a movement toward what can be called "Aboriginality." The other is a movement toward a more active role in the affairs of the wider Australian society, with eventual mergence. These two trends are not necessarily mutually reinforcing.

In this last point, Berndt states the essence of the problem of cultural pluralism in the case of the Aborigines. Nearly all part-Aborigines and a growing number of full Aborigines are so far removed from their traditional Aboriginal past that the essence of aboriginality for them consists of knowledge about and experience in situations of contact, conflict, and cooperation with the European society. Their "aboriginality" is very different from that of people who have lived their lives in an isolated tribal culture. The "aboriginality" of the part-Aborigines is that of a subculture of the more comprehensive Australian culture, hemmed in by barriers which limit their opportunities and choices. In their attempts to develop an Aboriginal identity, they have sought two things — a satisfactory place WITHIN that system, and a satisfactory place OUTSIDE that system — and here lies the personal dilemma for many Aborigines and the social problem for the Australian society.

Such writing and consultation with policy makers have been responsible, I believe, for a development of policy that is seen in the following three quotations from men who were responsible for making government policy. The first is an essay on Commonwealth policy for Aboriginal affairs by the Minister for Aboriginal Affairs, Mr. William C. Wentworth IV. Mr. Wentworth, a member of the fourth generation of a pioneer family prominent in Australian political life, was contrasting the policy of ASSIMILATION with an emerging policy which approaches what we call cultural pluralism. He pointed out that some Aborigines favored one policy and some favored another (1969:182–185):

From my point of view the important thing is that they have been put forward by Aboriginals. And let me summarize them briefly and crudely. There are some Aboriginals who say, "We want to become part of the community at any cost. We want education. We want housing. We want to forget our old ways. We want to have every kind of white-wash poured over us." There are others who say, "We want to preserve our own ways. You mustn't try to destroy the whole of the Aboriginal past. You mustn't try to destroy the whole of our Aboriginal culture." I put this very crudely, because a summarizer must and should be crude. We have to find some way of reconciling these views of Aboriginals, different Aboriginals, because in their reconciliation a policy has to emerge. I want to speak about the government's view…. It is of course — everybody would agree with this surely — impossible to preserve for the Aboriginals the status quo. I am not speaking of the southern and assimilated Aboriginals. Nobody would believe, for example, that you could wall off Arnhem Land and leave it as it is, or leave it as it was perhaps, and let things go on there as they have gone on for the last few thousand years. Nobody would expect this. It is impossible. It would be rejected by everybody, I think — internationally, nationally and by Aboriginals. That is the first thing. The second thing is that we do not want to have any kind of compulsory and permanent apartheid in Australia. We work, not for a completely uniform society, but as we are involved in the general democratic framework, we work for some kind of pluralistic society where people are not all the same, although they have all the same rights, privileges and responsibilities. That is a society where they have the power to maintain for themselves, inside their own group, the characteristics of that group.... I quote from what was said officially in 1967 by our Aboriginals speaking of their development in a pluralistic society: "They may cherish, within the bounds of citizenship responsibility, their own languages, special customs, beliefs and values just as, for example, various immigrant or religious groups can do."

Dr. H. C. Coombs, the chancellor of the Australian National University, formerly head of the Reserve Bank of Australia, and chairman of the Council on Aboriginal Affairs, described four Aboriginal communities that have in recent years made notable progress toward the control and direction of their own future. He concluded as follows (1972:25):

Consideration of these examples leads, I think, to the conclusion that the life-style sought in each of them is practicable and modest. An Australian community committed to making it a reality for them and for comparable communities would be assuming no impossible or overwhelming burden. There is, however, one aspect of the aspirations of all these groups which I believe, will surprise most Australians: that is the emphasis in all of them on "separateness" and "distinctiveness;" on a future in which their Aboriginal identity would be apparent and acknowledged. There is no evidence to my eyes of any of the Aboriginal groups having chosen or being prepared to choose, as official assimilationist policy in the past assumed they would, to live by the same standards and to pursue the same purposes as white Australians.

Then, after a Labor Party victory in the 1972 general election, the prime minister, Mr. Whitlam, made the following statement on April 6, 1973, to the Ministerial Australian Aboriginal Affairs Council:

The basic object of my Government's policy is to restore to the Aboriginal people of Australia their lost power of self-determination in economic, social and political affairs. The minister for Aboriginal Affairs, Mr. Bryant, will be introducing into Parliament, I hope during the budget session, legislation to enable Aboriginal groups and communities to incorporate for the conduct of their own affairs. We see these incorporated societies, set up for purposes chosen by their Aboriginal members, determining their own decision-making processes, choosing their own leaders and executives in ways they will themselves decide as the primary instruments of Aboriginal authority at the local and community level.

The Government will also set up, on the advice of Aborigines, procedures for the election of freely-chosen Aboriginal representatives from the various regions of Aboriginal population to form a consultative council with which the Government will confer on matters affecting Aborigines. Mr. Bryant has already convened initial meetings towards the establishment of this body.

Traditional Aboriginal societies have had close associations with specific areas of land, and there are many Aboriginal communities which have maintained that association substantially unbroken. In respect of land reserved for Aboriginal use and benefit it is the firm policy of the Government to vest such lands in the Aborigines, as far as practicable in ways which accord with traditional Aboriginal law and practice. Mr. Justice E. A. Woodward has been commissioned to confer with Aboriginal communities concerned and to advise the legislative and administrative actions required. His enquiry will also, of course, extend to land outside reserves. The Government will await with interest his recommendations in respect of those situations where traditional association can be established for such land outside reserves....

This policy of re-establishing the traditional association of Aboriginal communities with the land is linked with support for the preservation and development of Aboriginal languages and culture generally. A start has already been made in basing the education of Aborigines on literacy first in their own tribal tongue. Increasing support will be given to Aboriginal arts and Aborigines will be helped where they wish to do so to maintain the active ceremonial life on which these arts were traditionally based.

An opportunity for self-determination and independent action would serve little purpose if Aborigines continued to be economically and socially deprived. The Government therefore plans to help them as individuals, groups or communities, in crafts, trades and professions and as business entrepreneurs. To this end programs of socially valuable special work projects, vocational training, and grants and loans in support of enterprises, will be actively promoted.

CULTURAL PLURALISM IN NEW ZEALAND

The same progression in thinking and in policy from assimilation to pluralism is to be seen in New Zealand, but in a somewhat less dramatic form.

The government secretary for Maori affairs, Mr. J. K. Hunn, was assigned the task of surveying the circumstances of the Maori people as of 1960 and of reporting recommendations to the government for further steps. He collected data, sought advice from a variety of people, and wrote a report in 1961 which was almost immediately published as a government document. Mr. Hunn had apparently not expected publication of the report in that form, but it seems to have served a useful purpose, in that it stated a general policy which was widely discussed, and generally approved, so that it may be seen, now, as a landmark on the path of policy development. The Hunn Report tried to state a general policy, which would go beyond assimilation.

Possible relations between the Anglo and the Maori cultures were stated as follows (Hunn 1961:15):

Evolution is clearly integrating Maori and Pakeha. Consequently, "integration" is said to be the official policy whenever the question is asked. In theory, the alternatives are assimilation, integration, segregation, and symbiosis, which terms are intended to mean:

ASSIMILATION: To became absorbed, blended, amalgamated, with complete loss of Maori culture.

INTEGRATION: To combine (not fuse) the Maori and Pakeha elements to form one nation wherein Maori culture remains distinct.

SEGREGATION: To enforce a theoretical concept of "apartheid." One school of thought in New Zealand advocates "parallel development," which in essence is segregation under another name.

SYMBIOSIS: To have two dissimilar peoples living together but as separate entities with the smaller deriving sustenance from the larger (seemingly an attempt to integrate and segregate at the same time).

The concept of INTEGRATION involves some semantic difficulties, as it has been used in connection with ethnic relations in New Zealand, Australia, and the United States. It has been used with somewhat different meanings in the three countries and seems better omitted from the present discussion, though it clearly is an advance from ASSIMILATION toward CULTURAL PLURALISM.

A number of anthropologists and social psychologists in New Zealand have been thinking and writing about cultural pluralism during the past ten years. The most active ones have naturally been located in the North Island, where the great majority of Maoris live. Auckland University, Victoria University (Wellington), University of Waikato (Hamilton), and Massey University (Palmerston North) all have anthropology, education, and psychology staff members studying Maori culture There are substantial numbers of Maori students, especially at Auckland and Victoria Universities. To illustrate the influence of anthropologists, we will refer to two persons — Erik Schwimmer and Joan Metge.

Schwimmer, who was editor of *Te Ao Hou*, a Maori literary and cultural journal, put together a set of papers from various authors (1968), which show rather clearly the progression of thought and of social goals from assimilation to cultural pluralism, which he calls BICULTURISM. In his introductory chapter, "Needed — a new theory on Maori social development," he formulates a definition of cultural pluralism, with reference to the Maori and Anglo cultures in New Zealand in terms of two basic principles — INCLUSION and BICULTURISM.

The first term comes from the sociologist Talcott Parsons and signifies, in a situation involving two main cultures:

1. Equal civil rights for members of both groups.
2. Full sharing in the process of government and the exercise of power.
3. Equal opportunities, gained through equality of resources and capacities.

Biculturism means that each cultural group:
1. Accepts as legitimate the values of a second culture in the society.
2. Is to some extent familiar with the other culture.
3. Consciously reconciles the value systems of the two cultures, though choices may have to be made.

Schwimmer says clearly that to became a reality, biculturism requires: (a) education that makes the capacities and achievements of the two cultural groups equivalent; and (b) better housing and higher income for the group with the lesser socioeconomic status.

Joan Metge, in the department of anthropology at Victoria University, grew up in Auckland, knows Maori people intimately, and has built her career on studies of Maori culture. She closes her book with a chapter on "Maori and Pakeha" as follows (1967:213–218):

The Hunn Report defined integration as "to combine (not fuse) the Maori and Pakeha elements to form one nation wherein Maori culture remains distinct." Later statements, though little clearer, suggest that the Government interprets this to mean eliminating differences that involve inequality and discrimination, and helping Maoris to retain their language and culture if they want to. Translating this policy into action poses some interesting problems. Do certain differentiating laws involve unnecessary privilege or compensation for disability? What if the Maoris themselves prefer inequality to change?

Maoris generally accept "integration" as a goal, but often question Government implementation of it. They allege (for instance) that recent land measures, encouragement of urban migration, and the "pepper-potting" of Maori houses among Pakeha ones further assimilation rather than integration, and complain that not enough is done actively to foster Maoritanga. Most agree that their future is bound up with that of the Pakeha, and give little support to nationalistic or separatist movements. At the same time, they are determined to retain their own identity.

The large majority would endorse the ideal of integration as defined by the Presbyterian Maori Synod: "As we understand it, integration is the combination of the Maori and Pakeha peoples of the nation into one harmonious community in which each enjoys the privileges and accepts the responsibilities of their common citizenship, wherein there are no racial barriers and wherein, with mutual understanding and respect, each race is free to cherish its cultural heritage, that in this way the best elements of both cultures may be united to form the pattern of future New Zealand society."

The idea of fusion — the development of a truly New Zealand culture incorporating both existing cultures — is acceptable for the distant future, but arouses no enthusiasm as an immediate goal....

Year by year Maoris and Pakehas extend the area of their common culture by developing new patterns in association, in response to the same internal stimuli. This is particularly true in the fields of sport, soldiering and popular entertainment, in all of which Maoris have achieved national prominence. Recently also, several artists and writers, making use of ideas and techniques from both cultures, have produced work that adds an exciting new dimension to the arts in New Zealand. Prominent among these are the poets Alistair Campbell and Hone Tuwhare, artists Rau Hotere, Para Matchitt, Selwyn Muru and Theo Schoon, and the sculptor Arnold Wilson; but there are many more, especially (which is significant) among the younger generation....

Four factors in the situation give grounds for hoping that Maoris and Pakehas can not merely conflict, but effect a positive improvement in their relations. In the first place, both groups include some persons of mixed ancestry and many who have relatives in the other. Persons of mixed descent do not form a separate group. Maoris accept anyone with Maori ancestry as Maori; Pakehas accept those who look Pakeha without difficulty and those who look Maori if they "live up to Pakeha standards." Secondly, classification is extremely elastic. There is no clear-cut legal or administrative definition: the individual can largely make his own choice. Many claim to belong to different groups at different times, and more and more proudly assert with Peter Buck that they are BOTH Maori AND Pakeha. Thirdly, relations are both varied and open to change. Attitudes and patterns of behaviour differ from area to area, with economic status and education, and with individual personality and background. People act differently in different situations, and frequently change their minds in the light of experience.

Finally, both Maoris and Pakehas hold firmly to the belief that they are "one people," united in friendship and equality.

CULTURAL PLURALISM IN THE UNITED STATES

To speak of cultural pluralism in the United States brings to mind a diversity of cultures, in addition to the Anglo. There are the black or Afro-American, the Oriental-American, the Spanish-American, and the American Indian, not to mention the European ethnic groups such as Polish, Italian, Irish, Greek, Yugoslav. There is a definite movement toward a cultural pluralism that embraces all these groups. We will limit ourselves here to discussion of the American Indian in relation to the Anglo culture.

The architect of the "Indian New Deal," as the new policies of the administration of Franklin D. Roosevelt were called, was John Collier. Though not an anthropologist, his close professional and family associates were anthropologists, and he represented their views quite well. Ruth Underhill, Gordon Macgregor, Clyde Kluckhohn, and Laura Thompson were closely associated with him during the 1940's when his program was put into practice.

Collier's watchword was SELF-DETERMINATION for Indian tribes, on a tribal basis. He treated each tribe as a unit. The Indian Reorganization Act of 1934 gave each tribe the power to elect a tribal council, gave the tribal councils the power to make and enforce laws (with certain limitations) and to incorporate and conduct business enterprises.

Collier's policies held sway until about 1950, when there was a rever-sion to assimilation through the mechanism of terminating the res-ervations and dividing the land and other resources among the tribal members. That policy worked out badly and was abandoned after 1958, with only a few reservations terminated.

With the election of John F. Kennedy to the presidency, and with Stuart Udall named Secretary of the Interior, the urgent question of Indian policy came to the fore again. Udall appointed a task force to advise on Indian policy. This group contained people with a good deal of Indian experience. The chairman was W. W. Keeler, a part-Indian who was honorary chairman of the Cherokee tribe. Among the members were James Officer and Philleo Nash, both anthropologists. Mr. Nash, who had been lieutenant governor of the state of Wisconsin, was later ap-pointed Commissioner of Indian Affairs. President Johnson appointed another task force in 1966.

Both of these groups urgently recommended measures for assisting the economic development of Indians through tribal action. The emphasis was on tribal self-determination, with government financial aid when the tribe decided on a program of economic development. The general trend of government policy throughout the decade was toward greater self-determination. For example, all schools for Indians administered by the federal government were directed in 1968 to establish advisory boards from among the parents and local community leaders.

President Nixon's message to Congress on Indian affairs in 1970 was explicit on cultural pluralism. He said:

I am asking Congress to pass a new concurrent Resolution which would expressly renounce, repudiate and repeal the termination policy as expressed in House Concurrent Resolution 108 of the 83rd Congress. This resolution would explicitly affirm the integrity and right to continued existence of all Indian tribes and Alaska native governments, recognizing that cultural pluralism is a source of national strength (Nixon 1970: 17–18).

Thus the decade of the 1960's was following the direction charted in 1961 by the American Indian Chicago Conference when the Indians making up the Conference declared (1961:4):

In order to give recognition to certain basic philosophies by which the Indian People live, we, the Indian People, must be governed by principles in a democratic manner with a right to choose our way of life. Since our Indian culture is threatened by presumption of being absorbed by the American society, we believe we have the responsibility of preserving our precious heritage. We believe that the Indians must provide the adjustment and thus freely advance with dignity to a better life.

Several anthropologists made contributions to the development of Indian policy during the 1960's. Professor Sol Tax of the University of Chicago was one of the leaders in organizing the Chicago Conference of 1961. He and Professor Robert Thomas of Wayne State University kept the magazine *Indian Voices* going during most of this decade. Professor Murray Wax, a sociologist, and his wife, Rosalie Wax, have studied Indian schools in South Dakota and in Oklahoma and have recommended a type of instruction which fits the Indian culture and makes the Indian youth feel more "at home" in the school. Professor Nancy Oestreich Lurie of the University of Wisconsin at Milwaukee has made a useful analysis of cultural pluralism (see Leacock and Lurie 1971) in which she stresses the importance of ARTICULATION of Indians as GROUPS into the larger society. This is the desirable alternative to assimilation as INDIVIDUALS in the larger society. The technique for developing cultural pluralism, she says, involves Indian self-determination, organized intertribal activities, and diffusion of pan-Indian traits. Her stress on intertribal cooperation and pan-Indianism is a notable contribution to thinking about cultural pluralism. Also, she stresses a need for "a decent material foundation for existence, with Indian identity maintained and activity utilized as an essential component of satisfactory community life" (1971:419).

A school board member for the Rough Rock School on the Navajo reservation, John Dick, made the following statement in 1968:

We want our children to be proud of being Navajos. We want them to know who they are.... In the future they will have to be able to make many choices and do many different things. They need a modern education to make their way, but they have to know both worlds — and being Navajo will give them strength (Fuchs and Havighurst 1972:246).

FUNCTIONS OF EDUCATION FOR CULTURAL PLURALISM

What do anthropologists do, in their role as teachers, to foster the movement toward cultural pluralism? Their educational activities fall into three categories.

Education of Opinion Formers and Policymakers

They write, counsel, and speak to members of government, to journalists, and other people who take some responsibility for leadership on matters of public policy. Examples of this kind of activity have been given.

General Education of the Public

They write, lecture, and teach about the cultures of various ethnic groups, so as to increase the understanding of people and also the mutual respect of members of various cultural groups for one another. They prepare materials for adults and for school-age youth. Examples of anthropologists or sociologists who have been especially active in this connection are:
1.   UNITED STATES: John Collier, Jr., Malcolm Carr Collier, Robert Dumont, Estelle Fuchs, Fred Gearing, Clyde Kluckhohn, Nancy Lurie, Margaret Mead, Gordon Macgregor, George Spindler, Sol Tax, Murray and Rosalie Wax.
2.   NEW ZEALAND: Richard Benton, Bruce Biggs, Raymond Firth, John Harré, Patrick Hohepa, Joan Metge, J. R. McCreary, Ralph Piddington, James and Jane Ritchie, Erik Schwimmer, Rangi Walker, John E. Watson.
3.   AUSTRALIA: R. M. and C. H. Berndt, M. J. C. Calley, A. P. Elkin, P. M. C. Hasluck, F. Lancaster Jones, Lorna Lippmann, J. P. M. Long, B. Nurcombe, Marie Reay, C. D. Rowley, W. E. H. Stanner, Ronald Taft, C. M. Tatz, Betty H. Watts.

Education of the Minority Group

Members of the minority group or groups are a part of the general public for the kinds of education mentioned above. In addition, they are likely to get special attention due to their minority group membership. This special education is aimed at helping them maintain a group identity, pride in their group, and their tribal language. Anthropologists are likely to be involved in the selection or preparation of teaching material aimed at this goal.

CONCLUSION

Although there appears to be a substantial commitment to cultural pluralism in these three countries, at least a decade of social evolution will be necessary to work the concept into reality and to test its viability. The policy has been developed so far in a favorable environment. Young people in general appear to favor it. The Anglo society is permissive and regards it increasingly as an issue to be worked out by the minority cultural groups. The dominant society is willing to provide enough socio-economic support so that members of the minority groups will not have to suffer from sheer, abject poverty, which would probably make cultural pluralism impossible.

Still, the story is far from complete, and continued participation by anthropologists will probably be useful.

REFERENCES

AMERICAN INDIAN CHICAGO CONFERENCE
    1961   *The voice of the American Indian: declaration of Indian purpose.*
        Chicago: University of Chicago Press.
BERNDT, ROLAND M.
    1969 Introduction to Symposium on *Current problems among Aborigines.*
        Forty-first Congress of the Australian and New Zealand Association
        for the Advancement of Science.
COOMBS, H. C.
    1972 "The future of the Australian aboriginal." Cohen Memorial Lecture,
        University of Sydney.
ELKIN, A. P.
    1959 *Australian aborigines* (second edition). Sydney: Angus and Robertson.
        (originally published 1928).
FIRTH, RAYMOND
    1959 *Primitive economics of the New Zealand Maori* (second edition).
        Wellington: Government Printer. (originally published 1929).
FUCHS, ESTELLE, ROBERT J. HAVIGHURST
    1972 *To live on this earth: American Indian education.* New York: Doubleday.
HUNN, J. K.
    1961 *Report on department of Maori affairs* Wellington: Government
        Pinter.
LEACOCK, ELEANOR BURKE, NANCY OESTREICH LURIE, *editors*
    1971 *North American Indians in historical perspective.* New York: Random
        House.
MAYS, THOMAS J.
    1888 The future of the American Indian. *Appleton's Popular Science*
        Monthly 33:104–108.
MEAD, MARGARET
    1960 "Cultural factors in community-education programs," in *Community*
        education, 66–96. 58th Yearbook, Part I, National Society for the
        Study of Education. Chicago: University of Chicago Press.
MERIAM, LEWIS, *editor*
    1928 *The problem of Indian administration.* Baltimore: Johns Hopkins Press.
METGE, JOAN
    1967 *The Maoris of New Zealand.* London: Routledge and Kegan Paul.
MORISON, SAMUEL ELIOT
    1965 *The Oxford history of the American people.* New York: Oxford
        University Press.
NATIVE WELFARE CONFERENCE
    1951 *Policy statement.* Native Welfare Conference of Commonwealth and

State Ministers, September 3–4. Canberra: Government Printer.

NIXON, RICHARD M.

1970   *Recommendations for Indian policy.* Document 91–363, July 8, 91st Congress, 2nd Session.

PIDDINGTON, RALPH

1968   "Emergent development and integration," in *The Maori people in the nineteen sixties.* Edited by Erik Schwimmer, 257–269. Auckland: Blackwood and Janet Paul.

ROWLEY, C. D.

1970   *The destruction of Aboriginal society,* volume one. Canberra: Australian National University Press.

1971a   *Outcasts in white Australia,* volume two. Canberra: Australian National University Press.

1971b   *Aboriginal policy and practice,* volume three. Canberra: Australian National University Press.

1972   *The remote Aborigines.* Ringwood, Victoria: Penguin Books Australia.

RUSDEN, H. K.

1972   "Labor and capital," in *Racism: the Australian experience,* volume two: *Black versus white.* Edited by Frank Stevens, 16. Sydney: Australia and New Zealand Book Company (originally published 1876 as a letter in the *Melbourne Review* 1:78.)

SCHWIMMER, ERIK, *editor*

1968   *The Maori people in the nineteen sixties.* Auckland: Blackwood and Janet Paul.

SPINDLER, GEORGE D., *editor*

1963   *Education and culture: anthropological approaches.* New York: Holt, Rinehart and Winston.

STANNER, W. E. H.

1967   *After the dreaming.* Boyer Lectures, Australian Broadcasting Commission.

STRINER, HERBERT E.

1968   "A Program for the training, employment, and economic equality of the American Indian." Unpublished paper. Washington, D. C.: W. E. Upjohn Institute for Employment Research.

WAX, MURRAY L.

1971   *Indian Americans: unity and diversity.* Englewood Cliffs, N. J.: Prentice-Hall.

WENTWORTH, WILLIAM C.

1969   "The Role of the Commonwealth," in *Aboriginal progress: a new era?* Edited by D. E. Hutchison, 182–185. Perth: University of Western Australia Press.

Agents of Education and Development in Nepal

HUGH B. WOOD

Editors' Note: Nepal is a nation largely isolated from its neighbors, yet with sharp internal distinctions in social organization and cultural learning. Some of its strains of educational practice developed over hundreds of years and others were more recently incorporated from contact with the West (and the more "Westernized" East). Hugh Wood, a professor of education at the University of Oregon, has spent several years working in the organization and evaluation of a new national educational system for Nepal. In this paper he recounts some of the historical development of Nepal's current situation and analyzes parts of the new system and some of the problems it has encountered. In particular, he is concerned with the age-old battle between innovation and "tried and true" paths to success. People have a remarkable tendency to believe in innovation "for other peoples' children," and this intuition has a remarkable way of being borne out in the real world of education and social advancement. These individual manipulations are often brakes on national development, however. The questions posed by the seemingly human preference for advancement relative to one's closest competitors over aggregate advancement may be unanswerable. As Wood suggests, "In Nepal, time will tell."

Any discussion of education and development must be predicated on a common acceptance of the meanings applied to these terms. I intend the term "development" to include economic, political, and other cultural changes, which lead toward a greater degree of sophistication, as displayed by the so-called "more advanced" countries of the world. I use the term "education" much more broadly than institutionally; I include any activity that provides (to the recipient) new information, knowledge, and understanding, and leads to behavioral, and presumably cultural, change.

No attempt has been made to identify all of the facets or events in the educational spectrum of Nepal during recent centuries; rather, I have selected a few of the more obvious examples of "agents of education," and have tried to analyze some aspects of the impact these have had on Nepal's development.

The dearth of literature on Nepal has been a severe handicap to all who would study the country. My *Nepal bibliography* (1959a) and subsequent research uncovered fewer than 1,700 items that had been written in Western languages up to 1959 (about 10 percent of which have any real value). The Nepali and Indian language literature is sparse; the Chinese writings on Nepal are very limited; and the Sanskrit manuscripts concentrate on religion and dynasty records. Hence, much of what is presented here is based on personal observation, interviews, and other experiences which occurred during a six-year period of residence in, and subsequent visits to, Nepal.

LITTLE-KNOWN NEPAL

Geographically, Nepal extends for 550 miles east and west through the Himalayas between India and Tibet. The northern third of the country encompasses more than a score of peaks over 24,000 feet high, but contains some inhabitable valleys. The middle third (about forty miles wide) encompasses hundreds of small foothill valleys, surrounded by 8,000–10,000 foot ridges, and is extensively terraced for farming. The lower third of the country (about thirty miles wide) is part of the Gangetic Plains, and is the "rice bowl" of Nepal.

Nepal's 11,000,000 people are of mixed origin. Caucasian features are noticeable along the Indian border; Mongolian characteristics predominate in the north; but the majority, who live in the central valleys, are an admixture of the two races, the products, until recently, of extreme isolation. Similarly, the predominant religion of the south is Hinduism, of the north, Buddhism, with a delightfully harmonious mix of the two in the middle valleys. Centuries have produced and supported tribalism, closely related to a caste system which, in turn, is somewhat vocational in nature. This and geographic isolation have produced language variations, but Nepali, the national language, is quite universal today.

Historically, Nepal until about 1750 consisted of hundreds of independent principalities, which were determined primarily by geography. At that time, Prithi Narayan Shah, from the small state of Ghorka in western Nepal, successfully undertook to consolidate many of the independent units; his heirs continued his efforts and remained in power until 1846. At this time, Jung Bahadur Rana, the prime minister, usurped power and established a hereditary prime ministership, which lasted until 1951, when King Tribhuvan Bir Bickram Shah was able to regain power. His first actions included the solicitation of economic aid from India and America.

Politically, Nepal has experienced rapid change. Following the dictatorship of the Panas, King Tribhuvan and his son King Mahendra made efforts during the 1950's to prepare the people for popular elections and party government. Following less than two years of parliamentary government (1958–1960), King Mahendra dismissed the parliament and established a "partyless" benevolent monarchy with elected, nonpolitical advisory councils. This system remains in effect today under the recently crowned King Birendra.

Economic development, supported by foreign aid since 1952, has made typical progress and has brought improved agriculture, institutional education, some medical facilities, road building (only forty miles existed in 1950 in the entire country), a few bridges for the extensive trail system, air transportation, moderate industrialization, improvement in communication, tourism, increased nationalism, etc.

Finally, it should be noted that as we move northward through the country, we experience not only increasing elevations, but increasing isolation and provincialism, less development and change, greater "contentment" — in many ways we discern several distinct levels of development. The nature of these will become significant as we examine some of the agents of education.

SOME AGENTS OF EDUCATION

Education is essential to, and a product of, development. In each of the developing countries, we find agents of education that are peculiar and indigenous to one country as well as others that are somewhat common to all such countries, but often specific in their operation. I shall discuss several agents in each of these categories.

The Nepalese Porters

The origin of the porterage system in Nepal is hidden in the depths of history. Some of the trails, especially those leading to religious shrines, are paved with cobblestones, and there is some evidence that some of these were constructed or repaired as long ago as the seventh century. For the past two centuries this national network of trails has been limited only by the lack of permanent bridges, which reduces traffic during the monsoon period.

The porterage system (which includes some traders) is perhaps the first significant agent of education in Nepal. Formerly, the Nepalese villager seldom moved more than half a day's journey from his home; perhaps once or twice during his lifetime he would visit a shrine two or three days away. This has changed today; his mobility has extended to perhaps a full day's journey, and the number of exceptions has increased. A villager now travels to the capital or other center, or to other countries, or leaves his village permanently for more exciting and challenging centers.

Thus, the villagers have traditionally relied on the porters for information from the "outside world." The latter have been a significant agent of education, carrying information from village to village about improved methods of farming, of building fire pots and designing roofs, of weaving and dyeing, etc. They first brought the news of the sewing machine as it swept northward, and then they brought the machine itself. The porters brought the first cigarettes and kerosene to the villages, and more recently cheap Japanese cotton cloth. Information stimulated desire; desire led to buying, which in turn stimulated increased production.

During my residence in Nepal, I witnessed an interesting transformation of the porterage pattern in western Nepal. For many years, cigarettes and kerosene (and, more recently, cotton cloth) were transported by porters from an Indian railhead at Nepalgunj to Pokhara, forty miles north. In 1956 freighter plane service was inaugurated for this area. Transportation costs for cigarettes and cloth were halved, quantity was quadrupled. Many were concerned about the porters, who were now out of work; but the concern was needless. Most of the porters moved to Pokhara, increased in number, and fanned out to the east, the north, and the west from Pokhara to extend the "advantages of civilization" — cigarettes and machine-woven cloth — to many new villages (kerosene continued to be portered to Pokhara and the expansion of its distribution was much less rapid). Incidently, the porters provided these new villages with an agent of education.

Porters also carried news of political events, catastrophes, and even world events. But to the simple villager, this news was of less importance than legends and had little, if any, effect on his way of life.

Thus, the porter became a significant agent of education for many simple, local cultural changes in the village; he remains so today, especially in the more remote villages where more recent agents of education have not penetrated.

The Gurkha Soldier

The Gurkha soldier since the mid-1800's has been a most important agent of education. Informally at first, and later through formalized enlistment, he served in the British army, where he received the equivalent of an eighth grade education and, more recently, some severance vocational training. He had the opportunity to "rub" against Western civilization, both through his contact with the British soldier and later through service in Western countries. He absorbed not only formal "learning," but often some of the Westerner's concepts of human relationships.

During his twenty-year enlistment, he usually returned to his village several times, but his real educational impact began when he returned for "retirement" at about the age of thirty-seven. He commanded respect and attention. His pension provided financial independence. During his early years of retirement, he found pleasure in tutoring some of the youth of the village. (Institutional education was virtually unknown outside the Kathmandu Valley and Indian border regions before 1950.)

He, like the porter, brought new ideas and knowledge about agriculture, health, cooking, etc. to the village. But, as he became older, his status was enhanced, and he was permitted to challenge age-old concepts and beliefs. He often chided tradition, and, for the first time in the village's existence, someone made inroads into timeworn beliefs and created an interest and concern for national, if not international, events.

As India moved inexorably towards independence during the second quarter of this century, the Gurkha soldier carried support for this movement into the middle and northern hinterlands and prepared these areas for acceptance of Nepal's own revolution in 1950–1951, which overthrew the Ranacracy and restored power to the throne.

The "Rub of Culture"

Frances Dart (1963) has dealt with the "rub of culture" in Nepal at some length. This agent of education operated along the Indian border quite extensively, especially after the arrival of the British in India, and had political significance during India's struggle for independence.

This was augmented by several factors. Much of the border area was cut off from the rest of Nepal by uninhabitable, malaria-infested swamps and jungle. There is no natural border and, thus, there is an ethnic overlap in both directions. Trade is oriented to the south rather than to the north.

Thus, Indian beliefs, customs, and traditions were bound to rub off on the neighboring Nepalese. These were carried northward by visits to shrines, occasionally by relatives, and by business and political trips to Kathmandu and district headquarters in the midlands. It was in this border area of Nepal that the Nepali Congress Party came to life, flowered, and eventually led the revolutionary activities. (The proximity to the "escape hatch" — India — also undoubtedly prompted the party leaders to base their operations here.)

It has frequently been said that the Nepalese along the Indian border are more like Indians than Nepalese. The same might be said about the likeness of the northern Nepalese to the Tibetans. In general, however, the political allegiance is to Kathmandu. But the effect of "cultural rub" is strong on both borders.

Religious Institutions

Religion and its formal institutions in Nepal seem to have been rather innocuous as agents of education and are mentioned here more as exceptions than as models. The presence of two strong religions in the central valleys has, of course, affected the culture of these people, but change attributable to religion has been very slow. Modification of the two religions here has been comparatively sharp — sharing of deities, approval of meat consumption (perhaps because of climatic necessity), religious customs relating to birth, marriage, and death, etc.

However, two formal institutions associated with religion have failed to produce significant change. For centuries, the Buddhists have supported *gompas* [organized schools] to provide several years of training in prayer-reading to at least one male youth in each Buddhist family. Because the curriculum was confined to the skill of reading and the content of prayers, there appears to have been no substantial change in the institution or any resulting cultural change over the many centuries of the existence of these *gompas*. (It is believed that there were about fifty of these schools scattered throughout Nepal in 1952.)

A second institution, much more formal and extensive, and probably as old, was the Sanskrit education system, which included "primary schools," "secondary schools," and a "college." The purpose of the system was to train Sanskrit scholars who could copy, read, and interpret the thousands of Sanskrit manuscripts available in shrines and libraries throughout the country. Until about 1960, the curriculum was confined rigidly to Sanskrit studies; but the system, which has since expanded and become part of the present educational system, has added Nepali language, Nepali history, and some arithmetic to its curriculum. Here again, however, the rigid, narrow curriculum and the self-centered interests of the participants were not conducive to change and contributed little, if anything, to cultural change.

Foreign Visitors

The geography of Nepal and its politics up to 1956 discouraged foreign visitors. Missionaries traveling to and from Lhasa in the seventh century were told to "move on." Prior to the Rana regime, Nepal was inhospitable, to say the least, to the "foreigner"; the British, following a two-year war, 1814–1816, demanded a residency in Kathmandu, but didn't really achieve this goal until 1848. By that time the Rana dictators had assumed power and formally declared the country closed to all foreigners. Exceptions to this rule were the Tibetan traders and porters, Indians (if they did not impose), and individual British "residents." The latter were confined to the Kathmandu Valley and were usually escorted to and from the Indian border when such travel was necessary. With rare other exceptions — e.g. a Swiss engineer who built a power plant and visiting royalty who hunted in the Terai — Nepal had no foreign visitors until the advent of economic aid beginning in 1951–1952 and the arrival of the first tourists in 1956.

In spite of these limitations, however, the early British residents had a significant impact, especially in the Kathmandu Valley. The ruling Ranas were greatly impressed with the British achievements in India and imitated their customs and achievements in many ways. With considerable encouragement from the British (for obvious political reasons), the Ranas:

1. visited European capitals and brought back "curios of civilization," including knick-knacks such as grandfather clocks, crystal chandeliers, "Coney Island" curved mirrors to distort the viewer's features to the amusement of all, and primitive plumbing for their palaces;

2. sent their youth to British schools in India, and later established a British-type school and college in Kathmandu for their own children (education was forbidden, under penalty, to others);

3. encouraged the youth of Nepal to join the British army and later formalized British recruitment of the Gurkhas;

4. adopted many British trappings of government: courts, taxation, protocol, etc. (if they did not interfere with authoritarianism);

5. learned English (English was the instructional medium in the Rana schools), purchased English books for their personal libraries, adopted many English customs, abolished slavery (1926), anglicized their trade and businesses, etc.

The cultural, political, and economic changes resulting from this foreign contact were largely confined to the Kathmandu Valley, and many specifically to the Rana families, which, nevertheless, constituted the power structure and thus a potential force in Nepal's future.

As noted above, other agents of education interfered to change the course of history. Since 1952 hundreds of technical experts have had access to most parts of the country,[1] and since 1956 thousands of tourists with access to several of the more populated areas have also visited the country. The impact of these foreigners has followed the pattern found in most developing countries.

The "Trappings" of Development

While the agents of education noted above have continued to effect change, modern technology has been introduced, mostly since 1952, and has effected even more change. It is true that the earlier agents helped to set the climate for acceptance, and even desire, for these new technical devices, but conceptualize, if you will, the impact of:

1. air transportation, now serving some fourteen areas throughout Nepal and reducing the length of travel to the capital and India from up to thirty days to less than one day for much of the population and to an extreme of five days for all but a few of the others;

2. a north-south all-weather highway from the Tibetan border to the Indian border and major sectors of an east-west road now available, with military and political implications as well as severe cultural changes, for those who live adjacent to the new roads, and economic changes for many others;

3. radio services, including news and educational programs, telephone and other communication services, newspapers, expanding rapidly throughout the country, and the increasing availability of international information from Indian radio stations and newspapers;

4. institutional education through 7,500 primary schools, 1,100 second-

[1] Though perhaps not "technical experts" in the strict sense, the Peace Corpsmen, who are included in this category, have had special impact because of (a) their large number, (b) their actual residence "among the people," (c) their wide range of interest and activity, and (d) their competence in the native language.

ary schools, and 50 higher schools (1972) reaching into every corner of
the country, providing not only learning for youth but also adult education, first aid, and similar community services;

5. similar services in agriculture, health, business, industry, government (taxation, judiciary, planning), and the usual facets of development.

NEPAL AS A MODEL FOR STUDY

The development economist finds Nepal a neat model for study and
analysis partly because isolation has served to sharpen the delineation of
"periods" in economic development, and partly because of the existing
"levels" of development which may be used for comparison and contrast.
I should think that the anthropologist would find Nepal an equally
fertile ground for study, for similar reasons.

As an educational program design specialist, I found a unique situation
in 1953 when I was asked to assist in the development of an educational
system for Nepal. Nearly all other developing countries had been saddled
with European school systems, and, immediately upon gaining independence, they began a "band-aid" process of trying to adapt a foreign
system to their needs. An inventory of schools in Nepal in 1952 revealed
(a) about fifty *gompas*, (b) a Sanskrit system including a few primary
schools, three secondary schools, and a college, (c) a British system for
the Ranas and a few other elite, which included a few primary schools,
three high schools, and a college, (d) an increasing number (perhaps 100)
of vernacular schools near the Indian border (following Indian prototypes of British schools, but in the local language), and (e) a few "basic"
schools (following prototypes of Ghandi's indigenous schools in India)
in the process of being organized. The number of high school graduates
in all of Nepal, including those who had gone to India for schooling,
was about 1,000; college graduates numbered about 300. Less than one
percent of the population was in school.

Here was an ideal opportunity for a nation to design and develop a
school system truly indigenous to the needs of its people. In effect, it
was so designed (Pandey, Buhadur, and Wood 1956), and it is developing
to a major extent along these lines.[2] However, it is not difficult to discern
some of the obstacles to the full realization of such a dream.

---

[2] This is revealed by several interim reports and observations, including those contained in various issues of *Education Quarterly*, which has been published since 1957
by the College of Education, Kathmandu, especially 1959:1–77; other pertinent information is contained in Wood (1959b); Sharma (1962); Wood and Knall (1962);
Upraity (1962); and the *National education system plan for 1971–1976* (Ministry of
Education 1971).

First, the majority of the educational elite who designed the program were products of the British system, either the Rana-sponsored schools or the British schools of India. In spite of this, the DESIGN came out as an indigenous system.

Second, and more important, while the plan immediately won the "King's Seal" and the general support of the populace, the popular support was for "my neighbor's children; mine must have the 'superior' English education." Ability to speak English (available in the new national HIGH schools, but not primary schools) represented "educational success," and the English language soon found its way into the primary schools, displacing more practical, less academic parts of the curriculum.

Third, although the teacher training program included learning the content of the new curriculum of the primary and secondary schools, teachers, especially when pressured, tended to slight the content, which they had not personally experienced as youths, and to emphasize those aspects which would insure successful advancement through college, so often conceived as the true index of their own success.

Fourth, the two concepts of "voluntary terminal points in education prior to college graduation" and "TRAINING for a vocation" were totally incomprehensible to the populace — certainly inconceivable for one's own children!

So, the The national education system plan for 1971-1976, most recent report on education in Nepal, continues to chide the populace for straying from the original design and makes recommendations for returning education to manpower needs and other national goals. During its first two decades, the new institutionalized mass education in Nepal has been more indigenous than in most other developing countries — and it will be worthwhile for the economist, anthropologist, and educator to note the effects of this, if any, in their respective fields — but there has been, and will continue to be, a struggle to keep it indigenous.

THE CONFLICT BETWEEN INTEGRATION AND UNIQUENESS

In spite of Nepal's historic freedom from colonization and imperialism, it is caught up in the conflict between "trying to become like the Western world" and "retaining its uniqueness." Traditionally, we have assumed that integration ("making others like us") is essential to harmony. More recently, we have asked whether "coexistence" could not become something "beautiful" and harmonious.

Both nations and races need to examine this possibility. Paulo Freire, in his Pedagogy of the oppressed, points out that,

There is no such thing as a neutral educational process. Education either functions as an instrument which is used to facilitate the integration of the younger generation into the logic of the present system and bring about conformity to it, or it becomes the "practice of freedom," the means by which men and women deal critically and creatively with reality and discover how to participate in the transformation of their world.... As long as they [the oppressed] live in the duality in which TO BE is TO BE LIKE, and TO BE LIKE is TO BE LIKE THE OPPRESSOR, this contribution [self-liberation] is impossible (Freire 1972:15).

Obviously, an indigenous educational system, not a transplanted one, is essential to "the practice of freedom," the maintenance of uniqueness.

But if Nepal successfully adopts this stance in education, can it be sure of finding a world receptive to this notion of unintegrated, lovely coexistence? The process of creating a new national ideology, the rediscovery of the earlier uniqueness of the culture that reflects the true national character and aspirations of the people, and the resocialization necessary to achieve this unique and indigenous status require a great deal of change and much choosing (from the Rana period, the pre-Rana period, or what?); this may be too much to expect of Nepal, especially in view of the uncertainty of worldwide acceptance.

Ernest Shanahan points out that, "In order to mobilize the masses of people to promote social and economic development, the specificity of the heritage must be stressed, thus creating the necessity for a particularist curriculum in the country" (Shanahan 1972:11). On the other hand, Clignet emphasizes that, "This mobilization is only an indispensable tool for enhancing and accelerating the overall level of economic and political achievement of the entire social system and for making it more competitive in international deals and bargains." This necessitates a universalist curriculum. He goes on to emphasize that the leaders of these countries "... must choose between the formation of a particularist elite with deep roots in ... the local society or the formation of a universalist elite able to converse and compete freely with their counterparts ..." in other countries of the world (Clignet 1971:309). The existence of foreign technicians, educators, and advisors, ignorant of the demands of the local history, pretty well guarantees the latter course of events.

As it stands today, agents of education, including some of the schools, are contributing to the development of a universalist elite who are primarily concerned with directing the country's economic and political development. In the hinterlands, there is some evidence that the masses will cling to the particularist concept; and this possibility is supported by a strong set of "conservatives" in the populated centers who strongly defend traditional institutions and customs. Can a people reach a compromise between the two poles of this dichotomy in this fashion for a significantly long period? In Nepal, time will tell.

REFERENCES

CLIGNET, REMI
  1971   Damned if you do; damned if you don't: the dilemma of colonizer-colonized relations. *Comparative Education Review* 15:296–312.
DART, FRANCES
  1963   The rub of culture. *Foreign Affairs* 41:360–374.
FREIRE, PAULO
  1972   *Pedagogy of the oppressed.* New York: Herder and Herder.
MINISTRY OF EDUCATION, HIS MAJESTY'S GOVERNMENT OF NEPAL
  1971   *The national education system plan for 1971–1976, Nepal.* Kathmandu.
PANDEY, RUDRA PAJ, KAISER BAHADUR, HUGH. B. WOOD, *editors*
  1956   *Education in Nepal; report of the national education planning commission.* Kathmandu: Bureau of Publications, College of Education.
SHANAHAN, ERNEST J.
  1972   "Education and nationalism." Unpublished paper.
SHARMA, KULASHEKAR
  1962   *Primary education in Nepal.* Kathmandu: Ministry of Education.
  n.d.   Symposium: educational progress in Nepal. *Educational Quarterly* (Nepal) 3:1–77.
UPRAITY, TRAILOKYA NATH
  1962   *Financing elementary education in Nepal.* Oceanside, Oregon: The American-Nepal Education Foundation.
WOOD, HUGH B.
  1959a *Nepal bibliography.* Oceanside, Oregon: The American-Nepal Education Foundation.
  1959b *Six years of educational progress in Nepal.* Kathmandu: Bureau of Publications, College of Education.
WOOD, HUGH B., BRUNO KNALL
  1962   *Educational planning in Nepal and its economic implications.* Paris: UNESCO.

The New Education Plan in Nepal: Balancing Conflicting Values for National Survival

EDNA MITCHELL

> I know
> Where my efforts will end ...
> Against the wall!
> The hills and the mountains,
> The lofty crests of the Himalayas,
> The walls of flesh in flakes and fragments
> Are all standing before me
> Against the wall.
>
> MALLA (1972:52)

Editors' Note: In the following paper, Edna Mitchell explores the processes of implementation of plans for national educational programs in Nepal. Her paper comes directly after Hugh Wood's and takes up a different aspect of the conflict in the Nepalese situation. Mitchell describes the process of educational planning and decision making, itself a subject for anthropological observation, rather than the vicissitudes of local reactions. Her paper also deals with the problems of hybridization in the translation of one culture's educational practices into the situation of another. The forecast for Nepal's future is uncertain — the balancing of "Eastern and Western" values must continue, and it remains to be seen to what extent the educated elite gives way to a more common literacy and schooling. It is clear that the problems Wood describes still obtain and have their national policy counterparts as well. Both authors describe a bold and enthusiastic population, however, and so give a measure of optimism.

The lofty peaks of the Himalayas enshrouded in mist rise on the north; the hot, humid flatlands of the malaria-infested Terai stretch along the southern border; and together with the Kathmandu Valley, heartland of Nepal, they make up a nation of diversity, contrast, and complexity. Nepal provides a unique model for a study of the impact of contact between postindustrial societies and a preindustrial culture. Nepal, virtually closed to foreigners until the fall of the Rana Kings in 1950, had remained almost unchanged for centuries, preserving forms of production, trade, and social customs comparable in many ways to medieval Europe under the feudal system.

Under the leadership of the present monarchy (beginning with King Tribhuvan, continuing with King Mahendra Bir Bikram Shah Deva, and now through the efforts of His Majesty Birendra Bir Bikram Shah Deva), modernization of Nepal for economic competition and survival has become a national goal.

The strategic location of Nepal, a buffer between the Peoples' Republic of China on the north and India on the south, makes it a desirable target of influence for both of these powerful nations. The leaders of Nepal, in searching for the most fruitful way to provide both solidarity in a nation with diverse peoples and economic prosperity in a land of bare subsistence farming, have selected education as the instrument of top priority for developing the resources of the people.

This paper will focus upon the types of questions for which Nepal is seeking answers relative to the investment of money and manpower in education. Many of these questions plague the leadership of highly developed nations; but in the relatively fresh context of a country with few educational traditions to uphold, the issues seem much more clearly cut if not easier to resolve.

EDUCATION FOR WHAT PURPOSES?

Formal education in Nepal has traditionally been modeled on Indian education, which was modeled on eighteenth-century British patterns. As some Nepalis have remarked, "India took the worst of the British school plan, and we borrowed the worst from the Indians." While this is too severe a statement, it is nevertheless true that education in Nepal has followed a classical tradition for the elite few, and all higher education until very recently has been obtained in other countries.

New purposes for education were envisioned with the establishment of the constitutional monarchy in the fifties, and by the early sixties the concept of universal primary education as the basis for a democracy was accepted in principle. In 1951 the literacy rate was less than 10 percent. Strong efforts were made to expand educational opportunity, but for many reasons these efforts were not as successful as had been anticipated. By 1970 the literacy rate had climbed to what was optimistically reported as 32 percent.

A new National Education System Plan, which addresses itself to the problems of establishing clear objectives and setting priorities for optimal use of the limited financial resources available for education, was adopted for 1971 to 1976. The goal of universal primary education was delayed with a more realistic objective proposed for this five-year period. The revised goal is to double the primary enrollment from 32 percent to 64 percent of the children between the ages of six and eight by 1976.

The purposes of primary education now focus on the role of education in mobilizing manpower for nation building. The emphasis is on developing a stronger economic system through improved use of technology. There are other goals that relate to the creation of a population which would be aware of the modern world outside Nepal and the development of citizens loyal to the Crown.

The objectives of the New Education Plan are clearly slanted toward developing a modern nation with a strong economy relatively unencumbered by foreign commitments. The new plan clearly echoes national pride and determination to formulate a plan for the education of Nepalis which is designed by the Nepalis themselves.

The broad objectives are straightforward and provide a background against which other problems may be viewed. The achievement of the goals formally stated in the plan will be dependent upon how certain crucial questions are to be answered. Questions regarding who will be educated, what the content of education should be, how, and by whom, it will be taught — all are issues directly related to the purposes of educating a nation's people.

WHO SHALL BE EDUCATED?

The New Education Plan is intended to provide educational opportunities for a wide range of children and adults regardless of sex or geographical location. The nation is divided into seventy-five districts, with a developmental timetable which projects the implementation of the New Education Plan into all the districts within five years. The hope is ultimately to offer universal education.

The probability of achieving the desired changes in all districts within this time period is unlikely, given the severe problems of physical geography alone. The terrain in the mountains is impassable at times and communities are isolated from one another, making the attempt to provide schools as vehicles for education an inefficient technique.

Certainly the concept of equal education for boys and girls is a giant ideological step for Nepal to take. However, such a principle is far from being realized. The social traditions of the culture, similar to those of many other developing nations and industrialized societies, seem to make the education of women a luxury. An educated wife is more likely to be a social asset for her husband than an independent economic agent. In rural areas, particularly, it will be a very long time before the education of girls will be considered either desirable or necessary.

Therefore, the question of "Who shall be educated?" is being determinedly met in Nepal by a government that wishes to develop the human resources of its rural and village populations even though the belief in the value of education is not shared by all the people. The balance tips in favor of those who live in the Kathmandu Valley or near the larger towns such as Pokhara. Families which are affluent are more able to send their sons to school beyond the primary years. Only the affluent can reasonably encourage their daughters to attend school. The pyramid of an educated citizenry will be somewhat broadened at the base but will probably still be very narrow at the intermediate and higher levels of education for many years to come.

WHAT SHALL BE LEARNED?

Deciding upon the content for the new curriculum is a major task for Nepali leaders. Not only is it necessary to debate the scope and sequence of the subject matter, but the subject matter itself is being challenged. The older curriculum of classical studies (the Nepali version of the seven liberal arts of medieval Europe), with an emphasis on education of the intellect, is being challenged by the dictated priorities on vocational-technical education specified by the New Education Plan. However, there is danger of the new plan's being subverted in this regard. Even though there is to be an emphasis on vocational and technical skills, these subjects are not part of the curriculum until the secondary level, and the dropout rate may be so severe that those students remaining in school may well represent an elite group who will not relish the manual labor connected with some vocations.

Traditions which are rooted deeply in the culture tend to make people value education as a path to the intellectual–theoretical life. Only the man who is not educated may appropriately be expected to work with his hands or with tools. Of course, this tradition is not unique to Nepal, but it is at least as old as Socrates and the men of ancient Athens. Nepali educators are acutely aware of this dichotomy between learning and labor but have not yet discovered a way to overcome it. Some prevocational subjects are to be taught in the lower secondary school. Perhaps this area will be used productively to encourage pride in labor and to enhance the dignity of all work, which is a theme repeated frequently throughout the curriculum.

Many questions arise surrounding the selection of curriculum content. A major source of concern is how to provide for the survival of Sanskrit as a living language, continuing the practice of making all children learn the ancient language. Sanskrit is the source of all the religious writings, both ancient and modern, and is the language of official government documents. The Nepali language (Gurkhala) is derived from ancient Sanskrit. The Sanskrit scholars fear that a potential integrating experience, one which provides a strong sense of national pride, may be lost if the present plan to reduce the position of Sanskrit in the curriculum is successful. The plan calls for the maintenance of Sanskrit high schools throughout the nation, but Sanskrit scholars feel that not enough time is provided in the lower secondary school for students to develop the necessary background in Sanskrit to enable them to become proficient in all phases of the language by the time they graduate from the Sanskrit school. Actually, studying Sanskrit involves much more than learning a language; it involves learning a whole culture, including its history, politics, and religion.

The controversy over "What curriculum?" occurs in every discipline. Selecting and articulating major concepts in their field is a thorny problem for the most sophisticated educators. It is particularly difficult for scholars in Nepal because of the lack of time available for them to develop new integrated curricula while they continue to do their regularly assigned tasks.

Another difficult task which confronts Nepali educators is dealing with the expectation of creating a uniform curriculum to be used in every part of the country. The purpose of this uniformity is to ensure that the children in the villages will receive as fine an education as is provided in the Valley. It is assumed that if teachers' guides and materials are uniform, then children everywhere will be more likely to master the essential skills of reading and arithmetic as well as to learn the concepts of social studies and science. The Nepalis, however, indicate concern about incorporating the flexibility needed to meet unique problems in a local setting. For example, very few children outside the Kathmandu Valley speak Nepali as their native language; instead, they speak one of many dialects (which make communication between groups of Nepalis quite difficult). If the child is to have most of his instruction in Nepali, which he is also learning as a second language, how will his achievement of the goals stated in a uniform curriculum be affected? In the absence of an adequate supply of well-trained teachers who could make acceptable adaptations in the curriculum, it is necessary to write a prescribed minimal curriculum that teachers should follow as closely as possible.

HOW SHALL THEY BE TAUGHT?

The overall message of the New Education Plan emphasizes a changing world and the need for changing techniques of teaching and learning. A new curriculum heavily loaded with science and mathematics necessitates using teaching techniques and resources which encourage exploration, manipulation, demonstration, and experimentation. These terms are antithetical to the traditions of Nepali education. Nepali educators struggle, often in vain, to train teachers to use and value concrete experiences in learning concepts. There is very little in most classroom environments to support such unorthodox approaches. Classes are very crowded, classroom space is restricted in most cases, and resources are available in very limited amounts. It is exceedingly difficult to transport materials such as microscopes and chemicals to schools in the villages. However, to the surprise of many Westerners, these materials are quite often available, though infrequently used due to the crowded teaching facilities of the village schools. The forces of nature inhibit the use of many teaching materials which Westerners take for granted. For example, in the damp monsoon season, paper in books and charts deteriorates even inside the schoolroom, making it necessary for pupils and teachers to rely on recitation more than on reading or writing.

If it is difficult in the Western world to train teachers away from "teaching by telling," when we have for generations decried that as a teaching method, it is not hard to understand why progress in training teachers to use inductive methods and encourage more active participation on the part of students will be very slow in a nation like Nepal. Both the educational practices implanted in the schools by the example of other countries as well as some attitudes that have their basis in religion work together to inhibit the acceptance of teaching methods which involve small-group discussion or experimentation with maniuulative materials. The use of local materials and examples from everyday life for mathematics and science are being strongly suggested to teachers by the curriculum designers and by the education supervisors. However, teachers already in the classroom need intense in-service training before they can appreciate the importance of such approaches and use them imaginatively and creatively. The teachers who are being trained in the College of Education are more receptive to the new methods. Even they, however, have very limited resources for purchasing inexpensive and commonly used items from the bazaar which could become useful teaching aids. This problem raises the next question relating to teachers as a national resource.

WHO SHALL TEACH?

The New Education Plan makes predictions about manpower needs of Nepal for the next five years based on the major premises established by UNESCO. Recognition is made of the reverse status of available manpower with respect to that which would be desired. The greatest need is for a strong base of low-level manpower with practical technical skills and specializations. However, at the present rate of development, high-level manpower needs are being met while low-level resources are not being developed at the required rate. A realistic example of this problem is clearly seen in the status of the supply of teachers. The greatest need for teachers is at the primary level. With the expectation of doubling the primary enrollment, the number of teachers for that level would have to increase proportionately. Actually, more than twice the present number of primary teachers will be needed because not only is it estimated that enrollment will increase but it is hoped that the teacher-pupil ratio will be reduced. In a typical primary class the number of pupils for one teacher is forty-five to fifty. The goal is to reduce that load to about thirty pupils per teacher which, with no growth in enrollment, would require about 33 percent more teachers.

The shortage of teachers, both trained and untrained, is a critical problem. The establishment of colleges of education in several parts of the country has aided enormously in developing a new corps of teachers. However, salaries are only now being increased for the primary teacher whose salary previously was not enough to maintain a small family. Many young teachers in the city have to supplement their income by teaching at two or more schools at once or by working in hotels after school hours. Many promising young teachers have left teaching for other government posts as soon as they could find another position. As has been true all over the world, the status of primary teachers was very low — if they were not held in outright contempt — and the personal pride of the teacher until recently reflected that low esteem. With the new emphasis on the education of the teacher, these attitudes are changing. As long as teachers receive incomparably low wages, and as long as anyone who can read can teach, the low status of primary teachers will be unchanged. The New Education Plan attempts to alleviate part of that problem. It is staggering to anticipate the additional financial resources required to staff the New Education Plan, which calls for more teachers and significantly increased salaries. Some of the money will be provided by the national government, but a large part of it must come from local revenue sources.

Since the education of women has only recently received attention, teaching as an occupation has been traditionally a man's field. Women are now entering teaching in small but increasing numbers, particularly in the larger towns. Tables 1 and 2 show sex ratios in the schools in 1967–1968 (Tuladhar 1970: 240). (More recently available figures do not provide the numbers by sex.)

Table 1.   Primary school teachers

Year	Number of male teachers	Number of female teachers	Total	Percentage of females to the total
1964–1968	15,920	487	16,407	3

Table 2.   Enrollment in primary education by sex

Year	Number of boys	Number of girls	Total	Percentage of girls to total
1967–1968	375,721	66,530	442,721	15

These data may not accurately reflect the trend toward more education for women, but they do provide a clear picture of the possibility of a largely untapped human resource for teaching and learning — the women of Nepal.

WHAT ORGANIZATIONAL PLAN IS FEASIBLE?

A radical change in the organization of the schools and in the deployment of supervisory personnel is inherent in the design of the new plan. Primary education is to be a three-year block instead of a five-year program; grades four to seven will be the lower secondary school and grades eight to ten will be the upper secondary. All higher education will be under the jurisdiction of Tribhuvan University. The faculties of the university have been replaced by sixteen institutes. The colleges in parts of Nepal outside of Kathmandu are considered to be extensions of the institutes.

In order to implement the new curriculum and assist teachers and headmasters in improving education in their schools, a complex supervisory system has been established. Groups of specialists will be assigned to supervise and evaluate progress through regular visits to designated schools. Because of the limited numbers of available specialists, the large numbers of schools called for in the new plan, and the unavoidable difficulties of reaching many schools, supervisors are expected to make only semiannual visits to their schools. The ratio of supervisors to schools varies according to location and type of school. For example, the ratio in Kathmandu Valley and the Terai will be 1:30 for primary, 1:15 for lower secondary, and 1:10 for secondary. In the mountainous regions the corresponding ratio is 1:20, 1:10, and 1:7. Schools are required to submit monthly reports and maintain records of student performance which will be sent to the Ministry of Education in Kathmandu. The plan also provides for the encouragement of in-service education through the supervisors by arranging for the more successful teachers to tutor others or present model classes which the other teachers in the district can observe.

This overall plan for implementation provides for a district organization and a time schedule for phasing in the new plan. In the first year only two districts, Kaski in the hills and Chitawan on the Terai, changed to the new curriculum and organizational plan in three grade levels: grades one, four, and eight. Progress was evaluated and the changes made in the curriculum were subsequently channeled into the improved curriculum that was instituted in the succeeding phases. The second phase, in 1973, included thirteen more districts; in the third year fifteen more districts were added; until 1976, when all seventy-five districts would be operating under the new plan.

The country was further reorganized into three zones, each with a regional education office charged with the responsibility of coordinating and supervising the execution of educational policies and objectives within its zone. The regional office organizes the training programs and inspections described above.

District education offices have been established for each of the districts within the zones. These offices are directly charged with the administration and supervision of education within the district, with the exception of higher education, which is the responsibility of the regional directorate.

The systematic design of the New Education Plan provides for an integration of educational goals from the primary school through the university. The organizational arrangement also delegates the production of textbook and printed materials to a government printing operation whose major function is the preparation of educational materials.

The plan is designed to establish coordination between levels of the administrative hierarchy as well as to promote coordination laterally across disciplines. The organization of zones and districts is expected to ensure the extension of educational opportunity along with greater equality and improved quality in the curriculum.

ARE SOME BARRIERS INSURMOUNTABLE?

Some of the problems impeding the realization of Nepali educational goals appear to be soluble, but other barriers are deeply rooted in the culture or are inherent in the nation's topography. The achievement of some of the desired goals could require a major social reorganization. Many Nepali have noted the cultural, religious, and economic changes which are accelerating as contacts with industrialized nations increase.

A review of the barriers facing the New Education Plan shows geography, historical traditions, economics, and social and religious traditions all combining powerfully to slow down or regulate change.

The geographical nature of the country makes nearly impossible the distribution of educational materials. the dissemination of modern educational practices, and the development of the envisioned technological society. Climate and topography are both formidable foes of the New Education Plan. The problem of isolation, of the mountain tribes from Kathmandu as well as of the nation itself from the world, is almost insurmountable.

The political history of the country presents another cultural factor which provides little precedent for the development of an educational system based on democratic goals and ideals. Education for the participatory or representative government of people who have little awareness of a shared destiny is a difficult task, particularly when the political traditions are much closer to a system of feudal serfdom.

Economic barriers are similar to those faced by many developing nations: limited availability of natural resources and dependence upon other nations for many essential goods and services. Efforts to build a strong economic base within the country itself have been slow to materialize. Projects sponsored by other nations have often met with failure after the initial efforts were made. Too frequently such projects designed to boost the economy have failed to take into consideration both the complex interactions of Nepali attitudes and traditions and the local resources necessary for sustaining the effort after foreign advisors have gone. The inevitable confusion of conflicting advice from foreign sources has tended to reduce Nepali enthusiasm for those plans that promise much but are disappointingly slow to bring the promised rewards. Foreign assistance has come to Nepal from many sources other than the most obvious large nations such as the United States, Great Britain, India, China, and the Soviet Union. Japan, Switzerland, and even Lichtenstein have extended economic aid to Nepal. It takes a large amount of equanimity for a small nation to maintain its own national purpose while being courted by so many well-meaning suitors.

The effects of the economic pinch on education in Nepal are demonstrated in the critical lack of financial resources needed to support the massive education reforms suggested. The low wages paid to teachers discourage the most able students from seeking teaching positions. Limited textbooks and teaching materials, the need for more classrooms, and the anticipated increase in school enrollment all serve to create a critical financial situation during the implementation of the New Education Plan.

Furthermore, the social patterns and religious traditions in Nepal, while much less rigid than those of some other Himalayan nations, tend to inhibit the acceptance of modern ideas and contemporary teaching methods. While the caste system has been discarded by official decree, vestiges of it remain operable in every aspect of life. For example, the effort to teach the youth of the country the value and dignity of work (a specific goal of the new plan) is diluted by traditions which revere intellectual labor but relegate manual labor or work with animals to persons of low caste. The technical jobs which must be learned for industry or agriculture require practical application more than theoretical understanding. If personal attitudes or religious beliefs prevent a student from handling machinery or animals, what he learns about those experiences from a textbook will be of little real use to him. Such ancient traditions take a long time to change if, indeed, they can be changed through formal education.

Finally, the issues surrounding the methods of evaluating the effectiveness of the New Education Plan may tend to perpetuate some of the old problems. The use of evaluation instruments and examinations as well as observation is planned in order to broaden the methods of assessing pupil performance. The intent is to avoid the rigidity of the old examinations. However, the examination system still persists, as it always must if education is tied to the traditional institution of schooling. The use of examinations will therefore serve as a screening device, filter out people who do not meet certain standards, and thus inevitably relate progress in education to religion, caste, and economic status.

Reviewing the nature of the plans for educational reform in Nepal provides one with a pricture of the tremendous effort which has gone into the formulation of one of the most comprehensive, systematic, and logically based plans for vast educational improvement to be attempted by any developing nation. It represents a courageous and foresighted leadership and is a valiant attempt toward the goal of providing economic prosperity and political freedom for the diverse people of Nepal. The government of Nepal has chosen to use the already established educational system as its base for reform and in that choice has demonstrated the verification of belief in the value of ideas and respect for tradition. Meanwhile, Nepal's neighbor to the north, the People's Republic of China, has chosen a very different model of educational reform which emphasizes the development of basic practical skills at the primary level rather than attempting to teach ideas and concepts as well as (and, in fact earlier than) vocational technical skills.

Wherever the New Educational Plan takes Nepal in its first five years of operation, it is obvious that the problems to be confronted are complex and monumental. There is no turning back now as the leaders of this reform movement follow the nationalistic philosophy and determined purpose expressed by the late King Mahendra: "The task of uplifting this land of ours and our community in a proper way is our own and it is within our own abilities too."

REFERENCES

EESBEE
1972   Nepal's national education plan in brief. *The Nepalese Perspective* 8:18–24 (June).
MALLA, VIJAYA
1972   The wall. *The Nepalese Perspective* 8 (5) (February).
MINISTRY OF EDUCATION
1971   *The national education system plan for 1971–76*. Kathmandu: His Majesty's Government Press.
REED, H., M. J. REED
1968   *Nepal in transition: educational innovation*. Pittsburgh: University of Pittsburgh Press.
TULADHAR, TIRTHA R.
1970   "Recent trends in education development," in *Nepal: a profile*. Nepal Council of Applied Economic Research, 239–246. Kathmandu: His Majesty's Government Press.

SECTION THREE

Emerging Methodological Developments for Research Design, Data Collection, and Data Analysis in Anthropology and Education

PEGGY R. SANDAY

Editors' Note: In the paper which follows, Peggy Sanday looks at several of the current research-strategies which she finds promising in the field of anthropology and education. In particular, she attempts to make explicit the methodological rules and assumptions of each. Sanday's work is most concerned with culture contact and the transmission of culture to members of differing ethnic groups. Her statements have relevance for considerations of education internal to a particular social setting as well. As Sanday suggests in her conclusion, the very fact that in education anthropological research may be most likely to find a translation into application is a reason to push for increased methodological sophistication and "good faith" in science. Peggy R. Sanday is associate professor of anthropology at the University of Pennsylvania.

The work in anthropology and education exhibits the strengths and weaknesses which characterize the field of cultural anthropology in general. The major strength lies in the most frequently used method. This is to "seek consistently to penetrate social relationships in depth and to view behavior emphatically from the point of view of the participants themselves" (Murdock 1971:17). This is a strength which my own

This paper was written while receiving support from the Office of Education (Oeg-3-73-0003) and the National Science Foundation (GS 35680). The work being supported by these grants has significantly influenced and given direction to many of the ideas presented herein. I, therefore, wish to express my appreciation to these agencies for giving me the opportunity to develop these ideas.

I also wish to express my appreciation and gratitude to Antonia Pantoja, Executive Director of the Puerto Rican Research and Resources, Inc., for giving me the opportunity to develop in conjunction with the staff of this organization one of the methods described herein.

Evelyn Jacobs was responsible for writing part of the section on culture conflict. Her work with me in developing this technique is gratefully acknowledged, as is that of Arturo Marti, Julie Mathis, Eileen Rudert, and Roberto Aponte.

experience tells me is now widely recognized and valued by educators and educational administrators. For example, quite recently I had the experience of being joyfully welcomed by a commissioner of education at a state board of education where I was consulting for a day. When he heard that I was a cultural anthropologist, he wanted to know what he could read that would help him to understand, or at least would give him the appropriate tools to investigate, the processes occurring in his schools in a way that would aid him in the task of monitoring and formulating educational policy.

I found this brief encounter exciting, stimulating, and encouraging. It raised in my mind, however, the question of whether the methodological weaknesses in the work in anthropology and education would ultimately lead educators to reject the results of this work. The major weakness, as I see it — and it is typical, I might say, of all work in cultural anthropology — is that what passes as theory "includes remarkably few propositions which meet the basic requirements of science, that is to say, which explicitly state relationships between phenomena, specify precisely how these changes as relevant variables are altered, and support such statements with adequate validating evidence" (Murdock 1971:20).

The view held by most cultural anthropologists, including those working in anthropology and education, is that the other disciplines of the social sciences are more methodologically sophisticated, but that they depend far too heavily on information gathered by others or on superficial surveys which poll for ephemeral attitudes. According to Murdock, our sister disciplines, "construct sophisticated theoretical models, put them to the test with elaborate schedules or questionnaires, and publish the statistical results. But rarely, if ever, do they present the actual behavioral data they have collected" (Murdock 1971:17).

Unfortunately, in emphasizing description and the detailed presentation of the data collected (often from only few informants), anthropologists either neglect explanation or ignore some of the basic principles of verification in the explanations which they offer. If an explanation is to be generalized beyond the particular time and unique circumstances in which the observations were made, research design, techniques for collecting data, and analysis techniques must all be made explicit. Unfortunately, method is rarely discussed or made explicit by those working in the field of anthropology and education. George Spindler, one of the leading anthropologists working in education, has said, "As for methodology, it is doubtful that many clear claims to contributions can be made by anthropology, other than in a devotion to informants and informal participant observation" (Woolcott 1971:110). At a national conference on education and anthropology held in Miami Beach in 1968, the word method did not make its way into the discussions until the next to last session (Woolcott 1971:110). According to Woolcott (1971:110), "at that time someone made a cautious recommendation that although we 'probably are all using the same methods,' it might be a good idea to make these methods explicit."

This paper will review some of the current and more promising methods and attempt to make them explicit. The major method employed by the anthropologist is detailed observation of behavior *in situ*. Of the several thousand peoples on the face of the earth, there are few that remain completely undescribed by the anthropologist. There is now beginning to emerge a wealth of ethnographic detail on the school as a small society. The question which must be asked regarding most of this work is to what extent are the general statements derived from ethnographic observations distorted by observer bias. The work of Frederick Erickson provides a model of a technique which yields the same richness of detail that is found in ethnographies, while minimizing observer bias.

Erickson (1971:4) summarizes his research strategy by drawing an analogy to linguistic method. The linguist begins with a text from a tape recording of a speaker. He goes on to collect more texts from different individuals in different settings, in order to account for variation in situations as well as in individuals. Erickson employs these notions in doing ethnographic work in the schools. He uses the situational frame concept, which originated with Edward T. Hall. The situational frame is a behavioral segment which can be photographed and analyzed for verbal and nonverbal components. Situational frames are defined by six parameters: space (both location and proxemics), time, occupants (status relationships between frame occupants and their accompanying roles), activity, perception (of the frame by frame occupants), and control (who controls the frame and which frame occupants control the other occupants).

When behavior in a well-defined situational frame is recorded (i.e. videotaped or filmed), it is called a behavior record. Events are selected to be recorded because they seem important to the ethnographer as an outsider (i.e. they have "etic" significance). The participants in the event are then shown the videotape or film of their behavior. This is done in order to elicit from the participants THEIR perception of the setting and the events (i.e. the "emic" significance), and to elicit from them suggestions for new settings and events appropriate for filming. This procedure is continued until a corpus of behavior records is developed which includes a sampling of different situational frames and individuals. The ethnographer, like the linguist, can then check his hypotheses continually against the data until he has developed an ethnographic description that corresponds to the perception of the participants in the social system being described.

Behavioral observation techniques, such as the ones developed by Erickson, are especially suited for studies interested in the school as a socializing agent, that is, how the school becomes a setting in which culture is transmitted. The way culture is transmitted can be seen as an important causal variable that influences how children behave in school and the degree to which they learn the cognitive skills which are supposedly being taught. To my knowledge, no research has investigated this problem of behavior and learning, although a number of studies have addressed the question of how culture is transmitted.

A number of studies of schools, in this country and in others, have found that the school is a setting in which the culture of the larger society is recreated and hence transmitted. Parsons (1965), for example, reported in detail activities in the school in an Anglo-Chicano community which reinforce in the minds of the children the helper-helped relationship between Anglos and Chicanos in the wider community. Parsons used simple ethnographic tools, such as observing the number of times teachers asked Anglos to be helpers and Chicanos to assume the role of those helped.

In a similar vein, a number of studies of nonverbal communication in the school support this finding and provide a possible explanation for it. Byers and Byers (1972), using techniques developed by Hall and elaborated by others, made a film record of communication between two black and two white children and a white teacher in a nursery-school setting. The film was examined for contrasts in behavior between (1) the white children and the teacher and (2) the black children and the teacher. The author assumed that there would be cultural differences between the communication behavior of the white and black children and that the teacher's cultural background would be closer to that of the white children than that of the black children. The information on the film record supported this assumption. For example, one of the black children looked or glanced at the teacher thirty-five times and "caught her eye" or exchanged facial expressions with the teacher four of those times. One of the white children, on the other hand, looked or glanced at the teacher fourteen times and "caught her eye" or exchanged expressions eight of those times. It would appear from this information that the teacher does not pay as much attention to the black child as she does to the white child. Actually this is not the case. A careful analysis of the film indicates that the white child timed her glances at the teacher to catch pauses or general "searching-the-scene" behavior of the teacher, whereas the black child's attempts were not so timed. This and other similar instances, such as the difference between the way in which the teacher touched the white children and the black children, indicates that there is a communication gap which occurs at the unconscious level. The black children and the white teacher cannot communicate in a mutually rewarding manner because they do not know the appropriate language. This inability to communicate at an emotional nonverbal level can, the authors suggest, inhibit the black child's ability to learn from the teacher. This could eventually lead the teacher to treat the black children in the only way she knows how — that is, the way she has learned blacks are treated in the larger society.

Perhaps the most convincing study of cultural transmission in the schools is Leacock's study (1969) of teaching and learning in four city schools. Leacock examined what was being imparted to children in ordinary, city-school classrooms, and the specific differences in black and white, lower- and middle-income schools. The study investigated how and what children are learning in school, in order to arrive at a fuller understanding of what aspects of classroom life are most significant for their intellectual growth and understanding. Its purpose was to yield greater insight into the processes of teaching and learning, in the context of observing ways in which children are being socialized into various roles in American society (1969:9).

The second and fifth grades were studied in a low-income black school, a low-income white school, a middle-income black school, and a middle-income white school. Data were collected through observations of classroom proceedings and interviews with the teachers and children. All classes were observed from February through May. Two observers recorded the events in each classroom: one concentrated on the teacher and the children with whom she was immediately interacting, while the other focused on the children. Both observers recorded the time at the beginning and the end of transitions, interruptions, disciplinary episode, and any other slightly unusual indicents. The teacher-observers recorded as much of the teacher's verbatim evaluative, disciplinary, and motivating statements as possible; the general content and specific techniques of her teaching; and the names of all children she called on, referred to, or signaled. They also recorded the correctness or incorrectness of a child's reply to the teacher, and generally noted classroom reactions to specific teacher actions that the child-observer might not catch. The child-observers tried to record as much of the quality and atmosphere of the

class as possible in terms of child-to-child interactions, degree of attentiveness, content of elaborated or initiated statements by the children,
the behavior of a child after a significant interaction with the teacher was
closed, and the reactions of other children (Leacock 1969:11–12).

The results showed that the school experience of the low-income black
children contrasted sharply with that of white middle-income children.
It was found, for example, that the teacher working with white middle-
income, fifth-grade children took the children's lack of attention as a cue
to her, indicating the need for her to arouse their interest. On the other
hand, the teacher of the low-income black children attributed boredom
on their part to their presumably limited attention span. In general, the
expectations for the low-income black children were low, and there was
little respect shown for their ability to learn. It was found that the
contributions of the low-income black children would be cut off and
undermined, and that interest shown by the children would be stifled
with irrelevant personal remarks. It was also found that in these classrooms there was no attempt to "impose middle-class goals" on the
children, but rather a tacit assumption that these goals were not open
to at least the vast majority of them. The middle-class values that were
being imposed on them defined them as inadequate and their proper
role as one of deference. Lowered expectations on the part of teachers
were reflected in a low emphasis on goal-setting statements altogether.
In a three-hour period, clear-cut, overt goal-setting statements numbered
twelve and thirteen for the low-income black school, fifteen and eighteen
for the low-income white school, and forty-three and forty-six for the
middle-income white school.

These and other results indicate how the reality of the school experience
contributes to the progressive falling off of interest and the decrement in
cognitive performance of the black child. The value of a study like
Leacock's is that it provides vivid detail concerning the experience of the
black child in school. In discussing the relative role of the home, the
community, and the school in perpetuating the inequities in our society,
Leacock has this to say:

Social organization comprises an interlocking network of institutions, each
reinforcing the other, and the school can no more be entirely reponsible for
perpetuating inequalities in our society than can any other single institution.
However, the importance of the school is equally undeniable, and our data
indicate its complicity despite its formal commitment to ameliorating, rather
than aggravating, the difficulties of poverty (1969:204).

Two other studies, though quite different in method, lend support to
Leacock's emphasis on the role of the school. Henry (1971) observed two

black children in their homes and in their classrooms. The home environments were drastically different—one being supportive and loving, the
other totally lacking in what we believe to be important for the emotional
growth of a child. We would expect that the first child would perform
better than the second. Observations of the two children in school, using
Henry's "A cross-cultural outline of education" (1960), indicated that
they both performed about the same cognitively, but that the child from
the second home had more behavior problems. Observations of the
children in school further indicated that this second child had a teacher
who was interested in him and who planned so that he would perform at
the best possible level.

In my own work (Sanday and Staelin 1972) I am also finding evidence
of the effect of the school on the cognitive performance of children. The
methodology of this study is quite unique and, I think, has the potential
of being extremely useful in nationwide evaluation studies. The data were
taken from the cumulative school records of all the ninth graders in an
urban public school system. The purpose of the study was to examine the
correlates of the change in IQ (intelligence quotient) scores between
kindergarten and the eighth grade. The sample consisted of all those
children who had been in the school system during this period ($N =$
2,082). It was found that 66 percent of the white sample gained points,
while only 45 percent of the black sample gained. Furthermore, the
mean gain for the white sample was greater than for the black sample,
and the mean loss for the white sample less than for the black sample.
Using the variables that are included in the cumulative records, the next
step of this work will be to explain the patterns of change in terms of
home, individual, and school variables. The home and individual variables
noted in the records are:
1.   Number of brothers and sisters.
2.   Presence of father in the home.
3.   Identity of head of the household.
4.   Parents' education and occupation.
5.   Number of schools the child has attended.
6.   Number of grades repeated.
7.   Percentage of days absent.
8.   Percentage of days tardy.
9.   Number of different addresses.
10. Number of times mention is made in the records of child having
     social, work, or health and safety problems.
The school-related variables are:
1.   Proportion of new teachers each year.

2. Teacher/student ratio each year.
3. Racial composition of the school each year.
4. Average SES of peers in the school in the same grade each year.
5. Racial composition of the staff by the year.
6. Ratio of counselors to students by the year.

Preliminary analysis indicates that change in SES of peers is an important variable that is correlated with change in IQ scores. If SES of peers in school continues to prove as important as the preliminary analysis shows, and if the indication that children in lower-class schools are taught to accept and to expect a lower-class status continues to be evident empirically, we may begin to reach the level of scientific discourse which Murdock, quite correctly, notes is lacking in the field of cultural anthropology. We may find, for instance, that a school environment which is heterogeneous in class is the best single predictor of black children's cognitive performance over a period of time.

While the data provided in school records do not yield the richness of detail to be found in ethnographic work, the value of using school records as a data source outweighs this loss in information. First of all, it should be stressed that school records yield a rich, and as yet largely untapped, source of unobtrusive measures. IF educational policy is to be formulated on the basis of an appropriate data base, and IF the working of such policy is to be adequately monitored, then school records can be used to yield adequate sample sizes of representatives geographical areas without the extra cost of collecting data. The fact that the existing form of record keeping may not include all of the appropriate data only indicates the necessity of instituting a standardized and reliable form of record keeping.

Second, the emphasis on using the data in school records focuses attention on studying in detail the negative and positive influences of the school. While educational policy cannot influence family characteristics, such policy CAN plan optimal school environments. The studies discussed above indicate that the schools reinforce, rather than counteract, a trend that may begin in the home. The recent tendency to place all of the responsibility for a child's school performance on the home environment (see Jencks 1972) is simply a rejection of the overwhelming responsibility inherent in administering an enlightened public education system.

Before concluding this discussion on current research methodologies in anthropology and education, I want to discuss work in culture and cognition, the measurement of cultural and linguistic differences, and, finally, the body of research which Gearing calls intervention-research.

One of the prevalent views among those interested in cognitive processes in children is that in the subcultures or cultures of some children certain processes are present, while in the subcultures or cultures of other children they are not. For example, Jensen (1969) talks about two kinds of cognitive skills — associative learning and conceptual learning. According to Jensen, groups do not differ with respect to their use of associative learning. Jensen believes that whites possess conceptual ability to a greater extent than blacks and, thus, show superior performance in certain tasks.

The work of Cole and his colleagues (Cole, et al. 1971) seriously questions such statements. They utilize the experimental approach in an imaginative and innovative way. Their approach, which includes having subjects perform certain tasks, is applied within the ethnographic context. Careful ethnographic work is crucial to this approach, which Cole (1972) has called "an experimental anthropology of thinking," because of the guiding hypothesis that cognitive skills are closely related to the activities that engage those skills. The ethnographic work is necessary in order to specify the kinds of tasks that people in different cultures routinely encounter. Whenever the experimental evidence indicates that there is a lack of competence in some task which has been set up to measure some cognitive skill, the researchers look at their ethnographic observations to see whether that same lack of competence is manifested in routine activities. If it is not, this suggests that it is the experiment which is incompetent, rather than the subjects.

The major conclusion of this work (Cole, et al. 1971:233) is that "Cultural differences in cognition reside more in the situations to which particular cognitive processes are applied than in the existence of a process in one cultural group and its absence in another." An important part of the method in this research is to identify the naturally occurring activities and associated cognitive skills for given cultural or subcultural groups. The problem for the educator is to think of ways in which skills so identified can be transferred to the school setting. This may involve thinking of how cognitive processes can be freed from specific content and transferred to new content.

The works of Cohen (1971), and Cazden and John (1971) provide independent support for the importance of the relationship between culture and cognition. Cohen, using standard interview procedures and tests of cognitive styles, posits a relationship between primary-group structure and certain cognitive styles. Cazden and John (1971) review a number of studies which show how the duality of the Indian child's life affects children's learning style. All of the studies reviewed by them utilize standard interviewing procedures, including the administration of standardized psychological tests.

With the current interest and recognition of cultural pluralism in the schools, and of the importance of developing culturally targeted curricula material, I think it important to talk briefly about current techniques for measuring cultural differences. There are two general approaches to this problem. One approach emphasizes and describes differences in verbal and nonverbal communication as being the most crucial indicator of cultural differences. The sociolinguistic studies of bilingualism focus mostly on the linguistic aspects. After describing the way in which speakers alternate between grammatically distinct systems, investigators then proceed to study where and under what conditions alternants are employed. This is done either through surveys in which speakers are asked to report their own language usage, or by counting the occurrence of relevant forms in samples of elicited speech. According to Gumperz and Hernandez-Chavez (1972:87), "the assumption is that the presence or absence of particular linguistic alternates directly reflects significant information about such matters as group membership, values, relative prestige, power relationships, etc."

In my own work I have been specifically interested in methods for measuring cultural differences in ways in which data can be systematically collected so that any hypothesis which includes culture conflict as an important variable can be tested. In a recent study (Sanday 1972), I suggest two methods for measuring cultural differences. One is called the ethnographic method, and the other a marketing research method. The ethnographic method involves the elicitation from the groups studied of their major beliefs, values, attitudes, and ideas of what constitutes acceptable social performance. This means that one must first have some idea of what the subcultural group will be, and then proceed to gather data which will support or refute the hypothesis that a particular group posited is actually a distinct group culturally. Once a corpus of beliefs, values, attitudes, and standards for social performance is elicited the next step is to interview a random sample of those who see themselves, in some way, as being members of the group. If their response-rate is significantly different from the response-rate of another posited group, then we have some basis for suggesting subcultural differences.

The marketing research method is similar, but seeks to find differences with respect to attitudes toward something specific, such as a social program. This is an approach which is specifically problem-oriented and which seeks to find cultural segments (similar to the notion of market segments) in a population which is being targeted for some specific program, such as a special educational program, family income program, or the like. This approach, and some of the associated analytic procedures, are discussed in Sanday and Staelin (1971).

I am presently developing a method for measuring culture conflict in conjunction with the staff of the Puerto Rican Research and Resources, Inc., a research organization in Washington, D.C. which is specifically devoted to the study of the Puerto Rican's condition in the United States. At present, this organization is engaged in a project whose goal is to seek an explanation for the large drop-out rate of Puerto Rican high school students. We have selected two eastern states for the site of the research. The major hypothesis is that dropping out is a function of problems in language, racial discrimination, and cultural conflict between the culture of the school and the home culture of Puerto Rican students.

To measure culture conflict, we are employing Goodenough's treatment (1971) of the meaning of culture and are adapting a technique described by Goodenough (1969) for measuring status dimensions in our operationalization of culture conflict. Goodenough defines culture, in a general sense, as a "system of standards for perceiving, believing, evaluating, and acting" (1971:41). The culture of a group can then be viewed subjectively as the system or systems of standards a person attributes to a set of other persons. In other words, the standards that a person attributes to a particular set of others are for him the culture of that set. Going one step further, an individual's operating culture is the particular system of standards that he uses to interpret the behavior of others in order to guide his own behavior.

If there is a nonagreement in the operating cultures of individuals, there are a number of behavior alternatives: (1) contact is kept to a minimum, (2) contact is regulated to areas where differences are minimal, or (3) contact occurs, but there is misunderstanding and misinterpretation. The purpose of this research will be to ascertain empirically whether there is a nonagreement in the operating cultures of students and teachers.

To do this we will elicit from students, teachers, and parents a list of what they see as the major social identities in the home-school environment. Questions something like, "What are the types of students, types of teachers, and types of parents you have the most contact with in school?" will be asked. In addition to eliciting social identities, school-related behaviors will also be elicited. Questions like, "What are the types of activities you observe in the classroom?" will be asked. Once a corpus of behaviors and identities has been developed, the next step will be to create a list of acceptable social dyads, that is, pairs of social identities which, in fact, interact in the home-school environment. The final questionnaire will consist of a list of these pairs for each behavioral situation (verb). Informants will be asked whether the first member of the dyad can perform X action to the second member, where X equals the specific behavioral situation. Questions concerning whether failure to perform a certain behavior X is punishable will also be asked. These questions will be asked of teachers, parents, and students. Our aim will be to discover the extent to which the teacher's perception of acceptable behavior conforms with perception of dropouts and stay-ins.

This method is only just emerging. By the time the study is completed, it may be completely transformed. Preliminary interviews with a few dropouts and stay-ins indicate that further work is necessary in developing this as a tool, but that the method is yielding some interesting results. Once it is fully developed, it will become part of an interview schedule to be administered to a large sample of students, parents, and teachers.

I want to conclude by noting some of the methods presently being employed in what Gearing has called intervention-research. I might mention that all of the studies discussed above were selected because of their potential relevance for developing informed intervention strategies. In this section I will concentrate specifically on some of the methods employed in a few of the intervention strategies which have emerged from research in anthropology and education.

Anthropological curriculum-making and the development of techniques to bring about role change in teachers are two important areas in which anthropologists are currently working to bring about change in the schools. A number of anthropologists have been engaged in curriculum efforts at the primary, secondary, and college levels. For a review of some of these efforts see Gearing (n.d.). The importance of anthropological curriculum efforts, according to Gearing, is that through them the student discovers that he can vicariously enter the experience of other people, which means that he can discover how he is like them or how he is different. The anthropological message which is communicated in curricular materials involves the concept of cultural relativity, or the notion that all cultures of all people are to be equally respected and understood. This message is often in conflict with the teacher's or the school's emphasis on conformity to Anglo norms. Hence, the anthropological message may in fact compete with the processes of cultural transmission, both in the society at large and in the school in particular. It could be that, as Gearing suggests, such curricular materials are "out in front of the culture, anticipating and perhaps generating culture change ...."

Parsons (1970) has developed a technique to aid teachers and students in adopting new and more productive roles in the classroom. He assumed that it was first necessary to get teachers to change their role behavior, and that this could be done only by engaging the teacher in a process of self-confrontation. This self-confrontation, he decided, could best be accomplished through self-observation. On the basis of these assumptions, he designed what is called "Guided Self-Analysis."

This technique, described by Gearing, has three main features. A brief segment of classroom behavior is recorded on videotape. The teacher views the tape a number of times, each time performing a single coding task which involves focusing sharply on some very select aspect of the total behavior shown on the tape. After each viewing, the teacher performs a programmed analysis of the results. The preliminary evidence, derived from the pilot use of the Guided Self-Analysis technique by over 2,000 teachers, indicates that the behavioral changes induced by the technique are impressive.

In conclusion, I will comment briefly on the status of research in anthropology and education with respect to the weakness discussed in the introduction of this paper. I think that some of the work discussed in the body of the paper holds the promise of overcoming this weakness. In particular, I think that the work being conducted under the rubric of experimental anthropology, the work that Erickson is doing, and the work that I am doing with school records and with the culture conflict model hold the promise of meeting some of the basic requirements of science.

To meet the requirements of science is, in my opinion, the most important goal of research in anthropology and education. This is not an idle, ivory tower statement. Research results in anthropology and education have a far greater probability of being used to bring about change than other work in cultural anthropology. This imposes a greater responsibility on those who are reporting their results to state explicitly the relationships between the phenomena under study, to specify precisely how the phenomena change as relevant variables are altered, and most important of all, to support such statements with adequate validating evidence. By so doing, they can aid educators in the difficult task of formulating and monitoring educational policy.

REFERENCES

BYERS, PAUL, HAPPIE BYERS
  1972 "Nonverbal communication and the education of children," in *Functions of language in the classroom*. Edited by Courtney B. Cazden,

Vera P. John, and Dell Hymes, 3–31. New York: Teachers College Press.

CAZDEN, COURTNEY B., VERA P. JOHN
1971 "Learning in American Indian children," in *Anthropological perspectives on education*. Edited by Murray L. Wax, Stanley Diamond, and Fred O. Gearing, 252–272. New York: Basic Books.

COHEN, ROSALIE
1971 "The influence of conceptual rule sets on measures of learning ability," in *Race and intelligence*. Edited by C. L. Brace, G. R. Gamble, and J. T. Bond. Anthropological Studies 8. Washington, D. C.: American Anthropological Association.

COLE, MICHAEL
1972 "Toward an experimental anthropology of thinking." Paper presented at the joint meeting of the American Ethnological Society and the Council on Anthropology and Education. Montreal.

COLE, MICHAEL, JOHN GAY, JOSEPH A. GLICK, DONALD W. SHARP
1971 *The cultural context of learning and thinking.* New York: Basic Books.

ERICKSON, FREDERICK
1971 "The cycle of situational frames: a model for microethnography in urban anthropology." Paper read at the Midwest Anthropology Meeting. Detroit, Michigan.

GEARING, FREDERICK, O.
n.d. "Anthropology and education," in *Handbook of social and cultural anthropology*. Edited by John Honigmann. New York: Rand McNally.

GOODENOUGH, WARD
1969 "Rethinking 'status' and 'role': toward a general model of the cultural organization of social relationships," in *Cognitive anthropology*. Edited by Stephen A. Tyler. New York: Holt, Rinehart and Winston.
1971 *Culture, language, and society.* Addison-Wesley Modular Publications 7.

GUMPERZ, JOHN J., EDUARDO HERNANDEZ-CHAVEZ
1972 "Bilingualism, bidialectalism, and classroom interaction," in *Functions of language in the classroom*. Edited by Courtney B. Cazden, Vera P. John, and Dell Hymes, 84–108. New York: Teachers College Press.

HENRY, JULES
1960 A cross-cultural outline of education. *Current Anthropology* 1:267–305.
1971 "Education of the Negro child," in *Anthropological perspectives on education*. Edited by Murray L. Wax, Stanley Diamond, and Fred O. Gearing, 273–292. New York: Basic Books.

JENCKS, CHRISTOPHER
1972 *Inequality: a reassessment of the effect of family and schooling in America.* New York: Basic Books.

JENSEN, ARTHUR E.
1969 How much can we boost IQ and scholastic achievement? *Harvard Educational Review* 39:1–123.

LEACOCK, ELEANOR
1969 *Teaching and learning in city schools: a comparative study.* New York: Basic Books.

MURDOCK, GEORGE P.
  1971 "Anthropology's mythology." The Huxley Memorial Lecture. *Proceedings of the Royal Anthropological Institute of Great Britain and Ireland*, 17–24.
PARSONS, THEODORE W.
  1965 "Ethnic cleavage in a California school." Unpublished doctoral dissertation, Stanford University.
  1970 *Guided self-analysis system for professional development.* Education Series. Limited distribution by the author: 2140 Shattuck Avenue, Berkeley, California, 94704.
SANDAY, PEGGY R.
  1972 The relevance of anthropology for U.S. social policy. *CAE Newsletter*, September.
SANDAY, PEGGY R., RICHARD STAELIN
  1971 "A strategy for the analysis of attitudinal segments among the urban poor with implications for public policy." Unpublished manuscript.
  1972 "A diffusion model of the cultural determinants of differential intelligence between groups." Paper read at the 71st Annual Meeting of the American Anthropological Association. Toronto, Canada.
WOOLCOTT, HARRY F.
  1971 "Handle with care: necessary precautions in the anthropology of schools," in *Anthropological perspectives on education.* Edited by Murray L. Wax, Stanley Diamond, and Fred O. Gearing, 98–117. New York: Basic Books.

Intragroup Competitive Pressures and the Selection of Social Strategies: Neglected Paradigms in the Study of Adolescent Socialization

COLIN LACEY

Editors' Note: This paper has two distinct parts, each concerning a different branch of educational research. The first part discusses the processes of ranking, social categorization, and positioning in a form of British school boys. It is focused on the entire school lives of the boys combined with certain situational controls on possible intervening variables such as previous experience or family background. The second part is a report on an inquiry into the effects of various types of teacher-training programs on the attitudes and teaching practices of its students. Both parts relate to the question of what produces learning, whether introduced deliberately or not, in a school situation.

This paper discusses the findings of two studies on adolescent and early adult socialization, both of which were heavily dependent on social anthropological fieldwork methods carried out over a number of years in urban areas in a modern industrial society (the United Kingdom). In both cases, I lived in the environment of the institution I studied, participating as much as possible in its inner social life. The first institution was an English grammar school (pupil age: 11–18 years), the second a graduate teacher-education course (student age: 21–24 and over). This discussion raises a number of theoretical issues on the nature of socialization. The implications of these ideas for the interpretation of earlier work in the field and for the design of future research are also discussed.

In 1963 George Spindler wrote:

... education was not even listed as an area of application for anthropology in the encyclopedic inventory, *Anthropology today* (Kroeber 1953). Education is not in the subject index of the Decennial Index 1949—1958 of the *American Anthropologist* .... Only a handful of joint appointments in

education and anthropology exist in American colleges and universities.
Very few anthropologists have attempted to study the educational process
in our society (Spindler 1963: 53).

The last ten years have done much to remedy this situation in the
United States. In Britain, however, the present situation does not as
yet allow the writer to talk about even "a handful of joint appointments
in education and anthropology." To my knowledge there are none. It is
still axiomatic that any young anthropologist who wishes to study education within his own culture becomes a sociologist.

Coincidentally, it was in 1963 that I began my fieldwork in a sector
of the greater Manchester conurbation that in other publications I have
called Hightown. Despite my earlier years in training as a social anthropologist, I became known almost immediately as a sociologist. Yet
quite obviously my study of Hightown Grammar School contains all
the major elements of the social anthropological approach to the study
of a social system.

The major elements of the anthropological approach, which then distinguished it from contemporary British sociology,[1] were the methodological commitment to participant observation and the theoretical
concern with social structures viewed as systems. There was, however,
at the time an important challenge to classical anthropological theory.
Growing criticism among younger anthropologists of classical and of
some contemporary studies challenged the presentation of analyses as
functionally "closed" systems — systems that were purported to be in
dynamic equilibrium, with change seen in terms of cycles of fission and
fusion. To younger anthropologists it seemed that these systems were
in fact in the throes of the most rapid, open-ended revolutionary
change the world had yet seen.

The classical concern with the recreation of timeless systems led to a
number of shortcomings in the contemporary literature:
1. Relationships with external systems, especially rapidly changing
(modern) systems were neglected.
2. An emphasis on notions of structure and function led to neglect of
emergent social processes.
3. There was a simplistic view of socialization, with initiation ceremonies given a predominant place, and a preoccupation with the "continuity of culture,"[2] at the expense of emergent and changing cultures
developing among the younger generation.

[1] There have been substantial changes in British sociology over the last ten years.
These distinctions no longer exist in the way they did ten years ago.
[2] There are notable exceptions to this general rule, but mainly outside British
anthropology.

In my study of Hightown Grammar, I was concerned to avoid these pitfalls. The school was, therefore, viewed in the context of the community it served, and the study was given a historical dimension by tracing the changing function, within the community, of the education offered by the school. The major emphasis of the study was, however, the detailed examination of the social processes within the school. These processes were traced at the levels of the total year group within the school; at the level of a single class; and at the level of cliques and individual case studies within a class. Structure was neglected so that a picture of a developing process, where change was possible and perhaps imminent, could emerge. The material presented below identifies the social processes of differentiation and polarization and brings out some of the implications for the process of socialization which are suggested by these findings.

In the second part of the paper, some of these concerns are carried over into an examination of professional socialization among student teachers. The study referred to here is a recently completed study of an innovative teacher-education scheme at Sussex University. An emerging characteristic of adolescent socialization, identified in the review of the Hightown material, seems to have become an important or even determinant characteristic of early professional socialization by this stage.

HIGHTOWN GRAMMAR SCHOOL

Hightown Grammar is an exclusive secondary school for boys in a predominantly working-class urban community. At the age of ten all pupils in the Hightown junior schools took an examination which determined which secondary schools they would enter. Because of its academic standing, Hightown Grammar attracted a high proportion of the most able pupils in the town.[3] Within the state system, this school represented the major avenue into the universities and the professions.

A survey of the junior-school records of the boys in the school revealed that the vast majority of the entering students had been "good pupils" in their junior schools. They had been monitors and prefects, and only a few had not regularly been in the top half of their class.

The curriculum at Hightown Grammar School represented an exten-

---

[3]   It represented the educational goal for most parents with academic ambitions for their boys. Most of its pupils came from the top 10% of the Hightown final examination ranking. About 60% of its entering students came from the middle class, although the community was predominanly working class.

sion of academic studies for these pupils. Their timetables included subjects like physics, chemistry, biology, and foreign languages. Mathematics quickly moved from arithmetic to algebra, geometry, and calculus. There was some project teaching in the first two or three years, principally in English, geography, and history, but the bulk of the teaching became narrative- and textbook-oriented. The academic pressures implicit in the organization of the curriculum, the method of classroom teaching, and the volume of homework found explicit and sometimes ritual expression in the public award of academic prizes[4] and the weekly house-point competition. In other publications, I have described these characteristics of the school as amounting to a "pressured academic environment." The child entering this environment could expect pressures toward academic achievement from the school, his parents, and his peers, and also from his own image of himself and his past record of academic success at his junior school and in the selection examination. I have described these pressures toward academic achievement in some detail because they seem to me to be an important factor in the phenomenon I will describe here. In my experience they would be difficult to match in an American setting.

After observing and teaching in the school for a relatively short time, it became clear that although initially each cohort had been artificially more or less homogeneous as a result of the selection procedures, after they had been in the school a new heterogeneity in their school relations had begun to develop. This development was particularly noticeable among first-year boys, for, although they were generally more conformist and more enthusiastic and responsive to the teacher than the boys in other years, they had nevertheless begun to develop a set of expectations about particular boys who performed or behaved differently from the norm. At various times I noticed that not only did the class obviously anticipate particular attitudes or behaviors from certain of the boys, but their own behavior helped to bring them about:

On one occasion, for example, a master asked three boys to stay behind after the lesson to help him with a task calling for a sense of responsibility and co-operation. He called out "Williams, Maun and Sherring." The class burst into spontaneous laughter, and there were unbelieving cries of "What! Sherring?" The master corrected himself. "No, not Sherring, Shadwell." From the context of the incident, it was clear that Sherring's reputation was already inconsistent with the qualities expected of a monitor.

On another occasion, Priestley was asked to read, and the whole class

---

[4] As with many grammar schools, great prominence was given to outside academic honors won by pupils and former pupils. Scholarships to Oxford and Cambridge topped the hierarchy of honors.

groaned and laughed. A fat boy, he had been kept down from the previous year because of ill-health (catarrh and asthma) and poor work. He grinned apprehensively, wiped his face with a huge white handkerchief and started to read very nervously. For a few moments the class was absolutely quiet, then one boy tittered; Priestley made a silly mistake, partly because he was looking up to smile at the boy who was giggling, and the whole class burst into laughter. Priestley blew his nose loudly and smiled nervously at the class. The teacher quieted them and Priestley continued to read. Three lines later a marked mispronunciation started everyone laughing again. This performance continued, with Priestley getting more and more nervous, mopping his brow and blowing his nose. Finally, the master snapped, with obvious annoyance, "All right, Priestley, that's enough!" (Lacey 1970: 53).

In other words, the boys in the class collectively reinforced certain reputations. In the case of Sherring, they were actually policing the system of relationships established and recognized by the teacher.

Within the grammar school it was possible to see two distinguishable processes at work, structuring the relationships within the classroom and the year group — differentiation and polarization:

By DIFFERENTIATION I mean the separation and ranking of students according to a multiple set of criteria which makes up the normative, academically-orientated value system of the grammar school. Differentiation is defined here as being largely carried out by teachers in the course of their normal duties (1970: 57).

Differentiation proceeds through the teacher distributing rewards and punishments. I have called one class of rewards "short-term gratifications," because I wish to make clear that I am describing a flow of rewards that are more or less implicit in every situation. They can range from a smile or an approving nod to a five-minute eulogy on how well a boy has done in an examination. Rewards and punishments flow "differentially" to various boys in the class:

POLARISATION, on the other hand, takes place within the student body, partly as a result of differentiation, but influenced by external factors and with an autonomy of its own. It is a process of sub-culture formation in which the school-dominated, normative culture is opposed by an alternative culture which I refer to as the "anti-group" culture. The content of the anti-group culture will, of course, be very much influenced by the school and its social setting. For example, it may range from a folk music CND group in a minor public school to a delinquent sub-culture at a secondary modern school in an old urban area. In Hightown Grammar School it fell between these extremes and was influenced by the large working-class and Jewish communities of Hightown (1970: 57).

Polarization proceeds to a large extent outside the classroom, in conversations and interaction concerning the classroom and what the

194 COLIN LACEY

teacher has said or done. It develops where relatively unfettered and unpoliced interaction between boys can take place. The "antigroup" subculture is therefore an "underground" or "reactive" subculture which, nevertheless, increasingly makes itself felt within the classroom. Although the evidence for these two processes has been presented in detail elsewhere, I will recount some of it here, inasmuch as the pertinent publications are not generally available outside of England and inasmuch as the evidence reveals some of the characteristics of the processes under discussion.

Figure 1 represents the passage of a cohort of students through the the school in terms of their differentiation and polarization. The regrouping of pupils at the end of the first year, with the brightest 25 percent from each class going into the top stream (2 Express, or 2E), produces a new homogeneity which proceeds to be differentiated further during the second year.

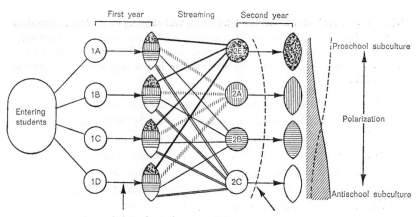

Figure 1. Differentiation and polarization associated with the streaming that takes place at the end of the first year

Quantitative Indices

The indices developed below were prepared from two questionnaires completed by all students who entered the school in 1962. One questionnaire was given at the end of the first year and one at the end of the second. The indices are designed to illustrate the processes of differentiation and polarization. On both occasions the boys were asked who had been their close friends over the last year. Unless they felt that they definitely could not do so, they were asked to restrict themselves to boys in the school and to six choices.

In the four UNSTREAMED first-year classes there was virtually no difference in the average number of times each boy was chosen (Table 1).

Table 1. Average number of times each boy in each first-year class was chosen as a friend *

Class	Choices per boy
1A	4.1
1B	4.1
1C	4.2
1D	4.5

* The choices were by boys in their own class and in the other first-year classes.

Table 2. Average number of times each boy in each second-year class was chosen as a friend

Class	(a) First year *	(b) Second year
2E	4.8	4.8
2A	4.5	4.6
2B	3.9	4.0
2C	3.3	4.3

* The choices in column (a) were made at the end of the first year and are the same as those shown in Table 1, but here they have been averaged for the class that each pupil was about to enter. The choices in column (b) were made at the end of the second year and have been averaged for the class in which the pupil had spent the year.

At the end of the first year, the higher up in the academic scale a boy was placed, the more likely he was to be chosen as a friend by a large number of his schoolmates.

At the end of the second year, when the boys were asked the same question, their responses revealed striking differences, and these differences were related to academic achievement. Column (b) of Table 2 shows that the year spent in a new class had hardly changed the overall positions of boys in 2E, 2A, and 2B, although the actual friendship choices for any one boy would have undergone considerable change. In contrast, the choices in class 2C had undergone a substantial change. In a class of thirty boys, the increase from 3.3 to 4.3 in the case of 2C represents an increase of something like thirty choices. That the new popularity of boys in 2C was brought about by the growth of a new set of norms and values, or the beginnings of the antigroup subculture, is demonstrated by Table 3. At this stage, the boys of 2C had become popular for the very reasons that they had been unpopular in the first year.

Table 3.   Distribution of friendship choices according to class: second year, 1963 *

Read ACROSS for choices made, DOWN for choices received by each class.

Class (number in each class in brackets)	2E	2A	2B	2C	Others	Total of choices made	Percentage of choices in own class
2E (31)	91	26	14	7	12	150	60.7
2A (31)	28	94	16	6	14	158	59.5
2B (28)	20	17	63	23	20	143	44.0
2C (30)	9	4	18	92	13	136	67.7
Total (of choices received)	148	141	111	128	58	588	

*   Figures are for students who entered in 1962, at the end of their second year.

The boys of 2E and 2A had proved academically successful, as reflected in their academic grading, and according to our hypothesis, they SHOULD have been influenced positively by it. Table 3 shows that academic standing did, indeed, have a marked positive influence on their choice of friends (e.g. 2E made twenty-six choices from among boys in 2A, fourteen choices from among boys in 2B, but only seven from among boys in 2C). There was no element in the organization of the school that could have brought about this result. Similarly, 2A made twenty-eight choices from 2E, sixteen from 2B, but only six from 2C.

This analysis was confirmed by another set of data which are, in many ways, complementary to the first. The second-year questionnaire asked, "What boys do you find it difficult to get on with?" Once again, the subjects were allowed to give up to six names, unless they felt that they could not possibly confine themselves to six. This time, however, many boys refrained from putting any names down, and only a few put down as many as six. Enough names were mentioned, however, to establish a pattern of unpopularity. Once again, the largest number of choices were made from among boys in the informants' own class (Table 4). The number of choices from other classes was always fewer than seven, with one notable exception: boys in 2C were named twenty-six times by boys in 2E, nine times by boys in 2A, and twenty times by boys in 2B, thereby eliciting the highest number of unpopularity choices, ninety-seven — compared with fifty-three for 2E, the next highest.

Table 4. Distribution of choices of unpopular boys: second year, 1963

Class	2E	2A	2B	2C	Others	Pre-fects	Total of choices made	Average number of choices received
2E	38	4	4	26	3	0	75	1.71
2A	5	33	1	9	22	1	51	1.45
2B	7	4	24	20	1	0	56	1.14
2C	3	4	3	42	3	6	61	3.23
Total (of choices received)	53	45	32	97	29	7	243	

Table 5. Sociomatrix: friendship choices within class 3E: third year, 1964*

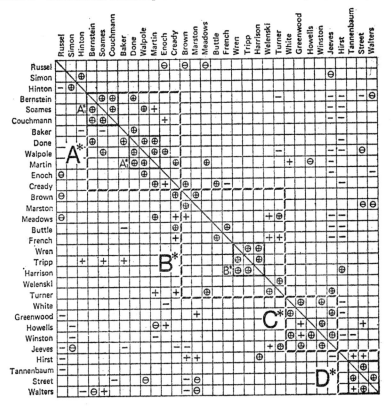

KEY
⊕ Reciprocated choices
+ Unreciprocated choices
— Dislikes (can't get on with)
⊖ Reciprocated dislikes
⌐⌐ Friendship areas
▢ Cliques

*   Students who entered in 1962.

The preponderance of unpopularity choices from 2C is to be explained by the antigroup development in 2C. These boys were now regarded as bullies and "tough eggs," who, in Badman's terminology, would rather be hooligans and have a good time than be nice little boys. They were aggressive and loudmouthed and were feared by many boys who were successful in terms of the dominant school norms. In Tables 5 and 6, there were no reciprocated choices between the top-third and bottom-third groups. This in itself does not prove polarity. We must show that this linear arrangement also concentrates "can't get on with" choices between the two extremes.

Table 6. Friendship choices between the three sections of the sociogram: top third, middle third, and bottom third*

Friendship choices made by		Friendship choices made from			
		Top	Middle	Bottom	Total
Top	Unilateral	25	2	1	28
	Reciprocated †	22	2	–	24
Middle	Unilateral	6	19	4	29
	Reciprocated	2	14	3	19
Bottom	Unilateral	3	8	22	33
	Reciprocated	–	3	16	19
Total:	Unilateral	34	29	27	90
	Reciprocated	24	19	19	34

* Dividing lines were drawn arbitrarily between the top eleven, middle ten, and bottom ten. If the lines had been drawn in any other position, it would have accentuated the difference between the three divisions.
† Reciprocated choices are counted each time they occur, i.e. not as pairs.

Table 7 shows that this polarity did exist: nineteen "animosity" choices were made by the top third from the bottom third, and fifteen were

Table 7. "Can't get on with" choices between the three sections of the sociogram: Top third, middle third, and bottom third

Negative choices made by		"Can't get on with" choices from			
		Top	Middle	Bottom	Total
Top	Unilateral	5	2	19	26
	Reciprocated	2	2	4	8
Middle	Unilateral	3	1	9	13
	Reciprocated	2	–	2	4
Bottom	Unilateral	15	6	5	26
	Reciprocated	4	2	–	6
Total:	Unilateral	23	9	33	65
	Reciprocated	8	4	6	18

made by the bottom third from the top third. The next highest figure was nine, made by the middle group from the bottom group. It is important to examine the nature of this polarity and get some idea of the characteristics that are associated with the members of each of these groups.

SOCIAL CLASS   The distribution of social-class background was very different among the three groups (Table 8). The table shows that boys in the "top third" were predominantly middle class, while those in the "bottom third" were predominantly working class.

Table 8. Distribution of manual and nonmanual parental occupations in the top third, middle third, and bottom third of the 3E sociomatrix

	Top	Middle	Bottom	Total
Parents with nonmanual occupation	9	5	3	17
Parents with manual occupation	2	5	7	14
Total	11	10	10	31

CLUB MEMBERSHIP   Membership in social clubs can be used as one index of whether a boy is oriented toward the normative adult-dominated school culture or toward the antiacademic, adolescent-dominated culture. Clubs were categorized in the following way:

1.   PROSCHOOL, ADULT-DOMINATED — school clubs, scouts, religious bodies and their youth clubs, libraries, golf and tennis clubs, etc.

2.   ANTISCHOOL, ADOLESCENT-DOMINATED — coffee-bar clubs, snooker and billards clubs.

Table 9 shows dramatically the extent to which the behavior of the three groups differed in this respect.

Table 9. Membership in clubs, categories 1 and 2, of pupils in the top third, middle third, and bottom third of the 3E sociomatrix

	Club membership			
	Top	Middle	Bottom	Total
Category 1 Proschool, adult-dominated	34	26	8	68
Category 2 Antischool, adolescent-dominated	1	1	14	16
Total	35	27	22	84

Theoretical Implications

Let us now take a step back from the concrete detail of the empirical situation and begin to examine in broader terms the process being illustrated and its implications for a view of socialization.

Dennis Wrong summarizes the sociological answers to the Hobbesian question of order in a twofold classification that also effectively summarizes the two main roots of socialization theory:

> The first answer is summed up in the notion of the "internalisation of social norms." The second, more commonly employed or assumed in empirical research, is the view that man is essentially motivated by the desire to achieve a positive image of self by winning acceptance or status in the eyes of others (Wrong 1961: 185).

In his influential article, Wrong elegantly and persuasively puts the case that the model of human nature implicit in these statements portrays an oversocialized conception of man. But he terminates the discussion at a crucial point. Man, he argues, is a neurotic, discontented animal for whom culture is a violation of his socialized bodily drives. Even though Wrong's apologies for a psychological view of man have the virtue of making the assumptions underlying this view explicit, we are left, nevertheless, without having examined the sociological advantages inherent in this powerful critique.

To me, the main benefit seems to be that our attention is forced to an awareness of the imperfect or partial nature of socialization and the existence of an essential element in man that remains outside both the processes of internalization of social norms and the conforming needs of his personality. I do not think that in theorizing about this element, sociologists or anthropologists need necessarily ascribe a psychological nature to it; in fact, following Gluckman (1964), I feel that it is important for us to remain naive about it. On the other hand, we should make our naive assumptions clear, describe our conceptions, and look for room in the theoretical sociological models we adopt to allow for the testing and refinement of these conceptions. We are, therefore, proposing that there is an element in man that stands above the usual socializing process as conceived by sociologists and that acts as commentator, judge, or director.[5] This "protected" self may even remain silent during the flow of interactions and impressions experienced by the individual. What I am saying is that man has purpose and will, and that sociologists and anthropologists must make room for them (a positive place — why make exceptions?), both in their models of the social process and in particular models of socialization.

---

[5]   Margaret Mead's writings, for example, illustrate that this is by no means a new proposal in theoretical works. It is, however, new in relation to empirical sociology.

Let us do this, in our case, by examining the processes of differentiation and polarization in the light of the two major strands of socialization theory outlined by Wrong.

It is quite clear from the earlier description that first-year boys are highly conformist with respect to teacher definitions of the appropriate behavioral norm (in dress, manners, etc.). And, interestingly enough, the friendship-choice analysis reveals that status in friendship is also correlated with academic achievement, suggesting that these pupils also accept the fact that academic differentiation provides them with a criterion for valued friendships.

At this stage, therefore, it looks like a straightforward matter of internalization. However, a problem emerges with the subsequent development of a subculture, for although some pupils proceed according to prediction and continue to conform to the "internalized" conceptions of behavior and academic performance, some start to behave in ways that suggest a rejection of these "internalized" values. Internalization as a way of "understanding" this phenomenon requires some elaboration.[6] Similarly, conformity with the expectations of friends needs considerable elaboration to explain why, among the boys who develop the subculture, there is a shift away from friendships with the more academic boys.

Two additional notions are required to explain these developments:
1. The Hightown Grammar School classroom is a relatively "closed" system of relationships, with limited teacher resources and rewards in terms of both short-term gratification (e.g. praise from the teacher) and longer-term successes (e.g. examination successes or admission to a university). I have used the term "competitive arena" to describe this aspect of the classroom.
Table 10 illustrates the way the classroom becomes a self-contained

Table 10.   Personal estimate of success in second year

Class	Regarded the past year as a success	Couldn't say	Regarded the past year as unsuccessful
2E	19	1	11
2A	24	–	7
2B	21	–	7
2C	24	2	4
Total	88	3	29

[6]   See Parsons (1951: 252 ff.) for one theoretical classification of possible elaborations.

"competitive arena" in which pupils compare themselves against each other. It shows that in 2E, eleven pupils regarded themselves as unsuccessful, despite the fact that they were in the top group, compared with only four pupils in 2C, who were in the bottom group. The difference can be accounted for only by the past experience of the two groups, the different sets of standards they have acquired, and the way in which their new experiences measure up to those standards. This view is confirmed by an analysis of the experience of the eleven boys who regarded themselves as unsuccessful in 2E. On the average, they dropped sixteen places in their second-year examinations compared with their first-year ones. The rest of the class dropped eight places on the average. During the year two of these boys had been considerably disturbed emotionally, crying during lessons, crying before school, and refusing to come to school. A third went through a similar period, and his father wrote to the school complaining that "the boy is utterly demoralized."

2.   The extreme competitive pressures described earlier highlight success and failure within the system. Success or failure is readily understood in terms that the classroom has established for itself and becomes knowledge that is immediately available to all members of the group.

Let us go back to the group of thirty boys entering the school. As soon as formal work begins, each action by the pupil (academic or behavioral) has meaning (1) in relation to the master and (2) in relation to what the other twenty-nine boys in the class can do.

Our friend Billy Green might be quite good at English, but if fifteen other boys in the class are better and maintain their advantage, no matter how much Billy Green tries to improve, he remains sixteenth, and his strategy for excelling at English fails. In fact, Billy Green's efforts to improve his own position can become part of the pressure that encourages the other fifteen to improve theirs. As we have seen, many of these pupils had been accustomed to playing the "good pupil" role in their junior schools. For a large number of these pupils this role is NECESSARILY no longer available. In our example, Billy Green's efforts in English and in other subjects are thwarted by his classmates and by the structure of rewards set up by the teacher.

The antigroup subculture is CREATED in the search for solutions to this type of problem, posed by intragroup competitive pressures.[7] Indi-

---

[7]   This analysis suggests that each cohort "creates" an antigroup subculture; there is little or no evidence that it is "learned" from older cohorts. For example, first-year boys make very few friendship choices from among boys in the second year, second-year boys have few friends in the third year, etc.

vidual pupils adopt strategies that they hope will provide personal solutions, and since there is a commonly recurring concern with the problem of "relative failure," there is sufficient coalescence, sufficient common ground in these adaptive strategies, to give rise to a recognizable subculture. Without some of the structural parameters that I have described, it is doubtful whether a similar development would take place. For example, in a Steiner school, with an explicit philosophy of cooperation and support within the classroom, no similar development takes place.[8] The sociogram reveals a loosely integrated classroom structure without distinct inclusive/exclusive cliques, in which half a dozen children who are either late arrivals or children with fairly marked behavioral problems are given the support of the "community" of the others.

The emergence of the antigroup subculture marks the emergence of the first "underground" culture expressed by this group of boys. That is, there comes into existence a second set of sufficiently coherent behavioral norms, sufficient mutual understanding which the boys are able to anticipate and manipulate to establish alternative reputations. For example, by the second or third year, a boy could make a statement like "Let's borrow your math book" and not elicit the response, "What do you want it for?" said in a surprised and hurt tone. Instead, the book would be tossed almost carelessly to the person making the request. It would be understood that THAT boy had made the request in order to copy the homework. By acceding to his request, the boy who supplies the book can enjoy the feeling of being "one of the boys" — of being openhanded and devil-may-care, even if he himself would never dare to come to school without the work completed. (Some boys, of course, would never be asked, and some would never make that sort of request.)

The existence of the antigroup subculture after the first year of school creates a new situation. Now most of the boys are put in the position at one time or another of choosing which shared meanings, which set of understood rules to adhere to in a given situation. A most dramatic example of this sort of choice was, in fact, demonstrated by a fifth-year boy:

Sherman was frequently top in 5B. He rarely misbehaved in class and was prominent in cooperating with teachers during lessons. On one occasion,

---

[8] The sociometric data were collected by Murray Webster for a master's dissertation. It is one of a number of school and classroom studies being undertaken at Sussex by graduate students.

however, I observed that after a lesson in which he was conspicuous for his enthusiastic participation, he waited until the master had left the room, then immediately grabbed an innocuous classmate's satchel and in a few moments had organised a sort of piggy-in-the-middle game. He passed the bag across the room, while the owner stood helplessly by, occasionally trying to intercept or picking up a fallen book. The initiation of this activity so soon after the lesson seemed to be a conscious demonstration of his status within the informal structure of the class. He was indicating that, although he was good at work, he was not a swot and would not be excluded from groups based on other than academic values (Lacey 1970: 86).

It was interesting to note how different boys reacted to having the satchel flung at them. Some entered eagerly into the "tease" and made fun of the luckless owner, while others tried to ignore its arrival — on their desk or at their feet. These boys were quickly brought into the game by the shouts or jeers of their classmates. To throw the satchel was likely to get them into trouble if a master came through the door; to ignore it was likely to get them the reputation of a "soft-arsed mard." Pupils found that both sets of values were important to them.

The manipulation of social strategies in situations of this sort brings to many adolescents a new awareness. The first step is the conscious manipulation of situations in terms of one or another set of subcultural norms. The next step is the awareness of that manipulation, and, therefore, the self-conscious recognition of an aspect of the self (the protected self) that lies outside the socialization influences of situation and biography.[9]

In the following quotation from the diary of a fourth-year boy he comes fairly close to recognizing this dualism and protected self in another boy, a newcomer to the school. After describing in detail the boy's various strategies, he writes, by way of explanation: "He is not naturally stupid, he is just a little cleverer than most people in deception. He is not clever enough, though, to maintain both an image [a good image] and a full-scale deceptive network. Enoch is, though." The good image corresponds to the boy's place in the proschool subculture, while the deceptive network represents his place in the antigroup subculture. The author of the diary correctly diagnoses Enoch as being relatively successful in this respect.

---

[9]   I am not postulating that there is a regular, or even a progressive, realization of the existence of the protected self by all individuals. I have observed, however, that there is a far greater consciousness of this self among university postgraduate students than among grammar-school pupils.

SUSSEX TEACHER-EDUCATION COURSE

The above-described review of some of the original findings of the Hightown research came about as a result of the insights obtained in a second piece of research, into the professional socialization of teachers. Certain features of the socialization process at Hightown, described above, were highlighted by some of the features noted also in early-adult socialization — in particular, the selection or creation of strategies to deal with different situations. The teacher-education research contained both macro and micro approaches to the study of change. Briefly, it was a study of the Sussex postgraduate-certificate-in-education course, against a background of four other teacher-education courses, chosen in order to represent some courses like and some unlike the Sussex course. Two of the schools (like Sussex) were innovative — York New Northern University and Brunel New Southern University; two were traditional — Soton Provincial South Coast University and Kings Metropolitan University (see Table 11). The material quoted in this paper is predominantly from the intensive study of the Sussex course.[10]

Table 11. Universities chosen by students who also chose Sussex

	Innovative	Traditional
Yes	York New Northern	Soton Provincial South Coast
No	Brunel New Southern	Kings Metropolitan

The Sussex course was designed to involve students concurrently in the two worlds of "the school" and "the university." Student-teachers were, therefore, assigned to schools in which they taught for three days a week under the guidance of teachers from the school (teacher-tutors, or T-tutors). During the other two days a week they attended university seminars in which they discussed their teaching experiences and examined theoretical approaches to education. In these university sessions they participated in two main types of groups: (1) the subject group, made up of all students teaching that school subject (twelve in number), supervised by a specialist in that subject (E-tutor); (2) the mixed group, made up of students from a variety of disciplines (also twelve), super-

---

[10] The 1970–1971 cohort studied was followed up for a year of their teaching career after their one year at Sussex.

vised by various theory tutors. The design of the Sussex course thus enabled the researchers to observe student-teachers in three different settings, all of which recurred every week.

In all four of the other university courses that were studied, school and university experiences were separated into discrete blocks of time. This separation enabled the students to adjust to the school and university situations over fairly long periods of time (one or two months).

My first insight into the effects of the different settings within the Sussex University course came as I attended seminars of the biology group and then met some of the biologists in their mixed-subject seminars. There was one biologist in the biology seminar who played what could be described as a "progressive" role, advocating child-centered techniques and liberal educational reforms; in the mixed seminar he became an advocate of formal academic standards and firm discipline. When I questioned him about this reversal, he found it difficult to accept that it had occurred, until I was able to detail some of the statements he had made and the context of the discussions. After much perplexed heart-searching, he resolved the problem by remarking that in the mixed seminar there were a couple of primary students "who really get my goat." It appeared to him that they were unrealistic in their outlook and needed to be brought back to earth. It became apparent that he felt that the biologists in his subject group were different. He could rely on their common sense and understand their outlook and problems — he therefore felt free to espouse progressive causes in the biology seminar.

In other words, the student composition of the seminar became a situational determinant of individual behavior, giving rise to two recognizable and different strategies. In this case, the emergence of distinct strategies pointed to the existence of a set of understood values and orientations within the biology group (a subject culture) that did not exist among the students in the mixed group. These incidents and many others like them encouraged me to look for more evidence of subject-culture differences and more examples of situationally determined strategies.

Attitudes Toward Tutors

The main situational difference was between the school and the university. To evaluate this difference, the students of all five universities were asked in the "end-of-year" questionnaire whether they felt that their T-tutors (school tutors) and their E-tutors (university tutors) differed in their ideas relating to five aspects of education, and whether they (the students) agreed with one or the other or both. The aspects were the following:

a. General views on the aims of education
b. Acceptance of new ideas
c. Curriculum
d. Relationships with pupils
e. The appearance of the teacher (dress, manner, etc.)

    The students were allowed five different responses:

1. Tutors did not differ
    If tutors DID differ,
2. student generally agreed with the teacher-tutor
3. student generally agreed with the university tutors
4. at different times student agreed with one tutor or the other
5. student resorted to some other method of coping with the difference.

In all five universities the students tended to agree with their university tutors rather than with their school tutors in the matters in question. The proportion of students who perceived differences in views between their E-tutors and their T-tutors, and who agreed sometimes with one, sometimes with the other, was consistently higher at Sussex than at the other universities. In other words, the Sussex course seems to produce some clear-cut differences in the perceptions of Sussex students, as compared with the rest.

Table 12. Students' perception of teacher-tutor/University-tutor differences regarding five aspects of education

(a) Average percentage who perceived differences

Sussex	York	Brunel	Soton	Kings
65.4	59.7	54.5	58.2	53.4

(b) Percentage of students who agreed with one tutor or the other at different times

Sussex	York	Brunel	Soton	Kings
29.2	18.5	20.9	19.8	16.6

(c) Above percentages (b) expressed as a percentage of those who perceived differences (a)

Sussex	York	Brunel	Soton	Kings
44.6	30.5	41.0	34.1	31.1

$x^2 = 12.88$
4DF. $P < 2.5$

It seems probable that the weekly cycle that includes both school and university experiences makes it possible for Sussex students to discern that differences exist. This perception is maintained throughout the year — because the school-university cycle is maintained throughout the year. Sussex students are under some pressure to find a way to live with these differences, and they seem to manage by agreeing with "both [the E-tutor and the T-tutor] at different times." Table 12 shows that not only do they follow this strategy to a greater extent than do students at the other universities (b), but that the greater incidence of this strategy is due both to the greater perception of differences and to the greater incidence of this strategy among those who perceive differences (c).

Let us look at some of the content of these strategies as reported by the students when they answered that there were differences and told how they coped with them:

1. IGNORING T-TUTOR: (a) [The tutors disagreed on] the role of English in the curriculum. I coped with [their difference of opinion] by ignoring my teacher-tutor. (b) Often it wasn't worth bringing the conflict with the teacher-tutor to a head, since there was a definite noncommunication and it was a waste of precious school time. It was more useful and peaceful to go away and do your own thing quietly.

2. DECEIVING T-TUTOR: (a) [I followed a policy of] evasion. (b) Although I disagreed with my teacher-tutor in [such matters as] discipline of children, approach to timetable, art work, and the importance of art and the story in the curriculum, the only way to cope was to concur with her when she was present.

3. DISAGREEING WITH BOTH TUTORS: (a) On most things they were [of] different [opinions], and I was [of an opinion] different from them both. It's too long to explain. (b) The teacher-tutor was at all times more recognizant of the concrete teaching situation, whereas the E-tutor preferred to talk in theoretical terms. I balanced the two viewpoints by recognizing the constraints which governed the thinking of each of them.

4. IGNORING E-TUTOR: (a) The teacher-tutor was, of necessity, more in favor of audio-visual methods than the E-tutor. This simply meant that in practical terms one used those aspects of the method in class which produced the best response, and discussed the philosophical impossibility of the entire exercise with the E-tutor. (b) [Concerning] introduction of the Nuffield A-level biology syllabus, the E-tutor favored it, while the T-tutor [received it with] qualified enthusiasm, preferring gradual incorporation of some curriculum material [from the syllabus] but not changing [to the new] syllabus [entirely]. I agreed with E in PRINCIPLE, but with T in practice.

The sense of "distance," and the sense of "I," as being apart from both "school" and "university," come through very clearly from these quotations. In only a very few cases did the student identify clearly with either the E- or the T-tutor, as in this example: "Teacher-tutor thinks that organizing and interesting children is of prime importance, and [that] our teaching must be centered around this more than around the [individual] child." This case was almost unique at Sussex, as evident in the replies to the student questionnaires. Yet in the seminars one frequently got the impression that students were agreeing and going along with members of the staff. At times it was evident that if the student felt the tutor was "unable to take" disagreement, the only way to cope was to "concur with her when she was present."

These strategies, common at this level of socialization, not only give the semblance of agreement concerning norms and procedures when there is no agreement but also allow the student to maintain a "view of the self" different from the views implied by some of his outward behavior. The model of socialization that emerges goes a long way toward explaining the very rapid changes that have taken place in some British schools after decades of relatively stable practice.

There is one final point to be made from these results. Let us examine the effects of an oversimplified view of socialization in predicting human behavior. Stones and Morris (1972) have criticized teacher-training schemes that emphasize school experience, holding that by keeping the student in school for longer periods of time and by putting more power into the hands of the practicing teacher, "all the pressures on the student are in the direction of conforming to the unadventurous stereotype" — the "sitting-with-Nellie" objection.

The Sussex scheme does both these things that Stones and Morris deplore. Sussex teacher-tutors are paid to give tutorials, and they also have an important role in the assessment of student-teachers. Sussex student-teachers spend more time in school than do students in any of the other four courses studied.

Stones and Morris assume that in these circumstances socialization proceeds by a simple process of identification and internalization. I hope I have given evidence to show that this is not necessarily the case. When he is put in a situation in which he is alternately viewing one institution from the standpoint of another and is constrained to exercise choices in his selection of strategies, the student becomes more aware of differences, more aware of "self" in relation to the selection of his strategies, and (I now add) both more critical and more radically critical in his approach to education.

Attitudes Toward Education

Evidence in support of the statement at the close of the last section may be found in the comparative study by questionnaire of attitudes toward education. The evidence, based on the following scales, indicates that, far from conforming, Sussex students adopt attitudes that constitute a radical criticism of schools as they are, and that they do so to a greater extent than any other group of students included in the study. The first three of the five scales used were developed in the 1950's by Oliver and Butcher (1962) and were widely used in the 1960's in research concerning teachers' attitudes. These scales — Radicalism (R), Naturalism (N), and Tender-mindedness (T) — are described briefly below. The last two scales — Liberalism and Progressivism — were developed more recently.

NATURALISM Naturalism presumes the existence of natural standards that reside within the child and emerge in a relationship with the child. It is, therefore, opposed to the imposition of external (absolute) standards in the moral, cultural, or academic sphere. Agreement with such statements in the questionnaire as "Naturalness is more important than good manners in children" and "The teacher should not stand in the way of a child's efforts to learn in his own fashion" is balanced against disagreement with statements such as "Character training is impossible

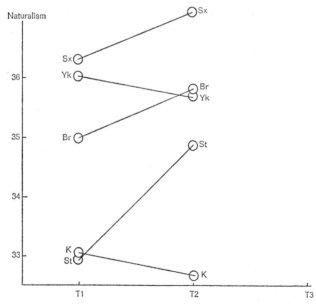

Figure 2. Naturalism attitude scores of Sussex, York, Brunel, Soton, and Kings students (based on scales developed by Oliver and Butcher 1962)

if there is no formal standard of right or wrong" to give a positive score on the Naturalism scale (see Figure 2).

RADICALISM   Radicalism is concerned with the allocation of resources to education and the distribution and availability of education. In general, more education, more equally distributed, is at the center of the concept. For example, option for "more nursery schools," "increased expenditure on adult education," and "comprehensive schools to be the normal form of secondary education" would give a positive score on the Radicalism scale (see Figure 3).

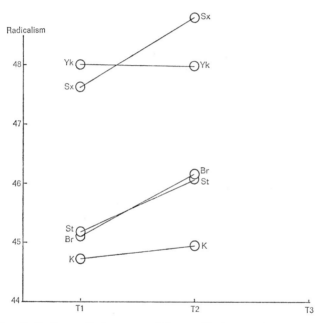

Figure 3. Radicalism attitude scores of Sussex, York, Brunel, Soton, and Kings students (based on scales developed by Oliver and Butcher 1962)

TENDER-MINDEDNESS   Tender-mindedness is OPPOSED to narrowly conceived vocationalism and instrumentalism in education, and OPPOSED to efficiency in fitting children into the "system." It is, therefore, a very negative concept and can only be viewed as an attitude in favor of protecting children from the demands of the future and of the "system." The tender-minded person would reject the statement "A scientific training offers good prospects for a career" as a reason for teaching science, and would reject the statement "A study of international affairs

Tender-mindedness

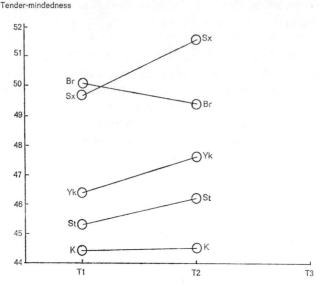

Figure 4. Tender-mindedness attitude scores of Sussex, York, Brunel, Soton, and Kings students (based on scales developed by Oliver and Butcher 1962)

should show which countries are our friends" as a reason for teaching international understanding (see Figure 4).

In other words, "a tender-minded attitude to education is one which regards children and others as persons to be treated as ends in themselves rather than as serving the interests of others, as represented, for example, by the demands of vocational efficiency or the interests of the State." Since the development of these scales, both educational policy and educational practice have moved considerably, and this has affected the scales. For example, some issues that had been controversial in the 1950's were widely accepted by the 1970's. As a result, scores made by individuals who would have been considered radical in the 1950's, in the 1970's were clustering near the top of the scale, giving a skewed distribution and thereby reducing the possibility for high-scoring individuals to register gain on the Radicalism scale.

Because we were particularly interested in change, we decided to augment the Radicalism scale with items more closely related to current preoccupations and more challenging to high-scoring radicals. The original intention of incorporating such items into the Radicalism scale was abandoned, due partly to lack of time and partly to the observation that the new items under consideration moved the focus of attention away from the politico-administrative level and towards the notions of participation and democracy in the school. This observation was borne out when the initial scores were seen to be as closely related to Naturalism as to Radicalism: Sussex R.49, N.45; York R.52, N.57; Brunel R.64, N.71; Southampton R.56, N.58; Kings R.61, N.47. The term Liberalism (in education), therefore, seemed appropriate to this new scale.

LIBERALISM   While this scale was initially conceived as a way of bringing the Oliver and Butcher Radicalism scale up to date, it was also thought relevant to bring in the issues of pupil participation (democracy), streaming (competition), and the issue of the unequal division of resources in favor of the poorer areas (compensation). A "disagree" response to "Children learn best in a highly competitive situation" and an "agree" response to "Older children should be allowed to make decisions in the running of the school" would give a positive score on the Liberalism scale (see Figure 5).

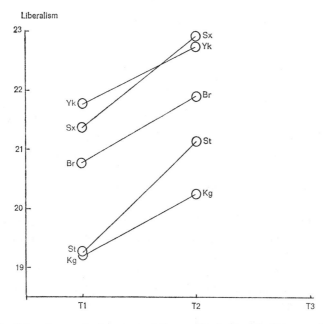

Figure 5.   Liberalism attitude scores of Sussex, York, Brunel, Soton, and Kings students

PROGRESSIVISM   The "relationships in teaching" question was designed to measure those attitudes toward the teacher-pupil relationship that seemed to typify the Sussex approach. The items were generated from

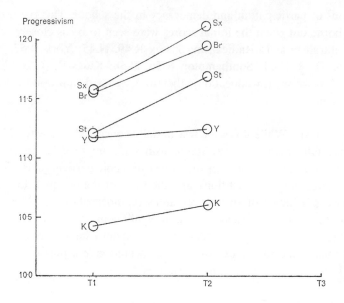

Figure 6. Progressivism attitude scores of Sussex, York, Brunel, Soton, and Kings students

notes taken during seminars and at keynote lectures, and an attempt was made to select aspects of the teaching relationship that were stressed and ones that were manifested frequently (see Figure 6).

I was unable to carry out a similar exercise at the other universities, so there is no direct evidence on whether these aspects were stressed equally there. Inasmuch as the items measured were developed from close contact with the Sussex course, it seems reasonable to make the assumption that they are likely to represent overall a much closer fit to the underlying philosophy of the Sussex course. The aim was to produce a scale sensitive to the sort of attitude change that proved most likely to occur at Sussex.

I felt that perhaps the attitude scales in general use heretofore had been less sensitive to the differences in emphasis between the approaches in different institutions. If so, a failure to isolate different patterns in different universities would not demonstrate that none had existed, but only that none had existed in the broad, rather general areas in which it has been usual to measure attitudes.

Scores on the five attitude scales are presented in Figures 2 to 6. The five universities are designated as follows: Brunel–Br, Kings–K, Soton–St, Sussex–Sx, York–Yk.

Discussion

On each of the five attitude scales, Sussex students end the year with the highest mean score. This occurred despite the fact that in three cases out of the five, Brunel or York started the year with higher scores. This suggests that there is an institutional effect, over and above a social-climate effect. The evidence appears to support the hypothesis that the Sussex teaching scheme produces changes in the attitudes toward education of the student cohort which are consistently more radical than those produced by the other universities.

In this case, therefore, Stones and Morris are clearly wrong. My argument suggests that they are wrong because they adopted a simplistic view of socialization and an "oversocialized conception of man." The tensions between the "world of the school" and the "world of the university" produced among Sussex students an enhanced realization of themselves as apart from either world, a realization of their protected self. It was this "distance" that contributed to the radical perspectives at Sussex.[11]

CONCLUSION

This paper aimed to illustrate that a more complex view of man is required in empirical sociology. We have attempted to show how empirically derived concepts, intragroup competitive pressures, and the selection of social strategies raise new issues relating to the nature of man and his relationship to society.

REFERENCES

GLUCKMAN, M., *editor*
    1964   *Closed systems and open minds: the limits of naivety in social anthropology*. London: Oliver.

LACEY, COLIN
    1970   *Hightown Grammar: the school as a social system*. Manchester: Manchester University Press.

OLIVER, R. A. C., H. J. BUTCHER
    1962   Teachers' attitudes to education, the structure of educational attitudes. *British Journal of Social Clinical Psychology* 1:56–69.

---

[11]   We are unable in a paper of this length to go into a more detailed analysis of the way the tensions between the worlds of school and university contributed to increases in radicalism. We hope to do this in future publications.

PARSONS, TALCOTT
  1951   *The social system.* Glencoe, Ill.: Free Press.
SPINDLER, G.
  1963   *Education and culture.* New York: Holt, Rinehart and Winston.
STONES, E., S. MORRIS
  1972   *Teaching practice, problems and perspectives.* New York: Methuen.
WRONG, D.
  1961   The oversocialized conception of man in modern sociology. *American Sociological Review* 26.

Notes on the Social Organization of High Schools

CRAIG JACKSON CALHOUN and FRANCIS A. J. IANNI

Editors' Note: This paper is a preliminary organization of material from a large comparative study of high school social organization. The authors present a scheme for the analysis of interaction in institutional settings of which high schools are an example. There is also discussion of the role of various informal associations or "quasi-groups" in the organization of complex societies in general and educational institutions in particular. The authors assume that the social organization of a high school will greatly affect the learning process of the students and that an approach to this organization as a whole, rather than as a fragment — such as a formal curriculum — will be the most productive way to find out what, in fact, does go on in schools.

In any social institution there is a formal system which describes for members what is supposed to occur. While this system serves as the backdrop against which most of the formal rules of the institution are cast, no one believes that it describes reality. There is also an informal system within any institution which, while it is not fully apparent to participants, can often be discovered by observation of actual behavior. While they appear in juxtaposition, it is impossible to understand either of these systems without recourse to the other. Moreover, the social organization of any institution is the amalgam of the two, for it is the interface between the institutional rules of the formal system and the individual and group manipulation of those rules in the informal system which constitute the social organization of the institution.[1]

This research was supported in part by a grant from the Ford Foundation, to which we express our gratitude.
[1] This is analogous in some ways to the argument between those culturalists who, like some followers of Lévi-Strauss, argue for the primacy of rules and those social anthropologists who argue for the primacy of actual behavior. Primacy is not a relevant

This paper is a discussion of the social organization of three high schools — one rural, one suburban, and one urban — in the eastern section of the United States. In particular, we are concerned with some of the constants in social organization which emerge from an examination of these three cases. In addition, we delineate a scheme of analysis which has proven useful in looking at these three cases comparatively and which we suggest may have some utility for similar comparative studies.

The analysis focuses around three constants of human behavior which are immediately apparent to the observer in the high school. These are the sorting of actors into categories, territoriality, and the making and breaking of rules. We suggest that these three domains provide keys to understanding the statements, actions, and explanations of the members of the high school institution.

The research on which this paper is based in part has taken place over the past year and is still in progress. Three field teams have been studying the three high schools using a method of intensive participant observation. The high schools in question vary on a number of criteria. One is in a small town and draws from a catchment area including several rural townships. It has a student population of approximately 700. The second is in an upper middle-class suburb of a major city. The suburb is composed chiefly of single family dwellings occupied by commuting executives and their families. It has approximately 600 students. The students of both these schools are primarily white Protestants with some Roman Catholics. The third high school is situated in the "inner-city" area of a major metropolitan center roughly divided equally among black, Puerto Rican, Chinese, and white ethnic groupings. There are further subdivisions within these categories such as those of the speakers of various Chinese dialects and that between Italian Catholics and Jews.

We shall here give examples of the functioning of each of the three high schools seen through the three analytic foci. The intent of this procedure is not to explicate thoroughly the functioning of the schools, but rather to demonstrate the salience of the three domains — sorting, territoriality, and the making and breaking of rules.

It is a universal operation for human beings to distinguish classes among those with whom they interact. These classes are at any time capable of more or less general application. That is, a class established in any one situation may, but need not, be applied to any other. Further, the classes may, but need not, be abstracted. For example, it is common

---

distinction. Neither the cultural (formal rule) nor social (individual and group manipulation) reality is complete without the other, as most experienced field workers have known all along.

for high school teachers to have abstract conceptualizations of "good students" and "bad students" and to sort certain of the students of whom they have knowledge into either of these categories. On the other hand, while it is less common for teachers to use other, more abstract, conceptions such as students who "threaten" or "support" them, these are still salient categories for many of the teachers we have observed.

Sorting of students into categories or classes takes place among students, by other students, by teachers, and by administrators. Similarly, teachers and administrators are sorted by members of each category, including their own. It is interesting to note that these very categories, along with those of ancilliary personnel such as teachers and custodians, form one of the most basic examples of sorting in the school situation. These are probably among the most ascriptive of the school statuses, and yet they still contain an element of manageable ambiguity. Teachers who "act like students" or who "make friends with the principal" are common figures of disparagement by their fellows. It would seem that creating ambiguous situations at the borders of these classifications is a threatening activity. One of the reasons "teachers' pets" are so disliked is their symbolic violation of their basic classification.[2]

The distinction between ascribed and achieved status in the sorting procedure is an important one. As the two terms are normally used in the sociological literature, they leave an important facet of their potential meaning unresolved. A status may be traditionally termed ascribed when it is given to an individual regardless of his personal effort. Note that this is not simply effort to gain the status which we exclude, but all effort. This does not take into account the processes of decision and recognition involved in the establishment of ascribed status. A status based on kinship is generally considered ascribed. It is by no means inviolable, however. As Moore has shown for the Chagga (1971), a process exists whereby a middle (as opposed to eldest or youngest) sibling may be edged from his family identification in a situation of land shortage. This is a situation of "ascribed" status being manipulated, not, as it happens, by the "ascribee" but the "ascriber." Sometimes it occurs that the ascriber can be manipulated by the ascribee. This is, of course, a large part of Goffman's statement in regard to stigma and other situations where "passing" becomes an appropriate operation (1963). Further, we

---

[2]   Colin Lacey, in his reports (in this volume and elsewhere [esp. 1970]) on his study of Hightown Grammar, describes the particular importance of certain ways in which a classroom pet can manage his relations with peers by behaving as a ruffian outside the classroom. Lacey's subject seems clearly to recognize the importance of maintaining symbolic membership.

suggest that a certain amount of active participation is frequently needed to maintain an ascribed status.

The further point should be made that statuses are ascribed *vis-à-vis* a certain social field. This field may be large or small. The ascription process is that in which persons are given statuses outside of their immediate control. Since control is in large part a skill, and variable, it must be emphasized that ascription/achievement is a continuum, and one may only productively talk about the extent of ascription.

In many school situations certain characteristics of sorting are established outside the school and carried over into it in greater or lesser degrees. The distinctions on ethnic lines in our urban school and on town of residence in our rural school serve as examples of this. Other characteristics are more clearly established within the school system itself. Of these, some, such as many good student/poor student distinctions, are established quite early in the student's school career. Reports are passed in writing or by word of mouth from elementary to junior high to high schools. Perhaps in some ways more important, this classification is often internalized and/or transferred into the student social field. Thus, a cohort of students will have accepted a certain amount of self-sorting by the time they reach high school. New students often will have an internalized image of where they belong on such a stratification continuum and will place themselves accordingly.

Other criteria for classification are particular to the high school institution. These may be influenced by reputation or other outside information, but are not primarily determined by external sources. Examples include much sorting of students as supportive or disruptive, of teachers as friends of the administration or as proponents of teacher solidarity. The ability of a principal to win battles with the higher levels of administration, or to bring in funds may make of him a "leader" or a "nuisance."

Frequently, these various sorting procedures result in the establishment of important social boundaries. Networks, at certain levels, are found to have many more links within certain classifications than without. This is of course predictable. Two related functions of this are more directly interesting. These are: one, the implications of the development of socially functioning classificatory units for the analysis of small groups generally in complex societies; and two, the importance of individuals who are able to function for one classificatory unit *vis-à-vis* others, or who are able to exist on the perimeters. Let us examine these two points more closely.

Discussions of social ties in complex societies often follow an implicit argument of degeneration from *gemeinschaft* to *gesellschaft*. This is apparent whether one follows Redfield's folk society (1947) into the cities or Gluckman's multiplex ties (1955) from Africa to the monoplex West. We do not wish to disagree fundamentally with these observations. Rather, we would point out, as these social theorists have sometimes themselves, that there is a gap left in the picture. Observations of complex societies by anthropologists have yet to produce so thorough a picture as we have gained for smaller-scale societies. Thus, we do not know whether or not there are emergent or even established social forms replacing some of the functions fulfilled by small-group ties in other societies. Classificatory affiliations may form such a unit. We are not suggesting that these aggregates are functionally similar to tribal kin groups, for example.[3] They are not, inasmuch as schools are not tribal societies. Neither are schools segments of tribal societies. They are a different form of social organization and, as such, have different social properties and processes. However, it is perhaps more a point of similarity to suggest that intervening units of the sort we have described do exist. The point is simple: there is not a complete transition from group to individual. What is at one level an increased social independence still requires its collectivities. Individualization may then mean, on a social level, classification. Classification is a different thing from membership in a corporate group, but the absence (hardly complete) of group[4] does not make it possible to treat large numbers of people as individuals. There must be an organization.

To the extent that classificatory affiliations become important, t here is a need for individuals who can mediate their boundaries. One classification voiced by students in the suburban high school and observed to be broadly relevant was that between "jocks" and "freaks." The distinction appears to be chiefly one of life-style and appearance, the former category being composed of relatively traditional youths, athletes, and

[3] Adrian Mayer has cogently discussed "The significance of quasi-groups in the study of complex societies" (1966). The classificatory affiliations we describe do not seem to have solidified to the extent Mayer requires for definition of a quasi-group. They are, however, a construct attempting to cope with a similar analytic weak point. See also Note 4 on "groups."
[4] It should be questioned to what extent there is, in fact, a disappearance of group. Rather, there may be a disappearance of ASCRIBED groups. One must form affiliations without such strict social parameters. Some affiliations may still be corporate groups — unions, political parties, social groups, and the like. It is possible that the classificatory affiliations described are not conceptually separate, but are on their way toward eventual incorporation. This incorporation may be upcoming, or it may be permanently blocked by the nature of the institution. The trend could exist independently of its completion.

their hangers-on, the latter of youths with more counter-culture aspirations, longer hair, and the like. Most other characteristics did not vary with classification. Neither group showed significantly different academic performance, social-class background, etc. Still, there was little network overlap between "jocks" and "freaks," although both displayed a primary identification with the community/school as a unit. That is, freaks from Sheffield identified themselves as Sheffieldites in opposition to residents of other communities, even where those persons could be considered fellow "freaks."

Where two large categories in a relatively small social field have little overlap, it may be expected that those individuals who can function in both groups and/or between groups will occupy a special place in the system. Just as crosscutting ties such as age-sets link members of different subsocietal units in tribal situations, there are crosscutting networks in those situations where sociologists find networks the more valuable analytic schema.[5]

In some ways, the effort the individual expends to control the process of his being sorted by himself and others may be seen as his effort to manage his identity. The way in which someone works into a classificatory system is a very large part of his social identity. The desire to create and maintain a favorable identity may be safely postulated as a human universal. Indeed, a more basic universal would be the previous sentence with the word favorable deleted. Demarcations of all sorts are the stuff of identity; those demarcations which add autonomy are the opportunities for the management of identity. Some territorial demarcations are such opportunities.

The division of the school from the "outside world" is the primary territorial demarcation of the institution, and a number of others follow from and within it. There are faculty lounges, "senior courtyards," administrative offices and other territories which are formally distinguished and ruled "off bounds" to those who are not members of certain classifications. There are also less formal territories, which are still fairly clearly in the possession of some broad classes; student restrooms, for example, are seldom entered by the adults in the school and produce an area of significant autonomy.[6] When territories of this kind are infringed upon, people feel an outrage, a classificatory violation. The idea of one-way mirrors is strongly offensive (for a variety of reasons, perhaps

[5] The concept of figure-8 networks may be mentioned here. Networks are frequently schematically represented by circles. Where there is a single focus of contact between two networks the diagram may look like a figure-8.

[6] See Lopate (1973). This study is based on observations in our rural high school.

including modesty), but in at least one school a reversed window serves this purpose. The fact that this should be deemed important demonstrates the threat felt by administrators with regard to a territorial autonomy for students.

There are a number of other territories established within the school for smaller categories, usually more by convention than rule. These range from a particular bench usually occupied during a break by a particular group of students, to an area behind the gym or in a copse of trees used for smoking, to hallways in large part controlled by black students in our urban school. The violation of one of these territories not bound by formal rule would produce conflict of a different process and result than, say, the violation of a teacher's control over the territory of his or her classroom. In any such dispute over territorial control a battle for power is in progress. However, the violation of a formal rule produces a major difference. In the former case individuals are competing for power within the system. In the latter case the order of the system is being challenged.[7]

The definition of territory, then, is a symbolic demarcation in a structural system and as such is not unlike sorting. Instead of dividing people into categories, territory is divided into units. In the case of territory, however, there is the added dimension of competition over territory. The competition must be carried in aggregates or among classes. For example, challenges to a teacher's territorial right over a classroom are not simply between individuals but on one level are between the two classes, teacher and student. On another level it may be seen that the conflict draws in administrators on the side of "the rules" and thus of the teacher. Certain students may support the teacher's claim over that of the challenging student. Where the lines of demarcation are drawn becomes an interesting and revealing area for observation.

A great many rules relate to the definition of territories. The enforcement of the rules differs among a variety of sorting categories, however.

---

[7]   Leach has discussed this distinction succinctly, if less originally than he may suggest, in the introduction to his *Political systems of highland Burma* (1965): "Every real society is a process in time. The changes that result from this process may usefully be thought of under two heads. Firstly, there are those which are consistent with a continuity of the existing formal order. For example, when a chief dies and is replaced by his son, or when a lineage segments and we have two lineages where formally there was only one, the changes are part of the process of continuity. There is no change in the formal structure. Secondly, there are changes which do reflect alterations in the formal structure. If, for example, it can be shown that in a particular locality, over a period of time, a political system composed of equalitarian lineage segments is replaced by a ranked hierarchy of feudal type, we can speak of a change in the formal structure."

For example, a student considered "good" may be able to wander down a hall during class time, while a "bad" student would be stopped, even though the formal rule simply makes the halls "off limits" to students during class. In this way, the domains of sorting and territoriality overlap in the context of the making, breaking, and enforcing of rules.

Rules are always set up in bureaucratic situations. Their meaning, however, only becomes clear with consideration of the patterns of enforcement followed. This does not mean that the structure of the formal rules system is irrelevant, only that it is insufficient to explain the social behavior involved. The proliferation of rules has two interesting aspects. First, the particular rules which are chosen have particular causes, reasons, and motivations behind their selection. Second, a range of rules is provided which can then be drawn into action to support virtually any stand of a person of higher rank (greater interpretive authority) versus a subordinate individual.

One question which becomes interesting is "to what extent can a person of low relative rank demand enforcement of a rule against a person of higher structural position?" On some occasions examination of a situation in which this has occurred will reveal either particular strength in the position of the lower ranked individual or weakness in that of the higher-ranked person. A student, for example, may be able to prove a point to a teacher of marginal status, or to one who has recently had a dispute with the principal. Another question is to what extent an invocation of a rule can be undone. Can (or will) a principal always override a utilization of a rule with which he disagrees, or does the invocation of the formal rule carry a weight of its own, sometimes comparable to the authority of the principal. This varies from situation to situation even where the same actors are involved. It is difficult for a principal to continually override teachers' judgements on the rules, even where he has both the authority and power to do so. If he does, he may both alienate the teachers and reduce whatever ideological significance or respect the rule system may have. On the other hand, one aspect of rank in a social structure may be seen as the degree of interpretative authority an individual has *vis-à-vis* the system of rules. What individual or collective interpretations can he overrule, and which can overrule him?

It may be deemed to be a function of any institution to protect the integrity of the system of rules which, to an extent, defines its existence and boundaries.[8] For example, in one high school we studied, students

---

[8]   A school, for example, is less a building or a set of individuals, than it is a series of situations in which a common set of rules are seen to apply. Whether or not the rules

were granted the use of a space called the senior lounge. Periodically the school administration would announce a suspension of the students' privilege of using the lounge, stating that the unauthorized prevalence of eating in the lounge was the cause. This was against the rules. There was always eating in the lounge, however, and there was no continuing attempt to police it. Apparently, the administration's actions centered more directly around a symbolic issue. The issue in this case seemed to be the periodic demonstration of administrative authority and its corollary, the prevention of an assumption of student autonomy.

Briefly, then, the organization of the school seems set up around the demarcation of identity and the subsidiary identification of power. This power may be within or without the authority structure. To an extent the school is an organization lacking in significant autonomy for its members. This reinforces the tendency to spend a great deal of effort and power enforcing boundaries. The situation is further complicated by the fact that the adolescents who form the major constituency of the school are marginal characters *vis-à-vis* society. The idea of autonomy for these marginal characters — people who are inevitably engaged in crossing boundaries — is anathema. These are people against whom one must be protected. Since there is a limited amount of power and autonomy in the school, much of the protection must be symbolic. That is, one cannot successfully prevent students from violating the symbolic boundaries, so emphasis falls on occasional enforcement and punishment rather than prevention.

In some instances administrators see teachers as posing similar threat to their autonomy and identity. The organization of teachers' associations and unions particularly produces this fear. Again, we interpret the root condition as being the lack of significant autonomy in the operation of the school. The three processes through which we find it easiest to see the mediation between formal structures and informal systems highlight the identity question well. From different perspectives, sorting, territoriality, and the making and breaking of rules are all identifying procedures.

REFERENCES

GLUCKMAN, MAX
   1955   *Custom and conflict in Africa.* Glencoe, Ill.: Free Press.

are actually found to be uniformly applicable is not as relevant as the extent to which they are perceived as applicable, and thus a part of the framework of negotiation in the situation.

GOFFMAN, ERVING
  1963   *Stigma*. Englewood Cliffs, N. J. : Prentice-Hall.
LACEY, COLIN
  1970   *Hightown grammar: the school as a social system.* Manchester: Manchester University Press.
LEACH, EDMUND R.
  1965   *Political systems of highland Burma.* Boston: Beacon Press. (Originally published 1954 by the London School of Economics and Political Science.)
LOPATE, CAROL
  1973   "The battle of the bathrooms." Paper presented to the American Anthropological Association symposium on "The Social Organization of High Schools," New Orleans.
MAYER, ADRIAN
  1966   "The significance of quasi-groups in the study of complex societies," in *The social anthropology of complex societies.* Edited by M. Banton, 97–122. A. S. A. Monographs 4. London: Tavistock.
MOORE, SALLY FALK
  1971   "Ritual concord and fraternal strife: Kilimanjaro 1968–69." Paper presented to the American Anthropological Association symposium on Secular Rituals, New York, 1971. Mimeographed. (Revised version forthcoming in *Secular rituals* [tentative title]. Edited by V. Turner. Ithaca: Cornell University Press.)
REDFIELD, ROBERT
  1947   The folk society. *American Journal of Sociology* 52:293–306.

American Culture and the School: A Case Study

HERVÉ VARENNE

Editors' Note: How is it that people come to learn the rules of their culture? How do schools present these rules, and how do they work out the interface between a cultural ideology and rules which may violate it but, nonetheless, operate in the school as well as outside? These are prominent questions which Hervé Varenne, an assistant professor of home and family life at Teachers College, Columbia University, raises, and for which he begins the analysis of possible answers. Varenne presents specific data from a suburban American high school (gathered as part of the study discussed in more general terms by Calhoun and Ianni in the preceeding paper) and uses it to illustrate the processes of definition, categorization, and mediation operative in culture and school.

I.   The following is a short report on research I am presently conducting on cultural behavior within an American high school and the relationship of the principles underlying this behavior with only the superficially unrelated principles which underlie the very concept of "school" and formal school organization in American culture. This research is a continuation and deepening of work which I began a few years ago when I became interested in developing a new statement of American culture that would be more systematic and holistic than the previous attempts (Mead 1965; Brogan 1944; Gorer 1948; etc.).[1] I feel that it has become

---

This research is part of a wider project on the social organization of schools. This project is introduced in the article by Calhoun and Ianni (this volume). My own research within it has concentrated on one suburban high school, and my data comes solely from observations which I and two students, Patricia Caesar and Rodney Riffle, have made in that school. I want to thank them for the help and stimulation they gave me in my thinking about the school.
[1]   The result of this initial research, which involved a study of behavior in a small midwestern town, is available in Varenne 1972.

possible to do so because of the great theoretical advances which have
been made in recent years in the study of symbolic systems. Most relevant
to my attempt are the works of Schneider (1968, 1969), Dumont (1970),
and Lévi-Strauss (1964–1971).

I shall not here go extensively into the theoretical justification for
studying symbol systems structurally. Let it just be said that, beyond the
philosophical issues which structuralism justifiably raises, the main
import of the approach is methodological. Structuralism, I believe, will
offer to cultural anthropologists a way out from the serious methodological
critique which emphasizes that their work is impressionistic, personal,
unreliable, and altogether "unscientific." One of the problems lies in the
fact that the reader cannot follow the researcher's iourney from his data
to his formal presentation of his interpretation of them. The data, plus
the logic used, must become more readily available; and it is because of
the great methodological advance made by Lévi-Strauss in his *Mythologiques* (1964–1971) that there is much less that we have to accept from
him "on faith," as it were, and much more that we can follow step by
step, myth by myth, "text" by "text."

My own research differs greatly from his insofar as it involves "participant" observation, field notes, and their transcription and transformation to protect the informants. The "on faith" part of the process has
not been completely eliminated. Lévi-Strauss has often been criticized
for his "presence" in his summaries of the myths he uses. My problems
on this aspect are greater since the original field notes are not readily
available and the original situation is forever lost. The only true advantage
of a presentation of the discussion involving, first, a long "text" summary
of a field situation in as much of its phenomenological wealth as possible,
and then a step-by-step investigation, first of the structure of the text in
itself and then in the context of other such texts, lies in the fact that at
least the logic of the argument has become available to the reader. This
is something which I hope to begin to demonstrate here.

Before going further, I want to comment briefly on the position I
take here on the subject of seeing culture as a "system of symbols."
The concept of symbol is usually defined along the following lines which
I borrow from Schneider: "A symbol is something which stands for
something else, or some things else, where there is no necessary or
intrinsic relationship between the symbol and that which it symbolizes"
(1968:1).

The typical example involves the word "dog" in English, the word *chien*
in French, and the animal. The problem with this definition is that it
seems to imply that the "meaning" of the symbol lies in the "something

else," i.e. that to understand an aspect of a cultural system, one has to understand first aspects of other systems, usually the biological or physiological system. First, while it is easy to find an "outside" correspondent for a symbol like the word "dog," it is so difficult to find one for the symbols like "God" or "individualism" that often these symbols are left aside as impervious to scientific analysis. The real problem comes from the fact that this process of finding a correspondent to a symbol in "something else" is that it violates the principle that the cultural system is a system *sui generis* and that everything which happens within it must be explained by aspects of this system. And, indeed, empirical studies of classification systems have shown that our system of arranging dogs, colors, philosophical concepts, or deities is idiosyncratic to us and certainly not universal; the meaning of the word "dog" is thus not given by referring it to the animal, but rather by showing that it derives from the distinction that we make between certain domestic animals on the basis of such things as retractable or nonretractable claws, shape of the body, ability to climb trees, typical habits, "psychology," etc.

A symbol is, thus, nothing else than a part of a total structure of communication, a unit as defined in contrast to other units of the same level. The work of a cultural anthropologist thus resides in identifying the elements (symbols) of the system, in determining their context — what other symbols the original symbol is related to and how — in exploring small systems first and then larger ones, and so on until the researcher has reached the level in which he is interested.

II.   The case study under consideration is a somewhat lengthy description of one period of the Sociology V class of Mr. Charles Taylor, eleventh and twelfth grade teacher at Sheffield High School.

Taylor is around thirty-five. He has an M.A. in sociology from a large state university and is presently in the process of working on his dissertation. He has a neatly trimmed beard, wears his hair slightly longer than most teachers in the school, and his clothes have a stylish mod cut that make him stand out as he walks the corridor without directly threatening the rather conservative teacher dress code that is considered appropriate in the wealthy white suburb. Taylor is a vocal proponent of the concept of "individualized instruction" by which a student is allowed to progress in any subject at his own speed according to his ability. He is one of the favorite teachers of the progressive principal, and, with his support, Taylor has taken over the chairmanship of the social studies program in the school and has transformed the curriculum almost radically in a way that is considered exemplary by many teachers and administrators, not only in the school system, but also in the neighboring school systems which maintain close relationships with Sheffield.

Sociology V is open to anybody in the high school who has completed four years of history and sociology. In practice, of the twenty-nine students, all are seniors except for two juniors who are considered exceptionally brilliant by all their teachers and who will indeed graduate at the end of the year. Most of the seniors in the class are also the type of students that have received early acceptance from such universities as Harvard or Princeton on the basis of their total performance in the school. Many of them can be found in the "advanced" classes of departments in the school that have not yet been "individualized" in the proper sense.

The curriculum of Sociology V consists mostly of the review of current sociological problems in the United States with a little consideration given to international problems that interest the United States most directly. Many periods are given to reading about the subject; the work asked from the students is mostly reports on specific points, some of which are presented and discussed in class. The period I am now going to describe was devoted to the discussion of one of those reports. The report had to do with the controversy that was agitating a nearby community: a planning board had decided that a low-income housing project ought to be built there, and groups of residents were up in arms in an attempt to prevent the project from being built.

At the beginning of the period, Taylor asked one student to come to the front and lead the discussion. He himself went to the back of the room where he spent the rest of the period observing what was going on and rarely intervening except to remind the leader that he should not monopolize the discussion too much and be certain that all students, even the most shy, could speak at one point. The leader started the discussion with an opening statement using rather strong words against the project and in favor of the right of people to live with people they like and, thus, to refuse to admit people in their community whom they wouldn't like. One or two approving voices were heared until a long-haired, rather sloppily dressed student, whom I knew had been accepted by Harvard, started arguing that the opposition to the project was not a matter of private freedom, but of racism, and that it was unconstitutional to prevent anybody from buying or renting property wherever he wanted. The discussion continued in this vein for the fifty minutes, dominated mostly by five or six students, with two or three on each side of the controversy. From time to time other students succeeded in placing a word, but this was rather rare. The atmosphere was often riotous as several students were talking at the same time. Tempers flared several times, and nasty comments were sometimes exchanged between two individuals. Then the bell rang. The discussion stopped at once. Conversations of the usual type between small groups of individuals began immediately, and the students walked out of the room. Taylor thanked the leader of the discussion and then walked out himself.

Later, two further comments were made to me about that class. First, two students who had remained rather quiet during the period came to me and asked "What side are you on?" They explained to me that all discussions in that class turned out to be basically the same. The class divides itself in two groups, the "liberals" and the "conservatives," and the students line themselves up in the same way on all issues. Later, Taylor, the teacher, explained to me that he thought it good that students speak up about such problems in order to build up their confidence in themselves and their ability to verbalize their opinions. He said, however, that students were often disturbed by such discussions and that he tried to minimize the negative effect that those discussions have by not discussing the personal aspect of the exchanges afterwards.

Let us try to analyze this case study in some detail. We have seen, among other things, that:

1. INDIVIDUALIZED INSTRUCTION is considered PROGRESSIVE and BETTER.
2. INDIVIDUALIZED INSTRUCTION does NOT seem to make MUCH DIFFERENCE in terms of which students belong to the most advanced grades.
3. Substantive differences of opinion exist among students.
4. One side of a discussion is defended in terms of the RIGHT OF PEOPLE TO CHOOSE THEIR FRIENDS. The other side in terms of the RIGHT OF PEOPLE TO DO WHAT THEY WANT.
5. To verbalize substantive differences draws out hostility which is considered bad.
6. To emphasize the right of choosing one's friends and thus excluding others is "conservative"; to emphasize the right to do what one wants outside or beyond any social group is "liberal" if not radical.

A set of interrelated questions can now be asked:
What is individualized instruction?
Is the fact that individualized instruction is considered "progressive" related to the "progressive" liberal side of the discussion?
Is the difference between liberal and conservative related to social structural definitions or to logical properties of an ideological structure?
Can we explain why expressing substantive differences of opinion in a face-to-face encounter is considered disturbing and dangerous?

III. The next methodological step in a full-blown investigation would be to present another text from the field notes telling of another situation where some of the elements we isolated are present. This could be curriculum discussions about the value of individualized instruction or verbal exchanges at an informal meeting of a clique, just as well as it could be another classroom situation. Lack of space will, of course, prevent us from following the complete unfolding of the structure as it should properly be done. Let us go back, then, to an "on faith" approach and investigate how we could answer the questions we asked.

"Individualized instruction," we are told, is the process by which children in a classroom are no longer treated as part of a group, but as individuals. It is assumed by proponents of that system that "traditional instruction" is based on a model by which instruction is passed from the teacher to the class as a whole with the responsibility falling on the child for internalizing that instruction. This is considered inadequate insofar as it does not take into consideration the fact that each child is a unique system that may have different interests or capacities. Individualized instruction is, thus, a refusal to assign *a priori* social, intellectual, or psychological characteristics to a certain person. For people of this tendency, assignment of characteristics can only be made through an in-depth analysis of each case.

It is interesting to note here that "individualized instruction" as a slogan is rather closely identified, on the one hand, with a small clique among the teachers as well as with "permissiveness" in discipline matters, lessening of the overall quality of education in the school, and political liberalism. Some people will identify the clique with the ideology. In fact, teachers partisan to individualized instruction may be politically conservative, and some very liberal teachers may not be accepted among the ranks of the modernists. Thus, even though there is a clear logical continuity between the political position which emphasizes the right of individuals to live wherever they want and their right to be taught at their own speed, a person may not feel uncomfortable standing on different sides of the issue depending on the substantive area on which an ideological choice must be made. Empirical reasons for special choices ranged from pragmatism, "things work better this way," to social considerations. For example, it appeared to be difficult for an older, female teacher who was very liberal in her politics and practiced something very much akin to individualized instruction to come out publicly as a partisan of this technique because the clique that was vocal in its partisanship was composed mainly of younger male teachers.

The preceding discussion can shed light on our next question: Is the opposition between groups considered to be "liberal" or "conservative" to be understood as deriving solely from cultural definitions of the social world? In other words, do both conservative and liberal cliques in the school consider their world to be divided in such groups BY DEFINITION? This would, of course, go against the view the liberals have of themselves as considering only the characteristics of individuals in their interrelationship with them, and as refusing to lump individuals into predefined social groups. So, could we find another theory that would account for the fact that there ARE liberals and conservatives in the school, and that there are group differences in the face of the fact that at least one of those groups refuses to define its world on such terms. The other plausible hypothesis is that the division of the school into groups is not based on a

definition of the social world, but rather that it derives from the properties of other systems of human behavior, the social system in particular.
Symbolic identification would then be derived from contradictory aspects
of a single ideological definition. Let us see how this would work.

The school records about individual children are organized alphabetically, according to the spelling of the last name of the children. In recent
years even communication between the administration, faculty, and
children has been arranged in the same way as "home rooms" have been
assigned, also according to alphabetical position. All informants consider the alphabet a totally "artificial" means of classification, insofar
as it is agreed that it does not imply anything as to the personality of
the child. And the fact that it is a more convenient manner of handling
a large population is seen as a valid consideration only in such situations
when the personality of the child is not involved. There is no conservative/
liberal split on the subject: both place the same values and limitations
on the alphabet. The relevance of this discussion to our analysis is that
it implies a generally accepted differentiation between two aspects of a
human being: (1) a human being is a self-sufficient unit within the total
universe of the species, i.e. it possesses a reality in itself beyond its
relationship to any other human beings; (2) this biological uniqueness
within a species is considered irrelevant to the reality of the being as a
human which is defined in psychological terms. On the one hand, a
human being is a biologically defined organism which can be dealt with
in complete disregard for its psychological reality since all such organisms
are similar. On the other hand, a human being is also a psychologically
defined individual who cannot be treated in terms of his belonging to a
social group because each individual is unique.

The problem with this definition of human reality is that it says nothing
about social organization, about the fact, indeed acknowledged by all
informants, that cooperation between human beings is necessary for
them to survive. But there is no abstract model for such interaction
except the alphabet, which is also considered the least suitable because
of its artificiality. On the other hand, one is told that total reliance on
individualism would lead to a destruction of society, chaos, or the like.
It was, for example, argued by the students that the alphabetically
organized home rooms were not effective because the students were not
with their friends and that they couldn't care less about the students
who were lumped together with them on the basis of their last name.
It was thus decided that for certain occasions home rooms would be
reorganized on the basis of choice after an election, so that friends would
be with friends to the largest extent possible — ad hoc groups with

234 HERVÉ VARENNE

no substance created for a particular purpose by a bunch of "individuals."

We could show now in great detail how the whole social organization of the school can only be explained in terms of ad hoc groups based on a common decision to share certain types of activities of services. The native word for these groups is "cliques" — pronounced with a short "i" by the students in the school. These groups rarely develop a strong identity. It is very difficult to draw empirical boundaries for them because a fair amount of communication takes place between cliques coupled with the fact that there are no marked rituals of interaction where belonging to a clique would be stressed or reinforced. Similarly membership is not set *a priori* by any rule even when an individual can be most easily typified because of his exterior appearance or his participating in a marked activity such as athletics. A person with all the social attributes necessary to be considered a "jock" may decide to relate mostly with the "freaks" because he will say he is "really a freak." Somebody who has never made the athletic teams may say that he is "a jock at heart," even though he sports long hair and wears dirty jeans regularly. Cliques are based on mutual acceptance and membership is considered to depend on life-style choices rather than on ascribed social roles. Thus, the opposition jocks/freaks, like the opposition liberal/conservative, is not based on a necessary opposition between jocks and freaks, or between liberals and conservatives.

The process of informal organization of students and teachers within the school thus consists of, first, the creation of a small group through chance and/or psychologically defined life-style choices. Then, it becomes necessary to identify the cliques for communication about them to exist. For this symbols are borrowed from the outside, the national media, for example. These become accepted as representing more or less adequately the group they refer to. Thus one should not try to understand jocks or liberals in Sheffield by looking at abstract definitions of jockishness or liberalism that one could postulate to exist in the larger American culture. The definition of the notions can only be derived from the actions and beliefs of the appropriate cliques in Sheffield, and thus one cannot expect the definition to be the same either synchronically from one locality in the United States to another or diachronically from one period in American history to another. Indeed, since "liberalism" is not a coherent whole but rather a label for a clique, it is possible for one person to be both "conservative" and "liberal" at the same time on different issues. This simply means that the pattern of behavior which the "liberal" clique of Sheffield exhibits is not the same as that of the more influential clique which controls the mass media and the intelligensia.

There is nothing intrinsically liberal about stressing the rights of individuals as abstract units versus the stressing of the rights of individuals after they have formed their groups of cliques. And if we could relate individualized instruction and the rights of individuals as abstract units with liberalism, it is because it appears that generally it is the same people in the administration and faculty of the school who hold these positions. What remains the same among all teachers and all students and thus provides the basic cultural model that is necessary for Americans to communicate among themselves, and uhich a foreigner or a cultural anthropologist can recognize as "typically American," is the belief that human society is based on the voluntary association of human beings whose social reality is grounded in psychology.

We can now fit the perceived danger of disagreement within this intellectual structure. Society, we have seen, is not a natural process for my informants; it must be built out of recalcitrant units which are not made with an inherent capacity to fit within a social structure. Interpersonal relationships are problematical, and when they exist, as within a clique, they are based on similarities rather than differences. A clique is not a team; its organization is not oriented towards a goal for the realization of which each unit contributes something. Everybody participates equally within a clique, and he contributes the same things. Thus, difference is tantamount to destruction of the clique and will trigger the tendency on the part of other members to reject the differing individual unless, of course, that individual has already left the clique. The larger the scale, the more dangerous for the individual is this expression of real difference. At the level of the clique, at the time of an interaction, there is rarely much of a problem because the boundaries between outside and inside the situation are fairly clear and differences are rarely aired. In larger situations, like the classroom, several cliques meet on a neutral ground that the teacher may then define as a clique in itself, a small community. When this teacher then sets up a discussion, the level of stress goes up. Differences will be expressed since they do exist. The situation is altogether an artificial one, but stress will be high since, given the definition of the situation, those differences should not exist.

IV. The preceding is, of course, all too brief to do complete justice to the complexity of the definitions involved. It was only intended to be an illustration of a type of analysis that can be brought to bear on behavior in a school. But what could be the relevance of such an analysis for educators, one could ask. This relevance may not be directly apparent especially since the data we used seems so commonsensical as to render any attempt at scientific treatment almost silly. Other people will argue that what is needed is not a study of beliefs which can be shown to be scientifically wrong, as those beliefs we discussed can indeed be shown to be, but rather of "real realities" in which more people must be made to believe. Those are supposedly the proper subjects to study for someone who wants to call himself a scientist. Let us comment briefly on these attitudes.

Cultural phenomena are "real realities" of their own particular order, and the fact that their properties are not so blaring as those of other systems of human behavior makes it more urgent that they should be explored systematically. On the other hand, a good cultural analysis must go beyond the perception of its culture which any individual within it may have. Cultural anthropology may be the science of the commonsensical; it is not common sense.

Once common sense has been accepted as a valid subject for science, what can we say is the use of this science for people who are interested in applied situations, as educators are? The failure of many programs based on the analysis of situations by social scientists or psychologists is often explained by reference to the complexity of human behavior. This complexity exists, to be sure; but the failure of the human sciences until now has been the failure to take into account that complexity and the attempt to reduce behavior to a few single components on which it would then be easier to act. A successful human science will be one which will take into account the fact that it is only at the level of analysis that one can distinguish between the biological, the social, and the cultural. Real behavior is one, and applied programs work at that level. Thus, these programs must take into account all aspects of behavior, particularly the fact that the program itself will be subjected to analysis on the part of the people to which it is applied, and that this analysis will be based on the common sense of the people — on their culture. If a program is perceived as going against a certain aspect of this culture, it will probably be rejected or transformed into something possibly quite different from what it was intended to be. Willy-nilly, it will be made to fit the model of the world the natives have, and the designers of programs must take this into account if they ever want to succeed.

Furthermore, it is a mistake to believe that a native social scientist has a sufficient knowledge of his culture to prevent that from happening. He has little knowledge of the actual theoretical working of a cultural system; furthermore, the symbols which a native will stress may not be those which another native of the same culture would stress or understand. Within a certain community, a "liberal" American may not at all understand a "conservative" one because he will not see clearly where the significant difference lies. As we saw earlier, the difference probably has nothing to do with politics, but rather with certain social and cultural consequences of the definition of society as being composed of a bunch of individuals. The usefulness of the works of a cultural anthropologist is thus double. On the one hand, he can explain the locus and the theoretical property of the cultural system in any society or situation. On the other, he can give a more adequate description of an actual cultural situation.

REFERENCES

BROGAN, D. W.
1944   *The American character*. New York: Vintage Books.
DUMONT, LOUIS
1970   *Homo hierarchicus*. Translated by M. Sainsbury. Chicago: The University of Chicago Press.
GORER, GEOFFREY
1948   *The American people*. New York: W.W. Norton.
LÉVI-STRAUSS, CLAUDE
1964–1971   *Mythologiques*. Paris: Plon.
MEAD, MARGARET
1965   *And keep your powder dry*. New York: William Morrow. (Originally published 1942.)
SCHNEIDER, DAVID M.
1968   *American kinship: a cultural account*. Englewood Cliffs, N. J.: Prentice-Hall.
1969   "Kinship, nationality and religion in American culture: toward a definition of kinship," in *Forms of symbolic action*. Edited by V. Turner. Proceedings of the 1969 Annual Spring meeting of the American Ethnological Association. Seattle: University of Washington Press.
VARENNE, HERVÉ
1972   "Individualism, community and love in a small midwestern town." Doctoral dissertation, University of Chicago.

Education in Africa: Myths of "Modernization"

ELEANOR BURKE LEACOCK

Editors' Note: What happens when social, political, and economic situations cause the items of one culture to be rated desirable by the government or people of another? Certain prices and practices are adopted and amalgamated into a new system. In this paper, Eleanor Leacock, who holds the anthropology chair of the City College of the City University of New York, traces some of the history of "Western" education programs in Africa and details some of the fallacies, problems, and successes of their operation. She compares the Zambian educational progress she has observed to New York City schools she has seen. Some of the current problems of the latter are shared by the Zambians, but they have been spared many. Leacock sees problems as the result of much of American education, and while she sees some mitigating factors as well, she fears too much of the same result in Africa. "Modernization," she suggests, has become a mythic concept, and not necessarily a good one.

In the industrializing nations of Africa universal free public education is widely seen as the key to national development. Western educational models have great influence, and advice and assistance are sought from Western educators. Paradoxically, this coincides with a period in the West in which public schools have been coming in for particularly heavy criticism. Although often cited as the means through which a

This is part of a larger report entitled "Primary schooling in Zambia," Number ED 067 729, available from ERIC Document Reproduction Service, PO Drawer O, Bethesda, Maryland, 20014. A fuller version is being prepared for publication by the Institute for African Studies, University of Zambia, which sponsored the study. The research on which this paper is based was conducted in 1970. It was supported in its pilot stage by the Louis M. Rabinowitz Foundation and carried through to completion with the assistance of a grant from the Bureau of Research, U.S. Office of Education. In Zambia I was assisted in my research by Ernest Phiri and a team of interviewers and translators: Ellias Chikago, William Daka, Wills Kaira, Samson Mwanza, Vincent Phiri, Phillip Zulu, and Sabel Zulu.

citizenry can be trained for humanistic and innovative thought, it is becoming increasingly clear that educational institutions, especially at the lower levels, have in fact acted to encourage unquestioning compliance and even outright bigotry. And, although generally said to provide an avenue for reinforcing democratic institutions through enabling equality of opportunity, the evidence increasingly shows that schools act instead in large measure to maintain the occupational hierarchy across generations.

My own understanding of educational problems in the West was deepened in the course of two studies. An analysis of elementary schooling in New York City documented some of the processes that lead often well-meaning and hard-working teachers to miseducate children. The research revealed ways in which the predominantly SOCIALIZING function of schools, as they operate within the framework of Western social-economic institutions, acts to the detriment of children's EDUCATION (Leacock 1969, 1970). Strongly prescribed styles of behaving and communicating, that link success in school with the acquisition of so-called middle-class white patterns, take precedence over training for thinking. Little leeway is given for artistic, expressive thinking in a free-floating exploratory way; and only superficial attention is given to systematic "scientific" thinking, that is, how to state problems, seek sources of reliable information, observe, compare, classify, evaluate evidence, and draw conclusions.

The second study concerned the teaching of interdisciplinary social science theory and method at a college level.[1] Among other things, the project illustrated to me the failure of present educational practices to lay a foundation for the humanistic and rational approach to living that is essential if a citizenry is to deal effectively with the problems of the contemporary world. Both projects revealed how much myth and magic there is in our schooling despite constant appeals to the name of science. A limited, mechanistic, and static view of natural phenomena, and a judgmental, moralistic approach to social phenomena pervade all educational levels.

Such criticism of education in the United States may seem picayune and irrelevant, for have we not, after all, built a scientific and technological plant that has placed men on the moon; have we not raised the human life expectancy to three-score years and ten? Indeed we have, but we are now being forced to recognize that this same technological

---

[1]   The project in the teaching of interdisciplinary social science theory and method was carried on in the Department of Social Sciences, Polytechnic Institute of Brooklyn.

plant is threatening to render the earth uninhabitable for humankind, and we find ourselves stymied at every turn in attempts to understand and control our presently murderous course. Nonetheless, bemused by our material standard of living and overlooking the fact that it is at present totally dependent on our grossly unequal consumption of the world's resources (which we, in fact, consume most inefficiently and wastefully),[2] countries that are now vastly expanding their school systems seek the advice that Western experts have to offer.

The questions therefore arise: what directions are the fast-growing educational systems in Africa taking? What is the nature of Western influences upon them? The nations of Africa do, of course, state their strong intentions of borrowing selectively as they frame their designs for contemporary living. They wish to choose as they see fit, both from the West and the East, and always with a view to how innovations can be adapted to their particular circumstances — their present needs and their cultural traditions. Unfortunately, however, this commitment to social and cultural autonomy is often at odds with the lack of full economic independence from the neocolonial bonds with which most African nations have to contend. Furthermore, the resulting difficulties are exacerbated by the enormous pressure African governments are under to achieve more quickly than is realistic the level of material comfort for their people that is commonly (and incorrectly) assumed to be enjoyed by the overwhelming majority in Western countries. And finally, recognition of the need for alternatives to Western-style education conflicts both with the institutionalization of nineteenth-century patterns of Western schooling introduced into Africa by the missions and with the tendency to see Western-style education as the avenue for achieving material success. Important experiments with alternative forms are under way, but at this writing they are not yet widely influential.

It was with a view to exploring both the nature of contemporary Western influences on educational practices, and what the bases are for African alternatives, that I visited Zambia during the spring and fall months of 1970. In both city and countryside I gathered material that pertained to three relationships: (1) The relationship between the role school played in preparing children for adult life and the attitudes towards

---

[2] "The United States, with 6 percent of the world's population, uses a third of the energy output" (*Science* 1973). As another statistic, the United States consumes more than one half-of the world's nonreplaceable raw materials. In the *Sierra Club Bulletin*, September, 1965, Hugo Fischer, administrator of the Resources Agency of California, estimated that, given the current rate of growth and consumption, the United States in 1982 would have 9.5 percent of the world's population consuming 83 percent of all raw materials produced by the entire world.

schooling held by children, teachers, and parents. (2) The relationship between the school curriculum and children's out-of-school experience. (3) The relationship between Western influences on teaching styles and curriculum content, past and present, and the understanding of today's most forward-looking educators as to how children can be prepared in school for a creative, humanistic, and rational approach to the mastery of social and technological problems.

In Zambia, I spent most of my time in the capital city of Lusaka, where I observed classrooms in three primary schools. The rest of the time I spent in a village near the provincial capital of Chipata, near the Malawi border, where I observed classrooms in two rural and one small city school. I also observed children at play and at work in whatever situations presented themselves. I am greatly indebted to the Zambian research assistants who worked with me to gather additional data: interviews with children, teachers, parents, and other adults; descriptions and explanations of games and other children's activities; translations of children's songs and stories, and of those classroom sessions that were conducted in Cinyanja (the language taught along with English in Zambia's central and eastern provinces).

I am writing up the body of this material elsewhere.[3] What I want to discuss here are some negative aspects of the role Western social scientists can and do play as research workers and consultants in relation to educational programs and policies, when they are not sensitive to their own biases and when they choose to ignore the realities of economic and political constraints on African countries. Westerners all too commonly accept and work from an ill-formulated series of assumptions about "traditional" societies and processes of "modernization" that both idealize Western schooling and underrate — or indeed may outright derogate — the scientific and intellectual content of African life and culture. These assumptions run parallel to assumptions about the "culture of poverty," a concept that was elaborated and introduced into educational parlance in the United States during the sixties as a supposed explanation for poor school performance on the part of children from low-income homes. At the same time as it was being argued that the home backgrounds of poor and of black children were robbing them of the motivation and the ability to succeed at school, the study of New York City schools in which I and my colleagues were engaged was revealing some of the mechanisms whereby expectations of failure were being

---

[3]   In addition to the research report, "Primary schooling in Africa," an article entitled "At play in African villages," is already available as part of a special supplement in *Natural History Magazine* (December, 1971).

projected onto these children, albeit often unwittingly, by hard-working and well-intentioned teachers.[4]

Some children have indeed been deeply hurt by conditions of dire poverty and demoralization and need special attention. Most children of the poor, however, have diverse abilities and coping skills. They are eager to learn and their parents are eager for them to learn, as evidenced by the enormous energy that community people have expended in efforts to improve educational opportunities for their children. It is school, in effect, that destroys children's interest and that plays an active part in socializing them for "outsider" roles (Lauter and Howe 1970). In his criticism of education in Third World nations, Ivan Illich (1970) discusses the extent to which schools are structured to keep poor children out of avenues for social and economic advancement, rather than to let them in.

Basically, the "culture of poverty" concept was built around an implied contrast between active, able, rational, goal-oriented, middle-class people, and fatalistic, incapable, traditional, impulse-ridden, lower-class people.[5] As such, it expressed in slightly new form old stereotyped views of class, ethnic, and/or racial inferiority that have long rationalized unequal opportunities for children who are lower class or nonwhite (see Drucker 1971). Similar stereotypes also appear in supposedly objective studies of how poorly African children are prepared for "modern" education by their home backgrounds. One can read of school difficulties as caused by "the presence of conservative, traditional, and primitive cultures often antagonistic to both the modern literary-humanistic and the science-rationalistic value systems (DeWitt 1969:125), or of the "basic intellectual hindrances to national development" in cultures that

[4] A point tested in the ingenious study by Robert Rosenthal and Lenore Jacobson (1968). A recent dissertation by Mary Ruth Harvey (1972) reports "virtually no inclassroom social behavior differences between children of low-income and high-income (black, white and racially mixed) schools at the 2nd grade level," but "extremely significant findings with respect to teacher treatments and 'feedback systems' in the low- and high-income classrooms, ... of a nature from which ultimate differences in social behavior and academic performance between low- and high-income (in expected directions) could be predicted." Harvey continues (personal communication), "examination of other data (curricula, attitudinal, etc.) supports the picture of low-income children being quite literally 'taught' how to fail and how to conform to negative stereotypes."

[5] Oscar Lewis writes "traits include a high incidence of material deprivation, of immorality, of weak ego structure, confusion of sexual identification, a lack of impulse control, a strong present-time orientation with relatively little ability to defer gratification and to plan for the future, a sense of resignation and fatalism, a wide-spread belief in male superiority, and a high tolerance for psychological pathology of all sorts" (1965:xlvii). For further discussion of the poverty culture concept, see Leacock (1971).

provide "little in the way of scientific concepts" to children (Poole 1968:57, 62). In most cases, however, such assumptions are implied rather than overtly stated.

As was the case in New York City, a close look at children in and out of school in the East African nation of Zambia rendered such statements meaningless. Children's out-of-school life was rich in experiences on which to build a "humanistic" and "rationalistic" curriculum. Furthermore, the "conservative traditionalism" of the schools was not so much that of autonomous African society, but that of mission school authoritarianism as it persists in the contemporary economic and political context of neocolonialism.

The varied influences, past and present, of the schooling introduced into Africa by missionary educators are complicated to unravel. On the credit side, the early mission schools introduced literacy itself, the tool that gives access to worldwide communication and to the accumulated body of written knowledge about natural processes and about human history. Moreover, these schools were sometimes taught by impressive and dedicated individuals. On the debit side, they were characterized by harsh discipline, rote teaching, and a curriculum that stressed European history and the classics. In other words, they introduced a body of largely irrelevant ritual knowledge, such as languages no longer spoken and some mixture of myth and fact about Europe and the classical Mediterranean world, as essential for entry into avenues for training in Western law, politics, science, and literature, or, at the very least, for entry into clerical jobs in the lower echelons of the colonial administration.

The closest counterpart of the mission school in traditional African society was the schooling prior to initiation, when adolescents mastered certain social and ritual lore before they were formally entered into adult status. Such schooling was rote and authoritarian. By contrast, however, the learning of technological and social skills took place in the free context of play, participation, and experimentation, as has been recorded in descriptions of traditional African practice (Kenyatta i.p.; Mair 1965; Read 1960; Edel 1957). Furthermore, the experimentation through play, and practice through work, of the children I observed in Lusaka and in the countryside near Chipata, was rich in cognitively meaningful experience, often of precisely the kind cited by contemporary educational theorists as affording a sound basis for learning.[6]

Another complication introduced into the African scene from the West is the standardized ability test. Along with the acceptance of

---

[6]   As presented, for example, in the manuals of the Nuffield Mathematics Project, such as *Beginnings* (Nuffield Mathematics Project 1970).

Western models for education, there has been the increasing tendency to equate school performance with ability and to adopt "intelligence tests" to select students for admission to secondary schools and universities. What such tests measure, however, has long been recognized as the previous training and experience of a given child, which are virtually impossible to separate from whatever "innate intelligence" may mean. Since tests have traditionally been constructed by middle-class Western-trained social scientists along lines that are familiar to them, their use in the West has acted to reinforce institutionalized patterns of educational and occupational discrimination by race and class. Although the prevalence of testing has been cogently and repeatedly criticized, the use of tests to determine chances for advancement in school or in a job has not decreased. Instead, the pervasive use of testing has itself influenced the designing of curricula. Since the way in which most intelligence tests are constructed presupposes that intelligence is based on thinking along the formal lines of a logical proof, and since the relation between test-taking ability and various kinds of creative thought remains obscure, the effect of this influence has been pernicious.

In the study of African children, the problem of testing has been compounded by the fact that Western researchers have all too commonly observed the children's performance in formally structured situations that involve the manipulation of unfamiliar materials in unfamiliar ways. Understandably, African children have been found "lacking" by comparison with Western children. Fortunately, some researchers have become more sophisticated about differences in culturally patterned skills and have found that varying the test to fit children's previous experience, and finding ways to present them in more familiar terms, can reduce group differences between African and Western children to the point where they disappear altogether (Cole, et al. 1971).

Yet the fundamental problem of what is being tested for remains, and it is complicated by questions about the relation between cultural traditions and individual thought processes. African writers, philosophers, and statesmen have for some time commented on the greater sense of community they see as characterizing Africa (by comparison with the competitive individualsim of Europe) and the greater sense of identity with the natural environment; and anthropologists have long been interested in recording non-Western ideologies and symbol systems. However, appropriate deductions have often been made about the effect traditional world views and mythologies may have on the carrying out of practical, "rational" technological activities. The historical interweaving of speculative thought and group experiences embodied in one or another philosophical system has been treated as if it arose as a direct reflection of individual thought process, or as if it directly affects individual thought in a one-to-one relation. In other words, the assumption has been made that the body of scientific knowledge accumulated in the West is the direct product of "rational" and "abstract" individual thought processes, precisely those processes that intelligence tests presume to tap. The existence of various Western mythologies is ignored in such reasoning, as are the variety of non-Western technologies. And non-Western children are found to have less "ability" for "scientific" reasoning than Western children.

The Western mythology that surrounds such thinking is nicely illustrated by a newspaper article on Albert Einstein (*New York Times* 1972:26). Einstein wrote about "thinking" as the process through which "sense impressions" move to "memory-pictures" and become ordered in a "concept" that may or may not be connected with a word or "a sensorily cognizable and reproducible sign." When it becomes so connected, it is communicable. When thinking about light waves, Einstein imagined himself in a "thought experiment" to be "riding through space, so to speak, astride a light wave and looking back at the wave next to him." However, in contradiction to the pictorial imagery Einstein speaks of himself as employing, the newspaper article reporting the second example was entitled, "The Einstein papers: the childhood of a genius displayed a gift for the abstract." If it was the great scientist Einstein, it must have been "abstract" (see also Schlipp 1959:7).

The point is that tests which measure what children can do with "logical" and "abstract" problems, to see IF they are able to learn "science," are constructed according to a series of confusions. The products of experimentation and considered judgement are everywhere in Africa, e.g. the technologies of agriculture, animal domestication, leather work, wood work, pottery and brick making, metallurgy, upon which African societies were built. And today, the activities children carry on by themselves reveal the foundation upon which training in conscious conceptualization can be built. Although African countries have made tremendous strides in creating new educational materials set in an African context as far as formal content goes, they are still constructed in terms of Western models that are inadequate, not only for African children, but for children generally.

Not only in children's out-of-school experiences are there rich and virtually untapped potentials for curriculum development, but these also exist in certain qualities of teacher-student and student-teacher classroom interaction. The classrooms I observed shared the problems that have been noted for school life generally in the newly industrializing nations. The limited amount of teaching materials and equipment is an important one. Although Zambia has accomplished an enormous amount in making available new primers and workbooks written for Zambian children, as well as teaching manuals, charts, and other aids, the rapid expansion of primary education has made it extremely difficult to produce these in adequate supply. Also, the prevalence of rote teaching (although considerably modified by comparison with older practice); the great emphasis on English and mathematics to the detriment of science, social studies, and creative activities; and the strict discipline in the classrooms even with the first and second grades — all contrast with the contemporary emphasis in the West on the active participation of children in the educational process. However, while good experimental schools in the West can be found as models for what education COULD be, the "freedom" of the ordinary Western public school is no more than some mix of children's bored and frustrated rebelliousness and the teacher's inconsistent authoritarianism and lack of rapport with the children; and lessons supposedly based on "discussion" or "involvement" or "experimentation" are superficial and manipulative. On the other hand, several features of the Zambian classrooms I visited contrasted with New York City classrooms in ways that seem to me of great importance in the learning process. Among these were:

1. The ability of the children to share, even pens and rulers, and to bend three heads over one reading book, when necessary, without shoving and jostling for place.

2. The protection of the children from the anxiety of individual performance through teaching methods largely based on group recital. However, the children did have the chance to perform individually in many lessons when they were called on to raise their hands. Children did, it is true, subject each other at times to harsh criticism by somewhat derisive laughter. Some teachers accepted this; others, however, chided the children for laughing at classmates. In any case, the structuring of the lessons strongly emphasized the group.

3. A quality of supportiveness on the part of the teachers that might seem in contradiction to the general strictness and "authoritarian" atmosphere of the classroom. There has been much confusion surrounding social-psychological research on education in the United States, especially that which in the past centered on a so-called authoritarian versus democratic classroom style. Strictness was virtually equated with rejection and lack of respect for children and permissiveness with a "democratic" acceptance. However, when strictness means the defini-

tion of a clear-cut structure for work and of high demands for performance, it is not the same thing as harshness and punitiveness. Furthermore, so-called permissiveness, when it becomes a matter of cajolery and manipulativeness, can be very nonsupportive to children. In any case, the teachers I observed in Zambian classrooms were strict, and would on occasion hit the children, but were not derisive or undermining, with one or two exceptions.

4. A last feature of many Zambian classrooms that presented itself strongly to me as an observer was a certain sense of teaching as a performance, a sense of style about it. Style is, of course, a highly individual matter, and one never knows when one may run into a teacher who possesses a quality of real artistry. On the whole in the West, however, teacher training schools threaten to replace this sense of personal style with the characteristically "school-teacherish" voice, mannered, controlled, superficial. The teacher role in Zambia seems to have taken on something of the traditional style of storytelling, legal disputation, or public discussion, where great attention was paid to skill in oral presentation. Some teachers were clearly enjoying having their teaching observed and showed skill in presentation that was not derived from formal education, reacting sensitively to the mood of the children, winning them back from inattention with a change in pace, a humorous illustration. Even some of those who were clearly nervous and constrained at being observed by an outsider began to enjoy displaying their skills as they relaxed.

The present curriculum, with its great emphasis on English, however, constrains this skill. The assumption is that children must first become literate in English in order to be prepared to learn more effectively later on, but the highly formal mode of teaching fails to integrate language learning with content of real meaning and use to them. The detailed manuals and lesson plans, while on the one hand an enormous accomplishment and advance, can mislead an insecure teacher (especially, I should add, when being observed) who feels he must be followed without deviation. I observed several sessions with nice interchange with the children on the basis of experiences of their own outside of the structure of the lesson plans, indeed, as examples of the kind of content and style that should be expressed in the manuals.

Finally, as impressive as the strides are that have already been taken in curriculum development, the task that remains is enormous. Not only in relation to science, but also in relation to history texts and reading materials, there is a pressing need to take account of the real events that were taking place both up to the European invasion of Africa and over the last some four and a half centuries in Africa. As research into African history proceeds and as rich new materials become available for school texts, there is a great need for people to rework them. An article in the *Zambia Mail* (1970) addressed itself to this problem. One hopes it will not be too much longer that children will have to work through such lessons as those I heard being read both in Lusaka and in a Chipata classroom: "Many years ago, there were no big roads in Africa. There were only many narrow little roads which led from one village to another .... In those days men did not travel about very much ...." Some of the children who read through such texts have grandfathers who still talk of the vast migrations which their fathers and grandfathers, in turn, knew from their youth. Their style and their content remain to be fully embedded in curriculum materials, both for African children and for enrichment of our thinking about education generally.

REFERENCES

COLE, MICHAEL, JOHN GAY, JOSEPH A. GLICK, DONALD W. SHARP
    1971   *The cultural context of learning and thinking.* New York: Basic Books.
DE WITT, NICHOLAS
    1969   "Some problems of science education in the developing countries of Africa," in *The social reality of scientific myth, science and social change.* Edited by Kalman H. Silvert. New York: American Universities Field Staff.
DRUCKER, ERNEST
    1971   "Cognitive styles and class stereotypes," in *The culture of poverty: a critique.* Edited by Eleanor Burke Leacock. New York: Simon and Schuster.
EDEL, MAY M.
    1957   *The Chiga of western Uganda.* New York: Oxford University Press.
HARVEY, MARY RUTH
    1972   "Differential treatment of upper-income and lower-income children by the public schools." Unpublished dissertation, Department of Psychology, University of Oregon.
ILLICH, IVAN
    1970   *Deschooling society.* New York: Harper and Row.
KENYATTA, JOMO
    i.p.   *Facing Mount Kenya.* New York: Random House.
LAUTER, PAUL, FLORENCE HOWE
    1970   How the school system is rigged for failure. *New York Review of Books* (June 18).
LEACOCK, ELEANOR BURKE
    1969   *Teaching and learning in city schools: a comparative study.* New York: Basic Books.
    1970   "Education, socialization, and 'the culture of poverty,'" in *Schools*

against children: the case for community control. Edited by Annette T. Rubenstein. New York: Monthly Review Press.

LEACOCK, ELEANOR BURKE, editor
1971   The culture of poverty: a critique. New York: Simon and Schuster.

LEWIS, OSCAR
1965   La vida. New York: Random House.

MAIR, LUCY P.
1965   An African people in the twentieth century. New York: Russell and Russell.

New York Times
1972   Article appearing in the New York Times. March 27, page 26.

NUFFIELD MATHEMATICS PROJECT
1970   Beginnings. London: W. and R. Chambers and John Murray.

POOLE, H. E.
1968   The effect of urbanization upon scientific concept attainment among Hausa children of northern Nigeria. British Journal of Educational Psychology 38.

READ, MARGARET
1960   Children of their fathers. New Haven: Yale University Press.

ROSENTHAL, ROBERT, LENORE JACOBSON
1968   Pygmalion in the classroom: self-fulfilling prophecies and teacher expectations. New York: Holt, Rinehart and Winston.

SCHLIPP, PAUL ARTHUR, editor
1959   Albert Einstein: philosopher-scientist. New York: Harper.

Science
1973   Editorial. Science 180 (4091).

Zambia Mail
1970   "Education needs Zambian authors." Zambia Mail. October 3.

Violence in Urban Public Education in the United States

WOODROW W. CLARK, JR.

Editors' Note: In this paper Woodrow W. Clark, Jr. attempts to give a comprehensive "contextual" picture of different sorts of events which may be termed
"violence" as they occur in American public schools. He draws on field observations of students and schools of various economic levels in order to give
substance to an application of linguistic and other varieties of "rule theory" in
his analysis. His paper deals with one of the most often phrased problems of
educators and policy scientists, but it puts it into an entirely new theoretical
framework. As new applications of this sort continue to be worked out, we
may expect anthropology to make more and more significant contributions
to educational theory and practice.

"The ultimate kind of power is violence" wrote Mills (1956:71). Assuming that Mills meant both physical and psychological violence, he
posed issues which other scholars are beginning to research. Coser (1956)
soon posited the constructive and functional aspects of conflict. However,
the most positive proclaimer of the virtues of violence is Franz Fanon,
the French scholar, in the late 1950's. Heretofore, philosophers like
Sartre (see especially 1963) and Camus battled over the meaning of
existentialism in contemporary society. The roots of violence can be
traced back into antiquity (Rubinstein 1970). However, the 1960's "brought
violence home" with the burning of numerous American cities and the
willful destruction of property. "Violence is as American as apple pie,"
asserted Stokely Carmichael (1968).

The hysteria associated with American cities burning and property
being threatened — "Those Negroes are coming over here next" — could
only be soothed by the declaration of the Nixon administration for
"law and order." The city fires have been less frequent. There is probably
no causal relationship between city fires and the Nixon regime. Other

institutions, such as prisons, are the new volcanoes.

However, the public schools have always been centers of violence. Stabbings, rape, beatings, and gang wars have existed for decades. Physical violence has become a way of life for most urban students. The schools become the focal point for violence in cities since they are the institutions for enculturation into American society. The values and norms of the dominant American culture are forced daily upon students from a variety of cultural backgrounds.

Upon closer examination, schools commit psychological violence upon students. Whether they are urban or suburban, schools are institutional ghettos. The result is the psychological destruction of the student. The increasing number of dropouts reflects this kind of mental anguish. Consider also the large numbers who are drop-ins; that is, students who stay in schools but have been mentally destroyed. The dropouts, in many cases, are probably the "wiser" students in that they escaped perhaps before it was too late.

Space does not allow for an elaborate analysis of the topic of violence (Clark 1971a, 1971b). In the short space available three factors will be considered. The first concerns the school as the context for analysis. Second is physical violence as the event under study. Third is the use of formal linguistic methods as an approach to analyzing violence and its influence upon schools and students.

THEORY

Before discussing the data, some preliminary remarks must be made about the theoretical perspective. Drawing heavily upon the recent research in generative semantics, far-reaching implications can be made for our study. Robin Lakoff (1972) explained the current view of linguistics as being a synthesis of syntax, semantics, and programatics (i.e. culture). Previous distinctions which were made between these areas for convenient analytical purposes are no longer valid. This view is shared by the generative semantics school of linguistics (George Lakoff, James McCawley, and Paul Postal, et al.) as opposed to the transformationalists (Chomsky 1965). The paradigm change (Kuhn 1972) is significant to anthropologists working in the area of ethnoscience and linguistic methodology.

Another theoretical perspective in this study is to take an event and analyze it. Consider this statement by Paul Bohannan (as quoted in Burnett 1973:12–13):

It is only with the introduction of the concept of the recurrent events that social change can be understood, for the simple reason that all events do not fit into such cycles that are predictable to actors in this situation. There are, everywhere and no matter how rarely, *unpredictable events, which disrupt the institution and its characteristic events. Such disrupting events by changing the nature of the cycle lead to new adjustments within all the institutional systems and hence to new repetitive event systems.* At one level of generalization, the nonrepetitive events are equivalent to what the computer analysts call random shock. At another, they comprise history. (Emphasis added).

Public schools have been studied by social scientists from many perspectives. However, most attention is given to the classroom situation. Indeed these situations and the events that take place within such a setting can be characterized as "recurrent" events. As Burnett puts it: "The regularity does not guarantee that every child will have the experience, but it greatly increases the possibility and probability that the child will have that experience" (1973:12).

Our study focuses upon the "unpredictable events" which Bohannon emphasized. In particular, our analysis concentrates upon a riot that took place before school hours on the school grounds. The riot became recurrent since there were two actual large confrontations with violent outcomes within the period of a week. The event(s) "cycle lead to new adjustments within all the institutional systems and hence to new repetitive event systems." (Bohannan cited in Burnett 1973). From a historical perspective these violent events are common and recurrent by generations within any public school.

CONTEXT

Rosewood High School is located in a moderately large city (200,000) in the Midwest. The city has two major industries: agribusiness and a university. The university students are counted for population census purposes (revenue sharing and state tax dollars) but are disenfranchised politically from voting. The city has a moderate nonpolitical mayor, but the area generally votes Republican in local, state, and federal elections. Rosewood is one of three high schools spread throughout the city. Each school has about 2,000 students. Racially, each school has between 11 to 15 percent black students; the rest are white. Rosewood is the newest of the schools (completed in 1965) and is situated in the upper middle-class area of the city. Black students must be bussed in or driven to school. Few walk — not only because of the distance (about 1 1/2 miles), but also because the only routes go through the all-white community.

The black section of town is called the North End and is typical of most black ghetto communities (Clark 1970). On the fringes there are working-class black and white families in the same neighborhood. The few professional black families in the city have moved out of the North End into the more fashionable larger homes in the white middle-class community.

The high schools have been integrated for many years. The oldest city high school (Ravenswood) borders the student, black, and low-income white ghettos. The overcrowding in this school necessitated the construction of a new high school. Rosewood is beautifully situated upon a hill with vast amounts of land surrounding it, including a complete track and field, parking lots, and open playground space. On the south side of the high school is Maplewood Middle School with about 1,000 students.

Wood Valley Public School System is a unified district. The high schools and elementary schools are coterminous. There are about 18,000 students in the district serviced by three high schools, six middle schools, and twelve elementary schools. As districts go, Wood Valley is fairly well-off economically. With a major university within its borders, the district has an ample supply of well-qualified teachers.

The district central administration could be labeled liberal. Again, this is partially due to the university omnipotence. Several years ago the district was the scene of two significant United States Supreme Court cases dealing with the schools. One involved the separation of religious instruction from the public schools; the other case involved the right of a teacher to use controversial materials in the curriculum.

Since that time, the district administration has been creative and supportive of innovation. The same is not true at the individual school site level. The state teacher's association dominates, with the local AFL-CIO union barely getting enough members to warrant a chapter. The union is not recognized by the central office. Within the high schools the administration and staff are conventional and conservative. New teachers bringing creative ideas are a function of the graduate school population at the university. Those staff members who stay within the district are permanent, life-long residents of Wood Valley. They tend to view education as a secure, safe, and stable occupation.

Social stratification within the schools is a major consideration when analyzing the context in which physical violence takes place. Greater change and creativity can be detected on the part of the students. As in any institutional setting, the creativity and outspokeness on the part of one group (students) will lead to a direct threat on another group (staff). Using Goffman's actors and audience approach (1959), consider the three major casts of characters at Rosewood High School.

The administration of Rosewood is headed by Dr. Hartz Mountain, who has his education degree from the university. Dr. Mountain is a quiet, unassuming, small, white man. He believes in strict adherence to rules, although he fails to make them explicit or enforce them equitably. The vice-principals are life-long residents of Wood Valley who have risen through the teaching ranks. The teachers themselves, like the administrators, are all whites from middle-class backgrounds. There are two teacher groups: the resident and the transient. The former are Wood Valley born and bred, virtually products of the area. The latter are university student wives and graduate students. In most cases the resident group is conservative and very conventional in its approach to education. The transient teachers are aggressive, young, and often union members who want to try and experiment with all sorts of teaching methods and materials.

The second group of actors in the school is the students. Racially, there are white and black students. However, contrary to many studies on high school students, the classification of school students should be on a socioeconomic scale. There are the rich, the working-class, and the poor students. Analyzing each group will prove useful.

The wealthy students of Wood Valley all attend Rosewood High. Each high school takes students from geographical areas; the wealthiest area of the city falls within the Rosewood attendance area. These students drive their own cars (usually new), buy expensive clothes, and take expensive vacations. They perform better than any other group in school on tests and with grades. They are the school leaders. There are a few black students in this category. Drugs are common. Family problems are even more common. The father works and the mother belongs to several social clubs.

Working-class (or middle-class) students come from a variety of backgrounds. The parents both work, a situation which leads to family problems different from those of the first group. Solutions to family discussions are usually violent and psychologically damaging to the entire family. Cars are an important factor to students in this group. They are a symbol of power, authority, and respect. Usually the student has a job to pay for the car and it's "fixed up" for looks and speed.

The poor students are predominantly black; however, an increasing number of transient welfare white families fall into this category. Surprisingly enough, the poor students are being surpassed by the other two groups in numbers of dropouts and failures. Families are often broken up. This category of student was allegedly responsible for the riots.

The pressures exerted by the administration to achieve and perform by the norms set by the wealthy students placed the poor students in a no-win situation. The poor students were constantly being "put down." For example, special programs were created to get these "behavioral" problem students out of the schools. One such off-campus program was originally intended to service all the high schools, but 70 percent of the students were coming from Rosewood High via the recommendation of Dr. Mountain. Several other instances reflected the school administration's lack of equal treatment in enforcing rules and regulations. At one point some wealthy students were caught smoking and only warned, while some poor black students were suspended immediately for the same offense.

EVENTS

The stage is set. The characters are described. The curtain opens. In early fall of 1971, minor fights broke out at Rosewood. Dr. Mountain claimed that he had 1 percent more black students than the other high schools. This would mean, that he had 20.5 more black students. The implication is that within that group Dr. Mountain could find his problem(s) and solve it (them).

Dr. Mountain took two steps to correct the situation. First, he either suspended or referred to the special off-campus program at least eighteen students (mostly black). Second, he enforced school rules more rigidly. However, he was more lenient on the black middle-class students and more severe on the white poor students. The group most directly affected was all the poor students. White students hated all black students. Dr. Mountain assumed the problem to be racial: "After all, black and white students are different. How can they exist together?" This was the principal's analysis of the situation.

One incident in early November finally provoked a confrontation between poor white students and poor black students. A white student in a wheelchair was deliberately set on fire in the boys' bathroom. The student claimed that two black "boys" did it. Talk spread. Rumors flew. The principal had been warned of trouble. Yet on a Wednesday morning in Mid-November at 8:10 A.M., fifty male and female black students walked off their buses into a large group of white male students swinging clubs and chains. Dr. Mountain was nowhere to be found. Some students claim he hid under his desk. The police were not summoned until 8:26 A.M., and failed to arrive for another fifteen minutes. An investigation was under way to determine the reasons for the police "delay." By that time it was too late: twenty-seven students (almost all black) were hospitalized, several severely injured.

A second riot occurred the following Monday. Several hundred poor white students attacked a group of poor black students in the school parking lot after school. This time the black students were prepared. The result was more injuries, police, and community hysteria. The schools were closed for a week. Parent meetings were called. Dr. Mountain blamed the "race riot" on outside troublemakers. He felt that there were several black students who helped to cause the trouble. Suspensions were handed out to thirty-five black students and ten white students. Other schools in the district reported outbreaks of violence as a protest against the suspensions. Dr. Mountain claimed the suspensions were "for the students' own protection."

Throughout the week, discussions between students, administrators, and parents took place. Dr. Mountain continued to point his finger at the black troublemakers. After some lengthy and heated arguments, students and parents alike uncovered Dr. Mountain's approach to education: replication of white upper middle-class values and norms. A public outcry was expressed by the end of the week. Finally, on the Sunday before Thanksgiving, the black and white communities demanded the resignation of Dr. Mountain. The superintendent considered the demand carefully. Then on Sunday evening Dr. Mountain spoke in a local television interview. He restated his original claims. This time, however, he accused the community people of meddling in matters that were best handled by professional educators and implied that integration of the schools was at the root at the problem of violence. By Monday afternoon he was relieved of his duties.

Since this event took place, Rosewood has gone through some changes. The district has put more black teachers and administrators into the school and has structured the high school administration in an innovative manner: one high school for the whole district with three separate campuses. The problems still exist and many issues remain unresolved. The new administrator for all the high schools came from a poor white background. This has made a difference. Prior to the new assignment, he was principal of one other Wood Valley High School (Ravenswood). He had taken the position after a series of riots in the late 1960's which had caused the previous principal to resign. His record was impressive: he was fair and equally just with all students. His background allowed him to handle a variety of difficult problems and potentially violent eruptions. For example, after the Rosewood riot his school was the only quiet one in the district. Finally, he did not push upper middle-class values and norms on any students. His educational philosophy included equality and open access, not molding students into predetermined roles.

RULES

Linguistics and Anthropology

With the descriptive data presented, the next step is to theoretically inter-relate the information. In two previous works (Clark 1972, 1973), the use of current linguistic theory and methods in the analysis of sociocultural phenomenon had been explored. The analogy between language and culture (Whorf-Sapir Hypothesis) assumes a direct cognitive processing. The use of language describes a cultural perspective and outlines the thought patterns of a particular people. Tyler sees "the formal analysis of culture, like a grammar, (which) is concerned only with what is expect-ed and appropriate" (1969:13). Earlier Tyler states the goal of cognitive anthropology as being "an attempt to understand the organizing princi-ples underlying behavior" (1969:3). He goes on to state: "The object of study is not these material phenomena themselves, but the way they are organized in the minds of men. Cultures then are not material phenomena; they are cognitive organizations of material phenomena" (1969:3).

At this point, a lengthy discussion of these issues would be counter-productive. The "formal analysis" in cognitive anthropology is based on structural linguistic notions. Chomsky (1965) has labeled such linguistic work as "taxonomic linguistics," implying that such work is narrow. In anthropology the interest in using structural linguistics has spread to related areas such as cultural transmission (Gearing 1973) and medical anthropology (American Anthropological Association 1973) among others. However, the use of structural linguistics in these areas may not be appropriate.

Our concern is in analyzing events and processes. Tyler points out that "neither prediction of actual events nor specification of developmental processes is a necessary component of a theory of culture" (1969:13–14). Yet he correctly qualifies that bold assertion in a footnote by stating that he does not want "to imply that such a theory is incompatible with the study of change and development. The point is that a theory of de-scription constitutes a different order of theory than that required for processes of change" (Tyler 1969:21, Note 10). Goodenough elaborates on what is involved in describing a people's culture as "their standards for perceiving, believing, evaluating, and acting" (1970:104).

This is precisely the point. The usefulness of cognitive anthropology must be seen in the descriptive realm of anthropological study.

Clearly, the use of structural linguistic analysis provided the linguists with the same sort of data. The time is ripe for another paradigm: the analysis of change and development in the light of current linguistic theories and methods. The attempt to explain, derive rules, analyze processes, and relate events can best be seen through the use of current linguistic thinking.

LINGUISTICS   Briefly, the argument goes in generative semantics that the linguist (and other social scientists) is interested in showing the interrelationships of elements in a language. Traditionally, the study of language contains three components: syntax, semantics or meaning, and phonetics or sounds. Chomsky (1965) has argued that the linguist need only be concerned with the study of syntax. Phonetics was already well accounted for by structural linguistics. Semantics was the concern of other social scientists. The generative semantists (G. Lakoff 1970a, 1970b, 1971; McCawley 1970) argue that language must be the study of all these areas together with the addition of pragmatics or cultural influences (R. Lakoff 1972).

In brief, Chomsky sees language as having deep and surface structures. The former "determines its (language) semantic interpretation;" the latter "determines its (language) phonetic interpretation" (Chomsky 1965:16). Transformations are then performed on the elementary parts of the deep structure yielding the surface structure.

Thus the syntactic component consists of a base that generates deep structures and a transformational part that maps them into surface structures. The deep structure enters the phonological component and undergoes phonetic interpretation (Chomsky 1965:135).

Chomsky concludes on the final effect of a grammar by stating it must

...relate a semantic interpretation to a phonetic representation — that is, to state how a sentence is interpreted. The relation is mediated by the syntactic component of the grammar, which constitutes its role creative parts (1965:136).

The arguments made by generative semantists against the transformationists are summarized in an earlier work (Clark 1971c). At this point let us emphasize three factors that relate to our current discussion. First, unlike Chomsky's view of a grammar, Lakoff posits a grammar being "thought of as generating triples of the form (L.S.C.) where L is a logical structure, S is a surface structure, and C is the class of contexts in which S can be used to express L" (1971:11). Such a theory of grammar denies the need of a deep structure (Lakoff 1971) which contains lexically marked items independent of the grammar. There is no artificial distinction between surface and deep structures (McCawley 1970).

Second, consider the notion for a rule of grammar. The Chomskian view uses phrase-structure rules and transformations as only "local rules" (Lakoff 1970b). Such local rules are limited in scope to defining well-formedness conditions only on individual phrase-makers and on pairs of successive phrase-markers in a particular derivation (Lakoff 1970b:627). The generative semantists argue for three kinds of rules: (1) local rules, (2) global rules, and (3) transderivational rules, with well-formedness conditions on each (Lakoff 1971:13). Without elaborating on the rules, the point is that there are rules relating structures which allow for an explanation of particular phenomenon provided that well-formedness conditions are met.

Finally, Lakoff argues that "the rules of grammar for a language are not separable from the rules that relate logical forms and surface forms" (1971:13, 15). Furthermore, he makes a claim that the recursive ability of rules in syntax is not independent of logical structures (Lakoff 1971: 15–16). The grammar of a language generates the triple form (L.S.C.) and not sentences (see Figure 1).

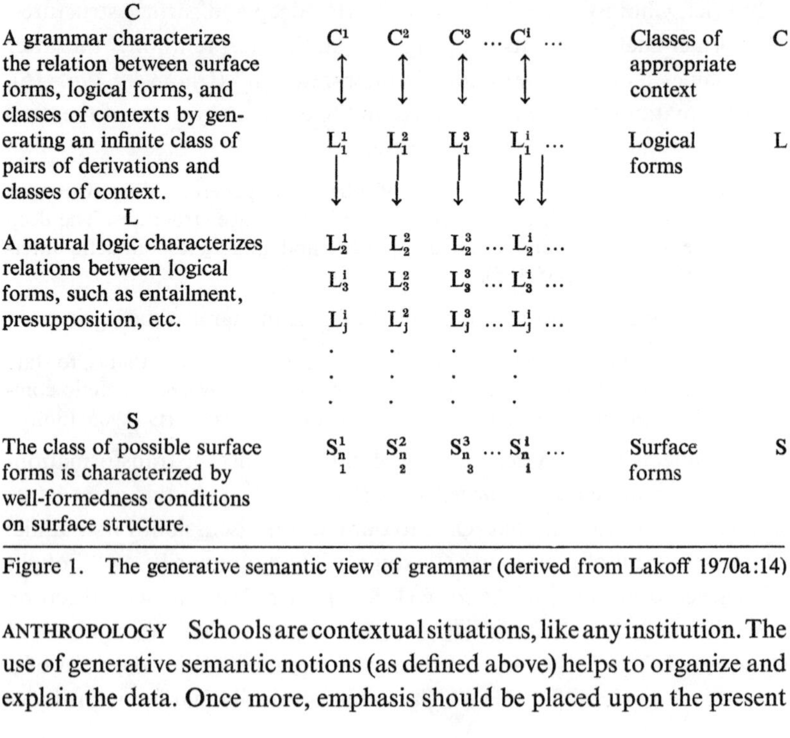

C
A grammar characterizes the relation between surface forms, logical forms, and classes of contexts by generating an infinite class of pairs of derivations and classes of context.

$$C^1 \quad C^2 \quad C^3 \ldots C^i \ldots \qquad \text{Classes of} \quad C$$
$$\uparrow\downarrow \quad \uparrow\downarrow \quad \uparrow\downarrow \quad \uparrow\downarrow \qquad \text{appropriate context}$$

$$L_1^1 \quad L_1^2 \quad L_1^3 \quad L_1^i \ldots \qquad \text{Logical} \quad L$$
$$\downarrow \quad \downarrow \quad \downarrow \quad \downarrow\downarrow \qquad \text{forms}$$

L
A natural logic characterizes relations between logical forms, such as entailment, presupposition, etc.

$$L_2^1 \quad L_2^2 \quad L_2^3 \ldots L_2^i \ldots$$
$$L_3^1 \quad L_3^2 \quad L_3^3 \ldots L_3^i \ldots$$
$$L_j^1 \quad L_j^2 \quad L_j^3 \ldots L_j^i \ldots$$

$$\cdot \qquad \cdot \qquad \cdot \qquad \cdot$$
$$\cdot \qquad \cdot \qquad \cdot \qquad \cdot$$
$$\cdot \qquad \cdot \qquad \cdot \qquad \cdot$$

S
The class of possible surface forms is characterized by well-formedness conditions on surface structure.

$$S_{n_1}^1 \quad S_{n_2}^2 \quad S_{n_3}^3 \ldots S_{n_i}^i \ldots \qquad \text{Surface} \quad S$$
$$\text{forms}$$

Figure 1.   The generative semantic view of grammar (derived from Lakoff 1970a:14)

ANTHROPOLOGY   Schools are contextual situations, like any institution. The use of generative semantic notions (as defined above) helps to organize and explain the data. Once more, emphasis should be placed upon the present use of linguistics in change and development theory rather than upon the applications made by cognitive theorists who are describing cultures.

The current analysis is incomplete, especially in the area of logical representation. The data takes the form of Figure 2. Phonological rules from a generative semantic perspective provide the model. The context is provided (/) with clear relationships shown (→) such that roles and functions are derived from the context and transmitted within a certain point in time for the event (—). The rules are then cyclic in that they individually or collectively feed back into each other (recursion).

The entire set of rules is recursive, meaning that the rules take place against another point in time (another event). Since these rules are related to physical violence, the recursive function would be related directly to a similar event. The following set of rules can be made now (Figure 2).

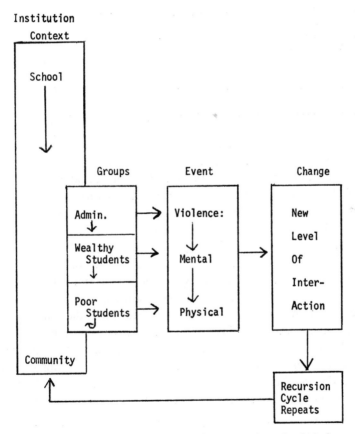

Figure 2. The school data: rules apply either on the horizontal axis (→) or on the vertical axis (↓). The rules are unilineal but are recursive. The result is a new level of interaction meaning that change has taken place

The first class in Table 1 yields a conflict situation with the second. However, the conflict is in the nature of gentlemanly argument, disagreement, and intellectual rationalization. The resultant rules can coexist. The violent conflict occurs between the second and the third classes producing rules that are bipolar. Here the violence is often psychological until a physical outburst relieves the frustration and anxiety. The third class and rule relate directly into the fourth since the two have the same common logical need for survival. Mention is not made of the upper- and working-class students since their role is marginal in the actual violence of the riot. The upper-class students are the models from which the school-site administration generated its rule.

Table 1.

Classes of context (C)	Logical forms (L)		Surface forms (S)
1. District/ administration	*Conventional, prosperous community* →		Educational change and reform
2. School-site/ administration	*Middle-class background*	→	All students must have upper middle-class values, norms, and standards
3. Poor students/	*Struggle for survival*	→	Enculturate and lose identity
4. Community/	*Struggle for survival*	→	Schools reflect needs and concerns

Before leaving the evidence presented, one thing is clear: the economic status of students influences the functions of education. The recent California Supreme Court Case (Serrano 1972) ruled that it was unconstitutional to have educational systems based upon a district's wealth. The evidence above and data collected by researchers (see Coleman 1966) indicated that the disparity between groups of students based on socioeconomic status is damaging to educational goals. In our study, the result of such a difference was a series of riots. However, the same discrepancy might surely influence learning and the educational process itself. As a result of the data presented above, the behavioral role of an administration favoring a certain normative pattern or model leads directly to violence against a particular group (mental, then physical).

The rules reflect a series of events, characters, and groups of people. The distinctions between each group depend upon the roles and functions of each. As Toch in *Violent men* (1969) quotes Colin McGlashan:

The black kids and the white cops — their pride, their fear, their isolation, their need to prove themselves, above all their demand for respect — are strangely alike: victims both, prisoners of an escalating conflict they didn't make and can't control (1969: vi).

The point is similar to that made about language by Lakoff: one cannot make artificial distinctions between people. In the school data, the administration acted out of a fear that was similar to that of the poor students. Within the context of the schools, there are cycles which produce change as Bohannon emphasized earlier (in Burnett 1973). The events become history. An understanding of the rules that govern these events will be instructive to future generations and may be transferable to other institutions. Some day the result may be a universal set of rules for all institutions.

CONCLUSION

In the near future, with enough interest and professional dialogue, there can be more precise and lengthier research into the areas suggested here. Immediate attention should be given to the three direct results of the research. First, theoretical and methodological clarification of issues in linguistics must be made since they might prove enlightening to anthropologists. From the data presented, the recent developments in the field of linguistics (since 1967) can be seen as extremely active in probing new ways to view and analyze problems. The important function for anthropologists would be to use some of the theories, methods, and perspectives developed by linguists. The long tradition of scholarly borrowing, especially in these two fields, is precedent enough.

Another area for investigation suggested by this study relates to the notion of institutions themselves. For example, how alike are schools, prisons, and office jobs? What are the roles and functions of individuals in each kind of setting? What are the rules for each? What kind of events are common to all institutions: mental and physical violence? Is there a universal set of rules that governs all institutions? These and other questions about the nature, use, and organization of institutions provide a rich source of data about the fabric of any developing culture.

Finally, there are issues directly related to the schools which anthropologists must further consider. In particular, as anthropologists, there is a need to address ourselves to the research and evaluation of schools and educational programs or projects where vast amounts of money and time are spent by local, state, and federal authorities. Currently, evaluation of educational programs and institutions comes primarily from educational psychologists. These modern-day "rat runners" are using schools as mazes and students as experimental rats. The results are predictable and dangerous. The analytical and evaluative skills of anthropologists must be more expediently utilized in order to counterbalance the extremely,

overbearing influence of psychologists (see Clark i.p.). The Street Academy
sites, through the Urban League, are attempting to take some anthropological approaches to program evaluation (Jackson 1973). Burnett (1973)
has outlined several evaluative processes used by anthropologists in the
analysis of culture-base educational curriculum. Other possible evaluative
measures could include: (1) linguistic-semantic descriptions, (2) rules and
cycles, (3) cultural self-rating scales, and (4) case or family histories.
Anthropologists interested in educational research must move into
evaluation; otherwise later generations may all be turned into little rats
going through a series of institutional mazes whether or not it is school,
or work, or hospitals, or prisons, or mental institutions, or....

REFERENCES

AMERICAN ANTHROPOLOGICAL ASSOCIATION
  1973   Program of the annual meetings, New Orleans.
BURNETT, JACQUETTA, et al.
  1973   "Toward culture-based educational development." Unpublished man-
         uscript, University of Illinois, Urbana.
CARMICHAEL, STOKELY, CHARLES V. HAMILTON
  1968   Black power. New York: Random House.
CHOMSKY, NOAM
  1965   Aspects of the theory of syntax. Cambridge, Mass.: M.I.T. Press.
  1973   Language and mind (second edition). New York: Harcourt, Brace and
         World.
CLARK, WOODROW W.
  1970   "Political structure of neighborhood black gangs." Bloomington:
         Central States Anthropological Association.
  1971a "La violencia and political conflict in Bogotá, Colombia." New York:
         American Anthropological Association.
  1971b "Violence in American public school education." Dissertation propos-
         al, University of Illinois, Urbana.
  1971c "Verb initial order in black standard English." Champaign: Champaign
         Illinois School System.
  1972   "Linguistic rules in anthropological research." Unpublished master's
         thesis, University of Illinois, Urbana.
  1973   "Linguistic rules in analyzing public schools." Tucson: Society for
         Applied Anthropology.
  i.p.   "The Anthropological evaluation of educational programs." Chicago:
         American Educational Research Association.
COLEMAN, JAMES S., et al.
  1966   Equality of educational opportunity. Washington, D. C.: U.S. Govern-
         ment Printing Office.
COSER, LEWIS
  1956   The functions of social conflict. New York: Free Press.

FANON, FRANZ
  1963   *The wretched of the earth.* New York: Grove Press.
GEARING, FRED O.
  1973   Where we are and where we might go: steps toward a general theory of cultural transmission. *Newsletter: Council on Anthropology and Education* 4(1): 1–10.
GOFFMAN, ERVING
  1959   *The presentation of self in everyday life.* New York: Anchor.
GOODENOUGH, WARD H.
  1970   *Description and comparison in cultural anthropology.* Chicago: Aldine.
JACKSON, BARBARA, *editor*
  1973   *Evaluation and documentation plan: Experimental Schools Street Academy Projects.* Cambridge, Mass.: National Urban League.
KUHN, THOMAS
  1972   *The structure of scientific revolutions.* Chicago: University of Chicago Press.
LABOV, WILLIAM
  1969   The logic of nonstandard English. *Florida Reporter* 7(1):60–74.
  1970   *The study of nonstandard English.* Champaign: National Council of Teachers of English.
LAKOFF, GEORGE
  1970a Linguistics and natural logic. *Synthese* 22: 151–271.
  1970b Global rules. *Language* 46(3):627–639.
  1971   "Introduction to the version of linguistics and natural logic," in *Handbook of cognitive psychology.* Edited by J. Mehler, 1–18.
LAKOFF, ROBIN
  1972   Lecture notes. University of California at Berkeley, Fall 1972.
MC CAWLEY, JAMES
  1970   "Syntact and logical arguments for semantic structures." Paper presented at the Fifth International Seminar on Theoretical Linguistics, Tokyo, August 1970.
MILLS, C. WRIGHT
  1956   *The power elite.* New York: Oxford University Press.
RUBINSTEIN, RICHARD
  1970   *Rebels in Eden.* Boston: Little, Brown.
SARTRE, JEAN PAUL
  1963   "Introduction," in *The wretched of the earth* by Franz Fanon. New York: Grove Press.
  1972   *Serrano v. Priest.* 96 Cal. Rptr. 601/487/P.2d/1241.
TOCH, HANS
  1969   *Violent men.* Chicago: Aldine.
TYLER, STEVEN, *editor*
  1969   *Cognitive anthropology.* New York: Holt, Rinehart and Winston.

Some Characteristics of Police Science as a Career-Related Program in Higher Education

ANDREW W. COUCH

Editors' Note: In the following paper Andrew Couch describes some of the factors which operate to distinguish a career-related police science program from other curricula in higher education. His thesis includes the suggestion that the close tie to concrete professional ambitions produces narrowly defined student interests and certain defferential relations to instructors. The latter is perhaps the more interesting phenomenon. One of the ostensible purposes often ideologically stated for American higher education is a "broadening" of the students' backgrounds. It appears from Mr. Couch's work that in fact certain characteristics of some institutional frameworks militate against this added breadth. Rather, the educational experience may be only an extension of a group solidarity. It is important for social scientists, public administrators, and politicians to understand the ways in which their theories and arguments of fact are subject to permutation or disregard due to the social factors of a professional situation. Further, it seems from Couch's paper that extensive further work with an aim to elucidating the input of police programs to this process would be in order.

In this paper I relate those characteristics of a Bachelor of Science program in Police Science and Administration that I regard as generic to all career-related programs in higher education. The material presented was gathered through intensive study of programs at two colleges in Southern California. Comparisons were made with a number of other programs and a variety of secondary sources. This paper is anthropological in that my primary methodology was participant-observation; I was a regularly matriculated student in the police science program, and none of my contacts, fellow students, or instructors knew me in any other capacity. I originally enrolled in the police science classes because I saw the academic setting as a means by which I could become acquainted with the policemen as "people" rather than study them in their role in the criminal justice system. In this paper I will confine my observations to a police science program in higher education, highlighting those aspects I feel are common to all such career-related programs.

METHODOLOGY

My first exposure to law enforcement education was at Los Angeles City College. I was a student in anthropology at the University of Southern California when I enrolled in a police science class at Los Angeles City College (LACC). The subject was criminal investigation, which sounded interesting, and I wanted to interact with the policemen in the class in a context of postulated equality. After completing three police science classes at LACC, I no longer viewed this exposure to policemen as a lark, but as an opportunity to study them. I therefore matriculated in the Bachelor of Science program in Police Science and Administration at California State University, Los Angeles (CSULA). Two differences between the institutions are important:

1.   LACC is a two-year institution, whereas CSULA offers a baccalaureate degree; with more classes, CSULA affords more exposure to policemen.

2.   LACC draws its student population from central Los Angeles, as opposed to CSULA, whose students come from all over Southern California, thereby maximizing my opportunities to interact with the greatest variety of policemen.

At CSULA, I tried to be as inconspicuous as possible. I maintained a conservative appearance, hair cut short and clothes slightly out of fashion. I tried to impersonate the typical police science student.

According to police science department statistics (which I obtained while preparing a term paper for a police science class), roughly 50 percent of police science majors at CSULA are employed in the criminal justice field. Thus I was not an oddity by not being so employed. In all of my conversations with my contacts, I tried to avoid the subject of my outside identity. I never deliberately misled anyone; I just did not volunteer any information. If the subject was broached, I said that I was a preservice student, too young to be employed by a police agency. In all such situations, I was never stigmatized for not being a policeman. It was perfectly acceptable for someone to study police science while he awaited his twenty-first birthday, and my age was not known. However, at times my fellow students were surprised that I was not a policeman; I take this as some measure of my success at blending in with them.

I am fully aware that some anthropologists believe the researcher is morally obligated to inform his subjects that they are being studied. I purposely did not so inform the police science department and my fellow police science students for two reasons: my research was rather mundane, adequate for impressions and certain areas of knowledge, but by no means pretentious; and I knew that such a revelation would totally alienate my contacts. The opinion of social scientists generally held by the policemen I encountered is such that it would have precluded any meaningful interaction with them. Their hostility would have activated the Hysenburg Uncertainty Principle to such an extent that my observations would have been restricted to the means by which policemen display contempt, and the observer would have indeed become the observed. I appreciate the reasoning employed by those anthropologists who argue that the social scientist is obliged to identify himself as such to his subjects; however, I do not accept it in this situation.

CHARACTERISTICS OF CAREER-RELATED PROGRAMS IN HIGHER EDUCATION, AS ILLUSTRATED BY THE POLICE SCIENCE AND ADMINISTRATION PROGRAM AT CSULA

These are some of the characteristics of the police science program at CSULA that I believe are a function of its career-related nature and are common to all such career-related programs.

1. Most full-time instructors are former practitioners in the field.
2. Career-related programs employ current practitioners as part-time instructors, contending that such adjunct faculty bring the latest developments in the field into the classroom.
3. Instructors are often hired on the basis of their accomplishments within the field, and their success within the field largely determines the relative esteem afforded them by students.
4. Students either aspire to practice within the field, or are employed within it at the entry level, and view their education as the means for advancement within the field.
5. Students are principally interested in the courses within the field and generally have little use for other courses, such as general education requirements or electives.
6. Students within career-related programs form recognizable cohorts predicated upon their perceived commonalities of interest.
7. Students in career-related programs who are already employed within the field, albeit at the entry level, are more assertive within the classroom and within the cohort.

Points 1 and 2 are both obvious and well documented in the literature. Who better to teach police work than a policeman? This assumption is based on a relative dearth of writing within the field, which serves to emphasize the lecture technique. There are few books which purport to instruct in the proper method to investigate the report of a prowler, for instance, and none do it adequately. An instructor who is a practitioner within the field can relate his personal experiences and thereby advise his students on what techniques he has found to be particularly effective. A part-time instructor who is a full-time practitioner can bring the very latest developments in the field into the classroom, and certainly the technological and social revolutions make the police service a constantly changing profession.

The notion that instructors are viewed in terms of their success within the field, both by the administration that hires them and by their students, is a personal observation that is nonetheless easily explained. If one had a choice of several policemen (or carpenters or electricians) for an instructor's position, one would be hard put not to hire the most successful, for those qualities and skills that made him the most successful would be worthy of imparting to his students. Because career-related programs are so instructor-dependent, with instructors serving as models for their students to emulate, the importance of providing the best possible models is obvious. What is not so obvious, and what I found startling, is that the instructor's accomplishments within the field are the sole basis for his evaluation as an instructor, and that bad instructors who were successful practitioners are still regarded as good instructors by school and students alike. In completing the requirements for the Bachelor of Science degree in Police Science and Administration, I was exposed to nineteen police science instructors; and of the nineteen, only the two who happened to be nonpolicemen were held to be bad instructors, to be avoided if possible. I base this statement upon my conversations with fellow students and upon the information supplied by the grapevine operated by the cohort of police science students that I will discuss later. One of these instructors was a ranking bureaucrat in the county probation department. In theory at least, the probation department and police agencies are allies in the war against crime; police agencies apprehend offenders, and the probation department reports to the court its recommendations of appropriate sentences for the convicted and supervises those placed on probation. In the eyes of the policemen in these police science classes, however, police agencies and the probation department are at cross-purposes. Policemen arrest offenders so that they will be incarcerated for as long as possible, yet the probation department often recommends lenient sentences and fails to adequately supervise those placed on probation (or so say the policemen). Worse still, the probation department burdens police agencies with paperwork regarding juvenile offenders and criminal records, thus wasting the police officers' time, which should properly be spent on the street fighting crime. For these reasons this instructor was disliked and avoided; his association with the probation department damned him. His ability as an instructor was not considered; and in point of fact he was better than average for the department.

The other unpopular instructor whom I personally experienced was a lawyer who had been a deputy district attorney but who now was in private practice. He had the unfortunate habit of illustrating a point of law by relating a situation in which he had employed it in successfully defending his client. This alienated his students, for they could empathize strongly with the policemen involved in each case; and when this instructor defeated them, he defeated his students as well. Several times this instructor was openly ridiculed for releasing criminals to prey on society, and his explanation that he was merely playing a role in the adversary system of American justice did little to abate such criticism. This instructor was also one of the better instructors in the department, yet he was also unpopular because he was perceived by his students as working at cross-purposes to the interests of the students.

The reason these two instructors were unpopular with their students (and apparently with the police science department, for their contracts were not renewed after the quarters in which I had them) is unique to law enforcement education. They lacked the ideological credentials necessary for acceptance by their students. Charles Tenney (1971) suggests that one reason that law enforcement education programs require that their instructors have police experience is that this guarantees that the instructors' attitudes and beliefs will conform to what is perceived as the law enforcement outlook. My observations of the student reaction to these instructors who lacked the appropriate ideological credentials support Tenney's claim.

However, police experience does not ensure that an instructor will be well received by his students. Some of the instructors with this qualification are more popular than others, and I believe that the more popular instructors are so regarded on the basis of their success as policemen and not on their abilities as instructors. This is more apparent when one considers the less popular instructors. To a man, they were assigned to police districts with a low crime rate; they were therefore not on the front lines of the war against crime. This severely eroded their credibility. For example, I can recall one such instructor describing some aspect of narcotics law enforcement and being defiantly asked, "When was the last time you saw a hype?" Unfortunately, it had been three or four years, and the hapless instructor's credibility suffered.

Those instructors with police experience who were popular were successful policemen. One who comes to mind was the commander of the division with the highest crime rate in Los Angeles. His lectures were nothing more than a reading of a notebook he had compiled on the subject. His exams were very difficult, and his grading was arbitrary. Worse still, he was often late for class. Yet the class waited for him and regarded him highly, I believe, because he was what everyone aspired to be. He had rank and a job that was seen as important by his students. The class anticipated with pleasure the moments when he would relate some personal experience, so that it could vicariously realize his success. If someone missed a class and asked a classmate what had transpired, the classmate would retell the instructor's stories, ignoring the lecture material. This instructor was more popular than most because he was what his students wanted to be; this suggests that students in career-related programs may want less to learn about the field than to be initiated into it.

This is substantiated by points 4 and 5. Students in career-related programs either aspire to practice within the field or are employed in it at the entry level. Police science department statistics reveal that 50 percent of all police science majors are not currently employed in the criminal justice system; of the remaining 50 percent that are so employed, 77 percent are at the entry level and 63 percent have been employed three years or less. It is apparent then that few police science students are well established within the field.

Point 5 contends that they have little interest in education *per se*, because I believe career-related students view their enrollment in higher education programs not as an opportunity to learn about the field, but as necessary in itself for their success within the field. My conversations with my fellow police science students indicate that they have little use for courses outside the police science department. The reasons cited vary somewhat; some feel that they are stigmatized for being police science students. (Computer-print-out class rolls list certain biographical information, such as each student's major.) Whatever the reasons cited at any point in time, they all distill into the feeling that the students are there to get a degree in police science and not to take courses in geology, or sociology, or whatever. Police science students take the maximum allowable number of police science classes; and when driven to take classes in other departments by academic regulations, somehow gravitate to the health and safety department, which offers classes in first aid and public health and other subjects vaguely related to the police profession. I believe that the health and safety department was selected as a refuge largely by chance. Its main attraction is that police science students know that they won't be alone, that there will be a significant number of police science students in the class. I base these remarks on a questionnaire I distributed to fifteen percent of the police science majors partially as a project for a police science class. My data indicated that few police science students enroll in classes outside of the police science department that might bear some relationship to the police profession. For example, few students venture into criminology or abnormal psychology, which one might expect would benefit someone entering the police profession. When asked why more students did not enroll in such classes, some cited their disaffection with the social sciences, others claimed that they were too difficult. However, from my conversations with my fellow police science students and our academic advisors, I conclude that these students are enrolled in a career-related program not so much to learn about the field they hope to enter as to get a degree that they see as a prerequisite to success within that field. I believe that this is a function of career-related programs because of the marketability of the degree. It is viewed by prospective employers as some qualification for a position, as opposed to a degree in the liberal arts, which purports to denote learning within a subject area. This acknowledgement of the motives of career-related students is not that startling, when one considers that the orientation of the program is toward the career, and that the classroom experience is valued in terms of its simulation of job situations. Inasmuch as the best learning occurs on the job, it is easy to discount the learning opportunity afforded by the degree program. The issue is more complex than this; some might construe it as an outgrowth of pragmatic anti-intellectualism. For my purposes here I merely wish to observe that students in career-related programs seek a degree, not necessarily an education.

Above I mentioned that police science students gravitate to the health and safety department for additional units to complete degree requirements because they know that there will be other police science students in the classes. I believe this supports point 6, that police science students form recognizable cohorts predicated upon their perceived commonalities of interest. These students share classes, ambitions, perceptions of hostility from social scientists and others; in short, there exists a homogeneity lacking in noncareer-related programs. This cohort operates a grapevine, which keeps its members abreast of job opportunities within the field, student opinions of instructors, and other news of common interest.

This cohort has a geographic identity, a patio adjacent to the police science department classrooms, and a coffee machine.

Within this cohort, and within the classroom, police science students currently employed in the field are the most assertive: point 7. This is attributable, in part, to their greater familiarity with the field, to the fact that they are now what the preservice students hope to be, and to their experience (however limited), which allows them to exchange anecdotes with their instructors; this reaffirms my contention that career-related programs view experience as the best teacher. Thus, those with more experience are more learned.

CONCLUSION

I have illustrated these seven characteristics of career-related programs in higher education with examples drawn from my experience with a Bachelor of Science program in Police Science and Administration at California State University, Los Angeles. I suggest that they are generic to career-related programs because they can best be explained in terms of the career-related nature of the program and the students. My experience with a graduate program in the field of education supports my contention that these characteristics are universal among career-related programs. In this analysis I may have implied certain value judgements, for example, that I thought it was wrong for instructors to be evaluated not in terms of their teaching ability but in terms of their professional success. I did not intend to, because all degree programs have their faults, and certainly career-related programs are no more deserving of criticism than any other. My observations are made purely to collect information and not to make judgements. One bias I will admit is my belief that one can best evaluate any learning experience from the learner's perspective. While the instructor has a perspective on the subject area that the student lacks, and thus may be better equipped to evaluate what the student may need to learn, the student knows what he wants to learn, and how he wants to learn it, therefore defining the optimum learning experience. Thus, participant-observation, though time-consuming, is the best method by which to evaluate any learning experience.

REFERENCES

TENNEY, CHARLES
1971   *Higher education programs in law enforcement and criminal justice.* Washington, D. C.: U. S. Government Printing Office.

The "Greening" of the American College of Switzerland: A Descriptive Study of the Radicalization of a Conservative Community

R. J. WELKE

Editors' Note: In this paper, R. T. Welke of the University of Maryland describes the process and some of the results of an initial radical action in what he describes as "a conservative community." Here Welke is looking less at the direct "teaching" aspect of the school than he is at its structure as an organization. As such, it should be viewed in relation to the other papers in this section. Each looks at a different school situation from the standpoint of a social system, rather than in terms of content or society-wide effect. The practical import of Welke's statement is apparent. If school administrators do not attempt to account for the pressures and problems which the social system of the school produces for various of its member constituencies, then they will be faced with a continual and probably accelerating series of the sort of revolts described here. In particular, we suggest that the infringements the school makes on the identity and autonomy of adolescent students (and indeed quite often on teachers) are the source of much of this dissatisfaction.

On April 4, 1972, the entire student body of the American College of Switzerland began a boycott of food facilities. That evening the students outlined certain changes they wanted, including the resignation of the dean of instruction. On April 5, they began a classroom boycott — again 100 percent effective. On April 6, the faculty unanimously voted to adopt a resolution which discussed and analyzed the low college morale, the intimidation, coercion, and unresponsiveness of the administration, as well as a number of ways to improve the situation.

The dissension was purely internal to the college, having no direct connection with Vietnam, racialism, or any other such issue. But the college, seemingly overnight, became "radicalized." The response of the administrators was not unexpected. They eventually employed selective pressures and punishments against those who, they assumed, were responsible for the unrest. No effort was made by the administration until much later, and then half-heartedly, to determine WHAT was responsible. The radicalization did not, of course, occur in a vacuum: there is an organization within and against which our topic developed.

The only administration *per se* is the board of trustees of Leysin American Schools, S.A., an organization which operates primarily under laws applying to the hotel industry. The usual administrative positions — president, dean, registrar, etc. — do exist, but they are chiefly clerical positions, for any policy decision or purchase, however minor or insignificant, must be cleared through the board's representative. The board has delegated operational and managerial authority to one of its members who resides on the college premises as chancellor, founder, and executive director. This man and his wife, the board secretary, in fact have full power by themselves to speak for the entire board, as they have been granted *signature collective à deux*. This couple runs the college, the affiliated high school, and two international ranger camps. These two have recently boosted their son into the only other powerful position in the corporation, director of business affairs.

The prime purpose of this enterprise is profit, not education. This corporate goal, understandable in itself, has provided the root of numerous troubles in the past. For example, operating expenses of the enterprise, when in excess of investment revenues and other sources of income, are written off against the academic fees paid by the students. The remainder is then applied against the originally allotted academic budget for the year. In this way the executive director can and does claim that the college operates in the red. The fees in themselves are high enough for any boarding college, but the return on such expenditures is often negligible. For a number of years the students have frequently publicized conditions they considered intolerable: the type and quality of food served them; inefficient laundry services; lack of study facilities and insufficient lighting in their dormitory rooms; the general condition of the dormitories; the presence of rats and cockroaches in various dorms; frequent breakdown of facilities; poor academic resources; the high mandatory fees and the numerous, often inflated, extra charges that accompany them.

The faculty has long been on record as opposed to the slip-shod admissions standards, lack of tenure, policies of hiring and retention, the high turnover rate of faculty, facilities generally, uninformed administrative meddling in program structure, attendance policies, grading and textbook policies, chicanery in personnel management, departmental budget manipulations, and administrative demission of AAUP guidelines. The faculty association, a local formality somewhat resembling a university senate, is vested only with the responsibility of organizing faculty parties and excursions, and even this recognition came grudgingly from the executive director.

But the purpose of this paper is to describe how a collection of individuals with a peculiarly significant set of common traits, faculty and students alike, managed to forge a full community feeling, and how this feeling at length disintegrated through manipulation and exaggeration of the very traits which served the unification. While the author was present throughout the "greening," though not initially intending to prepare a paper on it, he did nevertheless take copious notes and assiduously collected documents. From this base, despite the dearth of prior studies of similar events in like situations, the author has attempted to arrive at some of the *semina motuum* and their wider implications. His ultimate dissociation from the college, and his pending court case, attest to the practical risks Professor Tax noted in his essay on action anthropology (Tax 1964: 248–258).

In recent advertisements the college has been described as a traditional university, though in reality it is a relatively small coeducational college of never more than 300 students and about 25 full and part-time faculty. Most students are from affluent families, residing in more than thirty different nations. Who are these radicals? The majority are sons and daughters of middle- and upper-class Americans. There are also ex-military officers and aristocrats from the Third World. Nearly all are sons and daughters of bankers, diplomats, or corporation presidents. Approximately two-thirds carry an American passport, but only half of these reside in the United States. This pattern is repeated among the other nationalities. One estimate is that two-thirds of the students do not reside in their countries of origin. And all are again dislocated when they arrive at the American College in Switzerland. Furthermore, many of these families change residence frequently, about every two or three years. Finally, although the statistics have understandably not been made available to the author, a large proportion of the students — one-third is apparently not an extravagant estimate — come from broken homes.

With perhaps the single exception of students of French, the prime attraction of the college, as it now operates, is something other than an education. Often, the college fills the function of a "sitter," providing a stable focus in a "safe" environment for children of far-flung parents. Many of the students have yet to live in one locale for more than two years. The college and the town of Leysin thus become home.

On the other hand, many of the Asian students see the college as partially preparatory for upper-division education in the United States or

England — they are able to steep themselves in an English-speaking environment with the comfort of not being too far from home. These Asians are usually business students. Finally, and probably unfortunately, the college provides a last chance for many students to boost their grade averages and at the same time preserve their often well-developed ego-centrism, which would not be the case in a larger school with education as its primary goal.

Alien, largely rootless, and often anomic individuals discover here a place populated by kindred spirits. They demand no responsibility and are accorded none. Their day is planned for them by a stern but generally undemanding, fatherly congerie of administrators. They ease themselves, ratchetlike, through the quarterly sequence of courses, phlegmatically fulfilling the prescribed though banal cultural ritual of the degree quest, under the tutelage of dislocated, insecure, easily intimidated, and usually short-term faculty members. Indeed, until the radicalization happened in 1972, the faculty was treated as a class of migratory workers, a group tolerated only by the necessity of erecting an educational front for the exchange between the monied clientele and the credit and degree con-ferring proprietors. Thus the nature of the inherent conservatism. The net result for the faculty was that in order to be sure of a job for the next academic year, the instructor had to carefully curb both word and deed in the presence of administrators while making every effort to please or charm the clientele.

Faculty and students, however, suddenly asserted themselves and tried to define both their responsibilities and rights. But did this unanimous desire simply burst forth spontaneously? Did a choice exist as clear and unimpugned as taking one of two paths? Factors contributive to their rather existential choice varied between faculty and students; but all factors converged upon one seemingly unproductive yet pivotal condition — total alienation.

Individual faculty and students felt treated in a way that attacked their self-respect. Children of wealthy parents found themselves forced to eat poor food and live in substandard dormitories. Some claim to have been coerced, by threat of blackmail, to spy on their fellow students for any infractions of college rules, any rumblings of protest. Suspect individuals were singled out and castigated.

The faculty felt deprived of professional accord, were upset by inade-quate facilities, and amazed at the cavalier way salary manipulations were used to appease or punish. Both students and faculty, over the years, had accumulated long lists of grievances; but, as the administration hardly responded to these, the general feeling was that change and improvement were hopeless. Divide and rule tactics were skillfully employed by the administration, and the students and faculty alike, though individually, exhibited unmistakable frustration and cynicism. The pervading low morale sought and found releases: black humor, drunkenness, drug use, gossip, sarcasm, and backbiting. Student complaints were met by lack of response; faculty complaints were met by overreaction. The five forms of alienation were all present: normlessness, powerlessness, meaningless-ness, self-estrangement, and isolation. Administration-fostered divisive-ness created mutual suspicion. The de-emphasis of education and the blatant appeals to profit resulted in a decline of purpose among the faculty and finally a college-wide apathy. Cultural diversity, lingering intimidation, and the universally poor conditions reinforced this alien-ation. Depression was genuine and pervasive, a potentially fertile ground for breeding a strike. How a collection of fragmented, culturally disparate people transformed themselves into a community of purpose poses an intriguing problem.

There were certain catalysts which aroused the faculty and gave it a feeling of unity. But the student body had been threatening some form of action all year. A confident administration dismissed these threats as unrealistic. For the students would not act if the faculty, serving as an administrative instrument, meted out the administrators' various punishments in response. The faculty was contractually obligated to support the institution during crises. This was naturally read as support of the administration. Since the faculty had been so thoroughly fragmented, any possibly sympathetic faculty member could easily be singled out for immediate dismissal.

But the faculty's attitude was effectively changed for it by the admin-istration on two crucial days. On January 25, the faculty association convened and, in a very innocuous way and apparently for the first time, moved to suggest certain improvements in the college and its operation. Within twenty-four hours the faculty was called to a meeting where, as a body, it was threatened with loss of jobs by the administration for having the temerity to even discuss change. This meeting in actuality rendered the strike possible, and, ironically, the administrator who presided became the students' target until he resigned his post.

For the first time the faculty was treated as a collectivity by the ad-ministration, as a body without cadaverous implications. This mass intimidation provided the spark of camaraderie among the faculty, the first feeling of mutual support. But that afternoon the faculty was also presented with an example of what could happen to all. After a minor confrontation between two professors, one was singled out to receive the full flood of administrative calumny, and that professor resigned. From that afternoon the faculty as a whole came to share with the student body one common goal — better treatment.

During the next two months the climate continued to deteriorate. There were more debates, more resignations, while the students began to circulate more and more petitions. Finally, on April 4, the students announced their food boycott. Alternative facilities were arranged with local restaurants. That evening the student leaders held a meeting to present the reasons for the boycott. The atmosphere was ecstatic. A class boycott was announced, which was to continue until certain operational conditions at the college were improved. The faculty association convened to discuss the seriousness of the student attitude and ended by adopting a resolution condemning the administration on several counts, as well as suggesting numerous ways to create an academic environment and avert any further uprisings. The dissension and unrest continued, with gradually diminishing intensity, to the end of the school year. The administration was notably unresponsive to the requests for change. Thus, although the "strike" was technically successful, the result was not.

The conduct of faculty and students during the spring quarter was both interesting and significant. The students were orderly and self-controlled. They ignored the administration both by disciplining themselves and by debating changes, even attempting to implement some of them. The faculty participated in meaningful decisions by mapping out plans for long-range college improvement and the ameliorization of work conditions. Both faculty and students achieved for the first time a feeling of participation. Both evidenced this feeling by calling for a restructuring of organizational authority flow that would incorporate an upward as well as the downward influence in policy and decision making. The strike, in effect, served as a release mechanism for both segments of the community, and faculty and students treated each other as adults with rights and valid opinions. The strike had the effect of transmuting frustration and cynicism into purpose and hope.

But why the unanimity? The student boycotts were 100 percent effective, and the faculty unanimously adopted its resolutions. The pressure of one's peers may be invoked to account for the student solidarity, but the faculty arrived at total agreement only after long and heated debates. A plausible suggestion is that certain dominant personalities emerged in each group and guided the rest to the desired stance. But for the faculty this is easily refuted. For the students, however, the issue is more complex. They did have a leader with charisma of a kind and his role cannot be minimized. But the involvement of almost all of the students was so intense that they finally refused to submit to one man's leadership. A likely explanation is that all individuals involved, in varying degrees of truculence, could simply no longer tolerate the *selv'oscura* in which they lived and worked, thus needing minimal pressure and little leadership.

How did the administration respond? Its response was late, and initially ineffective when it finally did come. Two weeks after the strike began the administration consented to negotiate with the faculty and students. But toward the end of the quarter its reaction moved into higher gear. A number of senior students were told that their graduation was in jeopardy. Faculty members without new contracts were told that they would have to wait until conditions returned to "normal." There were rumors that the school might be closed down, affecting everyone. Some faculty members were fired, and fifteen of the twenty-five did not return for the 1972–1973 academic year. During the summer a number of students were notified that they were not welcome back. Finally, the remaining students and faculty received board notification in September that any act construed as injurious to the organization would result in dismissal without notice and possible suit for damages.

How did faculty and students react to this? When the administration acted by threatening to withhold graduation or even the quarterly sum of credits; by implying the nonrenewal of an individual contract; by hinting at personal damage suits; the individuals capitulated to the administration and ceased their protest. The solidarity evaporated, and fear and alienation resumed their primacy.

As of the fall of 1973, the last date for which we have full information, conditions had certainly not improved. If anything, they seemed to have become worse. In the first part of the school year there were two student demonstrations of protest. A number of students darkly predicted that the school would not last through December.* The protest at that time seemed to be moving to a different plane, however. Lawyers and public officials were being contracted and informed. The goal seemed to be to bring public and official pressure upon the administration without risking the uncertain results of direct confrontation. The wake of incidents at the college seemed to be creating a demand in Berne for reforms in legislation governing the operation of the *société anonyme*, and all private international schools in the Canton de Vaud — and there are many — were likely to be visited by various government inspectors. The events may

---

* As this volume went to press, the American College of Switzerland was still in existence. — *Editor*.

have reminded some Swiss of the historic confrontation between William Tell and the Landvogt.

The dilemma faced by both groups can be linked to Heidegger's concepts of "absence" and "presence." The underlying choice for both faculty and students was whether they were to remain deprived, perhaps voluntarily, of their humanity, or to assert their "presence" and assume the attendant responsibilities. The latter choice was made and demonstrated, and the aftermath of this *rite de passage* has left a palpable mark on both the college and its administrators.

The uprising of students and faculty at a small college high in the Swiss Alps has another, superficially trite, implication. No matter how diverse in origins, no matter how wealthy or poor, no matter how alienated or uprooted, there is a point beneath which abuses of any people's integrity and self-respect cannot penetrate without unleashing dire — if temporary — consequences for the abuser.

REFERENCE

TAX, SOL
    1964   "The uses of anthropology," in *Horizons of anthropology*. Edited by Sol Tax, 248–258. Chicago: Aldine.

"The Schooling Process": Some Lakota (Sioux) Views

BEATRICE MEDICINE

Editors' Note: It has become commonplace in recent years to hear students referred to as an "oppressed minority," and there may indeed be much truth in this judgment. Perhaps more remarkable is the extent to which the liberal American critics of education who make such judgments have been blind to the plight of those who are a double minority and who are often doubly oppressed. Occasionally a tract has appeared on urban blacks, who were easily accessible to the slumming or more serious educationist, but few have had the vision or taken the effort to look at the problems of those minorities not so close at hand, much less to talk with them and give serious attention to their views. To be sure, anthropologists have now and then published comments on native American education, but these have usually been attempts to reconstruct some indigenous system of cultural transmission, not to deal with the reality of the current situation. The current situation includes schools, as well as traditions, and to understand it one must have the views of those who attend the schools, those who do not, and particularly those who are at the same time both members of the community and educators. These views must also be seen as valid, not merely as obstacles to be overcome. In this paper Bea Medicine, herself a Sioux as well as an anthropologist, provides a sensitive summary of the views expressed by a number of trained educators and members of the Lakota community on "the schooling process." We hope this will be part of an ever-growing movement to change the dominant conception of native Americans from one in which they are the objects of anthropological study and government action to one where they are the subjects of their own lives. Sioux are educators as well as educated, they are to be listened to as well as talked about. Even more fundamentally, native Americans must be able to control education and the rest of purposeful action in their communities to an extent similar to the rest of the nation. There is no reason why they, more than others, should have to ask before being able to do. We all make concessions to society, but we are by no means all equally enfranchised members.

It is important to realize that with the increasing articulateness and sophistication evidenced among many native American groups, it is imperative that some consideration be given the viewpoints and attitudes toward education which comprise efforts for meaningful education for these indigenous populations.

Increasingly, it should be apparent that it is impossible to speak of THE American Indian. Therefore, a holistic view of "Indian education" is an impossibility. More significantly, a caveat exists that no one person — either native or anthropologist — is able to speak authoritatively for native Americans relying on their expertise about "my people." This is a generally recognized rule among most tribal enclaves. For despite the trend toward pan-Indianism on some levels, tribalism is still a strong and vibrant force in contemporary native American life. Tribalism can be tied in with regionalism in some instances, but such is not the case with the Teton or Western Sioux. There is a greater emphasis upon band membership based upon the older concept of the Seven Council Fires (*ocheti sacowin*). In such an atmosphere there is need for the presentation of statements and agreements which various persons of a specific tribe attempt in the wide area of education relevant to that group.

This paper will focus upon a meeting of Lakota (Sioux) persons who met at the tribally owned motel, "Land of Gall Inn," on the Standing Rock Indian reservation in South Dakota in August 1973. The purpose of the meeting was to deal with curriculum development in "Lakota studies." The meeting was initiated by the director of one of the emerging Lakota community colleges from Pine Ridge, South Dakota. Besides the director, the group included two instructors of Lakota language, the older women who were involved in tribal programs and had worked in the tribal governments from Cheyenne River and Standing Rock reservations. There were two younger Sioux men who had finished B.A. degrees in linguistics and education. One was teaching in *Sinte Gleska* [Spotted Tail] Community College, Rosebud reservation, and the other was instructing at Lakota Higher Education Center (a community college on Pine Ridge reservation).

The individuals so far delineated were actual residents of the reservations in the state of South Dakota and included all the bands of the Teton (Western) "Sioux" groups. A significant point regards language: the persons involved were all speakers of "Lakota," vernacularly called the "L" dialect. It is one of the three dialects of the Siouan language group, which also includes Dakota and Nakota. More importantly, the individuals in attendance at this native-initiated conference were from the so-called "grass roots" segments of the western Dakota reservations. The four reservations are Cheyenne River, Pine Ridge, Rosebud, and Standing Rock.

Additionally, one Lakota person teaching in an institution of higher education, but in another state, was invited as a resource person. Another, a female Sioux directing an Indian studies program at Black Hills State Teachers College where the majority of Sioux students in the area attend, was also present. Her natal reservation is Standing Rock. One other female Sioux, originally from Pine Ridge, with community college and university teaching experience in Washington state, was present. As this person was from the *tiospaye* [extended kin group] of the tribal government allied against the urban militants represented by the American Indian Movement (AIM), there was a period of initial tension as the meeting began. It is critical to realize that the *tiospaye* is very closely tied to the factions which are current in contemporary reservation life. Extended kin, whether the kin still reside in off-reservation or urban centers, is an important factor in the total thrust of interpersonal relations on various reservations. Thus kinship affiliations are an important fact in Lakota Indian social and political life of the present day. The first question usually posed to a returning Dakota whether he is returning for a visit, the summer "pow-wow" cycle, or permanent residence is: "Who are you?" This is a necessary reference point to place one in proper kin behavior and also to assess the returnee's possible political orientations.

One nonnative person (white male) connected with a community college in an eastern Dakota-speaking community was present. The writer, representing Lakota (Sioux) Indians and the discipline of anthropology in university teaching, taped the sessions. I live in Standing Rock, where I still maintain a home and vote in tribal elections. My main function was to listen to the discussion and attempt to relate the curriculum discussions to developments in other native studies departments throughout North America and in general to comment on educational directions in other fields. This is significant, not because I was invited, but because it indicates the increasing reliance upon indigenous people who have some credibility with local tribal peoples. It further points to the diminishing role of the "expert on Indians."

The two-day meeting opened with the question: "What is education?" It was agreed that it should be anything in which learning was involved — "not just school." The need was to "define and analyze the educational process as it pertains to Lakota people." Interestingly, much of the discussion was in the Siouan language, Lakota dialect. There was an easy flow from English to Lakota, with much of the discourse using the phrase "you know what I mean." This was not an effort to exclude the one non-Indian and one native non-Lakota-speaking individual. It merely shows the ability to utilize both languages in the formulation of questions, ideas, and discussion. The use of nonverbal communication was evident and was primarily used to indicate closure of topics and agreement. There was little disagreement on the points presented.

The discussion leader was the eldest man, affiliated with Lakota Higher Education Center as a Lakota language teacher. He made a chart — "Elders are wise people." This led to his statement that:

One of the most liberal educational philosophies that we have, and it should be rightfully pursued — is that what is taught at home must also be taught in the classroom, and what is being taught in the classroom must be taught at home. It shouldn't be that when an Indian child comes from a home stepping into a classroom that it would be a different world — another world, and that he has to change himself, adjust himself to those situations and once he steps into his own home he would have to be another person — what his learning activities are should not change from one setting to another. That is the educational goal that we are promoting.

But on the other hand, BIA [Bureau of Indian Affairs] rules are guilty of this. Because they have wide recruitment programs, we get people from Texas, from Florida, from New York and all different places. These people have never seen an Indian, not knowing what he is like, not knowing his life, let alone knowing his life-style. They would step into the classroom and begin to promote and push their own values and expect the Indian people to accept them at face value or blindly, not respecting what they have learned at home. This is where the alienation process has come in, as some experts claim. The bureau doesn't seem to care too much, at least that I know of. Being a school board member, I'm trying to promote an orientation program of some type that these people — non-Indians — first entering into the Indian field must be oriented to conditions and situations on the reservations. The emphasis should be placed on respecting that child as a learner — as an Indian learner. In doing that, we wouldn't have so many "push outs" as we have here. When I went to school — in reading John Artichoker's handbook [Artichoker 1959], they had 95 Indian students pursuing four-year education programs. He interviewed them. Within one quarter, he lost thirty-five of them. He only had a handful that he had to work with in order to complete the pamphlet that he was writing. We have a greater number of Indian people at this level [college]. Speaking of college centers and Indian studies programs — at Black Hills University — I think the atmosphere is a lot better than what we had to face at one time. The monies come by a lot easier than at that time [when this elder was going to college in the 1940's]. We had to borrow the money from the tribe, and we had to wait maybe six months before we could get to it, and this type of situation. Nowadays, they have the grant system. Money is no worry to them, at least in part. And yet, we still have a large percentage of people dropping out.

BM: Why do you think students are dropping out when money is easier to get?

SMD: I think it is through the use of words from the teacher to the scholars.[1] You have to be able to communicate with the scholars. You must use the right words in order to do this. If you do this, you have the scholar's trust and he has confidence in you. The process of learning what you are trying to teach him is easier.

GOF: *Wasicus*[2] [white people] call this rapport.

SMD: I don't care what they call it!

This verbal interchange sets the tone for the meeting and the Lakota etiquette is met. After the long speech by the eldest man in which he covers a wide variety of points which he sees as important, I ask a GOF: question showing my attentiveness, but also establishing my perogative to continue to ask questions. The oldest female (SMD) responds to my questions with her opinions. This allows the director (GOF) to break into the discussion, utilizing our word for "whites" (*wasicus*) and one of their concepts, "rapport." This is done in a humorous fashion to which she responds. The director has subtly entered the discussion and the "give-take-and-ask" atmosphere is under way.

The director of the Dakota Higher Education Center then explained testing procedures used at Black Hills State College. He mentioned the results of a study he had conducted using the Vocational Inventory and the ACT scores from computer results. The implications of the tests were summarized.

Their preference was to work with things; they didn't want to have anything to do with people. The girls' emphasis was health. This was beyond the fifty percentile. The boys were taking forestry, range management and so on.... Indications were that being a teacher, an administrator, and those kinds of things were last on the Inventory.

Obviously teachers and administrators present negative models. Implicit in vocational tests are their biases toward vocations. As a result, he indicated that there were some attempts at restructuring some

[1] In using this term, the speaker indicates students. In this case, she is referring to Sioux Indian students on all educational levels.
[2] It is interesting to note that the English plural *s* is added to a native term. A native variant might be *wasicukipi*. You will note *wasicup* used later in discussion.

courses in industrial arts. He explained the ACT test. "One interesting phenomenon revealed that every year the freshmen were ranking on an equal basis with the seniors in college. The students coming in on the GED were only 2 percent behind." His interpretation "means that on the college level, Indian students have very little difference in academic capabilities."

A younger male colleague stated, "I don't think we'll ever solve the problem until we [i.e. Lakota educators] get into high school." At this point the lone non-Indian made a strong plea for a "two-track system." He stated, "I don't care where you go to school, you're not going to get a diploma until you get academics. Students can get straight F's and go down to the shops and be tremendous."

The same younger male countered "Why can't we develop a suitable curriculum in elementary school to deal with what you're saying?" It is apparent that this individual is aware that pupil alienation has its roots earlier. He also pointed out the problems of the social setting in the classroom. He mentioned aspects of the "political rapport" between elementary-school and secondary-teachers. Of the "many lacks," he noted complete disregard of team teachers, teachers-aides, and absence of "open-mindedness." Het said, "I've never encountered anyone who was so good that he could sit down and listen — even though he's as smart as the kids." He stated that teachers were "balking" at his suggestions as a teaching interne, but "they have the prestige of having a degree and in their first year of teaching." When queried as to who these teachers were, he answered *Wasicup*. Further, he said, "We, *Lakotaki* should set up our own curricula." The non-Indian re-emphasized, "Many kids couldn't get academics; they don't have it now." This shows great unawareness of the aims of the Lakota people.

After this, the Lakota director replied: "The situation is such that the Department of Public Instruction of South Dakota, Bulletin 99 or 95, restricted language: '. . . that no ancient language be taught.' It took an act of the state legislature to modify that — to include our own native tongue. Teaching the Lakota language in elementary or high school classroom would be in violation of South Dakota law, and whoever is teaching it can lose his or her teaching certificate as a result." After this statement, the leader of the session produced the actual document and read it. This repeal provided the beginning of meaningful education for Lakota people. It also showed awareness of legal procedures that can be circumvented. The director again showed his respect for elders (and wisdom) by not producing the document himself.

The director resumed: "To sell this education business, we must deal with the community people. I think we should promote Indian studies, but we have to do a good job of selling. Otherwise, we can't do it."

A woman from Cheyenne River reservation used the Johnson-O'Malley Act as an example. Lack of knowledge as to their proper share of federal funding is a real detriment to Indian education. She emphasized that in most cases, "bad feelings at school had to be overcome before involvement is begun, and this cannot be done overnight." She raised another critical issue: "There is a problem. When a new tribal council comes in, one administration throws everyone out, and school board members put in their own people. If we say, 'We are the people,' we must start from scratch."

Again, the director shows his astuteness in Lakota social organizational features for he recognizes that each community on these four reservations tends to be unique. He indicates the need for understanding the communities, but he is also calling to our attention the futility of high-level planning without community involvement. This allows for the input of the other eldest woman, who is referring to a well-documented issue (see *An even chance*) in misuse of federal funds for children in public schools. She also reminds the group of the power of the tribal councils and the quite prevalent practice of tribal councils or school boards who often reelect members of the same clique or faction on the reservations.

The leader of the conference attempted to summarize:

The inner core of the whole problem would have to dwell within the classroom — where factions and values are being staged, where the battles of the mind are taking place. The learner has to have confidence in the giver. In order to take his word or his word to be worth anything to the learner, that confidence will have to be gained. Many schools have failed to send their teachers out to their [students'] homes and family visitations are to be acquainted with their students' homes. Once the learner knows that the teacher knows Mama and Papa, and Mama and Papa know the teacher, then this should improve his learning activity in the classroom. They see things on neutral grounds. They should have interests in common in the education of that child. All learning processes are hard. Learning in English alone, I couldn't pass first grade for three years. I gues I was pretty cute then, the teachers just kept me.

Again, we see the verbalization ending on a note of lightness. The younger Lakota male then commented:

It is very difficult when you go into the classroom and get the *wasicu wicoyake* [the way to learn the English language and to live the white way] teaching concept. You got that in your mind, but at four o'clock you get on the bus and go home and start thinking Indian again. White learning deteriorates. You see where the stuff you learn leaves. All friends come over, and you go out playing "cowboys and Indians" or play cars in the dirt, maybe. Well, the next morning you go back to school, and find yourself a "slow learner." As the semester goes on, you get further behind. So that has to be modified. The melting pot is no more than a myth because all it does is strengthen the middle-class values and the lower economic level of people have never been reached by the American education system — public education system. The Negroes have become poorer and they will be getting worse. While the American education system is growing and prospering, the parochial schools, in order to comply with state regulations, have been falling off.

This is a great statement which needs no explanation. As this speaker is only in his mid-twenties, it shows the longevity of meaningless education for the Lakota people, in general.

Essentially, these Lakota educators — for this is their self-image — see the educational process as an ongoing one. Ideally, they appear to desire smooth transitions for Lakota individuals on all levels of the superimposed transfer points.

They seem exceedingly aware of the structures of the agencies and institutions impinging on their lives and the lives of their children and grandchildren. The futility of trying to change the Bureau of Indian Affairs (BIA) educational policy is implicit in their remarks. Therefore, they are looking to other areas for change, namely Lakota studies. Underpinning this attempt is the desire to reassess traditional values and incorporate them in a meaningful learning situation for future generations of Lakota people.

Perception of schools as social systems and institutions predominates as a general tendency. Therefore, these Lakota educators are knowledgeable about teacher cliques, institutions, and the need for restructuring the educational system. The crux of the problem lies in curricula development. This was one area which needed precise and experimental approaches. To this end, they planned to have a special five-week session at one of the Lakota community colleges in the summer of 1974.

As a direct result of this meeting, a strong effort to enforce changes in the schools of education in all teacher-training institutions in the state was attempted. In order to be an accredited teacher in South Dakota, a course in Lakota language and culture was placed before the state legislature. These were to be taught by Lakota people.

REFERENCES

ARTICHOKER, JOHN JR., NEIL M. PALMER
  1959　*The Sioux Indian goes to college.* Institute of Indian Studies and
      State Department of Public Instruction.
NAACP LEGAL DEFENSE AND EDUCATION FUND
  n.d.　*An even chance.* Published by the NAACP Legal Defense and
      Education Fund with the cooperation of The Center for Law and
      Education, Harvard University; 10 Columbus Circle, New York,
      N.Y. 10019.

The Role of the Anthropologist in Experimental College Evaluations: Some Personal Observations

THOMAS K. FITZGERALD

Editors' Note: Thomas K. Fitzgerald has produced one of the most immediately practical papers in this volume. He has analyzed certain parts of the situation which obtained when a campus of the University of North Carolina began an experimental residential college program. What can the anthropologist contribute to such a program, he asks, and in particular, how can he aid in evaluating its success or failure? Fitzgerald has certain ideas on answers to these problems. In addition, he offers insights gleaned from his own experiences which should be of value to anthropologists who find themselves in similar situations. Educators may learn something concerning both programs and the use of anthropologists.

There has been a movement in the 1970's toward experimental education and self-directed learning as manifested in the experiments in educational reform variously labeled cluster colleges, residential colleges, living-learning centers, and the like. A primary concern that they all share is the attempt to eliminate the dichotomy felt to exist between the formal (or academic) and informal or residential aspects of the undergraduate experience.

The search for innovation and relevance in planning and developing such programs has called for an increase in the demand for systematic evaluations. If an experimental program is, indeed, to be an experiment, then some sort of evaluation is mandatory. Social program evaluation is the accumulation of facts in order to provide information about the achievement of the program's requisites and goals. Tripodi, et al. list three major components in any social program evaluation: (1) program efforts, (2) program effectiveness, and (3) program efficiency (1971:11-12). The unique contributions, as well as some special limitations, of the anthropologist to social program evaluations in the school will be examined.

SOCIAL PROGRAM EVALUATION

PROGRAM EFFORTS refer to the actual description of the type of activities involved. For example, as evaluator of the Residential College at the University of North Carolina at Greensboro, it was my responsibility to include in report form a brief history and description of this educational program over a two-year period (Fitzgerald 1972). Such a description typically includes statistical survey data (environmental variables as well); curricular accounts (instruction organization, student services, and the like); descriptions of living conditions; and a general thematic assessment stating the goals and objectives that the college perceives for itself. Too often social program evaluation is equated, *in toto*, with program efforts. Normally the director of the project describes and justifies the educational operation in a written report to the chancellor, and this report is taken to be the evaluation!

Any fair assessment of an experimental program can be meaningful only in terms of a clearly formulated set of objectives, namely those goals and objectives set by the group itself. The anthropologist's earliest task, then, is to find out what it is the people in the program hope to accomplish. PROGRAM EFFECTIVENESS, therefore, is concerned with the consequences or outcomes of program efforts. In relation to the goals set by the group itself, program effectiveness asks whether or not intended outcomes have been obtained as a result of program efforts. Unlike program efforts, however, program effectiveness calls for some sort of empirical study in order to discover the consequences, both intended and unintended, of such an experiment.

Evaluation of PROGRAM EFFICIENCY goes one step further. It asks what are the relative "costs" of achieving such outcomes. In other words, the anthropologist must consider the consequences, anticipated and unanticipated, in terms of some larger structure rather than merely in terms of itself (in our case, the larger university, but the larger culture is another possibility). A program might conceivably produce the kinds of things for which it was designed yet still be unsuccessful in relation to its external environment(s). The anthropologist, with his or her traditional sensitivity to structural complexities, can then be a great asset in avoiding oversimplification in analyzing and evaluating such educational programs.

THERE IS A ROLE FOR ANTHROPOLOGISTS

It is my opinion that the anthropological approach lends itself admirably to the description of program efforts and has an even greater contribution to make in the analysis of the structural complexities in the program efficiency stage. Although evaluation is not synonymous with any particular formalized research technique, certain methods are more compatible than others with the objectives of these "unstructured" experimental settings. Typically, for example, residential colleges lack computers and teaching machines; and the participants, in fact, are somewhat hostile to highly technological procedures. (As an aside, before I entered the scene as evaluator of our residential college, a psychologist — with his battery of tests — had just been thrown out!) The concern of the college, of course, was that any evaluative research not be disruptive to the natural flow of things and that the researcher refrain from any unnecessary structuring of its environment. With the traditional anthropological techniques (participant-observation, open-ended questionnaires, and various interviewing procedures), I found that one was able to gather a great deal of data "in the field" while causing little or no disruption to the ongoing activities of the college.

In short, the experimental college setting is a new area for anthropologists to exploit. As our methodology is both adaptable and nondisruptive, such a field situation is a "natural" for educational anthropologists. There is, then, a real role for anthropologists to play in evaluative research in the school.

The anthropological approach, however, lends itself to certain areas of evaluative process better than to others. Program efforts and program efficiency, we have established, are both compatible with anthropological methodology; program effectiveness, however, with its emphasis on empiricism and controls raises some problems in this particular setting. I would like to turn now to the limitations of the anthropological approach.

SOME PROBLEMS ENCOUNTERED

The very unstructuredness of much of the anthropological research in educational contexts can become its principal weakness. One is too often faced with questions that are not fully answerable using the traditional ethnographic approach. There are, to be sure, ways of getting around this dilemma. After rapport has been firmly established and any dangers of disruption to the continuation of the program allayed, one may borrow from other disciplines those techniques appropriate to one's research needs. In the case of multidisciplinary research, this practice is straightforward and easy. Unfortunately, borrowing from other disciplines sometimes poses an identity problem for certain anthropologists. It is not uncommon these days to hear the complaint among anthropologists that educational anthropologists are becoming servants to education rather than making significant contributions to anthropological theory. This sort of psychological projection is unbecoming to a discipline that is, by definition, interdisciplinary.

Coupled with this notion is the role confusion felt by some anthropologists in educational research settings. So often, it becomes difficult to decide whom one is working for. And to aggravate this anxiety, one's anthropological colleagues too often feel that, rather than doing anthropological research, one is merely writing a report for the chancellor of the university justifying another questionable innovation. Educational-anthropological research in our own culture is still somewhat suspect in the anthropological community. Yet, to do good educational anthropology in experimental settings, one needs to extend one's reference group affiliations beyond the anthropological fraternity.

Finally, there are ethical considerations to make in doing evaluative research. Anthropologists are used to describing conflict situations, but evaluative research calls for involvement as well. Constant feedback between evaluator and program participants is a prerequisite to good social program evaluation. At every stage of its development, improvements need to be incorporated into an ongoing program. It is not sufficient to offer a finished product in the form of a report at the end of two years. The question, then, of how involved the anthropologist will become in policy making is an ethical question that each individual must answer. Sometimes, of course, the decision is not in our hands. Too often the administration does not understand the nature of an evaluation and, therefore, never allows the evaluator to enter into any sort of policy-making stance. In this case, the evaluation and the experiment suffer.

In summary, despite the need for a diverse number of methodological tools, some of which must be learned from other areas — despite the conflicts of interest, the accompanying problems of identity, and the ethical considerations — things are not as bad as some of us anthropologists have been led to believe. It is safe to say that anthropologists by virtue of their training are in a good position to make some real contribution to experimental college evaluations.

REFERENCES

FITZGERALD, THOMAS K.
    1972   "Evaluation of a residential college program UNC-G pilot project."
           Report to the Chancellor, The University of North Carolina at
           Greensboro, April 15.
TRIPODI, PONY, et al.
    1971   Social program evaluation. Itasca, Ill.: F. E. Peacock.

SECTION FOUR

Chicano Bilingual/Bicultural Education

HENRY TORRES-TRUEBA

Editors' Note: Bilingual/bicultural education is a goal which many educators and community spokesmen have claimed for years. Some school systems have even organized programs aimed in this direction, but this is only a very small beginning in the attempt to deal with one of the major educational issues in the United States today and a prototype for emergent problems in other parts of the world. How can we structure educational situations which make dual language capacity efficient and an advantageous part of the learning process? How can we help minority group members maintain their cultural identities in a politically lopsided plural society? Henry Torres-Trueba, a member of the faculty of the College of Education at the University of Illinois, looks at the programs which have begun, and more specifically, at the efforts to train teachers for those programs. One training course is described in detail and related to the "social reality" of the Chicano situation. It is not a perfect prototype, but it is one of the few available for consideration.

This paper is not a survey of the existing bilingual/bicultural (b/b) programs organized by or for the Chicanos. It attempts rather to explore the types, scope, problems, and philosophy of Chicano b/b programs based on information gathered from life histories, questionnaires, formal and informal interviews, and active participation in such programs.

INTRODUCTION

The b/b education represents for the Chicano community the single most important effort to change the traditional educational philosophy expressed in standard policies and institutions throughout the country. B/b programs are thus seen by the Chicanos as a major breakthrough in the ethnocentric rigidity of curriculum and the overall school orientation towards a presumed monocultural middle-class American student. Chicanos also see b/b education as an opportunity to build up personal pride, self-identity, and a more meaningful and sensitive school that recognizes the reality of our pluralistic American society. Finally, *La Raza* believes that b/b education ultimately will open the door to full Chicano participation in the socioeconomic opportunities that this country offers.

Two definitions are in order here: Chicano and b/b programs. "Chicano" has been, and still is, a controversial word. I use it here synonymous with Mexican-American, *Hispano, La Raza,* etc. Chicano is a term that has been applied to "radical" Mexican-Americans and, more recently, to all Mexican-Americans. Simmen (1972:56) has defined Chicano as "An American of Mexican descent who attempts through peaceful, reasonable, and responsible means to correct the image of the Mexican-American and to improve the position of this minority in the American social structure." This definition, although essentially correct, is restrictive. I would define Chicano as "A person of Mexican descent residing permanently in the United States, who perceives his culture as unique, that is, different from the Mexican and the Anglo cultures, and actively works to defend his cultural heritage and his social and civil rights, in order to improve his economic, political, social, and religious life."

We must now define bilingual/bicultural education. B/b education should be distinguished from remedial programs, from programs with English as a second language, and from bilingual programs which exclude the cultural component. The main purpose of the above programs is to facilitate the language change of the monolingual child, that is, from the native tongue of the child to the official language, English. In contrast with these programs, b/b education intends to train the child in two languages without his losing either one and to acquaint the child with a new culture without rejecting his own. The assumption is, contrary to what traditional remedial programs presupposed, that monocultural/monolingual education is an undesirable goal. The goal of b/b education is to enrich the child's human experience with two compatible and alternative languages and cultures. Traditionally, the American educational system has demanded that the culturally different child rapidly assimilate American culture and language, which are conceived as a homogeneous unit. The result, of course, was that the child would gradually see his people, his language, his culture, and himself as undesirable. Therefore, he would be psychologically damaged, divided, and impaired in his learning and intellectual development. B/b programs see the minority child and the Anglo child as being in equal need of enlarging their cultural universe and perceiving each other as acceptable and equally good.

In order to appreciate the scope and types of b/b programs, their underlying philosophy, and their significance for the Chicano, the reader must
be reminded of the facts of life which Chicanos must confront, and of
which they have become painfully aware.

CHICANO SOCIAL REALITY

1. The Chicano population, now the second largest minority in this
country, is calculated to be over five and one-half million, of whom 90
percent live in the southwest, representing at least 12 percent of the total
population of this area.
2. The ancestors of the Chicanos arrived in this country as early as 1609,
and they settled in what is today Santa Fe. They lived in rural areas for
many years; however, at the present time, over 80 percent of the Chicanos
live in metropolitan areas.
3. According to the 1960 census information, 56 percent of the Chicano
labor force works in factories, mines, and construction: 19 percent work
on farms; 17 percent in professional or clerical jobs; and 8 percent in
service occupations.
4. Unemployment for Chicano males is twice the national unemployment rate.
5. Thirty-five percent of all Chicanos in the southwest (1960 census)
have a family income of less than $3,000 per year, and in some areas of the
country, even the median family income is under $3,000 (Texas, for
example).
6. Chicano median education for men and women, twenty-five years old
and over, is 7.1 years of completed school (1960 census), compared with
12.1 for the Anglo population. Furthermore, while the Anglos have at
least 22 percent with one year or more of college education, Chicanos
count on only 6 percent to reach that level of education.
7. Twenty percent of the GI's in the Vietnam frontlines were Chicanos,
even though the total population of Chicanos represents only 3 percent
of the country's total population.
8. More important still is the fact that most Chicanos have experienced in
a variety of ways — sometimes overtly, sometimes in a subtle manner —
the psychological oppression of being segregated, laughed at, neglected,
despised, or abused not only by private individuals in the dominant
society, but also by its official authorities and its public institutions. They
see Anglo society as a hostile enemy that has used all possible means to
undermine Chicano culture and language.

In response to these sad and complex facts of Chicano social life, there is a unanimous and energetic opposition of Chicano educators and students who say loud and clear: "*Ya basta!*" [It's enough!]. Therefore, the Chicanos seek to strengthen their language and culture as a means of restoring personal and group respect, pride, and self-sufficiency.

The full significance of b/b Chicano programs can be appreciated only in this light. It goes beyond the utilitarian and immediate rewards of personal advancement and the advantages of having a school diploma.

TYPES AND SCOPE OF B/B CHICANO EDUCATION

At present, there are two main types of b/b programs: (1) programs for children (either monolingual or quasi-bilingual) during the first years of school from kindergarten to third or fourth grade, and (2) programs for bilingual teachers to train them in b/b education in order that they may effectively work with Chicanitos at all levels of education, from elementary through high school, either as teachers or administrators. The emphasis on Chicano language and culture is essential to both types of programs.

The aim of the scope of these programs is essentially the intellectual emancipation of the Chacano. The main long-range objectives of the first type of b/b programs as expressed by Chicano educators are:
1.   To help Chicanitos maintain or create a positive self-image.
2.   To provide cultural continuity for the Chicanitos as they move from their environment to the Anglo institution of learning.
3.   To develop and maintain pride in their cultural heritage and build a more definite self-identity without losing the benefits of formal education.
4.   To develop curricula on the basis of Chicano language and culture whereby the content and the means of communicating knowledge become relevant to the Chicano.
5.   To stop and counteract school discrimination against Chicanos.
6.   To upgrade the academic achievements of Chicanos.
7.   To encourage Chicanos to fully participate in the national life of American society.

The goals of the second type of b/b programs, i.e. those geared to train teachers in b/b education, are complementary to the goals of the first type:
1.   To train teachers who can create the proper classroom atmosphere where the Chicanitos can retain and develop a positive self-image.
2.   To equip teachers with the knowledge of Chicano culture necessary to build pride in their cultural heritage.

3.   To train teachers as agents of change in their respective institutions, stimulating them to make innovations in educational methods, techniques, and curricula.
4.   To make teachers the models for incoming Chicano students who aspire to higher education.

As an illustration of the content of the second type of b/b programs and the means of obtaining the proposed goals, I will briefly describe the Mexican American Education Project (MAEP) of California State University, Sacramento (CSUS), which was started under the tutelage of the anthropology department in the fall of 1968.

MAEP AT CALIFORNIA STATE UNIVERSITY, SACRAMENTO

The MAEP began with an Experienced Teachers Fellowship Program funded by the United States Office of Education. It started with only five experienced Chicano teachers, fourteen Anglos, and one black teacher. At that time CSUS had very few Chicano students and no Chicano faculty members. The program emphasized courses in culture, culture and personality, culture change, poverty, agents of change, and cultures of Mexico. The main objective was to sensitize Anglo teachers to the special needs of Chicano students. Community involvement was encouraged. In the next academic year, 1969–1970, most program participants were experienced Chicano teachers. The program was reorganized to prepare b/b teachers and placed instructional emphasis on educational techniques and curricular innovations. Since then, the MAEP has striven to strike a balance between the rigid M.A. degree requirements, the central course work, the particular needs of students, and involvement in the local Chicano community. Evaluations from faculty and students showed the need for a more flexible organization of the academic activities. In 1971–1972 the MAEP added the "early childhood" component to serve students' interests in the education of Chicano children at the preschool and first grade levels.

As it stands today, the b/b program at CSUS offers an M.A. in Social Sciences with specialization in Chicano Studies, and it requires a minimum of thirty-one semester units distributed as follows: twenty four-units or more in social sciences, of which nine units must be taken at the upper level in an area of concentration (anthropology, criminal justice, economics, geography).

HENRY TORRES-TRUEBA

Basic Course Work

First semester
ANTHROPOLOGY: Basic concepts of culture and culture change (6)
HISTORY: Readings in Chicano History (3)
INTERDISCIPLINARY I: Chicano Involvement in Education (3)
EDUCATION: Introduction to Bilingual Education (3)

Second semester
ANTHROPOLOGY: Anthropology and Education (3)
GOVERNMENT, SOCIOLOGY, ECONOMICS: Seminar in Social Sciences (3)
INTERDISCIPLINARY II: Chicano Education, Synthesis and Application (3)
Electives in Social Sciences or Education (3)
THESIS (4)

If a student feels sufficiently prepared in an area required by the present program, he or she may, upon approval by the director, change his or her course work. Furthermore, students are encouraged to take additional courses within the school regulations.

At the end of its fifth year the MAEP has prepared over one hundred b/b teachers with an M.A. in Social Sciences and Chicano Studies, who for the most part have returned to their school districts as teachers, resource persons, administrators, or counselors. Others have been hired by the state Department of Education or by federal b/b programs. A few others have continued their education towards a Ph.D. Much of the success of this program is the result of the leadership coming from the administrative and teaching staff and the intensive interaction of the students, faculty, and the local Chicano community. During the current academic year there are seven Ph.Ds. and four M.A.s teaching from the departments of anthropology, economics, education, history, government, and sociology. Six of these instructors are Chicanos (two of them with Ph.Ds.).

By interviewing the participants during the last two years, I have arrived at the following conclusions which indicate the effectiveness of the program and its fundamental philosophy of education. Thirty-nine Chicano graduate students working for their M.A. in Social Sciences were given questionnaires and interviewed. The results are as follows:
1. In terms of the impact of the MAEP on the life of the participants, 75.6 percent feel that the project made a significant change in their careers because: (a) it made them aware of their social responsibilities and personal capabilities; (b) it gave them the opportunity to obtain a

master's degree and helped them to orientate their education towards the Chicano community.

2. When asked about the project's capacity for producing innovative teachers, 91.9 percent of the participants replied that the MAEP had offered them a unique opportunity to design educational programs and techniques that will improve Chicano education.

3. Concerning the selection of project students, 83 percent consider selection practices fair and essentially based on the qualifications of the candidates, i.e. high academic performance and a strong commitment to improve Chicano education.

4. The aspirations of project students go beyond the masters level: 29.7 percent plan to continue towards a doctorate, and 43.2 percent see the project as an initial step in the increase of their own potential, though they are not inclined to continue academically for a doctorate.

5. A majority of these Chicano students (54.1 percent) feel the need to visit as many local schools as possible to assess the situation of Chicano education and to help Chicano students.

6. Most students, however, realize that during this year's training their primary commitment is to their academic work, especially through the use of the library (86.5 percent).

7. In spite of one emphasis on group solidarity, Chicano students feel personally responsible for the outcome of their school training (86.5 percent).

8. Chicano students have two main concerns about their academic performance: (a) the demands that course work and the master's thesis represent, and (b) the lack of familiarity with proper academic behavior (75.7 percent).

9. The previous concerns are consistent with the three major challenges that many Chicanos (64.8 percent) face in school in order to:

a. adjust to the academic environment, especially when there is a conflict between school and community responsibilities (21.6 percent);

b. have confidence in their own ability, experience, and judgement (27.0 percent);

c. place themselves culturally, educationally and politically (16.2 percent).

10. When asked about the relevancy of MAEP curriculum, 97.3 percent of the participants answer that between 50 and 100 percent of the curriculum is directly applicable to their needs as teachers and administrators in schools with heavy Chicano population.

11. Nevertheless, some students (21.6 percent) would like to see curricular modifications, and others (35.1 percent) would welcome a cut in extra-curricular Chicano meetings, which in their opinion are unproductive.

12. Three out of four students have no serious economic problems during the year of training at the MAEP.

13. According to the project participants, the most important need of the Chicano community is:

a. Educational upgrading via b/b programs (48.6 percent).

b. Political leadership and political power (21.6 percent).

c. Solidarity of *La Raza* (10.8 percent).

d. Ideological leadership and more doctors of philosophy (2.7 percent).

e. Other (16.7 percent).

14. Given the opportunity, 43.2 percent of the students would like to replicate the MAEP elsewhere, while others see themselves directly involved in elementary or high school teaching of Chicanitos (40.5 percent).

15. The ideal job for the project participant would involve direct contact with as many Chicanos as possible and offer opportunities for personal intellectual growth (67.5 percent).

16. The two most important targets of the students during training are: (a) to gain knowledge rapidly, and (b) to show academic ability (67.5 percent). Other targets are the enjoyment of time to read, write, plan, and to make lasting friendships with other Chicanos.

17. Two-thirds of the participants (64.9 percent) were elementary school or high school teachers before joining the MAEP; the remaining either were students or had jobs other than teaching.

18. During early childhood 2.7 percent learned English first and learned Spanish later (still as children). Nonetheless, the great majority (64.9 percent) learned Spanish first and English later. Only 18.7 percent of the students learned English exclusively during childhood. Finally, 13.5 percent learned English and Spanish at the same time.

19. In spite of the previous findings, and although all project participants are bilinguals to a degree, only 8.1 percent feel more fluent in Spanish than in English, and less than half of them (45.9 percent) feel they speak English as well as the Anglos. Less than one-third of the participants (27.0 percent) think they speak English better than they do Spanish, and only 18.9 percent are aware of having a slight accent in English.

20. In the home, 48.6 percent use both English and Spanish, 29.7 percent use English exclusively, and 16.2 percent use Spanish exclusively.

PROBLEMS OF B/B EDUCATION

The internal and external evaluations of the program at CSUS, and similar programs, also suggest serious problems that b/b education must face. During a major three-day b/b conference in Sacramento, December 8th through 10th, where most b/b Chicano programs were represented, Chicano educators and students expressed their areas of concern with regard to problems extrinsic and intrinsic to the programs.

Extrinsic to the Programs

1. Lack of institutional support at all levels. B/b education is sometimes considered unpatriotic, politically radical, and wasteful. Unstable and meager funding reflects this lack of support.
2. Rigid educational views that curtail curricular flexibility and innovative teaching.
3. Political rivalry among Chicanos and competition for the same meager resources that divides community support.
4. Departmental and school-structured divisions that curtail effective use of personal and material resources.
5. Traditional policies for distribution and use of funds on the part of federal, state, or local agencies.

Intrinsic to the Programs

1. Lack of models of b/b education which could be replicated and lack of information about existing programs.
2. Inadequate conceptualization and justification of particular methodologies, techniques, and curricular innovations of the programs currently operating.
3. Lack of adequate personnel to staff programs, especially personnel proficient in the languages involved.
4. Lack of critical self-evaluation to assess the achievement of proposed goals, the effectiveness of the techniques used, and the reorientation of the program.
5. Conflicting philosophies of education on the part of staff and participants.

Most Chicanos present at the Sacramento conference seemed to recognize that b/b programs have developed too fast in the last five years to have been able to reassess and coordinate their activities. Since cooperative action and coordination are somehow contingent upon the philosophy of education that underlies b/b programs, it is important, at this point, to discuss the two polar positions of Chicano educators.

ANTITHETICAL PHILOSOPHICAL POSITIONS OF CHICANOS

The "Within-the-System" Philosophy of Education

This philosophy insists on the institutionalization of Chicano programs, that they be incorporated into the existing institutions of learning with full status equal to any other educational program. By implication, this philosophy strives to incorporate the Chicano population into the mainstream of American society with rights and obligations equal to those of the Anglos. American society, nevertheless, is seen by these Chicano educators as a pluralistic society that has never been homogeneous and has ignored the educational needs of the minority students. Education would, in their opinion, open the door to social and economic oportunities for the Chicano students. The steps to be followed are: (1) legislative and financial support for the existing b/b programs, (2) an increase in number of the rank and file professional academicians and educators who would be working with Chicano students, serving as models for Chicano students, and acting as middlement between the educational institutions and the students, and (3) a gradual change from within the system of education to make it more tolerant of cultural differences and more responsive to the needs of Chicanos.

The "Out-of-the-System" Philosophy

The advocates of this philosophy of education do not want to infiltrate the American educational system which they consider rotten and crumbling. They want an entirely different structure, independent from the Anglo system, with its own goals, its own rules, and one in which the control remains in the hands of Chicanos themselves. Since the main assumption is that the Anglo educational system cannot be patched or restored because it is collapsing already, this educational philosophy stresses Chicano self-sufficiency, not competition with the Anglos; Chicano self-determination, not dependence on Anglo sources; Chicano creativeness, not imitation of the Anglos. The meaningfulness of learning that comes from human experience and the values of Chicano culture are to be maximized. They emphasize *carnalismo* [brotherhood] of all Chicanos, whether they are students or faculty, and de-emphasize ritual behavior between teacher and student. These are the major tenets of the "out-of-the-system" philosophy of education:
1.   True learning is part of life, based on personal experience, and there-

fore part of one's own culture, involving the whole human being, his intellect, his heart, his wishes, aspirations, and values. Therefore, learning must capitalize on the student's language, family structure, dietary and dressing patterns, religion, and beliefs.

2. Learning must take place as an exchange of ideas between teacher and student, and among students in a symmetrical relationship where the students' wishes, rights, and intellectual inputs are respected by the teacher and the flow of messages is balanced and meaningful. This symmetrical relationship would discourage the rigidity, dishonesty, and incoherence of instructors that inhibit the student's intellectual growth.

As an example of this "out-of-the-system" philosophy, D.Q.U. (Dewanahwidah-Quetzaltcoatl University), a Chicano-Indian university near Davis, California, has been mentioned by some Chicanos. I am not prepared, however, to evaluate this example. But where we draw the line between IN and OUT of the educational system constitutes a controversial issue not yet resolved. What is important here is to note the way in which some Chicanos perceive the Anglo educational system and their contribution to our understanding of that system.

SUMMARY AND FINAL REMARKS

Chicano b/b education is beginning to stand on its own feet, struggling between two opposite philosophies, but strong enough to become a symbol of intellectual freedom and a promise of a better future for the Chicano community. In the view of the Chicano staff and participants, b/b education goes beyond a fair share of the good things of life in American society: it means social recognition, respect, and self-determination. While Chicanos may complain at times that there are more chiefs than Indians, on many other occasions chiefs and Indians iron out their differences and work cooperatively, showing a true *carnalismo* and love for each other. Quietly, the "within-the-system" programs grow and show their fruits, thus giving *La Raza* a new sense of confidence and optimism.

REFERENCES

SIMMEN, EDWARD
1972 *Pain and promise: the Chicano today.* New York: New American Library.

The Ethnography of Communication
and the Teaching of Languages

E. ROULET

Editors' Note In this paper Eddy Roulet takes traditional language education to task for its emphasis on the learning of a "competence at language" rather than a "competence at communication." It is true that most language instruction is able to teach the grammar and structure of a language (just as most structural linguistics is able to analyze this facet of language), but it does not necessarily teach the rules of choice and usage in actual situations of social interaction. Roulet calls on sociolinguistics and other social sciences to make up for this lack, and he himself offers some suggestions for approaches. Roulet has stepped with a practical voice into an age-old question of the existence or utility of that which is not actualized or used. Of what value is any knowledge of language which does not enable the individual to carry out social encounters?

For a long period the teaching of foreign languages was dominated by traditional methods based on translating, directed primarily to facilitating access to the literary works of other countries. At the beginning of this century, under the pressure of the requirements (economic, administrative, touristic, etc.) of contemporary society, the need to teach foreign languages as instruments of communication was recognized. Educationalists gradually abandoned the traditional grammars as being of little use, as they do not deal with the spoken language in use at a given time. They turned to linguists who, after de Saussure and Bloomfield, introduced a more systematic concept of language and proposed new and more precise descriptions of the languages taught, particularly the oral code (cf. Roulet 1972). Thus a new field of research rapidly developed, i.e. linguistics applied to the teaching of languages. And so it is that, since World War II, methods and courses called "linguistic" have appeared. These were intended to allow students, through carefully graded structural exercises (pattern drillls), to acquire the automatic responses necessary for daily communication.

It is true that the results obtained with beginners, especially by audio-visual or audio-oral intensive measures, appeared at first to be quite impressive. Students were capable of understanding and producing more rapidly and more correctly numerous structures of the spoken language, and they obtained better results in second-chance tests. However, researchers gradually realized that this new approach also had major defects. We will recall just three of these here:

a.   These new courses do not appear to help one develop the capacity to express himself freely and to communicate in the various situations of daily life. Gumperz acknowledges: "It is fair to say that we have not been completely successful in providing students with the linguistic ability they need to communicate effectively in speech communities where these languages are spoken" (1965:82). This is the paradox set forth by Jakobovits concerning this new approach to the teaching of foreign languages: "The irony of the matter lies in the fact that the 'New Key' approach, unlike the traditional methods in which reading classical literature was considered a worthwhile activity in itself, does not attach an intrinsic value to grammatical knowledge per se, but views habit drills as means towards achieving communicative skills, yet it seems that these very activities are the chief roadblocks to attaining meaningful skills ('liberated expression', as it has been called)" (1970:84). Furthermore, many teachers had realized that the students who obtained good results in attainment tests were often incapable of holding a conversation in the foreign language (see Savignon 1972:154). It can be argued that the majority of audiovisual or audio-oral methods include a so-called exploitation phase, which should in fact help the pupil pass from the strict conditioning of structural exercises to a freer expression in situations of communication. But this is an illusion, for, as Savignon recalls: "When so-called 'directed communication' is introduced, it is not communication at all, as the structural frame, if not the lexical content, remains in the control of the instructor" (1972:153). In short, the courses do not permit attainment of the objective in view.

b.   These new courses, far from interesting students, seem to bore them, at times to the point of discouraging them from learning new foreign languages. Let us read Hester's evidence: "Everywhere, we see a tendency to abandon foreign languages, among various other disciplines, because they are a hindrance to the young learner's freedom, self-discovery, and natural 'creativity'" (1970:viii). It is difficult to see how one can develop the capacity for students to communicate in a foreign language if they do not feel the need to use it, because they are not given the opportunity to express their wishes and requirements.

c. If the principles of this new approach turn out to be relatively effective in the acquisition of the first elements of a foreign language, they seem to be of little application to other levels of teaching. This is undoubtedly not an accident if there are a great number of audio-visual and audio-oral courses for the first level of learning a foreign language, while such courses for advanced levels are rare and less systematic. "Unfortunately," write Allen and Widdowson, "the generous provision of basic courses has coincided with a striking lack of new material specially designed for intermediate and advanced students. As a result, students who have become accustomed to an orderly progression of graded materials, simple explanations and easily-manipulated drills during the first two or three years of language learning find that these aids are suddenly withdrawn when they reach the end of the basic course, and that they are left to fend for themselves with little or no guidance at a time when the language is rapidly becoming more difficult" (1972:2).

The balance-sheet of this "linguistic" approach for a complete change in the teaching of foreign languages thus appears very much less favorable than anticipated. It is advisable to ask why an attempt based on scientific data borrowed from psychology and linguistics, and which has received the benefit of considerable investments, has ended in this relative failure.

It seems to us that one can explain and try to repair the errors committed by examining three factors:

a. one must clearly state what is meant by "being proficient in a language as an instrument of communication";

b. one must ask whether structural and transformational generative linguistics, from de Saussure to Chomsky, supply the information necessary for the drawing up of the contents of a language course directed to inculcating this communicative competence; and

c. one must reexamine the principles for learning a foreign language which underlie these methods in the light of recent research in psycholinguistics.

We shall limit ourselves here to dealing with the first two points, which are of direct concern to the subject of this paper (for the third, see Roulet i.p.).

What does one mean by being proficient in a language as an instrument of communication?

First, it is not sufficient to be capable of reading and writing a sentence correctly, as in traditional teaching; nor is it enough to be capable of understanding and producing rapidly and automatically a correct sentence in response to certain elementary stimuli, as in audiovisual and audio-oral teaching. One must know how to use the sentences appropriately in a linguistic context and in a given situational context. In other words, one must now how, on the one hand, to combine these sentences into larger units of communication, such as text and dialogue, and on the other hand, to use expressions appropriate to certain situations of communication (Allen and Widdowson 1972:3-4).

Second, to be proficient in a language as an instrument of communication is not just to be capable of transmitting information and asking questions of the universe which surrounds us ("Mrs. Thibaut opens the door," "How many rooms do you have?," etc.) (see Ducrot 1972a:1–5; Gumperz 1965:84). Barthes noted appropriately in L'empire des signes: "Open a travel guide: there you will usually find a small vocabulary list, but this glossary will bear whimsically on tedious and useless things: customs formalities, post, hotel, hairdressers, the doctor, prices. Yet, what is travelling? It is meeting people. The only important vocabulary is that for arranging meetings" (1970:25). One may make this observation more general by replacing "glossary" with "language," and "travelling" with "living in a community." In fact, we speak less generally to describe the universe which surrounds us (what Jakobson [1963:213] calls the referential, cognitive, or denotative function of language) than to establish contact with other people (the phatic function), to express our attitude with regard to the person with whom we are speaking or the subject of the conversation (expressive function), or to make the other person act (conative function). Furthermore, this observation is confirmed by the fact (which might for a moment surprise and embarrass the creators of audiovisual material) that words designating many common objects do not appear in the summaries of basic French drawn up from recordings of conversation. If one thinks of the situation of a student landing in a foreign country, there is no doubt that the most important thing for him is to establish and maintain contacts with the natives in order to be able to participate as much as possible in the life of their community. Now, it may frequently happen that these contacts, that communication, may be hampered or strained, even when the referential content of the message is transmitted perfectly, through a simple failure to recognize expressive, phatic, or conative features of the dialogue. Consequently, to be proficient in a language as an instrument of communication is to master not only the referential function, but also the expressive, phatic, conative, and even poetic functions.

Third, and as a corollary, in order to be able to communicate satisfactorily in a linguistic community, it is not sufficient to know a pure, homogeneous, monolithic language. One must be capable at least of understanding, and if possible of using, the different varieties of language used in the community in question. "Without any doubt," writes Jakobson (1963:213), "for every linguistic community, for every person speaking, there is a unity of language; but this overall code represents a system of sub-codes in reciprocal communication. Each language embraces several simultaneous systems, each of which is characterised by a different function." This is a very important fact, because in communication with other people the choice of variety of language used often says more about the emotional, professional, and social relationships (present and future) of the speakers than the content of the conversation. To be proficient in a language as an instrument of communication is thus also to understand its principal subcodes and to know how to use them in appropriate situations.

To illustrate our remark, let us take a concrete example which is well known today by sociolinguists, but which has never been treated systematically in language courses: the use of expressions of address and greeting. In a great number of languages the speaker has a choice between two pronouns to address the person to whom he is speaking: *tu* and *vous* in French, *ty* and *vy* in Russian, *du* and *Sie* in German, *du* and *ir* in Yiddish, etc. Concurrently, the speaker generally has the choice between different forms of address: Christian name (James), family name (Wood), title plus family name (Mr. Wood), and different forms of greeting (*Salut!*, *Bonjour*, *Monsieur!*, etc.). In communication these choices often have a more important significance than the purely referential content of the message. This is because they give each speaker valuable information, especially in the first moments of a new relationship, about the attitude and feelings of the other to himself, and may exert a decisive influence on the development of this relationship (cf. the importance of using the familiar "tu" form in French, for example). For subjects expressing themselves in their mother tongue, the use of these forms with respect to the emotional and social status of the person to whom they are speaking is so automatic and natural that there is no problem. The same is not true for the foreigner. For if this use is controlled by features which are probably universal, the norms for their use differ from one community to another (see Brown and Gilman 1962; Brown and Ford 1961; Slobin 1963; Friedrich 1972). The failure to recognize the rules for the use of these expressions in a certain community, in comprehension as well as in expression, may have much more unfortunate consequences for the community life of a foreigner than errors, even serious and repeated ones, of grammar, vocabulary, and pronunciation. Now, language courses do not deal with these problems and language teachers generally only have a vague knowledge of the rules of the employment of these expressions.

We have now sufficiently described the requirements for the use of a language as an instrument of communication to be able to reexamine the contribution of linguistics to the teaching of languages. We can state at once that the principal linguistic theories which have been applied to the teaching of languages have been so scaled down in the definition of their objective, from de Saussure to Chomsky, that they do not furnish any information on the use of language as an instrument of communication. In fact,

a. they describe only the rules and not the use of the language; for, as Candlin writes, "Useful though such an input from several linguistic grammars may be, the question begged is clearly that if a pedagogical grammar is at the basis of LT materials, and if such materials have as their aim to lead the learner to 'knowledge' of the L2, then they, and the pedagogical grammar, must be as concerned with rules of language USE as they are with rules of grammaticality and well-formedness of sentences" (1972b: 58).

b. They deal only with the structure of the sentence and therefore neglect units of communication such as text and dialogue. Therefore, Widdowson writes, "If we are to teach languages in use, we have to shift our attention from sentences in isolation to the manner in which they combine in text on the one hand, and to the manner in which they are used to perform communicative acts in discourse on the other" (1972:69). For that, one must have at one's disposal a grammar of text, which presents the rules for combining sentences in a text, and a grammar of discourse, presenting the rules for the use of sentences in acts of communication.

c. They systematically study only the referential function, neglecting the other functions of language. Frake notes: "To ask appropriately for a drink among the Subanun it is not enough to know how to construct a grammatical utterance in Subanun translatable in English as a request for a drink. Rendering such an utterance might elicit praise for one's fluency in Subanun, but it would probably not get a drink.... Our stranger requires more than a grammar and a lexicon; he needs what Hymes (1962) has called an ethnography of speaking; a specification of what kinds of things to say in what message forms to what kinds of people in what kinds of situations" (1964:87–88). We shall return later to Hymes's contribution.

d.   They study only one variety of language, regarded as homogeneous and representative, and neglect the other varieties which form part of the verbal repertoire of a linguistic community.

The gap between the two approaches, the theory of the rules of language and the theory of the use of language, undoubtedly goes back to the distinction between LANGUAGE and SPEECH, as established by de Saussure in his *General linguistics course*. Language is a code, a system of social conventions common to all members of a community. Speech is the individual use of this code in daily communication. Therefore, linguistics will study the rules of language as a matter of priority, even exclusively, relegating the study of speech, if it is possible, to an indefinite period in the future. So it is that the distinction established by de Saussure is going to lead to a rapid and necessary developing of the study of the rules of language, but it is also unfortunately going to draw linguists away from the study of the use of language. De Saussure, in fact, as Ducrot notes (1972b:11), "identifies linguistic activity and individual initiative," thus relating all study of our linguistic activity to the linguistics of speech, which is regarded as of minor importance. This is the source of the neglect which has left to one side studies of the use of language, units of communication such as text and dialogue, and the different functions of language. Now, numerous features of these linguistic activities do not depend on our individual initiative and are governed by social conventions as hide-bound as the code of language. They may thus form the subject of a study which is just as strict.

The classic transformational generative theory of Chomsky, Katz, and Halle, though it constitutes a fundamental contribution to the theory and description of linguistics on other points, remains a THEORY of the rules of languages. It characterizes competence in the restricted sense, that is to say, the capacity to construct correct grammatical sentences independently of any linguistic or situational context, and it maintains the fiction of a monolithic language which is pure and homogeneous. "Despite the increase in the scope of linguistic descriptions," writes Gumperz (1965:82), "the new theory continues to make sharp distinctions between grammars and the social context in which utterances are used." Very varied elements are consigned to the domain of performance, as, in earlier days, they were consigned to the domain of speech, without distinguishing the individual psychopathological factors of social conventions. In short, though the classic transformational generative theory considerably increases our knowledge of the rules of language, it doesn't teach us anything concerning the use of language and its different subcodes in different functions as instruments of communication (see Roulet 1972).

Such a limitation of the field of study seems acceptable as long as one is merely preparing a theory of limited dimensions, but it becomes untenable once one tries to apply this theory to a concrete field of activities, such as the teaching of foreign languages. One must also not be surprised at the relative failure of attempts to apply linguistics to the teaching of languages. Linguistics, from de Saussure to Chomsky, is simply unable to supply the information necessary for the teaching of languages as instruments of communication.

Rather than start from the contribution of the most well-known linguistic theories and ask what they can contribute to the teaching of languages, it is better to start with the requirements to teach languages as instruments of communication in order to examine other approaches to language. Gumperz posed the problem clearly in 1965: "It seems necessary, at least for the purpose of applied linguistics, to reopen the question of the relationship between linguistic and social facts. More specifically, the question arises: given a grammatical analysis of the languages involved, what additional information can the sociolinguist provide in order to enable the language teacher to give his students the skills they need to communicate effectively in a new society?" (1965:84).

Now, alongside the flow of research of which we have spoken, a current has always existed which remained marginal for a long time before occupying, for some years now, an important place on the linguistic scene, and the preoccupations of this latter current are much closer to those of applied linguists. We wish to speak of what Hymes today calls the ethnography of communication.

As early as 1935, Firth rejected the traditional concept of a monolithic and homogeneous language. "There is no such thing as *une langue une* and there never has been" (1935:67). He observes that we all, according to the situation, play different social roles and that a certain variety of language corresponds to each role. He asserts, as a corollary, that speech is not an "endless chaos" and that conversation is much more structured than is generally believed. In fact, we are not all that free to say what we want in the way we want to, for our linguistic activity is controlled to a large degree by conventions linked to our role and the situation. Malinowski, in 1937, proposed an abandoning of the language-speech distinction and declared that the principal objective of linguistic study should be living speech in its context of situation: "The present reviewer, like most modern anthropologists, would plead for the empirical approach to linguistics, placing living speech in its actual context of situation as the main object of linguistic study" (1937:173). Finally, Troubetzkoy, in his *Principes de phonologie*, asserts during the same period, after K. Bühler, the necessity of making a systematic study of the expressive and appellative functions of language, along with the representative (or referential) function: "Among the phonic impressions through which we recognise the person of the subject speaking, and the emotional influence which he intends to exercise on the listener, there are those which, to be correctly understood, must be put together in accordance with well-defined norms which have been established in the language in question. These norms are to be considered as linguistic values; they belong to the language, and phonology must consequently deal with them" (1949:17).

These few references suffice to show that at the time of the first attempts to apply linguistics to the teaching of languages, a number of linguists were already asserting the possibility of and the need for a systematic study of the use of the different varieties of language. One may regret that they were not heard more by applied linguists and pedagogues.

It was only in the sixties that the study of the use of different kinds of language, under the impetus provided by Hymes and other sociolinguists and under the label of the ethnography of communication (or the ethnography of speaking), began to take shape as a field of research within linguistics and to undergo very rapid development. Hymes defined its objective in these terms: "This is a question of what a child internalizes about speaking, beyond rules of grammar and a dictionary, while becoming a full-fledged member of its speech community. Or it is a question of what a foreigner must learn about a group's verbal behavior in order to participate appropriately and effectively in its activities. The ethnography of speaking is concerned with the situations and uses, the patterns and functions, of speaking as an activity in its own right" (1962:101). This definition itself immediately reveals how much the preoccupations of researchers in the field of the ethnography of communication completely respond to the requirements of teachers (see Gumperz 1965:85).

The main feature of this approach is to examine the verbal activities of a linguistic community as a whole and to study all the varieties of language that it uses (i.e. its verbal repertoire), instead of sticking to the description of only one of its codes or subcodes. Verbal exchanges within a community are analyzed in situations of communication (hunting, meals, courting a girl), which are subdivided into incidents of communication which are more limited and essentially verbal (conversation), which are themselves formed by acts of communication (order, question, joke, etc.) (Hymes 1972).

Each act of speech or communication is analyzed in turn in terms of a certain number of components, which are meager at the present state of research: form and content of the message, framework (geographic, temporal, and pyschological), participants (speaker, the person addressed, listener), objectives intended, methods (i.e. intonation, spirit in which the action is committed), channel of communication (oral, written, telegraphic), varieties of language used (dialects, tone qualities, etc.), norms of interaction (expression in a whisper or silent listening, for example), norms of interpretation (with respect to the community's system of beliefs) and genres (poem, story, proverb, etc.) (Hymes 1972:58–65).

One may then draw up rules of speech or communication which relate these different components of an act of communication so as to give a formal description of the latter (Labov 1970; Ervin-Tripp 1972).

Very interesting results have already been obtained by describing the use of expressions of address, the importance of which we have already noted in communicative competence. Brown and Ford (1961), Brown and Gilman (1962), Slobin (1963), and Friedrich (1972) have isolated the different variables which govern the use of these expressions of address in English, Yiddish, and Russian, and Ervin-Tripp (1972) has recently shown that it was easy to formalize their rules.

Undoubtedly such an approach may contribute valuable information for the teaching of languages as instruments of communication. Unfortunately, its theory has still scarcely been outlined, their analysis patterns have only begun to be programmed, and descriptions are still rare and very incomplete. Now, it is very well known that applied linguists and teachers cannot wait for the eventual completion of the works of general practitioners in order to set to work.

The situation is less serious than it appears, for it is already possible, while waiting for the completion of more important and systematic descriptions, to draw inspiration from the principles of the ethnography of communication, to gather materials that are of use for pedagogical purposes, to redefine the objectives and the content of language courses — in short, to prepare and experiment with new courses.

In reference to this first point, let us cite the sociolinguistic survey on the French spoken in Orléans (cf. Blanc and Biggs 1971), which will provide teachers with a large amount of systematic data and authentic documents on the use of French by different persons from different environments in different situations of communication within an urban community.

As to the redefinition of the objectives and contents of language courses, this is illustrated by the attempts of Candlin (1972a) and Wilkins (1972). The first, after having drawn up an inventory of the components of a course aimed at teaching competency in communication with regard to the social roles, purposes, and attitudes of the people speaking, proposes a program for teaching the principal acts of communication: presenting information, expressing an opinion, introducing someone or something, suggesting, advising, agreeing, criticizing, etc. Wilkins, within the framework of the great project for teaching languages to adults which was launched by the Council of Europe, defines on a notational basis the principal functions of communication which should constitute the heart of a system of training by capitalizable units: modalities (certainty, necessity, conviction, doubt, etc.), assessment (judgments), argumentation (agreement, disagreement, refusal, concession, etc.), persuasion, enquiry or rational exposition, etc.

Although these two experiments are still at the draft stage, several attempts already exist for the preparation of and experimentation with language courses directed to teaching communicative competency. Gumperz, based on the knowledge he acquired during his sojourn and sociolinguistic research in India, prepared a course in Hindi and Urdu with Rumery (Gumperz and Rumery 1962) and tried it out at the University of California. It not only offers the most up-to-date constructions in these languages, but also teaches their use in an urban environment such as that of New Delhi. From the beginning the student is placed, with the assistance of prepared recordings and slides, in the most typical and frequently encountered situations of communication for a stranger arriving in this city. Gumperz (1965:87) describes the contents of the course in these terms: "After setting up a list of likely conversational situations and identifying each with respect to their cultural labels, these situations and the statuses of participants can then be graded in terms of their social complexity and in terms of the amount of knowledge of the culture that they require." Such an approach leads to excellent results in the acquisition of communicative competence, as is proved by the experiences of students who stayed in India after having taken the course. In addition (an interesting fact for the applied linguist and teacher), it offers a happy solution to the difficult problem of preparing lexical and grammatical progressions: "The initial assumption regarding the dependence of linguistic form on social setting receives partial confirmation from the fact that in our text grammatical grading of conversational material emerges as a natural consequence of contextural grading" (Gumperz 1965:89).

For a more advanced and specialized level of apprenticeship in a foreign language, Allen and Widdowson have prepared a scientific English course which no longer aims only to teach students to construct correct sentences, but encourages them to use these sentences adequately in different situations of communication. They recommend a whole series of a new type of exercise, some aiming to show how sentences are combined in the text, others showing how they are used in different functions of communication (see Allen and Widdowson 1972).

Finally, let us report the results of a recent comparative test on the relative effectiveness of the teaching of the rules and the teaching of the use of language with a view to acquiring communicative competence. The experiment is undoubtedly too simple for us to be able to draw any final conclusions from it, but it already provides some revealing information. Savignon (1972) describes an experiment in the teaching of French to beginning students at the University of Illinois: a control group used classic audio-oral teaching methods, with a language laboratory; a second group used materials consisting essentially of conversational exercises on French culture and civilization; a third used materials based on the carrying out of specific acts of communication. In this last group, which is of special interest to us here, the researchers particularly sought to enable students to use French in situations of communication from the first week of the course on without attaching importance to the linguistic accuracy of what was said. The results of the experiment, as reported by Savignon (1972:160), are striking: "To summarize, all students had received similar instruction in linguistic skills, and there was no evidence that one group knew more French than the other in terms of the level of linguistic competence attained. However, those students who had been given the opportunity to use their linguistic knowledge for real communication were able to speak French. The others were not."

We have tried in this brief survey of the contribution of linguistics to the teaching of languages to show that a linguistic theory and description could only be validly applied to the teaching of foreign languages if they took into account the use of different varieties of language to carry out acts of communication in different situations. The majority of linguistic theories and descriptions, from de Saussure to Chomsky, which have been used in applied linguistics do not fulfill this elementary condition. On the other hand, the ethnography of communication, as developed by Hymes and sociolinguists, completely answers the requirements for teaching languages as an instrument of communication. Consequently, it is advisable to guide research in applied linguistics and to modify the conception of language courses by taking into account the fundamental contribution of the ethnography of communication.

REFERENCES

ALLEN, J. P. B., G. H. WIDDOWSON
1972 "Teaching the communicative use of English." Edinburgh, mimeographed.
BARTHES, R.
1970 *L'empire des signes.* Geneva: Skira.
BLANC, M., P. BIGGS
1971 L'enquête sociolinguistique sur le français parlé à Orléans. *Le Français dans le Monde* 85: 16-25.
BROWN, R. W., M. FORD
1961 Address in American English. *JASP* 62:375–385.
BROWN, R. W., A. GILMAN
1962 "The pronouns of power and solidarity," in *Style in language.* Edited by T. A. Sebeok, 253–276. New York: Wiley.
CANDLIN, C.
1972a "Acquiring communicative competence," in *32nd Dutch Philologists' Conference.* Utrecht.
1972b "The status of pedagogical grammars," in *Theoretical linguistic models in applied linguistics.* Edited by S. P. Corder and E. Roulet. Brussels AIMAV; and Paris: Didier.
DE SAUSSURE, F.
1972 *General linguistics course* (critical edition of T.de Mauro). Paris: Payot.
DUCROT, O.
1972a *Dire et ne pas dire: principes de sémantique linguistique.* Paris: Hermann.
1972b "De Saussure à la philosophie du language." Preface to *Les actes de language,* by J. R. Searle, 7–34. Paris: Hermann.
ERVIN-TRIPP, S.
1972 "On sociolinguistic rules: alternation and co-occurrence," in *Directions in sociolinguistics.* Edited by J. J. Gumperz and D. Hymes, 213-250. New York: Holt, Rinehart and Winston.
FIRTH, J. R.
1935 The techniques of semantics. *Transactions of the Philological Society,* 36–72.
FRAKE, C. O.
1964 How to ask for a drink in Subanun. *American Anthropologist* 66(6): 127–132.
FRIEDRICH, P.
1972 "Social context and semantic features in the Russian pronominal usage," in *Directions in sociolinguistics.* Edited by J. J. Gumperz and D. Hymes, 270-300. New York: Holt, Rinehart and Winston.
GUMPERZ, J. J.
1965 *Linguistic repertoires, grammars and second language instruction.* Monograph Series on Languages and Linguistics 18:81–90.
GUMPERZ, J. J., J. RUMERY
1962 *Conversational Hindi-Urdu.* Berkeley: University of California, Institute of International Studies.
HESTER, R.
1970 *Teaching a living language.* New York: Harper and Row.

HYMES, D.
1962   "The ethnography of speaking," in *Anthropology and human behavior.* Edited by T. Gladwyn and W. C. Sturtevant, 13–53. Washington: Anthropological Society.
1972   "Models of interaction of language and social life," in *Directions in sociolinguistics.* Edited by J. J. Gumperz and D. Hymes, 35–71. New York: Holt, Rinehart and Winston.
JAKOBOVITS, L. A.
1970   *Foreign language learning: a psycholinguistic analysis of the issues.* Rowley: Newbury House.
JAKOBSON, R.
1963   *Essais de linguistique générale.* Paris: Minuit.
LABOV, W.
1970   The study of language in its social context. *Studium Generale* 23:30–87.
MALINOWSKI, B.
1937   Review of "Infant speech" by M. M. Lewis. *Nature* 140:172–173.
ROULET, E.
1972   *Théories grammaticales, descriptions et enseignement des langues.* Brussels: Labor; and Paris: Nathan.
i.p.   "Vers une grammaire de l'emploi et de l'apprentissage de la langue," in *Proceedings of the 3rd Congress of the International Association of Applied Linguistics.*
SAVIGNON, J. A.
1972   Teaching for communicative competence: a research report. *Audio-Visual Language Journal* 10:153–162.
SLOBIN, D. I.
1963   Some aspects of the use of pronouns of address in Yiddish. *Word* 19:193–202.
TROUBETZKOY, D. S.
1949   *Principes de phonologie.* Paris: Klincksieck.
WIDDOWSON, H. G.
1972   "Directions in the teaching of discourse," in *Theoretical linguistic models in applied linguistics.* Edited by S. P. Corder and E. Roulet. Brussels: AIMAV; and Paris: Didier.
WILKINS, D.
1972   *An Investigation into the linguistic and situational content of the common core in a unit/credit system.* Strasbourg: Council of Europe.

CONCLUSIONS

Education and the Problem of Continuity

CRAIG J. CALHOUN

Editors' Note: It is customary at the end of a collection of essays to offer a conclusion, an encapsulation of what has been "found" and revealed concerning the subject at hand. The fields of anthropology and education seem, however, to merit an exhortation more than a pat on the back. To a very large extent, we have arrived on the field of battle — and then hidden from the enemy. In this essay Craig Calhoun suggests that what is needed to unify the many disparate empirical enquiries going on is a perspective, a social, cultural, and historical context in which to set the problems of education. To this end he examines the relationship between individual and society, the inevitable instability of the latter, and its relation to the purposive character of education. Hopefully, a tentative point of departure will prove more useful than a false conclusion to the growing relationship between anthropology and education.

When we call the world in which we live "modern," we are generally distinguishing it from a "traditional" one. We are suggesting that this modern world is somehow free from the bonds of the past. Instead of maintaining a social order predicated on tradition, we attempt to make new decisions, to respond to new situations. In the process we ensure that there will be still more new situations. The ideologies of progress and rationality which govern us are geared to bring this "modernity" more and more into being. But in this our ideologies are perhaps on their last legs. With them we attempt to break away from bonds that have lost their strength as well as their utility. Westerners often regard it as "backward" for members of traditional societies to balk at ever-accelerating rates of change and cycles of crises. At the same time, millions of Westerners seek community in both illusory and practical forms.

Since at least the eighteenth century, education has been a popular cause of liberal reformers as they have sought to improve the moral and economic conditions of the working class. Epually often — and generally with epual disinclination to radical solutions — education has been put forward as the key to the "development" of Third World nations. But in many cases this development has amounted to simply a dissolution of traditional society or a weak and unstable syncretism of incompatible forms. As the essays in this book demonstrate, education can be in one view a process of enculturation and in another an instrument of social and cultural change (for better or worse). Education can be used in the attempt to produce community solidarity or individual distinctiveness. Educators throughout the world are currently grappling with means for encompassing multiple world views, languages, sets of expectations, rules. Moreover, educators are often presented with a double task: they are expected to act as the guardians of culture and stability, and at the same time they are expected to prepare their students to deal with new situations, that is, with situations in which their culture does not fit. To be sure, much educational practice may seem to avoid such a dilemma. But even where it does not consciously confront the issue, its social impact can only be understood through consideration of the way it relates to this problem. I shall attempt to show that one aspect of this problem — that of achieving continuity — is becoming increasingly dominant, even while most curricula and theories are focused on change. Our general problem, then, is to establish a context for the study of education.

I. This problem results, at its most basic level, from the existence of history. If we assume that societies do not form coherent and completely stable systems, then we must see change as pervasive.[1] A crucial aspect of any social situation is thus its IMMANENCE, the direction of change implicit in its organization as abstracted at any moment. Further, if we look at societies over time we see that rates of change are variable and may be accelerating or decelerating within any particular period. Now, the existence of history is not only a problem denied or avoided by some varieties of social theory and research; it is also a notion which ahs different meanings for different societies. It is thus that we suggest that

---

[1] Not all change is equivalent, of course, but some change is inescapable. As Marx notes, considering early agrarian communities: "The aim of all these communities is survival; i.e., reproduction of the individuals who compose it as proprietors, i.e., in the same objective mode of existence as forms the relation among the members and at the same time therefore the commune itself. This reproduction, however, is at the same time necessarily new production and destruction of the old form" (1973 [1939]: 493). At the very least, this is because the natural conditions of existence change, and the forces of production are developed in turn (leaving exogenous influences, for example, out of consideration).

history may not be an important — or even existent — REFERENCE (of the members) in highly stable, traditional social orders. Empirically, however, we note that there is some change. It is simply possible for the members of such societies to act on the assumption that the social order will not change. There is almost no place in the world today where effective long-term action could be based on such an assumption.

When we term a social order "traditional," we clearly characterize it by reference to the members' minds. Tradition involves attitudes and sentiments relating to the past. I contend, however, that traditional social order cannot be understood by primary reference to sentiments or by any such analysis of "efficient causes" (cf. Homans and Schneider 1955). To advocate an analysis based simply on efficient causes would be to advocate the sort of myopia with which any individual must necessarily view the workings of his own immediate society. This argument rests on the suggestion that social events take place over greatly varying "objective" durations. That is, put crudely, some things happen within the range of individuals' vision and action, and some things do not. Of course this vision and action may vary. Some individuals may encompass a broader scope than others; some social situations may make the extension of vision more important to the choice of action than others.

Social institutions, such as unilineal descent, are particularly unlikely to be historically the result of "adoption" by consciously deciding individuals. The adoption argument has had its influential proponents, however. Among them are Homans and Schneider, for example, who proposed it in opposition to (their erroneous characterization of) Lévi-Strauss's position (in 1949). Their misreading of Lévi-Strauss seems to follow, however, from the conclusions they wish to draw and the recommendations they wish to make for the future of comparative sociology and social theory. These recommendations and conclusions are individualist in bias and are geared toward a maximization of ends analysis, complete with the assumption that individuals are able not only to identify but also to achieve their ends. Their stance suggests that both the extent of individuality and the extent of maximization of ends are social constants. But this is not true. Further, this falseness and the reasons for it have important implications for social policy with regard to education. These include implications for the choice of conservative or liberal ideologies and of orientations which emphasize fitting the school to the students or the students to society. Although I do not adopt the latter position in its most obvious form, I think that serious attention to the problem of social order and continuity argues against the currently fashionable alternative.

In opposition to those who seek to apply exchange theory to traditional social orders,[2] I suggest that as individualization increases and persons turn their "maximizing attention" more to their personal ends, such long-term social institutions as unilineal descent must be destroyed or at least removed from their position of social centrality. Paradoxically, therefore, the very social institutions which Homans and Schneider set out to study have as an essential characteristic the limitation of the individuality on which these authors base their analysis. The stronger the unilineal descent system, the less applicable Homans's and Schneider's arguments. The "psychological preoccupation" for which Needham faults them with devastating criticism (1962:126) is largely the result of their assumptions — and they are nothing more than assumptions — about the nature of man. Though they wrote nearly two centuries later, they shared the fault for which Marx criticized "natural right" theorists and utilitarian economists alike: the assumption of the state of man in alienated, capitalist "civil society" as man's universal and inevitable nature.

What, then, is the relationship between society and the individual? We may divide the question into two components, treating first the relationship between context and individual identity, and then asking how sociality and individuality may variably characterize different populations. Of course, in neither case can we do more here than sketch the barest outline of a full discussion.

II.   The identities of social actors are established primarily through contraposition with other actors. This has not been taken as being as obvious as it might seem, we may note, particularly by sociologists and anthropologists writing on the concepts of status and role. Many of these seem to reify social positions (statuses) into independent units operating outside of actual social situations and interaction. Similarly they tend to take roles as given concomitants of statuses rather than as the actions of an actor. This is more than just a terminological dispute; it is a real problem in social theory.

A necessary condition of any identity is distinction from "other," from nonidentity, or, at the highest level, from nothingness. This necessity of the other implies as well the importance of the definiteness of the other. An identification by contraposition can only be as secure and as specific as each of the parties is to its counterpart. No identity (social or otherwise), then, exists at once, in itself, as an immediate unity. An actor's social

---

[2]   And in opposition to those who would make simple individualism the ideology of all educational programs or of all economic activity.

identity can only be achieved/expressed in terms of other social identities, and, further, this interrelation of identities is temporal. It occurs as extant and given at no one point in time, but is both determined and created over time.

True reality is merely this process of reinstating self-identity, of reflecting into its own self in and from its other, and is not an original and primal unity as such. It is the process of its own becoming, the circle which presupposes its end as its purpose, and has its end for its beginning; it becomes concrete and actual only by being carried out, and by the end it involves (Hegel 1967 [1807]:80–1).

Hegel is describing here both a progress of a single mind and of "Mind" in history. The important point to grasp is the idea of movement, of the partiality or unreality of any moment taken out of context, and of the organized nature of the temporal whole. One caveat must be added with regard to the great question of evolutionary theory: whether the "end" is indeed implicit in the beginning, and, if implicit, knowable. Perhaps the most satisfying resolution to this problem is simply to indicate that revelation would be as necessary to prove such an historical doctrine as it would the existence of God (cf. Kolakowski 1971:31–58).

Leaving this last aside, the reciprocal involvement of social elements with each other in the process of establishing their respective identities is clear. As Fortes observes, this is the key to a segmentary lineage organization:

A segmentary relationship between lineages or any other social units implies the existence of specificities and cleavages which have the effect of making each unit a determining factor in the emergence of other units (1945:233).

The "social elements" for which this is the case include all the symbolic units of social intercourse, even such "material" ones as commodities (bear in mind that it is their symbolic, not material, nature that is involved). As Marx observed, value relations are such that the bodily or material form of one object becomes the value form of another. In other words, a commodity's value cannot be expressed in and of itself, but is a matter of comparison: "The value of A, thus expressed in the use-value of B, has taken the form of relative value" (Marx 1970 [1867]: 59). In a note, Marx even remarks on the analogous formation of human identity (not only demonstrating his continuing affinity with Hegel, but anticipating in an aside a key insight of such modern psychologists as Erikson):

In a sort of way, it is with man as with commodities. Since he comes into the world neither with a looking glass in his hand, nor as a fichtian philosopher, to whom "I am I" is sufficient, man first sees and recognizes himself in other men (Marx 1970 [1867]).

Not only does "man" do this, and not only *vis-à-vis* other individual persons. Not only is this the means of first sight or initial identity. Social actors of all varieties (including both individuals and groups) have their identities only in relation to others. Where this does not at first appear to be true, it is because a process of abstraction has taken place. Such abstractions are statuses appearing in isolation from their contexts. The extent of actual identification by contraposition vs. abstraction is of course variable. Thus, in a highly stable society with a close-knit fabric of social integration, identification by contraposition is elaborate and highly specific; the extent of abstract identity is minimal. In our "modern" society a much greater part of the definition of social identities is abstract; contraposition is both more amorphous and more variable. In this indefiniteness others are still implicated, but to a very low extent: "Each is indeed certain of its own self, but not of the other, and hence its own certainty of itself is still without truth" (Hegel, 1967 [1807]: 232). The major characteristic (mechanism) or identity is thus weakened as social integration is weakened. Individuality destroys the means of individuality. This is a central paradox of society.

III. In a sense we have established individuality on the opposite end of a continuum from society. This continuum represents a (complex) sociological variable. We are not, for example, primarily interested in an existentialist conceptualization of the individual, that is, in his life for himself (although it is difficult to entirely ignore experiential aspects of individuality when considering alienation). We are interested in the extent and effects of individuality, not in the experience of it. Similarly, as Simmel comments, the connections involved in making up society may be exclusively matters of "consciousness," but

...this does not mean, of course, that each member of a society is conscious of such an abstract notion of unity. It means that he is absorbed in innumerable, specific relations and in the feeling and the knowledge of determining others and of being determined by them (1971 [1908]: 70).

Absorption and reciprocal determination are the stuff of society, from the (objective, not subjective) point of view of individuality. Thus we characterize individuality as independence, stressing the extent to which the individual in society (as opposed to in individuality) depends for his identity on his relations with other units. Conversely, we may refer to to society as dependence, stressing the multilaterally conditioned character of social action. The dynamics of INdependence, thus, are quite simply the factors which reduce the extent to which social units depend on each other.

There is no need to recount all the arguments which have been posed, especially by the founders of modern sociology, to show that the social is not reducible to lhe individual. Nonetheless, there is something to be learned from brief reference to a few of the most central. Generally, these arguments attempted to separate individual from social LEVELS, hoping to eliminate such reductionism as has recently returned to social theory with the neo-utilitarianism of exchange and transactional approaches. The early sociologists, however, tended to distinguish the social as category (perhaps for institutional reasons) and thus to lose from their theories and variable formulation of its extent.[3] Sociology and anthropology both continued (and compounded) this error as they took "society" for granted, both as boundary and as organization. Fortes argued against the former aspect of this problematic usage:

For the concept of society as a closed unit ... we must substitute the concept of society as a socio-geographic region, the elements of which are more closely knit together among themselves than any of them are knit together with social elements of the same kind outside that region. We must substitute a relative and dynamic concept for an absolute and static one (1945: 231).

Fortes here at least introduces the extent of "society" (in our terms) into his definition, if not into use as a variable of comparison among populations.[4]

Of the turn-of-the-century "founding fathers," it is Weber who, despite his excessive methodological and conceptual individualism, introduces and stresses the variable nature of sociation. He does this in the course of defining "social relationship," and does it through the introduction of the idea of mutually determined probabilities existing in sets of individual behaviors:

---

[3]   As in Durkheim (1964 [1893]), although he does link individuality to social solidarity. Surprisingly — and I think incorrectly — he sees this as a positive relationship, suggesting that both social solidarity and individual distinctiveness increase with the division of labor.

[4]   A sociologist who did bring this strikingly into the foreground was Sorokin (1936, 1957), although he sometimes overestimated the ability of his fellow sociologists to grasp his points: "There is no need to stress the fact that THE DEGREE OF FUNCTIONAL UNITY OR FUNCTIONAL INTERDEPENDENCE IS EVERYWHERE NOT THE SAME: it fluctuates from unity to unity; in some cases it is exceedingly close, in others looser, until finally it imperceptibly passes into either a mere external unity or even a mere spatial adjacency (1957:7; original emphasis).

And again, we have Merton offering a critique which has held too much relevance for too long: "It seems reasonably clear that the notion of functional unity is NOT a postulate beyond the reach of empirical test; quite the contrary. The degree of integration is an empirical variable, changing for the same society from time to time and differing among various societies (1957:26–27; original emphasis).

The term "social relationship" will be used to designate the situation where two or more persons are engaged in conduct wherein each takes account of the behavior of the other in a meaningful way and is therefore oriented in these terms. The social relationship thus CONSISTS entirely of the PROBABILITY that individuals will behave in some meaningfully determinable way (1925: 63; original emphasis).

The condition that Weber makes is that the behavior must be "meaningfully determinable" to an (actual or potential) outsider, not necessarily meaningfully determinable to any or every social actor. The latter, however, is probably an important condition of the former. The more people are able to understand the actions taken by their fellows, and to thus make their own actions consistent with them, the more likely is an outsider to see pattern instead of chaos in their behavior. It is in the connection between these two levels that the "interpretative" nature of Weber's sociology comes to the fore (see Gerth and Mills 1948:55). The sociologist must be able to understand the behavior of the actor, even if he uses different analytic categories.

Despite the (poorly worked out) hints of their masters, the followers of Durkheim, Weber, and Simmel seem to have found it easy to take up the position that the relationships between individuality and society were implicit in the structure of society — and then to ignore them as a topic of study. Great though this trio's contributions were, none of them provided the necessary conceptual connection between such a variable and social organization. It would not have been so difficult for any of these writers to incorporate this variable, one would think, for Marx had given it some pride of place in his writings years before. This he did with the help of (his ammended version of) Hegel's conceptualization of alienation and his own insight into the importance of appearances in effecting the continuation of the circumstances which produce them by causing people to act rationally on an insufficient basis in valid understanding. The latter is a primary point made in the discussion of the fetishism of commodities in the first chapter of *Capital* (1970 [1867]:76–87), and of eighteenth-century ideas of independent individuals and production in the *Grundrisse* (1973 [1939]:83–84). As to the former, witness this early and very Hegelian critique of the "rights of man" theorists:

None of the supposed rights of man go beyond the egoistic man, man as he is, as a member of civil society: that is, an individual separated from the community, withdrawn into himself, wholly preoccupied with his private interest and acting in accordance with his private caprice (1964 [1844]: 26).

The point Marx is making is that man neither always has been, nor everywhere equally is, nor need continue to be to whatever extent he anywhere is, either rationally or capriciously private. (Note the connection between private interest and caprice.) The tendency of philosophers and economists to be preoccupied with — or to take as a basic assumption — the individual, is part and parcel of the alienation produced by capitalism.

More specifically, capitalism increased the power of productive forces, but required a misconstruction of the conditions of social life in order to achieve and perpetuate its particular reified relations of production:

> The relative liberation of man from his direct dependence on nature is achieved by means of SOCIAL action. Nevertheless, because of the reification of the social relations of production, this achievement appears in alienated form: not as a relative independence from natural necessity but as a freedom from the constraints of SOCIAL ties and relations, as an everintensifying cult of "individual AUTONOMY" (Mészaros 1970: 258; original emphasis).

Marx not only conceived, in the absolute, of the noninherent nature of alienated individualism, but he noted that it obtained in varying degree. Further, he incorporated this variance into a theoretical analysis of social history as a central dynamic variable. Thus he criticizes those who misunderstand the nature of capitalist production relations in which individuals production confronts them as an objective relation which is independent of them (taking the form of commodities). He terms it

> ... an insipid notion to conceive of this merely OBJECTIVE BOND [of commodity-exchange relations] as a spontaneous natural attribute inherent in individuals and inseparable from their nature (in antithesis to their conscious knowing and willing) (Marx 1973 [1939]: 162; original emphasis).

Such a bond belongs, of course, only to a particular phase in historical development, not to "nature." The existence of such a bond merely demonstrates that historical production is still underway. Assessment of this historical process is a PRECONDITION of any discussion of social organization. One may only anticipate the ideal state of affairs:

> Universally developed individuals, whose social relations, as their own communal [gemeinschftlich] relations, are hence also subordinated to their own communal control, are no product of nature, but of history (Marx 1973 [1939]: 162).

Static analysis is thus inevitably inadequate, and where its temporal context is not considered, is actually misleading.[5] It is in the process of negating partiality, false or immediate wholeness and abstraction, that a subject realizes itself, according to Hegel. In the case of man this is a

---

[5]   Reality appears as a dynamic in which all fixed forms reveal themselves to be mere abstractions (Marcuse 1960:26).

mediated realization, as man self-consciously creates himself. That is, mankind becomes more human — in essence — over time, one aspect of which process is becoming more conscious of itself as making itself. This is the crucial concept to a coherent view of history (following Hegel and Marx). The coherence comes from the production of each historical stage by its predecessor (any supposition of ultimate purpose is unnecessary). The process is, in particular, one of manifold negation:

These stages are not merely differentiated; they supplant one another as being incompatible with one another. But the ceaseless activity of their own inherent nature makes them at the same time moments of an organic unity, where they not merely do not contradict one another, but where one is as necessary as the other; and this equal necessity of all moments constitutes alone and thereby the life of the whole (Hegel 1967 [1807]: 68).

Since humanity is inherently self-consciously self-realizing, stages in its social history are also stages in the history of its consciousness. In order for humanity to become more fully "self-mediating,"[6] its consciousness of itself and its situation must be improved. It is largely in support of more revolutionary improvements in human social consciousness aimed at greater self-realization of mankind — both at large and in individuals — that Marx criticizes Hegel's later emphasis on reconciliation and its germs in the earlier work.

Two of the stages which Marx sees are relevant here. The first is that of high sociation and low mediation. This is how Marx conceives of much "primitive society." The second stage is that of alienated individuality but with the development of the abilities which will EVENTUALLY allow for fuller mediation. Leaving aside the hoped-for eventualities, then, we contrast sociation with alienation. The virtue of socialism/communism, as Marx conceives it, is that humanity can attain the same degree of sociation as "primitive" society provided, but be much more directly and significantly self-consciously self-mediating. Individuals will be no more (or less) determined by their social relations, but collectively they will be more accurately aware of them, and thus more able to effectively take a hand in shaping them. Much doubt remains as to how this collective awareness is to manifest itself, and that is a problem which we will not solve here. Let us simply note that a characteristic of Marx's "ideal" is that persons should be neither isolated and alienated nor wholly absorbed (unconsciously) in their social determinations.

For Marx the process of narrowing the gap between the actual capabilities and the ideal potentialities of the individual

[6] "Meditation" refers to something positing itself, being subject and not merely object to transformations from one state to its opposite (see Hegel 1967 [1807]:80).

... is inseparable from the realization of the "truly SOCIAL INDIVIDUAL." The more the individual is able to "reproduce himself as a social individual," the less intense is the conflict between individual and society, individual and mankind (Mészaros 1970: 285; original emphasis).

This follows on Hegel's suggestion of the eventual unification of "impulses" and "duties" (1967 [1821]:29) in the ethical community.[7] Marx differs from Hegel here in suggesting that individuals can maintain a greater degree of self-consciousness (and control over their own actions) in the proposed ideal community. For both, a key element in the process of transformation is a change in the nature of social consciousness. It is this change which Hegel considers the ultimate value and meaning of education (1967 [1821]:29, 124–126).

IV. Both Marx and Hegel discuss education and related concepts primarily as writers concerned with eliminating an alienation which they see as on the rise. But as the papers in this volume make clear, this is not always what appears to educationists as the problem. Whether an escape from social bondage or from alienation is to be sought through education depends on the social situation under consideration. It is thus impossible to formulate absolute or universal statements about the role of education in social organizations. What, we must ask, are the differences between education leading towards more society (the *bildungsprocess* of Hegel, and in a sense Marx, following von Humbolt) or towards more individuality (the self-actualization model, for example, prevalent in much contemporary educational ideology)? How does education relate to the immanence of sociocultural organizations?

If we assume that change — not stability — is the universal condition of society, then education can never be simply "maintaining the status quo." Although change may happen more or less rapidly, the status quo CAN never be maintained. Education systems may thus attempt to forestall or impede changes which are in progress (or may in fact do so unintentionally). But since only a part of social life is the result of education, it may only be a partially conservative force. If it maintains the prominence

---

[7] "In an ETHICAL community, it is easy to say what man must do, what are the duties he has to fulfill in order to be virtuous: he has simply to follow the well-known and explicit rules of his own situation. Rectitude is the general character which may be demanded of him by law or custom. But from the standpoint of MORALITY, rectitude often seems to be something comparatively inferior, something beyond which still higher demands must be made on oneself and others, because the craving to be something special is not satisfied with what is absolute and universal" (Hegel 1821:107; original emphasis). Morality, in Hegel's usage, is the characteristic aim of civil society as he found it to be constituted. An ethical order was the goal of the reforms he suggested.

of certain ideas while their social context changes rapidly, it may well contribute to a decrease in what Sorokin would call consistency, or "logico-meaningful integration" (1957:9–17). Education, in other words, may either resist or be a part of the logic of a society's immanence. Whatever its relation to the LOGIC of immanence, however, education cannot help but be part of the society's change. If for no other reason, this would always be so because education must always be inadequate. There must always be unintended consequences (cf. Merton 1936). Situations must always arise in which courses of action are not "given" and the results of choices are not known.

As we have suggested above, the stability of social life depends crucially on the extent to which social actors are predictable to one another. As one's social environment becomes less predictable, one is led to plan over shorter and shorter spans of time. This in turn makes one less predictable to others. The process is self-accelerating. The spiral is also furthered by the extent of individuation. The more distinctive people are, the less predictable they are likely to be. But this is not the crucial factor. That, rather, is the fact that individuation is accompanied by an increase in the incidence of individual decisions. In other words, people are faced more and more with situations which are "new" enough to render received knowledge inadequately applicable. Under these circumstances they must make decisions. In a sense, then, we could say that a new decision is made to the extent that an action is taken on incomplete information. The more complete information — that is, the more certainty — there is in the anticipation and action, the more the actor may be said to be acting directly on values. It is only when he is uncertain that information becomes important. But the more important it is, the more difficult it is to get. Really adequate information can be had only when very little is required. Very little is required only when the situation is very much like other situations and the future appears stable. Faced with inadequate information, people make choices that are individual. That is, they select (consciously, unconsciously, and by virtue of their positions in society) from the available information, of which there is always more than they can handle. With this information they make decisions which inevitably fall short of ideals of perfect "rationality."[8]

To the extent that education emphasizes individualized decision making, it contributes to an increase in the rate of social change. Perhaps more exactly, it contributes to an increase in social instability which may in turn lead to greater social change. The reverse would also seem to be true:

[8]   See Simon on administrators who must "satisfice because they have not the wits to maximize" (1957: xxiv).

education emphasizing sociated action contributes to the production of social stability. That is, it helps to create the conditions for social stability, one of which is sociated action. It does not in itself create the stability, and indeed, it may even promote social change in the short run. This is because greater sociation is itself a change, and in terms of some widely spread ideologies a radical change. A value on individualism is pervasive in Western liberal culture (and, along with the ill-defined value on progress, is becoming more and more common in the Third World — or parts of it). The fact that this value is widely held does not mean, however, that it is consistent, either logically or practically, with all other widely held values.[9] The kind of individualism generally valued in the West is inconsistent with values on community, with many religious values (Weber notwithstanding), and with values on social (and economic) stability. Inasmuch as education for sociation is successful, it produces a condition for stability ONLY given a fundamentally different sociocultural system. Such immediate impacts as it may have on stability cannot be permanent. Indeed they are likely only to prove sufficient for the groundwork for rebellion stemming from general sociocultural dissatisfactions. In other words, unaccompanied by more fundamental changes it can (macrosociologically) only help to provide impetus to one side of the periodic fluctuations between liberation and retrenchment (*vide*, the 1950's followed by the 1960's followed by the 1970's, etc.).

We are talking, then, about education in larger terms than those of the immediate impacts of fluctuating pedagogical styles. Indeed, in this respect the fluctuation itself reveals more than the content of any style. We are considering education's sociocultural context in terms of fundamental tendencies in social organization. These tendencies vary only over relatively long time-spans or across very radical changes. The "tendencies" to which I refer are the interwoven patterns, principles, and productions of social organizations. They cannot be reduced to any single underlying principle, however profound (e.g. capitalism), or assumed to be a completely coherent system. It is in these tendencies that the smaller and larger practical problems of social organizations arise. No item taken from this context can be treated as displaying the same meaning as it displayed within it, sociologically speaking. It is in this sense that Hegel says:

Rulers, Statesmen, Nations, are wont to be emphatically commended to the teaching which experience offers in history. But what experience and history

[9] An overemphasis on values as such, and the assumption that simple generality of a value is sociologically conclusive is one of the problems with Parsonian theories of social change (see, for example, Smelser 1959, 1962).

teach is this, — that peoples and governments never have learned anything from history, or acted on principles deduced from it. Each period is involved in such peculiar circumstances, exhibits a condition of things so strictly idiosyncratic, that its conduct must be regulated by considerations connect with itself, and itself alone. Amid the pressure of great events, a general principles give no help (1929 [1837]: 345).

V. The question we must now pose is a difficult and perhaps insoluble one: How do sociocultural tendencies change? In some ways this is comparable to asking at what point an object under strain — say, a bridge — collapses, or at what point a wave breaks. The mathematical description of those physical events — as in catastrophe theory, a branch of topology — is still a subject of much debate.[10] Social events present still more complex problems in many respects, not least those of adequate empirical — especially quantitative — description. Still, two points must be made: The first is that however gradually sociocultural change may be seen to occur in history, there are nonetheless catastrophe points — points beyond which events move in a different direction, on a different surface. This is the meaning of RADICAL change — not that change is sudden, but that it is a change at root, singular, nonrepeatable, of essence rather than of quantity. Such changes are certainly not always — if ever — identifiable by the observer. None of the immediate events will reveal the radicalness of a change; that can only be seen in historical outcome. The span of relevant events may be infinitely long, but the point of radical change has no width.

The second point follows from this. Sociocultural tendencies change in such a way that their transformation cannot be managed. That is, it is not subject to conscious control. Further, an order cannot be changed without disorder; a tendency must BREAK DOWN in order to be replaced by another. This is not to say that conscious change is impossible, only that conscious determination of the results of radical change is. The complexity of the phenomena renders the probability of predicting specific results extremely small. The greater the uncertainty in the situation as a whole, the more difficulty there is in predicting any single (or more

---

[10] Catastrophe theory is an attempt to describe the shape (including the shape in time) of certain singularities. Rather than treating (as do linear algebra and most statistics) of averages, catastrophe theory treats of sudden changes in the linear nature of relationships, such as in conventional statistics are suggested by bimodal distributions. In other terms, where x and y are related to each other, catastrophe theory is concerned with situations where a decrease in x will not affect the relationship as the simple inverse of prior increase in x, after a certain point. Rather, the relationship will "jump" to a different course. Productive though applications of catastrophe theory may in future be, at present it is helpful primarily by way of metaphor. See Stewart (1975) for a general discussion.

accurately, partial) event. Thus the partial events with which social policy and social engineering deal are rendered more difficult to grasp as disorder is greater. Change of the radical sort which we are here considering can only take place amid disorder.

The causes of such disorder may be internal or external to any social organization, but the disorder cannot be "outside" it. The disorder must be OF it. There cannot thus be an orderly transformation of a tribal society into a bureaucratic or entrepreneurial capitalist state, though the disorder of the change may mlnifest itself in various wlys. Both political and personal instabilities may stem from such disorder, for example. Further, in this particular instance, we may add that the "modern" centralized political state and capitalist economy are likely to exhibit less social order than would a traditional tribal organization.

The mechanics of producing the disorder likely to lead to radical change may be entirely different from those which operate to establish a new order. More often, some particulars will continue while the overall combination shifts so as to change the tendency. In such cases the elements which emerge as dominant features of the new order are likely to be versions of those which were submerged under the old order. In this sense, there is continuity even through radical change. The new tendency, the new organization, is not a creation *ex nihilo*. Rather, it is created out of the dissolution of the old. In this it reflects both some of the aspects of the old order, and the process of change which gave birth to it.

VI.   In the introduction to this volume education was described in terms of continuity. In this essay I have attempted to show how continuity may be a characteristic of a social organization, or, may be in its absence the focus of numerous social issues or problems. The latter seems more and more often to be the case. This seems to be a major aspect of the common distinction between "preindustrial" and "industrial" nations. The former refers to those with a high degree of stability achieved through a tightly knit structure of social interdependence. Such societies are described with the aid of concepts like "multiplexity" of relationships and hierarchical inclusivity of corporations. Industrial societies, on the other hand, are seen as characterized by increasing differentiation of functional special-isms and atomization of social units. That such differentiation takes place apparent. What is debatable is the contention that it results in or is accompanied by greater integration.[11] Though a larger population may

---

[11]   As, for example, Smelser (see 1962 for a general discussion) who argues following the Parsonian line, and Durkheim (1964 [1893]; see also Note 3 of this article). With a related optimism, Horton describes African traditional thought as "closed" in

be brought into interaction, it seems a dubious usage to consider that indicative of greater integration. Contrary to Smelser, I suggest that while social "unrest" and/or change is generally followed by relative stability, there is not necessarily greater integration after it than before it. Rather, there is only greater integration after than DURING it.

Education is among the sociocultural activities which are differentiated with the creation of so-called industrial society. In other words, education ceases to be an intrinsic and indistinguishable part of the range of social activity and becomes subject to specific intentional manipulation. Rather than being governed by the complex interaction of institutions and events, it is governed by the (relatively) simple choices of individuals and groups. Accordingly, the likelihood of discrepancies between those educational choices and social organization as a whole is increased.[12] Efforts to achieve greater accountability or otherwise to bring the two back in line through "rational" means are doomed by their own inevitable inadequacy to run a hopeless race against growing complexity.

Problems associated with the differentiation of education from other sociocultural activities are discussed in several of the papers in this volume. Thus, for example, King notes the problems faced by planned communities in developing a means of enculturation which makes their own offspring likely or suitable members. Only highly institutionalized communities seem to have any considerable success in this respect, and they may succeed because they do not treat education as primarily an issue of distinct individuals. Rather, education is regarded as a part of the life of the group as a whole. Though more attention may be focused on some members than on others, this is not conceptualized as being for their benefit alone (in either sense of "alone"). Many "hippie" communes, on the other hand, incorporate a strong emphasis on "self-realization" and "self-reliance" as distinct from dependence on the community. Here education is at odds with the survival of the community, though this is not generally recognized by the members. Similarly, although an attempt is made to educate members into a life of community, most communal groups seem to find themselves with problems of the second generation.[13]

---

comparison with Western science (1967). In this he rather overestimates the rational (Popperian) PRACTICE of scientists. However rational scientists' ideologies, the social and intellectual realities of scientific advancement follow a somewhat different path (cf. Kuhn 1970; Merton 1973).

[12] A problem of dysfunctions of unintended consequences of purposive action (Merton 1936, 1957). See also Lee (1963 [1955]) for some interesting observations on "discrepancies in the teaching of American culture."

[13] Described by Spiro in his study of kibbutz children (1958). The problem of the second generation is simply that of discrepancies between what parents and children

The *Bruderhoff* studied by Zablocki (1971) recognizes the inevitable inadequacy of such education and treats the problem in a novel manner. Its solution is to require that all young people spend a period of time outside the community so that those returning will have made a choice to commit themselves — thus presumably demonstrating the success of earlier enculturations (and/or the unacceptibility of life outside). These returnees must be accepted, as must strangers, and must go through a further period of enculturation designed to secure their dependence on the community.

There are severe difficulties, then, in instituting an educational program which secures social values in the midst of our individualist culture. These are not wholly unlike, although different in content and direction from, the difficulties faced by European missionaries and educators who would transform indigenous cultures in Eastern Nigeria (see Nwa-Chil's paper). Aside from difficulties of implementation, there is the simple impossibility of taking all the relevant variables into account. The situations are too complex for perfect planning. As Leacock has observed, one prominent response of educators (in America and Africa) is to artificially abstract education from its sociocultural context. This amounts to practicing what Slater has called "the escalation of failure" (1970:40). The very problem confronting educators is (unsuccessfully) dealt with by increasing the factors which caused it in the first place and have failed to remedy it in the meantime. One reason for this is that it is only by drastically narrowing the range of educational approaches they consider that educators can produce any sense — however unreal — of dealing with a problem of manageable proportions. Examples of situations of this kind can easily be multiplied. They are in fact the stuff of our everyday lives as well as of our large-scale plans and collective policies.

It is a mistake, then, to treat of education as necessarily a force for either continuity or change. In many traditional societies education fits closely into the social order and works to reproduce it. More and more, however, education is the responsibility of specialized subunits. as such it becomes more subject to individual decisions and more productive of diverse results. Some aspects of this process may well be valued. But we must also remember that education of this sort becomes the source of discontinuities and contradictions in sociocultural organization. In essence, education can become part of the dissolution of society. We must not

---

are likely to think of a community which the former have chosen and built, but into which the latter were only born and raised. At the very least, the grass always seems greener on the other side of the hill.

think that society is simply THERE, given. It is not a conscious and complete
formal organization, like a state. As Ortega y Gasset said, "... a nation
is never formed .... The nation is always either in the making, or in the
unmaking" (1961 [1930]:134).

REFERENCES

DURKHEIM, E.
    1964   [1893] *The division of labour in society.* Translated by G. Simpson.
            New York: Free Press.
FORTES, M.
    1945   *The dynamics of clanship among the Tallensi.* London: Oxford Uni-
            versity Press for the International African Institute.
GERTH, H. H. ,C. W. MILLS
    1948   "Introduction: the man and his work," in *From Max Weber.* Edited
            by H. H. Gerth and C. W. Mills. London: Routledge and Kegan Paul.
HEGEL, G. W. F.
    1929   [1837] "Introduction to the philosophy of history," in *Hegel selections.*
            Edited by J. Loewenberg. New York: Scribner's.
    1967   [1807] *The phenomenology of mind.* Translated by J. B. Ballie. New
            York: Harper and Row.
    1967   [1821] *Philosophy of right.* Translated by T. M. Knox. London: Oxford
            University Press.
HOMANS, G. C., D. M. SCHNEIDER
    1955   *Kinship, authority, and final causes.* Glencoe, Ill.: Free Press.
HORTON, R.
    1967   African traditional thought and Western science. *Africa* 37 (1): 50–71;
            (2): 155–187.
KOLAKOWSKI, L.
    1971   "The priest and the jester," in *Marxism and beyond,* 31–58. Translated
            by J. Z. Peel. London: Paladin.
KUHN, T. S.
    1970   *The structure of scientific revolutions.* Chicago: University of Chicago
            Press.
LEE, D.
    1963   [1955] "Discrepancies in the teaching of American culture," in *Educa-
            tion and culture.* Edited by G. D. Spindler, 173–191. New York: Holt,
            Rinehart and Winston.
LEVI-STRAUSS, C.
    1949   *Les structaires elementaires de la parente.* Paris and The Hague:
            Mouton.
MARCUSE, H.
    1960   [1941] *Reason and revolution: Hegel and the rise of social theory.*
            Boston: Beacon Press.
MARX, K.
    1964   [1844] *Early writings.* Translated by I. B. Bottomore. New York:
            McGraw-Hill.

1970   [1867] *Capital*, volume one. Translated by S. Moore and E. Aveling. London: Lawrence and Wishart.

1973   [1939] *Grundrisse*. Translated by M. Nicolaus. Harmondsworth: Penguin.

MERTON, R. K.

1936   The unanticipated consequences of purposive social action. *American Sociological Review* 1: 894–904.

1957   *Social theory and social structure* (revised edition). Glencoe, Ill: Free Press.

1973   *The sociology of science: theoretical and empirical investigations*. Edited by N. Storer. Chicago: University of Chicago Press.

MESZAROS, I.

1970   *Marx's theory of alienation*. New York: Harper and Row.

NEEDHAM, R.

1962   *Structure and sentiment*. Oxford: Blackwell.

ORTEGA Y GASSET, J.

1961   [1930] *The revolt of the masses*. Translator anonymous. London: Unwin.

SIMMEL, G.

1971   [1908] "Conflict," in *Georg Simmel on individuality and social forms*. Edited by D. N. Levine; translated by K. Wolff, 70–95. Chicago: University of Chicago Press.

SIMON, H. A.

1957   *Administrative behavior* (second edition). New York: Free Press.

SLATER, P.

1975   [1970] *The pursuit of loneliness*. Harmondsworth: Penguin.

SMELSER, N. J.

1959   *Social change in the Industrial Revolution*. London: Routledge and Kegan Paul.

1962   "Mechanisms of change and adjustment to change," in *Economic development and social change*. Edited by G. Dalton, 352–374. New York: Natural History Press.

SOROKIN, P. A.

1936   Forms and problems of culture integration and methods of their study. *Rural Sociology* 1: 121–141, 344–374.

1957   *Social and cultural dynamics* (abridged version of 1937–1941 edition). Boston: Sargent.

SPIRO, M.

1958   *Children of the kibbutz*. Cambridge, Mass.: Harvard University Press.

STEWART, I.

1975   The seven elementary catastrophes. *New Scientist* 68 (976): 447–454.

WEBER, M.

1964   [1925] *Basic concepts of sociology*. Translated by H. P. Secher. New York: Citadel Press.

ZABLOCKI, B.

1971   *The joyful community*. Baltimore: Penguin.

Biographical Notes

CRAIG J. CALHOUN (1952) is currently in the Department of Social Anthropology at the University of Manchester on a post-graduate research studentship. He is a member of the staff of the Bureau of Applied Social Research and the Department of Sociology at Columbia University. Educated primarily at the University of Southern California, Columbia, and Manchester Universities he has been Research Associate in the Horace Mann-Lincoln Institute at Teachers College Columbia. His publications include "Continuity and change: the significance of time in the organization of experience " "General status; specific role " and "The social function of experiences of altered perception."

WOODROW W. CLARK JR. (1945) is an Associate in Education in the University of California, Berkeley, School of Education. He was previously Learning Coordinator at the Far West Educational Laboratory and was educated at the Ohio Wesleyan University, Northwestern, Roosevelt, and Loyola Universities, the University of Illinois and the University of California. His publications include "Causes, issues, and remedies of conflict and violence in American public schools," and *Conflict and violence in public education.*

ANDREW W. COUCH (1951) is currently at the Loyola University School of Law in Los Angeles. He has been doing fieldwork on various aspects of law enforcement in Los Angeles City and County for several years and was previously in the Department of Criminal Justice at the California State University, Los Angeles. He was educated primarily at the University of Southern California, California State University, and Loyola.

HERBERT G. ELLIS.   No biographical data available.

THOMAS K. FITZGERALD (1939) is now Associate Professor of Anthropology at the University of North Carolina at Greensboro. He was educated at the University of North Carolina, University of Paris, and Stanford University, and is the author of *Education and identity*, coauthor of *Culture, society and guidance*, and editor of *Social and cultural identity: problems of persistence and change* (forthcoming).

VLADIMIR GARDANOV is on the staff of the Institute of Ethnography in Moscow.

ROBERT J. HAVIGHURST (1900) was educated at the Ohio State University (Ph.D. in Chemistry) and at the University of Chicago, where he is now Professor of Education and Human Development. Since 1941 he has worked as Social Psychologist in a number of interdisciplinary teams studying human behavior and development in cross-cultural research designs. He has studied American Indians, New Zealand Maoris, and Australian aboriginals as well as American, Brazilian, and Argentine adolescents. In 1974 he presented the American Educational Research Association-Phi Delta Kappa Award Lecture on Cultural Pluralism and Education. He is the author of *The impact of Anglo culture on native societies: Australia, New Zealand and the USA; To live of this earth: American Indian education; American Indian and white children; society and education in Brazil; Comparative perspectives in education;* and *Las actitudes personales y sociales de adolescentes de Buenos Aires y de Chicago.*

FRANCIS A. J. IANNI (1926) is currently Professor of Education and Director of the Horace Mann-Lincoln Institute at Teachers College, Columbia University, and was formerly Associate Commissioner of Research in the U.S. Office of Education. He was educated at Pennsylvania State University. His recent publications have included *Black mafia, A State University.* His recent publications include *Black mafia, A family business: kinship and control in organized crime,* and *Cultural relevance: a reader in anthropology and education* (with Gerald Storey).

MILADA KALAB (1929), born in Czechoslovakia) is currently on the faculty of the Department of Anthropology at the University of Durham, Great Britain. She was educated at the Universities of Prague, Santiniketan, Bombay, and London and has done fieldwork in Cambodia, Thailand, and among the Naga tribes in India. Her publications include

"Changing values in Naga Hills and Manipur State," and "Study of a Cambodian village."

J. MICHAEL KING (1949) is currently doing fieldwork with communal groups in Santa Cruz County, California. Previously Assistant Curator for Ethnology in the Treganza Anthropology Museum of the California State University in San Francisco, he has done fieldwork with the Pomo and other native American groups, particularly with regard to the provision of health care services. He has been Archaeological Consultant to the state of California and was educated primarily at the California State University, San Francisco, and the University of California. He is the author of a modular educational program for teaching anthropology at the elementary school level.

COLIN LACEY (1936) is currently Director of Research in Education at the University of Sussex. He was educated at the Universities of Birmingham and Manchester and also held the post of Lecturer at Manchester. His publications include "Some sociological concommitants of academic streaming in a grammar school" (1966), *Organizational change in schools* (1970), *Hightown Grammar: the school as a social system* (1970) and *Sociologists and schools* (forthcoming).

ELEANOR BURKE LEACOCK (1922) is Professor of Anthropology and holds the chair of the Department of Anthropology at City College of the City University of New York. She was educated at Barnard College and Columbia University and has conducted fieldwork in Canada, East Africa, and the United States. She has authored, coauthored, or edited several books, including: *The Montagnais "Hunting territory" and the fur trade* (1954), *Toward integration in suburban housing, the Bridgeview study* (with Martin Deutsch and J. A. Fishman, 1965), *Teaching and learning in city schools: a comparative study* (1969), and *Culture of poverty: a critique* (1971, editor). Relevant recent articles include "Education, socialization and the 'culture of poverty'" (1970), "Theoretical and methodological problems in the study of schools," (1971) and "Primary schooling in Zambia" (1973).

BEATRICE MEDECINE (1924) is Visiting Professor of Native American Studies at Dartmouth College and an Educational Consultant to the National Congress of American Indians. She was educated primarily at the South Dakota State University, Michigan State University, and the University of Washington. Some of her recent publications include "The anthropologist as the Indian's image maker," "The anthropologist and ethnic studies programs," "The changing Dakota family," and several contributions to the Bureau of American Ethnology's *Handbook of American Indians*, a publication for which she also serves on the editorial board.

EDNA MITCHELL (1931) is Professor of Education and Head of Department, Mills College, Oakland, California. She received her B.A. from William Jewell College, Liberty Missouri, her Ph.D. from the University of Missouri at Kansas City, and did additional graduate work at the University of Colorado and the University of Hawaii. Her teaching experience includes preschool and elementary in both rural and urban schools, faculty positions at William Jewell College, Liberty, and Smith College, Northampton, Massachusetts. She has been a Research Project Coordinator for Mid-Continent Regional Educational Laboratory, Researcher for the Study of Metropolitan Problems in Education, and Regional Coordinator for a nationa research project on preschool education sponsored by I/D/E/A. She served three summers on the NEA/USAID team as Consultant to the Ministry of Education in Nepal. The summer of 1975 was spent in research on toys and play in Denmark. Publications include articles on curriculum development, career education, sex-stereotyping in children, cross-cultural perspectives on play, and a study of educated women in Nepal.

CHUDI. C. NWA-CHIL, born in Nigeria, is Lecturer in Sociology at the University of Dar-es-Salaam, Tanzania.

JUHA PENTIKÄINEN (1940) is Professor of Comparative Religion at the University of Helsinki. He received his M.A. from the University of Helsinki in 1963, a Phil.Lic. from Turku 1966, and a Ph.D. from Turku in 1968 with a dissertation on Nordic and North Eurasian folk belief. He has been Visiting Professor of Anthropology at the University of California, Berkeley, and Visiting Professor of Folklore at the University of Indiana, Bloomington. He has been the Chief Editor of *Temenos* since 1974, and Member of the Finnish UNESCO Council. His special interests include methodology of anthropological research, Artic cultures, and religious and psychological anthropology.

EDDY ROULET (1939) is Professor of General Linguistics at the University of Neuchatel, Switzerland, where he was also educated. In 1970 he was elected Vice-President of the International Association of Applied

Linguistics. Among his several publications are *Théories grammaticales et enseignment des langues, Theoretical linguistic models in applied linguistics* (with P. Corder), and *Linguistic insights in applied linguistics* (with P. Corder).

PEGGY R. SANDAY (1937) is currently Associate Professor of Anthropology at the University of Pennsylvania and was previously Assistant Professor of Anthropology and Urban Affairs at Carnegie-Mellon University. She was educated at Columbia University and the University of Pittsburgh. Her recent publications include "Subcultural variations in an urban poor population, "Analysis of the psychological reality of American-English kin terms in an urban poverty environment", "Genetic and environment", "Genetic and environmental componants of differential intelligence" (with Thomas Gregg), "On the causes of I.Q. differences between groups and implications for social policy", and "Education from an anthropological perspective: an empirical investigation of structural differences among blacks and whites" (in press).

HENRY TORRES TRUEBA is Associate Professor and Director of Bilingual Bicultural Education Graduate Programs for Latinos in the College of Education at the University of Illinois. Educated at the University of Pittsburgh, his major interests are in Latin American ethnography, cognitive anthropology, as well as bilingual, bicultural education. His publications include "Slash-and-burn cultivation in the tropical Amazon", "Faccionalismo en un municipio Mexicano," "Nahuat functionalism," "Bilingualism in the Southwest," and "Bilingual Bicultural Education for Chicanos in the Southwest."

HERVÉ VARENNE (1948), born in France, is Assistant Professor of Education at Teachers College, Columbia University. He was educated at the Université d'Aix-Marseille and the University of Chicago and has done fieldwork in a small village in southeastern France and in a small town in southwestern Michigan. He is the author of "Culture and stratification in an equalitarian civilization," "To melt or not to melt, acculturation and ethnicity in a small Midwestern town," and *Individualism, community and love* (forthcoming).

R. J. WELKE.   No biographical data available.

HUGH B. WOOD (1909) is now retired after thirty-five years as Professor of Education at the University of Oregon and as Educational Advisor to various governments and the United Nations. He was educated at the University of Colorado, and Teachers College, Columbia University. Among the more recent of his numerous books are: *Adult literacy in Malawi, The development of education in Nepal, Educational planning in Nepal and its economic implications,* and *Foundations of curriculum planning and development.*

Index of Names

Reay, Marie, 144
Redfield, Robert, 221
Reed, Donald R., 117
Riessman, F., 107, 108
Riffle, Rodney, 227
Ritchie, James, 144
Ritchie, Jane, 144
Roosevelt, Franklin D., 141
Rosenthal, Robert, 243
Roulet, Eddy, 7, 311–324
Rowan, Carl T., 111
Rowley, C. D., 134, 144
Rubinstein, Richard, 251
Rumery, J., 321
Rusden, H. K., 129
Rydzevskaja, E. A., 34

Sanday, Peggy R., 4, 173–187
Sarin, 69, 70
Sartre, Jean Paul, 251
Savignon, J. A., 312, 322
Schlipp, Paul Arthur, 246
Schmidt, I. J., 34
Schneider, David M., 228, 329–330
Schwimmer, Erik, 139–140, 144
Shah Prithi Narayan, 148
Shanahan, Ernest J., 157
Shannon, C. E., 15
Sharma, Kulashekar, 155
Simmel, G., 332, 334
Simmen, Edward, 300
Simon, H. A., 338
Sizemore, Barbara A., 123
Slater, P., 343
Slobin, D. I., 315, 320
Smelser, N. J., 339, 341–342
Smirnov, N. I., 34
Smirnova, Ja. S., 31
Sorokin, P. A., 333, 338
Spindler, George, 144, 174, 189
Spiro, M., 342–343
Staelin, Richard, 179–180, 183
Stanner, W. E. H., 134–135, 144
Steinmetz, S. R., 34, 35–36
Stewart, I., 340
Stones, E., 209, 215
Strunk, O., 19
Swanson, G. E., 107

Taft, Ronald, 144
Takalo, Marina, 23–24, 26
Tambiah, S. J., 71
Tatz, C. M., 144
Tax, Sol, 143, 144, 277

Taylor, Charles, 229–231
Tenney, Charles, 271
Thomas, Robert, 143
Toch, Hans: *Violent men*, 262
Torres-Trueba, Henry, 6–7, 299–309
Tribhuvan (king of Nepal), 148–149, 160
Tripodi, Pony, 293
Troubetzkoy, D. S.: *Principes de phonologie*, 318–319
Tuladhar, Tirtha R., 166
Turner, Victor, 77
Tyler, Steven, 258

Uchendu, V. C., 46
Udall, Stuart, 142
Upraity, Trailokya Nath, 155
Utley, Francis L., 13

Vajirappano, Huot Tath, 68
Vann Molyvann, 72
Varenne, Hervé, 5, 227–237
Vladimirtsov, B. A., 34

Walker, Lewis, 120
Walker, Rangi, 144
Watson, John E., 144
Watts, Betty H., 144
Wax, Murray, 143, 144
Wax, Rosalie, 143, 144
Weaver, W., 15
Weber, M., 333–334, 339
Webster, Murray, 203
Weinhold, K., 34
Welke, R. J., 6, 275–282
Wentworth, William C., 136
Whiting, John, 98
Widdowson, H. G., 313, 314, 316, 321–322
Wilkerson, D. A., 120
Wilkins, D., 320–321
Wilson, J., 51, 52
Wojciechowski, T., 34
Wood, Hugh B., 147–158; *Nepal bibliography*, 148
Woolcott, Harry F., 174–175
Wrong, Dennis, 200, 201
Wyatt, David K., 67

Yette, S. F., 111, 112
Yogamanda, Parmahansa, 89

Zablocki, Benjamin, 77, 78, 344
Zigler, E., 116
Zulu, Phillip, 239
Zulu, Sabel, 239

Index of Subjects

Abkhazia, USSR, 31–32
Aborigines, Australia, 127–132, 134–138
Altan-tobchi, 34
American Anthropological Association, 258
American Anthropologist, 189
American Association of University Professors (AAUP), 276
American College of Switzerland, 275–282
American Indian Chicago Conference (1961), 142–143
American Indian Movement (AIM), 285
Anthropology today (Kroeber), 189
Aros, 57–58
Arts University, Phnom Penh, Cambodia, 73
Atalychestvo (fosterage), in Caucasus, 29–38
"At play in African villages" (Leacock), 242
Auckland University, New Zealand, 139
Australia, 3; Aborigines in, 127–132, 134–138; Aborigines' Welfare Board (originally, Aborigines' Protective Board), 131; Commonwealth Council on Aboriginal Affairs, 134, 137; Labour Party, 137; Ministerial Australian Aboriginal Affairs Council, 137; Native Welfare Conference of Commonwealth and State Ministers (Canberra, 1951), 131; Social Science Research Council, 134
Australian National University, 134, 137

Beginnings (Nuffield Mathematics Project), 244
Benin, 55, 56
Biafra, 43
Black Hills State College, South Dakota, 285, 286, 287
Black students, United States, 105–125, 176–179, 255–258
Bonny, 56, 57
Brazil, 55
Brown vs *Board of Education in Topeka*, 110
Buderhof (communal group, New York), 75, 77–78, 343
Brunel New Southern University, England, 205, 207–215
Buddhism: Theravada, in Cambodia, 61–73; Zen, 84
Buddhist University, Cambodia, 73

California, communes in, 76–104
California State University, Los Angeles (CSULA), 268, 269–274
California State University, Sacramento (CSUS), 303–307
Cambodia, 2; Arts University, 73; Buddhist University, 72, 73; Khmer, 64, 66, 67, 68, 71, 72–73; Khmer Peace Committee, 72; Khmer Rouge, 72; Mohanikay monastic order, 65–66; Pali language, 64, 66, 68, 69, 71, 72, 73; Theravada Buddhism, 61–73; Thommayut monastic order, 65–66; Viet Cong, 72